Vital Statistics
on American Politics

Vital Statistics on American Politics

Fifth Edition

Harold W. Stanley
University of Rochester

Richard G. Niemi
University of Rochester

A Division of Congressional Quarterly Inc.
Washington, D.C.

Printed in the United States of America.

Library of Congress Cataloging-in-Publication Data

Stanley, Harold W. (Harold Watkins)
   Vital statistics on American politics / Harold W. Stanley, Richard G. Niemi. -- 5th ed.
     p. cm.
   Includes bibliographical references and index.
   ISBN 0-87187-793-7 (cloth)
   1. United States--Politics and government--Statistics.   I. Niemi, Richard G. II. Title.
JK274.S74 1995
320.973'021--dc20   95-35053
                                           CIP

To the memory of our colleague
William H. Riker,
whose writings ranged across
most aspects of American politics
and whose teaching and career helped create
a political science worthy of the name

Contents

Tables and Figures

Chapter 4   Political Parties

Chapter 5   Public Opinion

Chapter 6   Interest Groups

Chapter 8   The Presidency and the Executive Branch

Chapter 9   The Judiciary

Chapter 10   Federalism

Chapter 12   Social Policy

Acknowledgments

In preparing the fifth edition of this book, we owe a great deal to those who have helped us in the past. Each edition presents its own problems and challenges, but it is clear that we continue to draw on the efforts of those who have worked on the earlier editions; they are thanked in the previous acknowledgments. For this edition, Kimberly Maluski, Ken Tomaszewski, and Rory Austin shared the workload—the library searches, phone calls, faxes, reminders, and other efforts that go into updating our many tables and figures.

Several individuals provided assistance with specific tables or figures. Special contributions to this edition were made by Sheldon Goldman, Bruce Jacobs, William Keech, Tom Smith, and Tim Storey.

We thank a growing number of colleagues for reviewing the previous editions and for their helpful suggestions about specific tables, sets of tables, and entire chapters.

Barbara Silveri assisted with skilled typing of tables, as did Melinda Cuddy-Mueller. Fran Versace and her staff provided timely technical support that made typesetting practical and possible.

Our families provided understanding and encouragement on the many nights and weekends when we tracked down, validated, proofed, and typeset yet another table and figure.

At CQ Press David Tarr and Brenda Carter continued in their backing and encouragement. Jon Preimesberger once again edited the entire volume and supervised the production of the figures. Paul Pressau guided us through the typesetting. Kathryn Suárez ably managed the promotions and advertising.

Introduction

Locating material for earlier editions of this book involved a search of several hundred publications, ranging from the traditional to the obscure. For this edition we continue to draw upon this great array of sources. Considerable effort has gone into providing the most up-to-date, politically relevant information possible. Some of the material is from volumes that are not generally available. The most recent information is often unpublished. The data from standard sources are often difficult to trace with the historical continuity we have provided, even with extensive library resources, knowledgeable reference librarians, and time to spare. Combined with its broad coverage of subjects, this means that even more than before this book is an invaluable aid for the reader intent on understanding and keeping up with American politics. Along with the Guide to References for Political Statistics (beginning on page 407), it can serve as a fundamental reference volume for those who wish to keep informed about the American political scene.

The volume covers a wide range of topics. In addition to such standard subjects as elections, Congress, the presidency, and the judiciary, the book provides information on the media; interest groups; foreign, social, and economic policy; and a variety of issues related to state and local government. Coverage is not limited to "hard" data such as votes cast and offices won; rankings of public officials' reputations, content analyses of media coverage, and public opinion data about policy issues are included. The information ranges from simple lists to compilations of outcomes based on implicit analytical concerns. A historical perspective is maintained throughout; depending upon available data, the longest possible time periods are covered, even with public opinion data. The sources of material range from the findable to the fugitive: reference volumes, government publications, political science journals, monographs, the Internet, and press releases, among others.

The chapter organization follows that of most introductory American government textbooks. Readers will recognize, of course, that any such organization is somewhat arbitrary and that information relevant to a specific topic may be found in a variety of places. For example, public opinion data about specific policies are found in the policy chapters, while the public opinion chapter is reserved for more general topics such as party identification and liberal-conservative outlooks. The list of tables and figures, along with the index, should make use of the volume straightforward.

The Guide to References for Political Statistics provides help for those seeking data beyond that contained here. Literally thousands of tables and figures on the topics covered in this volume and on related topics can be found in the works cited.

The quantity and quality of statistical information have grown enormously in recent years, and this trend has yet to peak. The Internet potentially makes data overload just a click away. But statistics have a bad image. Even the numerically innocent can retort that "there're lies, damn lies, and statistics" and that "figures don't lie but liars can figure." But anyone seeking to understand politics—past, present, or future—would be ill-advised to take refuge in such skepticism. Increasingly, both public debates and political analyses contain points couched in or accompanied by statistics. Democracy turns in part on the ability of an informed public to follow such debates and analyses. Now more than ever, understanding politics requires an ability to comprehend numerical data and the assumptions behind them.

Although data are more essential and more readily available, the interpretive skills are all too often lacking. Unless one knows how to read them, tables and figures can be less than useful; they can be intimidating, incomprehensible, and boring. Yet properly understood, tables and figures can be a resource of considerable value and, surprisingly to many students, even intelligible and interesting.

This volume will not teach statistical methods, but it will foster a greater familiarity with the appropriate cautions about reading too much or too little into tables and figures. This introduction, the chapter introductions, and the guide are all intended to enhance the reader's understanding of how to make better use of tabular information. They are designed to help the reader to extract the maximum amount of information from tables, to understand the level of accuracy in tabular information as well as the various sources and kinds of inaccuracies, and to find additional information, including up-to-date information that must be found in serial publications rather than books.

Some readers, particularly students who are accustomed to working with numbers as they appear in textbooks, are sometimes frustrated, perhaps even mystified, when confronted with whole tables of numbers—not to mention a whole book of tables and figures. An important point of departure for these readers is to realize that this book is based principally on simple numerical data, not on the results of complicated statistical manipulations. The fanciest statistics presented are averages or medians. Regression coefficients, chi-squares, and the like can be revealing and useful, and increasingly political science has become methodologically sophisticated so that many journal articles are opaque to those without the ability to cope with advanced statistics. But this book fills a more fundamental need for a single volume encompassing a broad range of data about American politics and as such should be useful to the methodologically skilled and unskilled alike.

The figures and tables are easy to read. Many are merely lists, but very useful lists. They are often lengthy because they may cover as many as two hundred years. Long historical stretches mean change, and that creates some complexities, as, for example, when the names of the dominant parties change so that going back in time introduces unfamiliar labels. Footnotes to the tables and figures contain the necessary explanations as well as important qualifications and details; they must be read to understand the table or figure content. Following conventional practice, large numbers are sometimes expressed in units of thousands or millions to enhance readability. This, too, can lead to minor problems for readers unaccustomed to reading tabular material, but with a bit of practice any such difficulties should be overcome. In general, a little care and caution in reading and interpreting numbers is all that is required.

The Accuracy of Published Data

Errors in Data

The material selected for this volume is intended to be the most accurate, up-to-date information possible from the most reputable sources available. But anyone who has used statistical information realizes that it is almost never completely error free. This is inevitably true here as well. Consider, for example, Tables 13-4 and 13-5. Both are taken from the same governmental publication, fifty pages apart. The figures reported for total outlays, which appear in both tables, typically match. For example, the $195.6 billion total outlays for 1970 noted in Table 13-4 appears identically in Table 13-5. Similarly, the total outlays for 1975 through 1990 match almost perfectly. Yet inexplicably, the figures for national defense never quite match, differing by as little as $.2 billion and as much as $1.1 billion.

Why do such discrepancies and other kinds of errors (or what appear to be errors) occur? The answer varies.

Rounding. Sometimes what appears to be an error is simply a matter of rounding. For example, 20.2 plus 20.4 equals 41 if one adds and then rounds, but equals 40 if one rounds and then adds. Almost certainly this explains why the 1960 federal and state and local expenditures in Table 12-6 (24,957 and 27,337) do not add up exactly to the total shown (summing to 52,294 rather than 52,293). A similar sort of "error" occurs when percentages sum to 99.8 or 100.2 rather than to 100 plus or minus 1 percent.

Exact Date of Data Collection. Accurate interpretation of data depends on knowing the precise date of collection and the period covered. Sometimes this is obvious. For example, the unemployment rate "at the end of the year" may differ if the phrase means the average of the November and December figures rather than the December figures alone. The time factor can be more subtle—for example, if a U.S. senator-elect dies and someone from the other party is appointed to fill the seat, the number of Democrats and Republicans elected will differ slightly from the number of Democrats and Republicans who actually take office a few months later. Even seemingly similar time spans sometimes conceal important differences. Dollar amounts for given years are likely to differ if one uses calendar years rather than fiscal years.

Handling of "Minor" Categories. "Minor" categories may be uncounted, ignored, or dropped for analytical reasons. Often, for example, votes are given only for the candidates of the two major parties. The small number of votes for the Socialist, Libertarian, and Prohibition candidates, not to mention the stray ballots cast for Mickey Mouse or "none of the above," are unreported or lumped together under "other." Thus a vote may be correctly reported as 42.7 percent (of the total vote) and just as correctly reported as 42.9 percent (of the two-party vote). Occasionally minor categories create more complicated problems. For example, in New York State the same candidate may be nominated by two parties, such as the Democratic party and the Liberal party. The percentage of Democratic votes then differs from the percentage of votes received by the Democratic candidate.

Changes in Measurement Techniques. Changes in the way measurements are made can produce different figures and can lead to time series that are not fully comparable. A classic example is survey measurements, in which researchers "improve" the questions, only to find that they cannot measure change in public opinion because the new results are not comparable to those of earlier polls. Sometimes, however, changes are forced on reluctant researchers. For example, the "market basket" of items in the Consumer Price Index (Table 13-2) has changed over time. Fountain pens or carbon paper might have been reasonable items to include in the 1950s, but not in the 1980s; VCRs could hardly have been included until recently.

Ad Hoc Problems. All sorts of small discrepancies can occur, with ad hoc explanations for each one. An example that nearly everyone is familiar with involves the counting of presidents. Bill Clinton is usually said to be the forty-second president. But he is only the forty-first individual to hold the office; Grover Cleveland is counted twice because his two terms were separated by four years. So is the correct number forty-one or forty-two? It depends on precisely what one means. A less obvious problem occurs in counting Supreme Court nominations that failed. In 1987 Douglas Ginsburg was publicly announced as President Reagan's choice, but his name was withdrawn before it was formally submitted to the Senate. Technically, was he nominated? This kind of subtlety is exacerbated when we deal with events of the distant past. It would be easy, for example, to think that the two listings of the nomination of Edward King by President John Tyler are a typographical error. In fact, King was nominated twice, and the nomination was twice withdrawn in a fight between the president and Congress (Table 9-4).

Solutions to Errors in Data

Awareness that data may contain inaccuracies is no reason to ignore the data; nor is it an excuse to ignore the possible inaccuracies. A consideration of some "solutions" to data errors helps illustrate this point. The solutions, like the problems discussed above, are suggestive rather than exhaustive.

Sometimes errors are relatively obvious and can be easily corrected. Misprints occur, for example. One can encounter references to the 535 members of the House of Representatives when obviously the whole Congress is meant. Checking with alternative or more authoritative sources when mistakes are suspected can help remedy such problems.

Outlandish or illogical numbers should also be checked. A classic example of finding and explaining nonsensical results is the case of two researchers who were not willing to believe data from the 1950 census showing "a surprising number of widowed fourteen-year-old boys and, equally surprising, a decrease in the number of widowed teenage males at older ages."[1] They wrote a "detective story" about how they traced the problem to systematic errors in the way certain data were entered into the census records.

Another method—one that should always be used—is to check footnotes and accompanying text for exceptions and special comments. Recognize that the problem may not really be error, but misreading. Consider the table on U.S. casualties in Vietnam (Table 11-8). For 1973-1993 the bottom row shows there were no U.S. military forces in Vietnam but 1,118 battle deaths—surely an anomaly. But the note reveals that there were troops in Vietnam for nearly a month during this time—the zero indicates the force count as of 31 December 1973, and U.S. forces were withdrawn on 27 January 1973. In addition, forces dying of wounds incurred earlier or those who were missing and later classified as deceased are also considered battle deaths.

Another solution is what is formally called sensitivity analysis. When values are inexact or differ across sources, one needs to ask how sensitive the conclusion is to the precise values used. If the true values differed by some specified amount from the reported values, would the conclusion change? If not, one can be more confident about the conclusion. Similarly, if sources differ, consider the actual values from several sources. If the conclusion to be drawn does not vary with the different values, the discrepancies are only a minor problem. For example, almost any conclusion about social welfare expenditures would be the same whether 1973 expenditures were $213.3 (Table 12-5) or $212.3 billion (Table 12-7), even though the difference represents what in other contexts would be an astonishing one billion dollars.

In examining data over time, one way to avoid possible errors is to be sure the data are truly comparable. Again, one must check that the data were collected uniformly or know what the differences are over time and their probable effects. Occasionally guesses about probable error can be confirmed by formal tests. An excellent example is a study in which both old and new survey questions were asked. Differences that had previously been attributed to changes in the electorate over time were shown to be methodological artifacts.[2]

One should also examine data, perhaps especially data over time, for "outliers." If a series of values, say the percentages of votes for the Republican candidate in a given district, are 52, 56, 49, 85, 50, one must check the accuracy of the 85 percent. Is the 85 a transposition of 58? If 85 is the correct number, what is the reason for it? Was the candidate essentially unopposed that year? What conclusion should be drawn if the 85 were omitted?

Finally, after taking all reasonable steps to be sure the data are as good as can be obtained, checking multiple sources, and so on, one should indicate known errors. It is better to point out that there is some question about certain figures than to pretend that they are perfect. If a loftier reason does not come to mind, being straightforward about inaccuracies at least prevents readers from lobbing them back as if the author were too ignorant to even notice the problems.

Obtaining Additional Material

This book provides essential figures and tables, but the coverage is far from exhaustive. Many readers may want data with a slightly different twist or of another sort altogether. The Guide to References for Political Statistics should help orient readers who seek information beyond that contained here. In addition, the sources given for the tables and figures in this book should also be considered in such searches.

Data on current events can be found in newspapers, weekly news magazines, the *Congressional Quarterly Weekly Report*, and the *National Journal*. Indexes for the *Weekly Report, National Journal*, and for major newspapers are a valuable guide. The *National Newspaper Index, Newsbank, Nexis*, and the *National Magazine Index* cover many sources.

Readers need to appreciate how useful reference librarians are in the quest for information. Librarians for government documents collections are also invaluable resources. Interlibrary loans can help secure less readily available volumes, although principal reference works and current material seldom circulate in this fashion.

For some material, one may need to contact organizations that compile or disseminate the data. Various directories are available—of party organizations, interest groups, associations, research institutions, and state agencies. At the federal level, Congressional Quarterly's *Washington Information Directory* is a valuable guide to potential sources. The Council of State Governments, with directories such as *State Administrative Officials Classified by Functions* and *State Elective Officials and the Legislatures*, provides a similar service at the state level. (See also the references cited in the introduction to Chapter 10.)

Data and texts are becoming increasingly available in machine-readable form. Several commercial vendors offer on-line data services. *Nexis* provides newspaper and magazine articles in electronic form. Some government agencies also offer such access. The Internet has increasingly offered access to data holdings. For instance, recent census data in Table 3-1 were obtained through the Internet. While this may make the information widely available, it can also restrict ready access to the computer literate. The Census Bureau seized publication on the Internet as a cost-savings opportunity—the previously published studies would no longer be published or available in conventional form. As personal computers and the Internet proliferate in the years ahead, such opportunities will undoubtedly expand.

For this volume, machine-readable data constituted a valuable source for several tables and figures. Descriptions of available machine-readable data would require another volume. The Inter-university Consortium for Political and Social Research (ICPSR) at the University of Michigan has the largest collection of such data and publishes an annual guide to resources. Most major research universities are members of the consortium. To learn how to obtain data, one should contact the official university representative of the ICPSR.

These hints are merely starting suggestions for those who wish to go beyond this volume to track down particular pieces of information. We hope the reader will find the extensive coverage in this obviously nonexhaustive volume to be convenient and valuable.

Notes

1. Ansley J. Coale and Frederick F. Stephan, "The Case of the Indians and the Teen-Age Widows," *Journal of American Statistical Association* 57 (1962): 338.
2. John L. Sullivan, James E. Piereson, and George E. Marcus, "Ideological Constraint in the Mass Public: A Methodological Critique and Some New Findings," *American Journal of Political Science* 22 (1978): 233-249.

1

The Constitution

Constitutions are documents about rights and authority. At first blush, little about them suggests statistics. However, a great many numbers relate to the fundamental laws that govern the states and the nation. Such numbers, while significant, tend to be straightforward and simple: dates of constitutional revision and amendment, length of gubernatorial terms, requirements for voter registration, and so on. In addition, some important information is found in lists showing, for example, which state constitutions have a certain component, such as the line-item veto.

The image of the U.S. Constitution as a document written on parchment with quill pens is a powerful legacy from the past but a misleading image for understanding the Constitution in the present. The bicentennial year celebrations focused attention on the Constitutional Convention of 1787, but the U.S. Constitution has evolved dramatically over the past two hundred years (Table 1-3). The document, both in content and meaning, has changed as a result of civil war, formal amendments, and Supreme Court rulings. Amendments are not things of the past either; several have been proposed since the 1960s, and a few are still pending (Tables 1-5 and 1-6). Surprisingly, one of the very first amendments proposed, concerning congressional pay, was adopted only recently (Table 1-3).

The federal political structure, delineated in the Constitution, has also undergone significant transformations. For instance, the first ten amendments, the Bill of Rights, originally limited only the federal government, but Supreme Court decisions have interpreted almost all of these rights to limit state governments as well (Table 1-4). Other data about federal and state constitutions and their changes (for example, Tables 1-2, 1-8, and 1-18) also reveal the continuing evolution of the basic framework of the U.S. political system.

9

Because the federal constitution is a brief document that has been changed little during U.S. history, many may think that this is characteristic of all constitutions. State constitutions vary considerably in their length and in their age (Table 1-2). Some also have been amended frequently. Constitutional change has sometimes swept across the entire country, as when Progressives around the turn of the century mounted a major reform effort. Primaries flourish today as one legacy of the Progressive reform movement (Table 4-9). Progressive reformers also pushed the initiative, referendum, and recall; most states have constitutionally adopted at least one of these procedures (Table 1-7).

Constitutions attest to the fundamental values underlying the political order, supposedly capturing and constraining the prevailing political consensus. Although surveys have found public support for civil liberties such as free speech to be less than broadly based (Table 1-9), one of the major contributions of the U.S. Constitution is precisely the protection of minority rights against majority wishes.

Because individuals often fail to agree, even on so-called fundamental issues, and because any change in a constitution may have sweeping effects, constitutions attract controversy. And not surprisingly, data relevant to constitutional issues also reflect controversy. In a number of instances, public opinion has revealed clear majority preferences—on the balanced budget and school prayer (Table 1-6), for example—and yet legislators have failed to enact these constitutional amendments. This may be understandable, as when the outnumbered opposition is intense or raises legal impediments. The discrepancy between majority opinion and political action serves as a helpful reminder about the distinction between opinion and behavior and raises questions about the meaning, interpretations, and implications of such survey data.

Constitutions reach beyond the words they contain. Vital pieces of the political fabric, such as political parties, are not mentioned in the U.S. Constitution. But much that was unmentioned has increasingly come under the Constitution and the jurisdiction of the federal courts. Voter registration requirements, for example, were originally left to the states, but federal court decisions, the Voting Rights Act, and the "Motor Voter" law have caused greater uniformity among the states since 1965 (Table 1-17). Similarly, reapportionment of legislative seats, an area the federal courts initially refused to review because it raised "political questions," has changed dramatically since the early 1960s. With its "one-person, one-vote" ruling, the Supreme Court has imposed strict standards on legislative districts (Tables 1-15 and 1-16).

Constitutions are words, not numbers. But it is surprising how many statistics are relevant to the understanding of constitutions.

Table 1-1   The States: Historical Data and Current Populations

State	Population[a]	Date organized as territory	Date admitted to Union	Chronological order of admission to Union
Alabama	4,040,587	March 3, 1817	December 14, 1819	22
Alaska	550,043	August 24, 1912	January 3, 1959	49
Arizona	3,665,228	February 24, 1863	February 14, 1912	48
Arkansas	2,350,725	March 2, 1819	June 15, 1836	25
California	29,760,021	[b]	September 9, 1850	31
Colorado	3,294,394	February 28, 1861	August 1, 1876	38
Connecticut	3,287,116	—	January 9, 1788[c]	5
Delaware	666,168	—	December 7, 1787[c]	1
Florida	12,937,926	March 30, 1822	March 3, 1845	27
Georgia	6,478,216	—	January 2, 1788[c]	4
Hawaii	1,108,229	June 14, 1900	August 21, 1959	50
Idaho	1,006,749	March 4, 1863	July 3, 1890	43
Illinois	11,430,602	February 3, 1809	December 3, 1818	21
Indiana	5,544,159	May 7, 1800	December 11, 1816	19
Iowa	2,776,755	June 12, 1838	December 28, 1846	29
Kansas	2,477,574	May 30, 1854	January 29, 1861	34
Kentucky	3,685,296	[b]	June 1, 1792	15
Louisiana	4,219,973	March 26, 1804	April 30, 1812	18
Maine	1,227,928	[b]	March 15, 1820	23
Maryland	4,781,468	—	April 28, 1788[c]	7
Massachusetts	6,016,425	—	February 6, 1788[c]	6
Michigan	9,295,297	January 11, 1805	January 26, 1837	26
Minnesota	4,375,099	March 3, 1849	May 11, 1858	32
Mississippi	2,573,216	April 7, 1798	December 10, 1817	20
Missouri	5,117,073	June 4, 1812	August 10, 1821	24
Montana	799,065	May 26, 1864	November 8, 1889	41
Nebraska	1,578,385	May 30, 1854	March 1, 1867	37
Nevada	1,201,833	March 2, 1861	October 31, 1864	36
New Hampshire	1,109,252	—	June 21, 1788[c]	9
New Jersey	7,730,188	—	December 18, 1787[c]	3
New Mexico	1,515,069	September 9, 1850	January 6, 1912	47
New York	17,990,455	—	July 26, 1788[c]	11
North Carolina	6,628,637	—	November 21, 1789[c]	12
North Dakota	638,800	March 2, 1861	November 2, 1889	39
Ohio	10,847,115	May 7, 1800	March 1, 1803	17
Oklahoma	3,145,585	May 2, 1890	November 16, 1907	46
Oregon	2,842,321	August 14, 1848	February 14, 1859	33
Pennsylvania	11,881,643	—	December 12, 1787[c]	2
Rhode Island	1,003,464	—	May 29, 1790[c]	13
South Carolina	3,486,703	—	May 23, 1788[c]	8
South Dakota	696,004	March 2, 1861	November 2, 1889	40
Tennessee	4,877,185	June 8, 1790[d]	June 1, 1796	16

(Table continues)

Table 1-1 *(Continued)*

State	Population[a]	Date organized as territory	Date admitted to Union	Chrono-logical order of admission to Union
Texas	16,986,510	[b]	December 29, 1845	28
Utah	1,722,850	September 9, 1850	January 4, 1896	45
Vermont	562,758	[b]	March 4, 1791	14
Virginia	6,187,358	—	June 25, 1788[c]	10
Washington	4,866,692	March 2, 1853	November 11, 1889	42
West Virginia	1,793,477	[b]	June 20, 1863	35
Wisconsin	4,891,769	April 20, 1836	May 29, 1848	30
Wyoming	453,588	July 25, 1868	July 10, 1890	44
Total	248,709,873			

Note: "—" indicates one of the original thirteen states.

[a] As of 1990.
[b] No territorial status before admission to Union.
[c] Date of ratification of U.S. Constitution.
[d] Date Southwest Territory (identical boundaries as Tennessee's) was created.

Sources: Council of State Governments, *Book of the States, 1992-1993* (Lexington, Ky.: Council of State Governments, 1992), 659-660; population: U.S. Bureau of the Census, *1990 Census of Population and Housing: Summary Population and Housing Characteristics* (Washington, D.C.: U.S. Government Printing Office, 1992), Series 1990 CPH-1-1, 360.

Table 1-2 State Constitutions

State	Number of constitutions[a]	Dates of adoption	Present constitution Effective date	Estimated length (number of words)	Number of amendments Submitted to voters	Adopted
Alabama	6	1819, 1861, 1865, 1868, 1875, 1901	November 28, 1901	174,000	783	556
Alaska	1	1956	January 3, 1959	16,675	32	23
Arizona	1	1911	February 14, 1912	28,876	215	119
Arkansas	5	1836, 1861, 1864, 1868, 1874	October 30, 1874	40,720	171	81
California	2	1847, 1879	July 4, 1879	33,350	814	485
Colorado	1	1876	August 1, 1876	45,679	254	124
Connecticut	4	1818, 1965	December 30, 1965	9,564	29	28
Delaware	4	1776, 1792, 1831, 1897	June 10, 1897	19,000	[b]	123
Florida	6	1839, 1861, 1865, 1868, 1886, 1968	January 7, 1969	25,100	92	65
Georgia	10	1777, 1789, 1798, 1861, 1865, 1868, 1877, 1945, 1976, 1982	July 1, 1983	25,000	52	39
Hawaii	1	1950	August 21, 1959	17,453	102	86
Idaho	1	1889	July 3, 1890	21,500	189	109
Illinois	4	1818, 1848, 1870, 1970	July 1, 1971	13,200	14	8
Indiana	2	1816, 1851	November 1, 1851	9,377	70	38
Iowa	2	1846, 1857	September 3, 1857	12,500	52	49
Kansas	1	1859	January 29, 1861	11,865	118	90
Kentucky	4	1792, 1799, 1850, 1891	September 28, 1891	23,500	65	32
Louisiana	11	1812, 1845, 1852, 1861, 1864, 1868, 1879, 1898, 1913, 1921, 1974	January 1, 1975	51,488	92	54
Maine	1	1819	March 15, 1820	13,500	192	162
Maryland	4	1776, 1851, 1864, 1867	October 5, 1867	41,349	238	205

(Table continues)

Table 1-2 (*Continued*)

State	Number of constitutions[a]	Dates of adoption	Present constitution Effective date	Present constitution Estimated length (number of words)	Number of amendments Submitted to voters	Number of amendments Adopted
Massachusetts	1	1780	October 25, 1780	36,690	144	117
Michigan	4	1835, 1850, 1908, 1963	January 1, 1964	20,000	51	17
Minnesota	1	1857	May 11, 1858	9,500	207	113
Mississippi	4	1817, 1832, 1869, 1890	November 1, 1890	24,000	148	116
Missouri	4	1820, 1865, 1875, 1945	March 30, 1945	42,000	132	81
Montana	2	1889, 1972	July 1, 1973	11,866	32	18
Nebraska	2	1866, 1875	October 12, 1875	20,048	293	197
Nevada	1	1864	October 31, 1864	20,770	184	113
New Hampshire	2	1776, 1784	June 2, 1784	9,200	280	143
New Jersey	3	1776, 1844, 1947	January 1, 1948	17,086	57	44
New Mexico	1	1911	January 6, 1912	27,200	240	123
New York	4	1777, 1822, 1846, 1894	January 1, 1895	80,000	280	213
North Carolina	3	1776, 1868, 1970	July 1, 1971	11,000	35	27
North Dakota	1	1889	November 2, 1889	20,564	235	129
Ohio	2	1802, 1851	September 1, 1851	36,900	253	151
Oklahoma	1	1907	November 16, 1907	68,800	293	146
Oregon	1	1857	February 14, 1859	26,090	383	—
Pennsylvania	5	1776, 1790, 1838, 1873, 1968	1968[c]	21,675	26	—
Rhode Island	2	1842	May 2, 1843	19,026	102	56
South Carolina	7	1776, 1778, 1790, 1861, 1865, 1868, 1895	January 1, 1896	22,500	648	463
South Dakota	1	1889	November 2, 1889	23,300	191	99
Tennessee	3	1796, 1835, 1870	February 23, 1870	15,300	55	32
Texas	5	1845, 1861, 1866, 1869, 1876	February 15, 1876	76,000	518	353
Utah	1	1895	January 4, 1896	11,000	131	82

Vermont	3	1777, 1786, 1793	July 9, 1793	6,600	208	50
Virginia	6	1776, 1830, 1851, 1869, 1902, 1970	July 1, 1971	18,500	28	23
Washington	1	1889	November 11, 1889	29,400	158	88
West Virginia	2	1863, 1872	April 9, 1872	25,600	110	64
Wisconsin	1	1848	May 29, 1848	13,500	174	129
Wyoming	1	1889	July 10, 1890	31,800	102	61

Note: Constitutions as of January 1, 1994. "—" indicates not available. For more details on the constitutions, see source.

[a] The constitutions include those Civil War documents customarily listed by the individual states. In Connecticut and Rhode Island, colonial charters served as the first constitutions.

[b] Proposed amendments are not submitted to the voters in Delaware.

[c] Certain sections of the constitution were revised in 1967-1968. Amendments proposed and adopted are since 1968.

Source: Council of State Governments, *Book of the States, 1994-1995* (Lexington, Ky.: Council of State Governments, 1994), 19.

Table 1-3 Length of Time Between Congressional Approval and Actual Ratification of the Twenty-seven Amendments to the U.S. Constitution

Amendment		Time required for ratification	Year ratified
I-X	Bill of Rights	2 years, 2½ months	1791
XI	Lawsuits against states	11 months	1795
XII	Presidential elections	6½ months	1804
XIII	Abolition of slavery	10 months	1865
XIV	Civil rights	2 years, 1 month	1868
XV	Suffrage for all races	11 months	1870
XVI	Income tax	3 years, 6½ months	1913
XVII	Senatorial elections	11 months	1913
XVIII	Prohibition	1 year, 1 month	1919
XIX	Women's suffrage	1 year, 2 months	1920
XX	Terms of office	11 months	1933
XXI	Repeal of prohibition	9½ months	1933
XXII	Limit on presidential terms	3 years, 11 months	1951
XXIII	Washington, D.C., vote	9 months	1961
XXIV	Abolition of poll taxes	1 year, 4 months	1964
XXV	Presidential succession	1 year, 10 months	1967
XXVI	Eighteen-year-old suffrage	3 months	1971
XXVII	Congressional salaries	203 years	1992

Sources: Congressional Research Service, *The Constitution of the United States: Analysis and Interpretation* (Washington, D.C.: U.S. Government Printing Office, 1973), 23-44 (92d Cong., 2d sess., S. Doc. 92-82); *Congressional Quarterly Weekly Report* (1992), 1423.

Table 1-4   Incorporation of the Bill of Rights to Apply to State
Governments

Year	Issue and amendment	Supreme Court case	Vote
[1868	Fourteenth Amendment to Constitution passed][a]		
1897	Eminent domain (V)	Chicago, Burlington & Quincy RR v. Chicago 166 U.S. 266	9:0
1927	Freedom of speech (I)	Fiske v. Kansas 274 U.S. 380	9:0
1931	Freedom of press (I)	Near v. Minnesota 283 U.S. 697	5:4
1932	Counsel in capital criminal cases (VI)	Powell v. Alabama 287 U.S. 45	7:2
1934	Free exercise of religion (I)	Hamilton v. Regents of the U. of California 293 U.S. 245	9:0
1937	Freedom of assembly and petition (I)	De Jonge v. Oregon 299 U.S. 253	8:0
1947	Separation of church and state (I)	Everson v. Board of Education of Ewing Township 330 U.S. 1	5:4
1948	Public trial (VI)	In re Oliver 33 U.S. 257	7:2
1961	Unreasonable searches and seizures (IV)	Mapp v. Ohio 367 U.S. 643	6:3
1962	Cruel and unusual punishment (VIII)	Robinson v. California 370 U.S. 660	6:2
1963	Counsel in all criminal cases (VI)	Gideon v. Wainwright 372 U.S. 335	9:0
1964	Self-incrimination (V)	Malloy v. Hogan 378 U.S. 1	5:4
		Murphy v. Waterfront Commission 378 U.S. 52	9:0
1965	Right to confront adverse witnesses (VI)	Pointer v. Texas 380 U.S. 400	7:2
1967	Impartial jury (VI)	Parker v. Gladden 385 U.S. 363	8:1
1967	Obtaining and confronting favorable witnesses (VI)	Washington v. Texas 388 U.S. 14	9:0
1967	Speedy trial (VI)	Klopfer v. North Carolina 386 U.S. 213	9:0
1968	Jury trial in non-petty criminal cases (VI)	Duncan v. Louisiana 391 U.S. 145	7:2
1969	Double jeopardy (V)	Benton v. Maryland 395 U.S. 784	7:2

Note: Enumerated rights not incorporated: grand jury indictment, trial by jury in civil cases, excessive fines and bail, right to bear arms, and safeguards on quartering troops in private homes.

[a] The Fourteenth Amendment's due process clause is the basis for applying the Bill of Rights to the states.

Sources: Henry J. Abraham, The Judiciary: The Supreme Court in the Governmental Process, 7th ed. (Dubuque, Iowa: William C. Brown, 1988); votes: United States Reports (Washington, D.C.: U.S. Government Printing Office, various years).

Table 1-5   State Action on Proposed Constitutional Amendments

	Proposed amendment				
State	Reapportionment[a]	Equal rights[b]	Balanced budget[c]	Ban abortion[d]	Line-item veto[e]
Alabama	yes	n.a.	r	yes	n.a.
Alaska	n.a.	yes	yes	n.a.	n.a.
Arizona	yes	n.a.	yes	n.a.	yes
Arkansas	yes	n.a.	yes	yes	n.a.
California	n.a.	yes	n.a.[f]	n.a.	n.a.
Colorado	yes	yes	yes	n.a.	n.a.
Connecticut	n.a.	yes	n.a.	n.a.	n.a.
Delaware	n.a.	yes	yes	yes	n.a.
Florida	yes	n.a.	r	n.a.	n.a.
Georgia	yes	n.a.	yes	n.a.	n.a.
Hawaii	n.a.	yes	n.a.	n.a.	n.a.
Idaho	yes	r	yes	yes	yes
Illinois	r[g]	n.a.	n.a.[f]	n.a.	yes
Indiana	yes	yes	yes	yes	n.a.
Iowa	yes	yes	yes	n.a.	n.a.
Kansas	r[g]	yes	yes	n.a.	yes
Kentucky	yes	r	n.a.[f]	yes	n.a.
Louisiana	yes	n.a.	r	yes	yes
Maine	n.a.	yes	n.a.	n.a.	n.a.
Maryland	r[g]	yes	yes	n.a.	n.a.
Massachusetts	n.a.	yes	n.a.	yes	n.a.
Michigan	n.a.	yes	n.a.	n.a.	yes
Minnesota	yes	yes	n.a.	n.a.	n.a.
Mississippi	yes	n.a.	yes	yes	n.a.
Missouri	yes	n.a.	yes	yes	n.a.
Montana	yes	yes	n.a.[f]	n.a.	n.a.
Nebraska	yes	r	yes	yes	n.a.
Nevada	yes	n.a.	r[g]	yes	yes
New Hampshire	yes	yes	yes	n.a.	n.a.
New Jersey	n.a.	yes	n.a.	yes	n.a.
New Mexico	yes	yes	yes	n.a.	n.a.
New York	n.a.	yes	n.a.	n.a.	n.a.
North Carolina	r[g]	n.a.	yes	n.a.	n.a.
North Dakota	yes	yes	yes	n.a.	n.a.
Ohio	n.a.	yes	n.a.	n.a.	n.a.
Oklahoma	yes	n.a.	yes	yes	n.a.
Oregon	n.a.	yes	yes	n.a.	n.a.
Pennsylvania	n.a.	yes	yes	yes	n.a.
Rhode Island	n.a.	yes	n.a.	yes	n.a.
South Carolina	yes	n.a.	yes	n.a.	n.a.
South Dakota	yes	r	yes	yes	yes
Tennessee	yes	r	yes	yes	yes
Texas	r[g]	yes	yes	n.a.	n.a.
Utah	yes	n.a.	yes	n.a.	n.a.
Vermont	n.a.	yes	n.a.	n.a.	n.a.
Virginia	yes	n.a.	yes	n.a.	yes

Table 1-5   (*Continued*)

State	Reapportionment[a]	Equal rights[b]	Balanced budget[c]	Ban abortion[d]	Line-item veto[e]
		Proposed amendment			
Washington	r[g]	yes	n.a.	n.a.	n.a.
West Virginia	n.a.	yes	n.a.	n.a.	n.a.
Wisconsin	n.a.	yes	n.a.	n.a.	n.a.
Wyoming	yes	yes	yes	n.a.	n.a.

Note: "Yes" indicates state legislature approved the amendment or sent a petition to Congress for a constitutional convention; "n.a." indicates no action was taken or the state legislature rejected the amendment or a proposal to petition for a convention; and "r" indicates previous appeal was rescinded. The equal rights amendment was initiated by Congress and submitted to the states for ratification. The other proposed amendments were initiated by petition from state legislatures.

[a] Reapportionment: States acted to petition Congress for a constitutional convention on this issue following two Supreme Court "one-person, one-vote" decisions concerning how states were apportioned for their state legislatures. As a result, some states called for a convention to consider an amendment that would allow one house of a state legislature to be apportioned on a basis other than population.

[b] Equal rights: This amendment had a time limit for approval, which expired. As proposed by Congress and voted on by the states, it read: "Section 1. Equality of rights under the law shall not be denied or abridged by the United States or by any State on account of sex. Section 2. The Congress shall have the power to enforce, by appropriate legislation, the provisions of this article. Section 3. This amendment shall take effect two years after the date of ratification."

[c] Balanced budget: This proposed amendment has various forms. In its simplest form, Congress would be required to approve a balanced federal budget each year. In other forms there is a provision that a three-fifths majority of Congress could vote not to balance the budget in any given year.

[d] Abortion: Some states have called for a constitutional convention to consider an amendment that would ban abortions. The most common approach among the various proposed amendments is to apply the constitutional protection of due process against the denial of life and property to unborn children.

[e] Some states have called for a constitutional convention to consider an amendment that would give the president a line-item veto.

[f] The state did not endorse the call for a constitutional convention but petitioned Congress to propose a balanced budget amendment to the states.

[g] Passed by only one house of each of the state legislature.

Sources: Reapportionment: *Congressional Quarterly Weekly Report* (1969), 1372-1373; equal rights: Congressional Research Service, *The Constitution of the United States: Analysis and Interpretation* (Washington, D.C.: U.S. Government Printing Office, 1973), 43 (92d Cong., 2d sess., S. Doc. 92-82); balanced budget: Congressional Research Service, "Constitutional Convention: Political and Legal Questions," September 18, 1990; abortion and line-item veto: *Congressional Record* citations to state communications relating to constitutional conventions.

Table 1-6   Public Opinion on Issues Relating to Proposed
Constitutional Amendments (percent)

Proposed amendment/year	Favor	Oppose	Don't know or no opinion
Abortion amendment			
1985 (January)	38	58	. 4
1985 (September)	37	55	8
1987	25	69	6
1988	34	60	6
1989 (January)	29	68	3
1989 (March)	28	63	9
1989 (April)	27	65	8
1989 (June)	31	60	9
1989 (July)	27	62	11
1989 (October)	29	62	2
1990	21	73	6
1992	25	67	8
Supreme Court decision in *Roe v. Wade*			
1974	47	44	9
1981	45	46	9
1983	50	43	7
1986	45	45	10
1988	58	37	5
1989	61	33	6
1991 (June)	52	42	6
1991 (July)	56	37	7
1991 (September)	57	36	7
1991 (December)	64	30	6
Balanced budget amendment[a]			
1976	78	13	9
1981 (April)	70	22	8
1981 (September)	73	19	8
1982	74	17	9
1983	71	21	8
1985	49	27	24
1987	53	23	24
1989	59	24	17
Equal rights amendment[a]			
1975	58	24	18
1976	57	24	19
1978	58	31	11
1980	58	31	11
1981	63	32	5
1982	56	34	10
1984	63	31	6

Table 1-6   (*Continued*)

Proposed amendment/year	Favor	Oppose	Don't know or no opinion
Flag burning amendment			
1989 (June)	71	24	5
1989 (June)	67	29	4
1989 (July)	67	28	5
1990 (June)	68	25	5
1990 (June)	57	42	1
Supreme Court decision banning school prayer			
1963	24	70	6
1971	28	67	6
1974	31	66	3
1975	35	62	3
1977	33	64	2
1981	31	66	3
1982	37	60	3
1983	40	57	4
1985 (March)	43	54	3
1985 (September)	37	62	1
1986	37	61	2
1988	37	59	4
1989	41	56	3
1990	40	56	5
1991	38	58	4
Supreme Court one-person, one-vote decision			
1964	47	30	23
1969	52	23	25

Note: All results are based on national, adult samples. Questions: Abortion amendment: "Do you favor or oppose a constitutional amendment to ban abortions?," or very similar wording. *Roe v. Wade*, 1974-1986—"The U.S. Supreme Court has ruled that a woman may go to a doctor to end her pregnancy at any time during the first three months of pregnancy. Do you favor or oppose this ruling?" *Roe v. Wade*, 1988-1989—"The Supreme Court's 1973 *Roe versus Wade* decision established a woman's constitutional right to an abortion at least in the first three months of pregnancy. Would you like to see the Supreme Court completely overturn its *Roe versus Wade* decision, or not?" (Question did not include "completely" in 1988.) Balanced budget—"Have you heard (or read) about the proposal for a constitutional amendment which would require the federal government to balance the national budget each year? A proposed amendment to the Constitution would require Congress to approve a balanced federal budget each year. Government spending would have to be limited to no more than expected revenues, unless a three-fifths majority of Congress voted to spend more than expected revenues. Would you favor or oppose this amendment to the Constitution?" (Slightly different wording in 1976 and 1989.) Equal rights—"Have you heard or read about the Equal Rights Amendment to the U.S. Constitution which would prohibit discrimination on the basis of sex? Do you favor or oppose this amendment?" Flag burning—"Do you favor or oppose a constitutional amendment which would make it illegal to burn the American flag?," or very similar wording. School

(*Notes continue*)

Table 1-6 *(Continued)*

prayer—"The U.S. Supreme Court has ruled that no state or local government may require the reading of the Lord's Prayer or Bible verses in public schools. What are your views on this—do you approve or disapprove of the court ruling?" One-person, one-vote, decision, 1964—"As you know, the U.S. Supreme Court has ruled that the number of representatives of both the lower house and the Senate in all state legislatures must be in proportion to population. In most states, this means reducing the number of legislators from the rural areas and increasing the number from urban areas. Do you approve or disapprove of this ruling?" One-person, one-vote decision, 1969—"The U.S. Supreme Court has required states to change their legislative districts so that each member of the upper house represents the same number of people. Some people would like to return to the earlier method of electing members of the upper house according to counties or other units regardless of population. Would you favor continuing the present equal districting plan or returning to the earlier plan?"

[a] Of those who were aware of the proposed amendment (except 1984 for equal rights, 1976 and 1987-1989 for balanced budget). Between 88 and 91 percent of those asked were aware of the equal rights amendment. Between 48 and 66 percent of those asked were aware of the proposed balanced budget amendment.

Sources: Abortion: (1985, January 1989) Harris surveys; (1987) CBS/*New York Times* survey; (1988, October 1989, 1992) ABC/*Washington Post* surveys; (March 1989) *Los Angeles Times* survey; (April, June, July, 1989, 1990) Yankelovich, Clancy, Shulman surveys; *Roe v. Wade*: *The Gallup Poll* (Wilmington, Del.: Scholarly Resources, Inc., 1983), 140, *The Gallup Report*, January/February 1986, 17-18, October 1990, 17, *Los Angeles Times* survey, *The Gallup Poll* (New York: Random House, 1972), 1897, 2205-2206, Gallup Poll Surveys; school prayer: (1963, 1971) *The Gallup Poll* (1972), 1837; 1981, 1985 (September) ABC News/*Washington Post* survey; (1974-1977, 1982-1985 (June), 1986-1991) General Social Survey, National Opinion Research Center, University of Chicago; equal rights: *The Gallup Poll* (1982), 140, (1984), 242; balanced budget: *The Gallup Poll* (1972), 679, (1982), 125, 231, (1983), 127, *The Gallup Report*, September 1985, 10-11, July 1987, 8, February 1989, 3; flag burning: (1989 June, first; 1990, June, first) *Gallup Poll Monthly*, June 1990, 3-4; (1989, June, second) Yankelovich, Clancy, Shulman survey; (1989 July) *Los Angeles Times* survey; 1990 (June, second) Harris survey.

Table 1-7 State Provisions for Initiative, Referendum, and Recall

State	Initiative[a]	Referendum[b]	Recall[c]
Alabama		legislature and petition	all but judges
Alaska	direct	legislature and petition	all elected officials
Arizona	direct	legislature and petition	
Arkansas	direct	legislature and petition	all elected officials
California	direct	legislature and petition	all elected officials
Colorado	direct	legislature	
Connecticut		legislature	
Delaware		legislature	
Florida		legislature	
Georgia		legislature	all elected officials
Hawaii		legislature	
Idaho	direct	legislature and petition	all but judges
Illinois		legislature	
Indiana		legislature	
Iowa		legislature	
Kansas		legislature	all but judges
Kentucky		legislature and petition	
Louisiana		legislature	all but certain judges
Maine	indirect	legislature and petition	
Maryland		legislature and petition	
Massachusetts	indirect	legislature and petition	
Michigan	both	legislature and petition	all but certain judges
Minnesota		legislature	
Mississippi	indirect	legislature	
Missouri	direct	legislature and petition	
Montana	direct	legislature and petition	all elected or appointed officials
Nebraska	direct	legislature and petition	all public officers
Nevada	both	legislature and petition	
New Hampshire		legislature	

(Table continues)

Table 1-7 (*Continued*)

State	Initiative[a]	Referendum[b]	Recall[c]
New Jersey		legislature	
New Mexico		legislature and petition	
New York		legislature	
North Carolina		legislature	
North Dakota	direct	legislature and petition	all elected officials
Ohio	both	legislature and petition	
Oklahoma	direct	legislature and petition	
Oregon	direct	legislature and petition	all elected officials exc. Congress
Pennsylvania		legislature	
Rhode Island		legislature	certain elected officials
South Carolina		legislature	
South Dakota	direct	legislature and petition	certain municipal officials
Tennessee		legislature	
Texas		legislature	
Utah	both	legislature and petition	
Vermont		legislature	
Virginia		legislature	
Washington	both	legislature and petition	all but certain judges
West Virginia		legislature	
Wisconsin		legislature	all elected officials
Wyoming	indirect	legislature and petition	

Note: Initiative and referendum provisions may apply to Constitution, statutes, or both. See source for details.

[a] Initiative: Allows proposed state laws to be placed on a ballot by citizen petition and enacted or rejected by the electorate. "Direct" means measures may be placed on the ballot with a specific number of signatures and no legislative action; requirements for number of signatures vary. "Indirect" means a measure must be submitted to the legislature for consideration before it can be placed on the ballot.

[b] Referendum: State law passed by the legislature is referred to voters before it goes into effect. Referendum may be held by citizen petition or voluntary submission by the legislature. For certain types of decisions, such as tax increases, referendum may be a constitutional requirement.

[c] Recall: Voters are allowed to remove state elective officials in a recall election. Number of signatures needed ranges from 10 to 40 percent; percentage is based on last vote for the office in question or general election. Sometimes percentage is modified by geographical or jurisdictional restrictions.

Source: Council of State Governments, *Book of the States, 1994-1995* (Lexington, Ky.: Council of State Governments, 1994), 294, 305-306.

Table 1-8 Governors' Terms, Limits, Powers, and Other Statewide Elected Officials

State	Length of term in 1900	Length of term in 1995	Year of change	Maximum number of consecutive terms	Item veto[a]	Other statewide elected officials[b] Number of officials	Number of agencies
Alabama	2	4	1902	2	no	9	7
Alaska	[c]	4		2[d]	yes	1	0
Arizona	[c]	4	1970	2[d]	yes	8	6
Arkansas	2	4	1984	2[e]	yes	6	6
California	4	4		2[e]	yes	7	7
Colorado	2	4	1958	2[d]	yes	4	4
Connecticut	2	4	1950	No limit	yes	5	5
Delaware	4	4		2[e]	yes	1	1
Florida	4	4		2	no	7	7
Georgia	2	4	1942	2[d]	yes	12	8
Hawaii	[c]	4		2	yes	1	1
Idaho	2	4	1946	No limit[f]	yes	6	6
Illinois	4	4		No limit	yes	14	6
Indiana	4	4		[g]	no	6	6
Iowa	2	4	1974	No limit	yes	6	6
Kansas	2	4	1974	2	yes	5	5
Kentucky	4	4		2	yes	7	7
Louisiana	4	4		2	yes	7	7
Maine	2	4	1958	2	no	0	0
Maryland	4	4		2[d]	yes	3	3
Massachusetts	1	4	1920, 1966[h]	2[d]	yes	5	7
Michigan	2	4	1966	2[e]	yes	35	7

(Table continues)

Table 1-8 (Continued)

State	Length of term in 1900	Length of term in 1995	Year of change	Maximum number of consecutive terms	Item veto[a]	Other statewide elected officials[b] Number of officials	Number of agencies
Minnesota	2	4	1962	No limit	yes	5	5
Mississippi	4	4		2	yes	7	7
Missouri	4	4		2[e][i]	yes	5	5
Montana	4	4			yes	5	5
Nebraska	2	4	1966	2[d]	yes	5	5
Nevada	4	4		2	no	5	5
New Hampshire	2	2		No limit	no	0	0
New Jersey	3[c]	4	1949	2[d]	yes	0	0
New Mexico	4	4	1916, 1970	2[d]	yes	9	7
New York	2	4	1938	No limit	yes	3	3
North Carolina	4	4		2	no	9	9
North Dakota	2	4	1964	No limit	yes	13	11
Ohio	2[c]	4	1958	2[e]	yes	5	5
Oklahoma		4		2	yes	10	8
Oregon	4	4		2[e]	yes	5	5
Pennsylvania	4	4		2	yes	4	4
Rhode Island	1	4	1912, 1995[h]	No limit	no	4	4
South Carolina	2	4	1926	2	yes	8	10
South Dakota	2	4	1974	2	yes	9	7
Tennessee	1	4	1954	2	yes	3	1
Texas	2	4	1974	No limit	yes	9	7
Utah	4	4		3	yes	4	4
Vermont	2	2		No limit	no	5	5

Virginia	4		1[e]	yes	2	2
Washington	4		[j]	yes	8	8
West Virginia	4		2	yes	5	7
Wisconsin	2	1970	No limit[i]	yes	5	5
Wyoming	4			yes	4	4

[a] Provisions to override vary, requiring as many as two-thirds of the legislators elected. For details, see source.

[b] Popularly elected executive branch officials and the number of agencies involving these officials.

[c] Oklahoma was admitted to the Union in 1907, Arizona and New Mexico in 1912, and Alaska and Hawaii in 1959. Oklahoma, Alaska, and Hawaii have always had four-year gubernatorial terms. Arizona started with two years. New Mexico started with four years, went to two years in 1916 and back to four years in 1970.

[d] After two consecutive terms, must wait four years before being eligible again.

[e] Two terms only, whether or not consecutive, except Virginia: one term only, successive terms forbidden.

[f] Cannot serve more than eight years in any fifteen-year period.

[g] Cannot serve more than eight years in any twelve-year period.

[h] Massachusetts went from one year to two years in 1920 and from two years to four years in 1966. Rhode Island went from one year to two years in 1912, and from two years to four years in 1995.

[i] Cannot serve more than eight years in any sixteen-year period.

[j] Cannot serve more than eight years in any fourteen-year period.

Sources: Council of State Governments, *Book of the States, 1994-1995* (Lexington, Ky.: Council of State Governments, 1994), 50-51, 55-56, 320-321; length of term in 1900 and year of change: Congressional Quarterly, *Congressional Quarterly's Guide to U.S. Elections,* 2d ed. (Washington, D.C.: Congressional Quarterly, 1985), 454; *Book of the States,* 50-51; maximum number of consecutive terms: updated by the editors from texts of state term limit measures.

Table 1-9   Public Opinion on Civil Liberties, 1940-1994 (percent)

Issue/year	Allow[a]	Don't forbid[b]
Public speeches against democracy		
1940	25	46
1974	56	72
1976a	55	80
1976b	52	79

Issue/year	Allow to speak	Allow to teach college	Keep book in library
Atheist[c]			
1954	37	12	35
1964[d]	—	—	61
1972	65	40	61
1973a	65	41	61
1973b	62	39	57
1974	62	42	60
1976	64	41	60
1977	62	39	59
1978	63	—	60
1980	66	45	62
1982	64	46	61
1984	68	46	64
1985	65	45	61
1987	69	47	66
1988	70	45	64
1989	72	51	67
1990	73	50	67
1991	72	52	69
1993	71	52	67
1994	73	52	70
Admitted communist[c]			
1954	27	6	27
1972	52	32	53
1973a	60	39	58
1973b	53	30	54
1974	58	42	59
1976	55	41	56
1977	55	39	55
1978	60	—	61
1980	55	41	57
1982	56	43	57
1984	59	46	60
1985	57	44	57
1987	60	46	61
1988	60	48	59
1989	64	50	62
1990	64	52	64
1991	67	54	67
1993	69	56	67
1994	67	55	66

Table 1-9   *(Continued)*

Issue/year	Allow to speak	Allow to teach college	Keep book in library
Racist[c]			
1943[e]	17	—	—
1976	61	41	60
1977	59	41	61
1978	62	—	65
1980	62	43	64
1982	59	43	60
1984	57	41	63
1985	55	42	60
1987	61	44	64
1988	61	42	62
1989	62	46	65
1990	63	45	64
1991	62	42	66
1993	61	43	64
1994	61	42	66

Note: "—" indicates not available.

[a] Question: "Do you think the United States should allow public speeches against democracy?"
[b] Question: "Do you think the United States should forbid public speeches against democracy?"
[c] Question: "There are always some people whose ideas are considered bad or dangerous by other people. For instance, somebody who (is against all churches and religion/admits he is a communist/believes that blacks are genetically inferior). If such a person wanted to make a speech in your (city/town/community), should he be allowed to speak or not? Should such a person be allowed to teach in a college or university, or not? If some people in your community suggested that a book he wrote (against churches and religion/promoting communism/which said blacks are inferior) should be taken out of your public library, would you favor removing this book or not?" (Slight variations in wording across groups.)
[d] In 1964 the question was as follows: "Suppose a man admitted in public that he did not believe in God. Do you think a book he wrote should be removed from a public library?"
[e] In 1943 the question was as follows: "In peacetime, do you think anyone in the United States should be allowed to make speeches against certain races in this country?"

Sources: Public speeches against democracy: Howard Schuman and Stanley Presser, *Questions and Answers in Attitude Surveys* (New York: Academic Press, 1981), 277; 1943, 1964, and 1973b: National Opinion Research Center surveys; 1954: Samuel A. Stouffer, *Communism, Conformity, and Civil Liberties* (Garden City, N.Y.: Doubleday, 1955), 32-34, 40-43; 1973a: Clyde Z. Nunn et al., *Tolerance for Nonconformity* (San Francisco: Jossey-Bass, 1978), 40-43; data for all other years from General Social Survey.

Table 1-10 States with the Death Penalty, Number of Executions (1930-1994), and Number on Death Row (1995)

State	Method[a]	Number executed							Number awaiting execution[c]
		1930s	1940s	1950s	1960s	1970s	1980s	1990s[b]	
Alabama	electrocution	60	50	20	5	0	7	3	134
Alaska	none	0	0	0	0	0	0	0	0
Arizona	gas chamber	17	9	8	4	0	0	3	122
Arkansas	lethal injection	53	8	18	9	0	0	9	38
California	gas chamber or lethal injection	108	80	74	30	0	0	2	398
Colorado	lethal injection	25	13	3	6	0	0	0	3
Connecticut	electrocution	5	10	5	1	0	0	0	5
Delaware	lethal injection	8	4	0	0	0	0	4	15
District of Columbia	none	20	16	4	0	0	0	0	0
Florida	electrocution	44	65	49	12	1	20	12	350
Georgia	electrocution	137	130	85	14	0	14	4	106
Hawaii	none	0	0	0	0	0	0	0	0
Idaho	lethal injection or firing squad	0	0	3	0	0	0	1	20
Illinois	lethal injection	61	18	9	2	0	0	2	163
Indiana	electrocution	31	7	2	1	0	2	1	48
Iowa	none	8	7	1	2	0	0	0	0
Kansas	none	0	5	5	5	0	0	0	0
Kentucky	electrocution	52	34	16	1	0	0	0	28
Louisiana	lethal injection	58	47	27	1	0	18	3	43
Maine	none	0	0	0	0	0	0	0	0
Maryland	gas chamber or lethal injection	16	45	6	1	0	0	1	14
Massachusetts	none	18	9	0	0	0	0	0	0

State	Method								
Michigan	none	0	0	0	0	0	0	0	0
Minnesota	none	0	0	0	0	0	0	0	0
Mississippi	gas chamber or lethal injection	48	60	36	10	0	4	0	53
Missouri	lethal injection	36	15	7	4	0	1	10	94
Montana	lethal injection or hanging	5	1	0	0	0	0	0	8
Nebraska	electrocution	0	2	2	0	0	3	1	10
Nevada	lethal injection	8	0	9	2	1	0	1	69
New Hampshire	lethal injection	1	0	0	0	0	0	0	0
New Jersey	lethal injection	40	14	17	3	0	0	0	9
New Mexico	lethal injection	2	2	3	1	0	0	0	2
New York	lethal injection	153	114	52	10	0	0	0	0
North Carolina	gas chamber or lethal injection	131	12	19	1	0	3	3	143
North Dakota	none	0	0	0	0	0	0	0	0
Ohio	electrocution or lethal injection	82	1	32	7	0	0	0	137
Oklahoma	lethal injection	34	13	7	6	0	0	3	128
Oregon	lethal injection	2	12	4	1	0	0	0	14
Pennsylvania	lethal injection	82	6	31	3	0	0	0	182
Rhode Island	none	0	0	0	0	0	0	0	0
South Carolina	electrocution	67	61	26	8	0	2	2	58
South Dakota	lethal injection	0	1	0	0	0	0	0	2
Tennessee	electrocution	47	37	8	1	0	0	0	102
Texas	lethal injection	120	74	74	29	0	33	52	392
Utah	firing squad or lethal injection	2	4	6	1	1	2	1	11
Vermont	none	1	1	2	0	0	0	0	0

(Table continues)

Table 1-10 (*Continued*)

State	Method[a]	Number executed							Number awaiting execution[c]
		1930s	1940s	1950s	1960s	1970s	1980s	1990s[b]	
Virginia	electrocution or lethal injection	28	35	23	6	0	8	16	56
Washington	lethal injection or hanging	23	16	6	2	0	0	2	13
West Virginia	none	20	11	9	0	0	0	0	0
Wisconsin	none	0	0	0	0	0	0	0	0
Wyoming	lethal injection	4	2	0	1	0	0	1	6
U.S. government	lethal injection	10	13	9	1	0	0	0	8
U.S. military[e]	lethal injection	[d]	[d]	[d]	[d]	[d]	[d]	0	
Total[e]		1,667	1,284	717	191	3	117	137	2,976[f]

[a] In some states, method depends on when sentenced. For details, see source.
[b] Through December 31, 1994.
[c] As of January 31, 1995.
[d] One hundred and sixty executions have been carried out under military authority since 1930.
[e] The national total counts multiple death-sentence inmates once. However, they are included in the state total for each state where they are sentenced to death.
[f] Number of inmates; some are multiple-sentenced and are listed in each state.

Sources: Number executed in 1930s–1970s: U.S. Department of Justice, Bureau of Justice Statistics, *Sourcebook of Criminal Justice Statistics-1989* (Washington, D.C.: U.S. Government Printing Office, 1990), 631; method, number awaiting execution: NAACP Legal Defense and Educational Fund, *Death Row, U.S.A.*, Winter, 1994, 4–40, with 1995 change in New York law added by the editors.

Table 1-11   Public Opinion on the Death Penalty, 1936-1994 (percent)

Date	Favor	Oppose	Don't know
April 1936	62	33	5
December 1936	59	38	3
November 1937	61	33	7
October 1953[a]	68	26	6
April 1956	53	34	13
September 1957	47	34	18
March 1960	53	36	11
February 1965	45	43	12
July 1966	42	47	11
June 1967	54	38	8
January 1969	51	40	9
October 1971	48	41	11
February 1972	51	41	8
March 1972	53	39	8
November 1972	60	30	10
March 1973	60	35	5
March 1974	63	32	5
March 1975	60	33	7
March 1976	66	30	5
April 1976	67	27	7
March 1977	67	26	6
March 1978	66	28	6
July 1979	65	27	8
March 1980	67	27	6
March 1981	66	25	9
March 1982	74	21	6
June 1982	71	20	9
March 1983	73	22	5
March 1984	70	24	6
January 1985	72	20	8
March 1985	76	19	5
November 1985	75	17	8
January 1986	70	22	8
March 1986	71	23	5
March 1987	70	24	6
March 1988	71	22	7
September 1988	79	16	5
March 1989	74	20	6
March 1990	75	19	6
March 1991	72	22	6
March 1993	72	21	7
March 1994	74	19	6

Note: Questions: 1936-1937—"Are you in favor of the death penalty for murder?" 1953-February 1972, November 1972, April 1976, January 1981, January 1985, November 1985—"Are you in favor of the death penalty for persons convicted of murder?" All others—"Do you favor or oppose the death penalty for persons convicted of murder?"

[a] "Favor" includes those responding with a qualified yes or qualified no.

Sources: 1936 through February 1972, November 1972, April 1976, January 1981, January 1985, November 1985, and September 1988: Gallup surveys; others from General Social Survey.

Table 1-12 Frequency of Legal Abortions, 1973-1991

Year	Total Number of abortions (thousands)	Total Percentage of pregnancies terminated by abortion	White Number of abortions (thousands)	White Percentage of pregnancies terminated by abortion	Nonwhite Number of abortions (thousands)	Nonwhite Percentage of pregnancies terminated by abortion
1973	744.6	19.3	548.8	17.4	195.8	25.9
1974	898.6	22.0	629.3	19.6	269.3	31.6
1975	1,034.2	24.9	701.2	21.5	333.0	35.9
1976	1,179.3	26.5	784.9	23.0	394.4	38.9
1977	1,316.7	28.6	888.8	25.0	427.9	40.4
1978	1,409.6	29.2	969.4	26.1	440.2	39.6
1979	1,497.7	29.6	1,062.4	27.1	435.3	38.2
1980	1,553.9	30.0	1,093.6	27.4	460.3	39.2
1981	1,577.3	30.1	1,107.8	27.4	469.6	39.2
1982	1,573.9	30.0	1,095.3	27.1	478.7	39.2
1983	1,575.0	30.4	1,084.4	27.4	490.6	40.1
1984	1,577.2	29.7	1,086.6	26.8	490.6	39.2
1985	1,588.6	29.7	1,075.6	26.5	512.9	39.7
1986	1,574.0	29.4	—	25.9	—	39.8
1987	1,559.1	28.8	1,017.3	25.2	541.8	39.3
1988	1,590.8	28.6	1,025.7	25.0	565.1	38.9
1989	1,567.0	27.5	1,006.0	23.6	561.0	39.4
1990	1,609.0	28.0	1,039.0	24.1	570.0	39.6
1991	1,557.0	27.5	982.0	23.3	574.0	39.8

Note: "—" indicates not available. "Percentage of pregnancies terminated by abortion" indicates the percentage of pregnancies resulting in live birth or abortion terminated by abortion. The number of abortions per 1,000 live births is from July 1 of the year shown to June 30 of the following year.

(Notes continue)

Sources: Reprinted with the permission of The Alan Guttmacher Institute from: 1973-1981: Stanley K. Henshaw and Ellen Blaine, *Abortion Services in the United States, Each State, and Metropolitan Area, 1981-1982* (New York: Alan Guttmacher Institute, 1985). 64; 1982-1983: Stanley K. Henshaw, "Characteristics of U.S. Women Having Abortions, 1982-1983," *Family Planning Perspectives* 19(1) (1987): 6-7; 1984-1986 (total): Stanley K. Henshaw and Jennifer Van Vort, "Abortion Services in the United States, 1987 and 1988," *Family Planning Perspectives,* 22(3) (1990): 103; 1984-1985 (white and nonwhite): Alan Guttmacher Institute, unpublished data; 1986 (white and nonwhite), 1987-1988: Stanley K. Henshaw, "Abortion Trends in 1987 and 1988: Age and Race," *Family Planning Perspectives,* 24(2) (1992): 86; 1989-1991: unpublished data, Alan Guttmacher Institute.

Table 1-13 Public Opinion on Abortion, 1962-1994 (percent)

	Abortion should be legal under these circumstances						
Year	Mother's health	Rape	Birth defect	Low income	Single mother	As form of birth control	Any reason
1962	77	—	55	15	—	—	—
1965	70	56	55	21	17	15	—
1969	80	—	63	23	—	—	—
1972	83	75	75	46	41	38	—
1973	91	81	82	52	47	46	—
1974	90	83	83	52	48	45	—
1975	88	80	80	51	46	44	—
1976	89	81	82	51	48	45	—
1977	89	81	83	52	48	45	37
1978	88	81	80	46	40	39	32
1980	88	80	80	50	46	45	39
1982	90	83	81	50	47	46	39
1983	87	80	76	42	38	38	33
1984	88	77	78	45	43	41	37
1985	87	78	76	42	40	39	36
1987	86	78	77	44	40	40	38
1988	86	77	76	40	38	39	35
1989	88	80	78	46	43	43	39
1990	89	81	78	46	43	43	42
1991	88	82	79	46	42	45	41
1993	86	79	79	47	46	45	43
1994	88	81	79	49	46	47	45

Note: "—" indicates not available. Question: "Please tell me whether or not you think it should be possible for a pregnant woman to obtain a legal abortion [in the order asked in the survey] if there is a strong chance of serious defect in the baby? If she is married and does not want any more children? If the woman's own health is seriously endangered by the pregnancy? If the family has a very low income and cannot afford any more children? If she became pregnant as a result of rape? If she is not married and does not want to marry the man? The woman wants it for any reason?"

Sources: 1962 and 1969: Gallup surveys; 1965: National Opinion Research Center surveys; 1972-1994: General Social Survey.

Table 1-14   Public Opinion on Gun Control, 1959-1994 (percent)

Date	Favor	Oppose	Don't know
July 1959	75	21	4
December 1963	79	17	4
January 1965	73	23	4
September 1965	70	25	5
August 1966	67	29	3
August 1967	73	24	4
October 1971	72	24	4
March 1972	70	27	3
May 1972	72	24	4
March 1973	74	25	2
March 1974	75	23	1
February 1975	71	28	1
March 1975	74	24	3
February 1976	73	24	4
March 1976	72	27	1
March 1977	72	27	2
March 1980	69	29	2
March 1982	72	26	2
March 1984	70	27	3
March 1985	72	27	1
March 1987	70	28	2
March 1988	74	24	3
March 1989	78	21	2
March 1990	79	20	2
March 1991	81	18	1
March 1993	81	17	2
March 1994	78	20	2

Note: Question: "Would you favor or oppose a law which would require a person to obtain a police permit before he or she could buy a gun?"

Sources: 1959-1971: Gallup surveys; February 1975, February 1976: Survey Research Center, University of Michigan; others: General Social Survey. .

Table 1-15 Legislative Districting: Deviations from Equality in Congressional and State Legislative Districts (percent)

| | Congressional districts | | | State legislative districts | | | | | |
| | | | | Senate | | | House | | |
State	1960s	1980s	1990s	1960s	1980s	1990s	1960s	1980s	1990s
Alabama	38.6	2.45	a	665.4	8.50	9.22	317.7	9.80	10.20
Alaska	AL	AL	AL	467.3	9.77	11.70	75.6	9.99	15.50
Arizona	107.2	.08	a	704.7	8.40	9.85	151.4	8.40	9.85
Arkansas	54.2	.73	.73	88.4	9.15	9.27	150.9	9.15	9.52
California	451.4	.08	.49	1,528.4	4.60	1.60	118.9	3.60	1.80
Colorado	104.5	a	a	117.6	3.98	4.90	107.6	4.94	4.96
Connecticut	87.7	.46	.05	200.6	3.92	7.98	937.8	8.35	8.78
Delaware	AL	AL	AL	251.0	9.78	10.18	444.3	25.10	9.58
Florida	102.5	.13	a	710.7	1.05	0.86	592.5	0.46	4.99
Georgia	139.9	—	.93	746.1	9.99	9.95	954.9	9.94	9.95
Hawaii	AL	a	a	217.3	18.60	9.86	151.5	8.60	9.78
Idaho	45.8	.04	a	611.0	5.35	9.88	139.2	5.35	9.88
Illinois	65.2	.03	—	295.2	1.75	—	220.7	2.80	—
Indiana	96.0	2.96	a	130.9	4.04	2.19	162.2	4.45	3.36
Iowa	22.7	.05	.05	419.2	0.71	1.45	490.7	1.78	1.97
Kansas	38.2	.34	.01	599.5	6.50	6.89	381.8	9.90	9.72
Kentucky	60.0	1.39	a	208.6	7.52	6.13	185.9	13.47	9.91
Louisiana	66.8	.42	.04	259.6	8.40	9.78	364.2	9.69	9.97
Maine	8.6	a	—	114.0	10.18	—	167.8	10.94	—
Maryland	123.6	.35	a	443.5	9.80	9.84	258.0	15.70	10.67
Massachusetts	23.9	1.09	a	88.6	—	4.75	213.9	—	9.92
Michigan	156.7	a	—	306.1	16.24	—	142.4	16.34	—
Minnesota	25.2	.01	a	143.0	4.61	3.42	348.6	3.93	5.90
Mississippi	72.2	—	.02	251.9	4.61	8.96	359.8	4.90	9.97
Missouri	29.7	.18	.20	46.1	6.10	8.42	184.8	9.30	8.96
Montana	37.4	—	AL	648.6	—	9.51	161.6	—	9.97

State						[b]	[b]	[b]
Nebraska	26.8	.23	.20	99.5	9.43	3.81			
Nevada	AL	.60	a	754.6	8.20	2.28	730.9	9.70	4.55
New Hampshire	18.6	.24	.07	101.3	7.60	12.36	383.7	13.74	14.53
New Jersey	81.7	.69	a	305.2	7.70	4.60	93.2	7.70	4.60
New Mexico	AL	.87	.16	876.7	9.83	9.58	189.7	9.87	9.89
New York	29.5	1.64	a	81.6	5.29	4.29	120.6	8.17	9.43
North Carolina	55.6	1.76	a	249.6	9.46	9.94	204.7	9.66	9.97
North Dakota	10.8	AL	AL	288.6	9.93	8.71	103.7	9.93	8.71
Ohio	121.1	.68	a	72.8	8.88	13.60	122.6	9.67	13.60
Oklahoma	83.8	.58	a	629.2	5.60	3.93	293.9	10.98	6.13
Oregon	58.2	.15	a	74.3	3.73	1.69	69.7	5.34	1.89
Pennsylvania	59.6	.24	.01	222.1	1.93	1.86	249.8	2.82	4.94
Rhode Island	14.0	.02	.02	248.9	—	13.00	215.4	10.47	14.70
South Carolina	65.3	.28	a	400.6		1.00	108.1	9.88	5.20
South Dakota	92.6	AL	AL	170.9	12.90	9.47	145.2	12.40	9.47
Tennessee	101.8	2.40	—	183.2	10.22	—	211.8	1.66	—
Texas	167.0	.28	a	355.8	1.82a	9.98	111.9	9.95	9.99
Utah	57.2	.43	.02	154.9	7.80	7.60	224.4	5.41	7.94
Vermont	AL	AL	AL	120.3	16.18	16.36	2,088.4	19.33	17.62
Virginia	57.1	1.81	a	235.9	10.65	8.53	308.8	5.11	9.67
Washington	41.2	.06	a	217.5	5.40	a	158.4	5.70	9.96
West Virginia	32.0	.50	.09	372.4	8.96	9.98	188.9	9.94	0.92
Wisconsin	74.3	.14	a	110.7	1.23	0.52	171.7	1.74	9.97
Wyoming	AL	AL	AL	221.4	63.70	9.60	120.6	89.40	

Note: "AL" indicates at-large district (only one congressional representative). "—" indicates not available. Figures represent the absolute sum of the maximum percentage deviations (positive and negative) from the average district population. 1960s data are from 1962; 1980s data are as of April 1983; 1990s data are as of August 1994. The 1980 state house plans for Delaware and Rhode Island contained errors which increased total deviation, but which had not been corrected.

[a] Less than .01 percent.
[b] Nebraska's state legislature is unicameral.

Sources: 1960s: Robert G. Dixon, Jr., *Democratic Representation: Reapportionment in Law and Politics* (New York: Oxford University Press, 1968), Appendices A-B (copyright 1985, Regents of the University of California, all rights reserved); 1980s: Election Data Services, Inc.; 1990s: National Conference of State Legislators.

Table 1-16   Congressional Districts with a "Majority-Minority" Population

State	District number	Percentage of district total population				Representative elected in 1994	Party	Race or ethnicity
		White	Black	His- panic	Other			
Alabama	7	32.0	67.4	0.3	0.3	Hilliard	D	Black
Arizona	2	38.2	6.4	50.5	5.0	Pastor	D	Hispanic
California	8	44.3	12.4	15.7	27.6	Pelosi	D	White
California	9	44.1	31.0	12.0	15.9	Dellums	D	Black
California	16	37.5	4.8	36.8	20.8	Edwards	D	White
California	20	32.6	6.0	55.4	6.0	Dooley	D	White
California	26	34.2	5.7	52.7	7.4	Berman	D	White
California	30	15.2	3.0	61.5	20.4	Becerra	D	Hispanic
California	31	17.5	1.4	58.5	22.5	Martinez	D	Hispanic
California	32	23.6	38.2	30.2	8.0	Dixon	D	Black
California	33	8.1	3.8	83.7	4.4	Roybal-Allard	D	Hispanic
California	34	26.7	1.7	62.3	9.2	Torres	D	Hispanic
California	35	10.4	40.4	43.1	6.1	Waters	D	Black
California	37	12.0	32.2	45.2	10.7	Tucker	D	Black
California	46	35.6	2.2	50.0	12.2	Dornan	D	White
California	50	31.5	13.6	40.6	14.3	Filner	D	White
Florida	3	41.7	54.5	2.8	1.0	Brown	D	Black
Florida	17	19.8	55.7	23.0	1.5	Meek	D	Black
Florida	18	29.2	2.9	66.7	1.2	Ros-Lehtinen	R	Hispanic
Florida	21	25.6	3.3	69.6	1.6	Diaz-Balart	R	Hispanic
Florida	23	39.3	50.2	9.4	1.2	Hastings	D	Black
Georgia	2	41.3	56.3	1.7	0.7	Bishop	D	Black
Georgia	5	35.0	62.0	1.8	1.3	Lewis	D	Black
Georgia	11	34.1	63.8	1.1	1.1	McKinney	D	Black
Hawaii	1	27.6	2.4	5.5	64.5	Abercrombie	D	White
Hawaii	2	35.1	2.3	9.2	53.4	Mink	D	Asian
Illinois	1	25.9	69.3	3.6	1.2	Bush	D	Black
Illinois	2	24.6	68.0	6.6	0.7	Reynolds	D	Black
Illinois	4	26.8	5.5	65.0	2.7	Gutierrez	D	Hispanic
Illinois	7	27.2	65.2	4.3	3.3	Collins	D	Black
Louisiana	2	33.5	60.4	3.7	2.4	Jefferson	D	Black
Louisiana	4	32.4	66.2	0.9	0.5	Fields	D	Black
Maryland	4	31.1	57.7	6.4	4.9	Wynn	D	Black
Maryland	7	26.9	70.6	0.9	1.6	Mfume	D	Black
Michigan	14	28.8	68.8	1.0	1.3	Conyers	D	Black
Michigan	15	24.9	69.7	4.3	1.2	Collins	D	Black
Mississippi	2	36.5	62.6	0.5	0.3	Espy	D	Black
Missouri	1	45.8	52.2	0.9	1.2	Clay	D	Black
New Jersey	10	26.4	58.6	12.3	2.7	Payne	D	Black
New Jersey	13	42.3	11.4	41.5	4.8	Menendez	D	Hispanic
New Mexico	3	44.0	1.1	34.6	20.4	Richardson	D	Hispanic
New York	6	22.8	53.3	16.9	7.0	Flake	D	Black
New York	10	21.0	56.6	19.7	2.8	Towns	D	Black
New York	11	15.8	69.4	11.6	3.2	Owens	D	Black
New York	12	14.0	8.7	57.9	19.4	Velázquez	D	Hispanic
New York	15	14.0	36.8	46.4	2.8	Rangel	D	Black

Table 1-16   (*Continued*)

State	District number	Percentage of district total population White	Black	His-panic	Other	Representative elected in 1994	Party	Race or ethnicity
New York	16	4.2	33.2	60.2	2.4	Serrano	D	Hispanic
New York	17	29.1	37.8	29.1	4.0	Engel	D	White
North Carolina	1	41.4	57.0	0.7	0.8	Clayton	D	Black
North Carolina	12	41.4	56.4	0.9	1.3	Watt	D	Black
Ohio	11	39.3	58.3	1.1	1.3	Stokes	D	Black
Pennsylvania	1	36.0	51.4	9.9	2.6	Foglietta	D	White
Pennsylvania	2	34.1	61.8	1.6	2.5	Fattah	D	Black
South Carolina	6	37.1	62.0	0.6	0.4	Clyburn	D	Black
Tennessee	9	39.3	59.0	0.7	0.9	Ford	D	Black
Texas	15	23.9	1.0	74.5	0.6	de la Garza	D	Hispanic
Texas	16	25.0	3.3	70.4	1.3	Coleman	D	White
Texas	18	31.3	50.2	15.3	3.2	Lee	D	Black
Texas	20	32.3	5.5	60.7	1.6	Gonzalez	D	Hispanic
Texas	23	33.6	2.8	62.6	1.1	Bonilla	R	Hispanic
Texas	27	30.7	2.2	66.2	0.9	Ortiz	D	Hispanic
Texas	28	30.4	8.2	60.4	1.6	Tejeda	D	Hispanic
Texas	29	27.8	9.6	60.6	2.0	Green	D	White
Texas	30	31.4	49.2	17.1	2.4	Johnson	D	Black
Virginia	3	33.4	63.7	1.4	1.5	Scott	D	Black

Note: Districts listed are those in which the white population does not constitute a majority. Blacks elected from majority-white districts: Franks (R., Conn.); Wheat (D., Mo.); Asians elected from majority-white districts: Matsui (D., Cal.); Mineta (D., Cal.); Kim (R., Cal.)

Sources: District population composition, 1990 census: Election Data Services, Inc.; 103d Congress representative, party, race or ethnicity: "The Freshmen-Elect" (Washington, D.C.: Congressional Quarterly, 1994), November 12, 1994, vol. 52, supplement to No. 44, 10.

Table 1-17   Jurisdictions Subject to Federal Preclearance of Election Law Changes and to Minority Language Provisions of the Voting Rights Act

Coverage under preclearance provisions	Coverage under minority language provisions	
Alabama	Alaska (16)[a]	Nevada (2)
Alaska	Arizona	New Jersey (5)
Arizona	California (21)	New Mexico (26)
California (4)	Colorado (11)	New York (7)
Florida (5)	Connecticut (4)[a]	North Carolina (1)
Georgia	Florida (9)	North Dakota (3)
Louisiana	Hawaii (3)	Oklahoma (1)
Michigan (2)[a]	Idaho (4)	Oregon (1)
Mississippi	Illinois (1)	Pennsylvania (1)
New Hampshire (10)[a]	Iowa (1)	Rhode Island (1)[a]
New York (3)	Louisiana (1)	South Dakota (8)
North Carolina (40)	Massachusetts (5)[a]	Texas
South Carolina	Michigan (4)[a]	Utah (2)
South Dakota (2)	Mississippi (6)	Wisconsin (1)
Texas		
Virginia		

Note: "Preclearance" means that changes in elections laws must be approved by the U.S. Justice Department. "Language provisions" require covered jurisdictions to provide bilingual voting materials to members of specified minority language groups. Numbers in parentheses indicate the number of counties in the state affected by the provisions. If there are no parentheses, coverage is statewide.

[a] Number of towns, townships, cities, boroughs, or areas.

Sources: Preclearance: 28 *Code of Federal Regulations* Ch. 1 (7-1-89 Edition), 577-578; language: 28 *Code of Federal Regulations*, Pt. 55, Appendix, 611-615. *Federal Register*, vol. 57, no. 182, September 18, 1992, 43214-43217.

Table 1-18 Term Limits on State Legislators[a]

State	Lower house (years)[b]	Upper house (years)[b]	Year adopted	Percent support	Effective as of[c]	Mechanism[d]	Break in service[e]
Arizona	8	8	1992	74	2000	L	2 years
Arkansas	6	8	1992	60	1998 & 2000	L	lifetime
California	6	8	1990	52	1996 & 1998[f]	L	lifetime
Colorado	8	8	1990	71	1998	L	4 years
Florida	8	8	1992	77	2000	B	2 years
Idaho	8/15	8/15	1994	59	2002	B	contingent
Maine	8	8	1993	63	1996	L	2 years
Massachusetts[g]	8	8	1994	51	2002	B	2 years
Michigan	6	8	1992	59	1998 & 2000	L	lifetime
Mississippi			on ballot in 1995		2003	L	2 years
Missouri	8	8	1992	74	2000	L	lifetime
Montana	8/16	8/16	1992	67	2000	B	contingent
Nebraska	Unicameral	8	1994	68	2002	L	4 years
Nevada	12	12	[h]	70	1998	L	lifetime
Ohio	8	8	1992	68	2000	L	4 years
Oklahoma	12 years total in legislature		1990	67	2002	L	lifetime
Oregon	6[i]	8[i]	1992	69	1998 & 2000	L	lifetime
South Dakota	8	8	1992	63	2000	L	2 years
Utah	12	12	1994	[j]	2006	L	2 years
Washington	6/12[k]	8/14[k]	1992	52	1998 & 2000	B	contingent
Wyoming	6/12	12/24	1992	77	1998 & 2004	L	contingent

Notes: States have varying provisions for counting partial terms due to appointment or special election. In many states, limits are defined in terms of times elected rather than years served or contain a clause such as "or, but for resignation, would have served."

[a] Twenty-two states enacted term limits for members of Congress between 1992 and 1994—20 of those listed here, plus Alaska and North Dakota. (In addition,

(Notes continue)

Table 1-18 (*Continued*)

a federal as well as a state limitation was scheduled to be on the ballot in 1995 in Mississippi, and New Hampshire was about to enact term limits for members of Congress.) On May 23, 1995, the Supreme Court ruled 5-4 in *U.S. Term Limits v. Thornton* that these provisions were unconstitutional. In Florida, Michigan, Missouri, and Oregon, the term limits provision stated that, should any part of the law be declared unconstitutional, it is the wish of the voters that the expressed limits be respected voluntarily.

b Number of years an individual may serve before term limits are applied. A pair of numbers indicates that an individual may not serve more than a certain number of years over a longer period—e.g., six of the previous 12 years—whether or not those years are consecutive.

c The year in which incumbent legislators will first be excluded from ballots or prevented from serving.

d Strict term limits (L) prohibit service in the legislature. Ballot access restrictions (B) prevent a candidate's name from being placed on the ballot but do not prevent a candidate from being elected on write-in votes.

e Length of time an individual must "sit out" before serving (or having ballot access) again. The time may vary when the term limit law specifies that an individual may serve no more than a certain number of years over a longer period.

f Senators in office on November 6, 1990, whose office was not on the ballot on that date may serve only one additional term.

g Massachusetts law allows write-in candidates to be elected and serve, but they cannot be paid a salary or expenses if the stated term limit has been exceeded.

h Nevada requires two votes on the same question in order to amend the state constitution. It is expected that the term limit proposal will be on the ballot again in 1996. The level of support for the measure in 1994 suggests passage.

i No more than 12 years total in the legislature.

j Passed by the legislature in early 1994. In November, 1994, voters rejected an initiative that included additional term limit and other electoral reforms.

k No more than 14 out of 20 years combined in both houses of the legislature.

Sources: Texts of state measures. Percent of support: "22 States with Term Limits" (Washington, D.C.: U.S. Term Limits, n.d.) and Council of State Governments, *Book of the States, 1994-1995* (Lexington, Ky: Council of State Governments, 1994), 29.

2

The Mass Media

The mass media thrive on numbers. Nearly every American adult has heard of audience ratings games—serious games with millions of dollars and many individual careers at stake—played by television, newspapers, radio, and magazines. Will the top-ranked television show remain first in the ratings, and how much will it help the show that follows it? Can a "national newspaper," such as *USA Today*, be profitable? Will a radio station increase its audience ratings—and what kind of audience will it attract—by playing more hard rock? How many extra copies and how much more advertising will a weekly news magazine sell with excerpts of soon-to-be-published political memoirs—and how much can the publisher afford to pay for those excerpts? So much money is at stake that media organizations annually spend millions of dollars to find the answers to such questions.

Politics, as it relates to the media, also involves numbers. Some questions simply involve market share and audience, much like the questions noted above: How many and what kinds of individuals pay attention to political news stories, candidate advertisements, campaign debates, and so on? Of course, these matters, while very important, are relatively straightforward. More complicated and controversial are other matters that involve numbers. Some critics charge, for example, that television emphasizes only the "horse race" aspect of political campaigns (who is ahead and by how much) to the exclusion of issues (Table 2-6) and that both print and electronic media give too much emphasis to the very early presidential primaries and caucuses (Table 2-5).

Despite these concerns about numbers as they apply to politics and the media, data are not as publicly available as one might think or hope. General information on how many people watch, read, and listen to the media is readily obtainable (Tables 2-1 through 2-3), but specific information about political material is not. Some material is proprietary—for example, a candidate's private surveys—and therefore mostly unavailable to researchers or to students. But there are other reasons for the unavailability. One is that television is relatively new (serious coverage of presidential campaigns began only in 1952, and extended coverage only in the 1960s) and is still changing (televised House proceedings began in 1979 and Senate proceedings in 1986). This means that researchers have not yet settled on exactly what data are most relevant and therefore most in need of continued collection. This is especially true of data that go beyond sheer numbers of viewers. Note, for example, that some interesting information about television coverage has been tabulated for only two election cycles (Tables 2-6 through 2-10).

Fortunately, data collection and publication have expanded and improved, and researchers are beginning to see longer time series of significant information about politics and the media (for example, Tables 2-4 and 2-11 through 2-15 and Figure 2-2). Moreover, the media themselves are increasingly well preserved. Magazines are saved and are relatively well indexed. Major newspapers are widely available and well indexed, and small newspapers—though often kept only locally—combine to give widespread coverage of politics as practiced and perceived throughout the country. CBS News has published transcripts and indexes of its news programs since 1975 to facilitate research. Network television news programs since 1968 have been stored at Vanderbilt University; the archives are indexed and available to researchers. These efforts at preservation mean that studies can be made of the past as well as of contemporary events. Indeed, some of the most interesting studies of politics and the media are yet to come because they will be able to cover long expanses of time.

As in all areas of research, data about the media are rarely self-interpreting. One specific problem here is that the media both shape the news and reflect it. The shift in emphasis from parties to candidates (reflected in Tables 4-7 and 4-8, for instance) is a case in point. To some degree this shift simply reflects the weakening hold of political parties over American voters, a process that began as long ago as the turn of the century, well before the advent of television. On the other hand, the power of television to bring individual candidates directly into one's living room has accelerated the declining influence of party organizations in particular and of party affiliation more generally.

Problems of interpretation—especially whether the media cause or simply reflect events—thus make inferences about media influence difficult. The usual response to such problems of inference is to bring additional data to bear on the subject. With more data now becoming available, researchers can safely anticipate better answers to questions about media audiences, coverage, emphasis, and influence as they relate to the political process.

Table 2-1   Growth and Reach of Selected Media, 1950-1994

Year	Percentage of households with			Percentage of TV households with		Average TV viewing per day (hours)[e]
	Telephone service[a]	Radio sets[b]	Television sets[c]	Cable TV[d]	VCRs[d]	
1950	—	92.6	9	—	—	4.6
1960	78.5	96.3	87	—	—	5.1
1970	87.0	98.6	95	—	—	5.9
1975	—	98.6	97	—	—	6.1
1980	93.0	99.0	98	19.9	1.1	6.6
1981	—	99.0	98	25.2	1.8	6.8
1982	—	99.0	98	29.8	3.1	6.8
1983	—	99.0	98	34.0	5.5	7.0
1984	91.8	99.0	98	39.3	10.6	7.1
1985	91.8	99.0	98	42.8	20.8	7.2
1986	92.2	99.0	98	45.6	36.0	7.1
1987	92.5	99.0	98	47.7	48.7	7.0
1988	92.9	99.0	98	49.4	58.0	7.1
1989	93.0	99.0	98	52.8	64.6	7.0
1990	93.3	99.0	98	56.4	68.6	6.9
1991	93.6	99.0	98	58.9	71.9	7.0
1992	93.9	99.0	98	60.2	75.0	7.1
1993	94.2	99.0	98	61.4	77.1	7.2
1994	—	99.0	98	62.4	—	—

Note: "—" indicates not available.

[a] For occupied housing units. 1950 through 1980, as of April 1; thereafter, as of March.
[b] As of December 31. Estimated after 1987.
[c] 1970-1975, as of September of prior year; all other years as of January of year shown.
[d] Cable as of January; VCR as of February. Excludes Alaska and Hawaii prior to 1989.
[e] Calendar year data.

Sources: Telephone service: U.S. Bureau of the Census, *Statistical Abstract of the United States, 1992* (Washington, D.C.: U.S. Government Printing Office, 1992), 551; radios: Radio Advertising Bureau; television, 1950-1960: National Broadcasting Company, Inc.; television, 1970-1994, cable, VCR, and viewing: Television Bureau of Advertising, *Trends in Television* (New York: Television Bureau of Advertising, 1994), 3, 5, 7.

Table 2-2 Use of Television, Radio, and Newspapers, Cross-Section, 1994-1995[a]

	Total adult population (thousands)	Television watchers						Radio listeners		Newspaper readers	
		CNN[b]	Court-TV	Cable	Pay	Early[c] news	Late[d] news	Week-day	Week-end	Daily	Sunday
Age											
18-24	24,315	22.4	2.5	60.3	35.2	7.5	3.1	87.0	75.4	41.1	53.2
25-34	43,097	34.0	1.8	63.0	30.7	10.4	3.5	85.6	69.9	45.4	59.7
35-44	41,069	38.8	2.7	67.8	34.8	13.2	4.5	83.0	63.5	56.5	65.9
45-54	28,148	42.5	2.1	69.6	34.7	15.9	5.4	80.9	62.4	61.3	68.6
55-64	21,484	42.0	1.7	65.0	26.4	17.7	5.6	71.4	54.6	65.1	63.9
65 and older	31,496	36.3	1.5	58.1	12.0	19.9	6.3	54.9	46.0	69.9	66.4
Sex											
Male	90,694	40.4	2.1	65.6	31.3	14.0	4.9	80.5	63.0	57.3	63.6
Female	98,917	32.1	2.1	62.7	27.2	13.7	4.4	75.3	61.9	52.9	64.0
Race/ethnicity											
White	161,141	37.4	2.0	66.2	28.6	13.6	4.3	78.2	61.7	57.0	65.4
Black	21,597	29.8	2.5	52.3	34.8	16.4	7.5	76.9	69.4	45.7	57.6
Spanish-speaking	16,085	29.5	2.7	53.7	28.3	9.2	4.0	80.0	68.0	44.9	48.9
Other	6,873	26.7	1.0	51.0	23.5	10.7	4.3	71.4	56.5	35.4	44.6
Education											
College graduate	38,167	46.6	2.4	71.4	30.8	13.1	4.7	84.9	62.7	69.8	78.1
Attended college	49,065	38.7	2.5	68.0	34.1	13.1	5.1	83.4	66.7	56.2	68.3
High school graduate	65,245	34.1	2.0	64.2	29.7	13.9	5.0	77.0	62.6	55.6	64.4
Not high school graduate	37,134	25.5	1.4	51.1	20.4	15.1	3.4	64.6	56.2	36.9	42.0

Employment										
Full-time	103,609	38.7	2.2	68.1	34.7	12.2	4.3	85.4	66.3	57.3	66.9
Part-time	17,354	32.4	2.2	62.9	28.9	12.6	3.8	81.6	65.3	52.9	65.0
Not Employed	68,648	33.1	1.8	58.3	20.8	16.5	5.4	65.4	55.8	51.9	58.8
Household Income										
Under $10,000	19,445	21.6	1.1	46.0	14.4	13.5	4.2	61.4	57.0	33.8	38.7
$10,000-19,999	29,468	26.6	1.4	50.2	18.1	15.9	4.9	70.0	57.6	46.1	53.1
$20,000-29,999	29,193	32.3	1.4	58.7	24.4	15.8	4.6	74.8	63.3	50.8	59.9
$30,000-39,999	26,473	36.5	2.5	64.4	27.1	13.4	4.3	79.9	65.4	54.0	65.7
$40,000-49,999	21,931	37.1	2.1	69.2	34.2	14.0	5.0	83.6	64.4	58.4	67.2
$50,000-59,999	17,314	40.5	2.5	74.6	36.8	11.8	4.5	84.3	65.2	61.6	73.8
$60,000-74,999	18,340	47.3	2.7	75.8	37.9	14.1	5.3	83.6	65.9	67.5	74.5
$75,000 or more	27,467	49.3	3.0	78.6	44.0	10.8	4.5	86.3	63.2	69.3	79.3
Total	189,611	36.1	2.1	64.1	29.2	13.8	4.6	77.8	62.4	54.9	63.8

Note: CNN: the percentage of adults of the specified type who reported watching within the last seven days. Cable, pay: the percentage of adults in households having cable TV and pay TV, respectively. Early news, late news: the average percentage viewing at least one of these news programs the weeknight before the survey. Radio: the percentage of people listening to the radio at any time on a weekday or weekend during the average week. Newspapers: the percentage who read one or more daily newspapers, one or more Sunday newspapers. All percentages are based on 10,019 interviews between March and July 1994 and another 10,064 between September 1994 and January 1995. Percentages subject to sampling error; see sources.

[a] Data for earlier years can be found in previous editions of *Vital Statistics on American Politics.*

[b] Does not include CNN Headline News.

[c] Includes "ABC World News Tonight," "CBS Evening News," and "NBC Nightly News," Monday through Friday.

[d] Includes "ABC News Nightline," Monday through Friday.

Sources: Multimedia Audiences Report (New York: Mediamark Research, Inc., Spring 1995), 2-57; *Television Audiences Report* (New York: Mediamark Research, Inc., Spring 1995), 3-57.

Table 2-3   Newspaper Circulation, Daily Papers, 1850-1993

Year	Number	Circulation (thousands)	Circulation as a percentage of population
1850	254	758	3.3
1860	387	1,478	4.7
1870	574	2,602	6.5
1880	971	3,566	7.1
1890	1,610	8,387	13.3
1900	2,226	15,102	19.8
1904	2,452	19,633	23.4
1909	2,600	24,212	26.2
1914	2,580	28,777	28.6
1919	2,441	33,029	31.0
1921	2,334	33,742	31.7
1923	2,271	35,471	30.6
1925	2,116	37,407	32.3
1927	2,091	41,368	35.7
1929	2,086	42,015	34.1
1931	2,044	41,294	33.6
1933	1,903	37,630	29.6
1935	2,037	40,871	32.1
1937	2,065	43,345	34.1
1939	2,040	42,966	32.4
1947	1,854	53,287	37.0
1950	1,772	53,800	35.3
1954	1,820	56,410	34.6
1958	1,778	58,713	33.6
1960	1,763	58,900	32.6
1963	1,766	63,831	33.7
1965	1,751	60,400	31.1
1967	—	66,527	33.5
1970	1,748	62,100	30.3
1975	1,756	60,700	28.1
1978	1,756	62,000	27.9
1979	1,763	62,200	27.6
1980	1,745	62,200	27.3
1981	1,730	61,400	26.7
1982	1,711	62,500	26.9
1983	1,701	62,600	26.7
1984	1,688	63,300	26.8
1985	1,676	62,800	26.3
1986	1,657	62,500	26.0
1987	1,645	62,826	25.9
1988	1,642	62,695	25.6
1989	1,626	62,649	25.3
1990	1,611	62,328	24.9
1991	1,586	60,687	23.9
1992	1,570	60,164	23.1
1993	1,556	59,812	22.6

(*Notes continue*)

Table 2-3   *(Continued)*

Note: "—" indicates not available. Data are for English language newspapers only. In 1900 and earlier, figures include a small number of periodicals. In 1970 and later, the number of newspapers is for February of the following year and circulation figures are as of September 30 of the year indicated.

Sources: Daily papers, 1850-1967: U.S. Bureau of the Census, *Historical Statistics of the United States* (Washington, D.C.: U.S. Government Printing Office, 1975), 810; 1970-1993: *Editor & Publisher International Yearbook* (New York: Editor & Publisher), annual; population: U.S. Bureau of the Census, *Statistical Abstract of the United States, 1991* (Washington, D.C.: U.S. Government Printing Office, 1991), 7; 1991: U.S. Bureau of the Census, *Current Population Reports* (Washington, D.C.: U.S. Government Printing Office, 1992), Series P-25, no. 1087; 1992-1993: estimated by *Editor & Publisher*.

Figure 2-1 Growth of Congressional Press Corps, 1864-1993

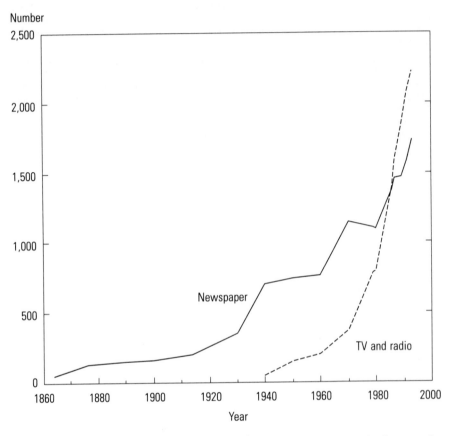

Note: Press corps members are those correspondents entitled to admission to the Senate and House press galleries and radio and television galleries. Prior to 1986, the number of press corps members was recorded approximately every ten years.

Sources: Samuel Kernell, *Going Public: New Strategies of Presidential Leadership* (Washington, D.C.: CQ Press, 1986), 57; updated by the editors from successive volumes of U.S. Congress Joint Committee on Printing, *Official Congressional Directory* (Washington, D.C.: U.S. Government Printing Office).

Table 2-4   Presidential News Conferences with White House
Correspondents, 1929-1995

President	Average number of press conferences per month	Total number of press conferences
Hoover (1929-1933)	5.6	268
Roosevelt (1933-1945)	6.9	998
Truman (1945-1953)	3.6	334
Eisenhower (1953-1961)	2.0	193
Kennedy (1961-1963)	1.9	65
Johnson (1963-1969)	2.2	135
Nixon (1969-1974)	0.6	39
Ford (1974-1977)	1.3	39
Carter (1977-1981)	1.2	59
Reagan (1981-1989)	0.6	53
Bush (1989-1993)	1.3	64
Clinton (1993-1995)[a]	1.1	29

[a] As of April 20, 1995.

Sources: Hoover and Truman through Carter: compiled by the editors from *Public Papers of the President* (Washington, D.C.: U.S. Government Printing Office); Roosevelt: Elizabeth Denier, comp., "List of FDR Press Conferences" (Hyde Park, N.Y.: Franklin Delano Roosevelt Library, n.d. [1991]); Reagan through Clinton: compiled by the editors from *Congressional Quarterly Weekly Report*.

Table 2-5 Media Coverage of Presidential Nomination and General Election Contests, by State, 1980-1992

State	1980 nomination Percent of news coverage		1984 nomination Percent of news coverage	1988 nomination Percent of TV news	1988 general election		1992 nomination Percent of TV news	1992 general election	
	CBS	UPI			Percent of TV news	Percent of electoral vote		Percent of TV news	Percent of electoral vote
Alabama	1	0	3	0	0	2	0	1	2
Alaska	0	0	0	0	0	1	0	0	1
Arizona	0	1	1	0	1	1	0	1	1
Arkansas	0	0	0	0	1	1	0	1	1
California	6	4	7	3	20	9	5	11	10
Colorado	0	0	0	1	1	1	2	2	1
Connecticut	2	2	2	2	1	1	3	1	1
Delaware	0	0	0	0	0	1	0	0	1
District of Columbia	1	2	0	1	1	1	0	1	1
Florida	3	2	1	2	2	4	4	7	5
Georgia	0	0	4	1	0	2	7	3	2
Hawaii	0	0	0	0	0	1	0	0	1
Idaho	0	0	0	0	0	1	0	0	1
Illinois	10	7	4	5	7	4	5	4	4
Indiana	1	1	2	1	0	2	0	1	2
Iowa	14	13	13	23	0	1	2	1	1
Kansas	0	1	0	0	0	1	1	0	1
Kentucky	0	1	0	1	1	2	0	2	1
Louisiana	0	0	1	0	0	2	2	2	2
Maine	4	3	2	1	0	1	2	0	1
Maryland	0	2	1	0	0	2	4	1	2
Massachusetts	7	3	3	0	2	2	0	0	2
Michigan	1	7	1	5	6	4	6	7	3
Minnesota	1	0	0	3	1	2	1	0	2

Mississippi	0	0	0	0	0	1	1	1	1
Missouri	0	0	1	0	2	2	0	4	2
Montana	0	0	0	0	0	1	0	0	1
Nebraska	0	1	1	0	0	1	0	0	1
Nevada	0	1	0	0	0	1	0	1	1
New Hampshire	14	15	19	17	0	1	23	1	1
New Jersey	1	0	5	1	5	3	1	5	3
New Mexico	0	0	1	0	1	1	0	1	1
New York	7	6	11	7	4	7	8	2	6
North Carolina	0	1	1	1	1	2	0	4	3
North Dakota	0	0	0	0	0	1	0	0	1
Ohio	4	2	2	2	9	4	1	7	4
Oklahoma	0	1	0	0	0	1	1	1	1
Oregon	1	1	0	0	1	1	0	1	1
Pennsylvania	9	7	6	4	5	5	4	4	4
Puerto Rico	1	2	0	0	0	0	0	0	0
Rhode Island	0	0	0	0	0	1	0	0	1
South Carolina	2	3	0	3	0	1	3	1	1
South Dakota	0	0	0	3	0	1	3	1	1
Tennessee	0	0	1	0	1	2	1	1	2
Texas	2	2	4	2	20	5	2	10	6
Utah	0	0	0	0	0	1	0	1	1
Vermont	1	1	2	1	0	1	0	0	1
Virginia	0	0	1	0	0	2	1	0	0
Washington	0	0	1	0	2	2	1	1	2
West Virginia	0	0	1	0	0	1	0	0	2
Wisconsin	6	5	1	4	1	2	2	2	1
Wyoming	0	0	1	1	0	1	0	0	1

(Notes continue)

Table 2-5 (Continued)

Note: Media coverage in a given state is the proportion of seconds of TV coverage or of column inches of print coverage of primary, caucus, or general election contests that mention the state. For 1984, media coverage of multistate stories is calculated by proportionately allocating coverage. For 1988 and 1992, media coverage of the nomination tabulates state contests mentioned—one story may mention several state contests. Media coverage of the general election includes only those stories discussing the presidential contest in a state.

Sources: 1980 news coverage: Michael J. Robinson and Margaret A. Sheehan, *Over the Wire and on TV: CBS and UPI in Campaign 1980* (New York: Russell Sage Foundation, 1983), 176, 177 (copyright © Russell Sage Foundation, used with permission), percentages calculated by the editors; 1984 news coverage: William C. Adams, personal communication, content analysis of *New York Times* and of ABC, CBS, and NBC evening news summarized in *Television News Index and Abstracts* (Nashville, Tenn.: Vanderbilt Television News Archives, Vanderbilt University); 1988 news coverage: Center for Media and Public Affairs content analysis of the ABC, CBS, and NBC evening news from February 8, 1987 through November 7, 1988; 1992 news coverage: Center for Media and Public Affairs content analysis of the ABC, CBS, and NBC evening news from January 1, 1991 through November 2, 1992; 1992 electoral vote: this volume, Table 3-2. For a discussion of data on television news coverage of the 1988 nominations, see S. Robert Lichter, Daniel Amundson, and Richard Noyes, *The Video Campaign: Network Coverage of the 1988 Primaries* (Washington, D.C.: American Enterprise Institute for Public Policy Research and Center for Media and Public Affairs, 1988). For a discussion of data on news coverage of the 1984 nominations, see William C. Adams, "As New Hampshire Goes . . ." in *Media and Momentum: The New Hampshire Primary and Nomination Politics*, ed. Gary R. Orren and Nelson W. Polsby (Chatham, N.J.: Chatham House, 1987), 42-59.

Table 2-6   Focus of Television News Coverage, 1992 Presidential Election

Period	Policy issues (percent)	Campaign issues (percent)	Horse race (percent)	Number of stories
Primary				
1991 (1/1-12/31)	47	33	20	211
Pre-New Hampshire (1/1-2/17)	43	35	22	190
Junior Tuesday (2/18-3/2)	18	31	51	104
Super Tuesday (3/3-3/9)	22	17	62	76
Midwest (3/10-3/16)	21	40	40	54
New York (3/17-4/6)	28	45	28	131
California (4/7-6/2)	39	31	30	273
Primary total (1/1-6/2)	36	33	31	1,039
General Election				
Pre-Democratic Convention (6/3-7/10)	49	34	17	247
Democratic Convention (7/11-7/19)	30	48	22	185
Pre-Republican Convention (7/20-8/14)	57	32	11	182
Republican Convention (8/15-8/23)	50	25	25	138
Labor Day (8/24-9/6)	53	31	16	77
Pre-Perot entry (9/7-9/30)	35	41	24	245
Pre-debates (10/1-10/10)	35	23	42	120
Debates (10/11-10/19)	23	25	52	124
Final days (10/20-11/2)	28	28	44	239
General election total (6/3-11/2)	40	33	27	1,558
Primary and general election total	38	33	29	2,597

Note: "Policy issues" involve concerns such as those detailed in Table 2-7; "campaign issues" concern candidate character; "horse race" coverage focuses on the contest—who's ahead, who's behind. Comparable data for the 1988 election can be found in Table 2-7, *Vital Statistics on American Politics*, 2nd or 3rd edition.

Source: Center for Media and Public Affairs content analysis of the ABC, CBS, and NBC evening news from January 1, 1991, through November 2, 1992.

Table 2-7 Television Coverage of Issues During the 1992 Presidential Campaign

Issue	1991	New Hampshire	Junior Tuesday	Super Tuesday	Midwest	New York	California	Pre-Democratic convention	Democratic convention	Pre-Republican convention	Republican convention	Labor Day	Pre-Perot	Pre-debates	Debates	Final days	Number of stories
General foreign policy	6	5	2	4	5	7	1	4	3	10	6	3	2	6	5	3	274
Persian Gulf	5	3	7	2	1	1	1	2	1	6	5	2	2	2	5	5	205
Defense spending	2	4	2	5	3	3	2	4	2	6	4	9	4	2	0	3	189
Asia	2	4	1	0	1	1	0	4	0	2	0	3	1	5	4	4	130
Soviet relations	2	1	1	0	4	4	1	2	1	0	1	1	0	2	0	1	77
Dealing with allies	1	1	0	1	0	2	0	2	2	2	1	1	1	2	3	1	72
Middle East	1	1	1	2	2	4	0	0	1	4	1	0	1	0	1	1	71
Iran-contra	0	0	0	0	0	0	0	0	0	0	0	0	2	1	4	5	51
Central America	1	0	1	1	3	0	1	1	1	0	0	1	0	3	1	1	42
Yugoslavia	0	0	0	0	0	0	0	1	0	4	1	0	0	0	0	0	30
Arms control	0	1	1	1	0	0	0	1	0	0	0	0	1	1	1	1	29
Panama	0	0	0	0	0	0	1	1	0	0	0	0	0	0	0	1	17
South Africa	0	0	0	0	0	0	0	0	2	0	0	0	0	0	0	0	10
Terrorism	0	0	1	0	0	0	0	0	0	0	0	0	0	0	0	1	5
SDI	0	0	1	0	0	0	0	0	0	0	0	0	0	0	0	0	4
Foreign policy total	21	19	16	15	18	22	7	20	13	34	20	21	15	23	24	25	1,206

																	Total
General economy	15	17	20	22	17	13	10	9	9	13	13	12	16	15	18	18	878
Taxes	6	10	11	11	11	12	6	5	6	8	10	9	9	8	9	7	507
Jobs	5	10	5	7	16	6	8	7	9	5	5	10	8	11	7	9	481
Health	6	7	2	5	3	2	3	4	3	3	4	5	4	3	3	4	245
Social welfare	3	5	3	6	4	5	6	3	3	3	3	3	4	2	3	2	222
Deficit	1	3	1	2	0	2	3	4	3	4	4	4	6	5	7	4	210
Other budget	3	3	2	2	3	2	1	0	0	1	4	4	4	2	4	2	140
Trade	1	3	4	2	3	2	1	2	1	0	0	5	2	3	2	2	114
Energy	1	1	1	4	3	2	0	0	0	1	1	0	2	3	2	3	68
Agriculture	0	1	2	1	2	1	0	0	1	1	1	3	2	2	0	1	60
Industrial policy	2	1	1	2	3	1	0	1	1	0	1	0	0	1	0	1	54
Inflation	0	0	1	0	0	0	0	0	0	1	0	0	1	0	0	1	21
Economic total	45	61	55	62	62	45	39	35	35	41	45	55	59	55	54	53	3,000
Civil rights	5	2	8	7	6	6	11	7	9	2	3	1	2	2	2	2	280
General social	7	2	3	1	2	3	11	4	4	3	4	3	4	3	1	1	248
Education	4	4	1	2	1	2	6	4	6	3	3	2	3	2	3	2	206
Abortion	3	2	1	2	0	4	4	4	6	7	6	2	2	1	2	2	202
Family values	0	0	0	0	0	0	5	4	4	5	9	6	4	1	3	2	177
Crime	3	2	1	2	2	4	6	3	4	5	2	0	3	2	2	4	163
Drugs	0	1	1	0	0	2	2	2	1	2	1	0	0	0	0	1	57
Women's issues	0	0	1	1	2	1	2	1	2	1	1	0	1	1	0	0	53
AIDS	0	1	0	0	1	2	1	0	2	0	2	0	0	1	0	1	44
Homeless	1	1	0	1	0	1	0	0	3	0	0	0	0	0	0	0	32
Social total	23	14	16	17	13	24	46	31	41	20	31	13	19	14	14	16	1,462

(Table continues)

Table 2-7 (Continued)

Issue	1991	New Hamp-shire	Junior Tues-day	Super Tues-day	Mid-west	New York	Cali-fornia	Pre-Demo-cratic con-vention	Demo-cratic con-vention	Pre-Repub-lican conven-tion	Repub-lican conven-tion	Labor Day	Pre-Perot	Pre-debates	Debates	Final days	Number of stories
Environment	2	3	2	0	2	1	3	6	3	1	1	2	2	4	2	3	147
General governance	1	1	1	1	0	5	3	2	3	1	0	0	0	0	1	2	84
Supreme Court	1	0	7	2	1	0	1	3	2	1	2	1	1	1	0	1	81
Other issues	2	1	3	2	0	1	0	0	0	1	0	6	1	1	0	0	61
Transportation	3	1	0	1	0	0	1	1	1	0	0	0	1	1	1	1	53
Role of government	1	0	1	0	0	0	1	0	2	0	1	1	2	1	0	1	51
Government ethics	1	0	1	1	4	1	1	0	0	0	0	0	0	1	3	1	34
Government management	0	0	1	0	0	0	0	0	0	0	0	0	0	0	0	0	9
Other total	11	6	14	7	7	9	9	13	11	4	4	11	8	9	8	7	520
Number of stories	676	549	216	167	116	248	549	526	330	463	459	232	683	307	240	427	6,188

Note: Issues were coded if the story mentioned that particular issue. More than one issue could be coded for each story. Table entries give each issue's times mentioned as a percentage of all issues mentioned within each time period. More precise indications of the time periods can be found in Table 2-6, this volume. Totals calculated before rounding. Comparable data for the 1988 election can be found in Table 2-7, *Vital Statistics on American Politics*, 2nd or 3rd edition.

Source: Center for Media and Public Affairs content analysis of the ABC, CBS, and NBC evening news from January 1, 1991, through November 2, 1992.

Table 2-8 Television News Coverage of the Candidates and Parties, 1991-1992 (percent)

Candidate/party	1991	New Hamp-shire	Junior Tues-day	Super Tues-day	Mid-west	New York	Cali-fornia	Total pri-mary	Pre-Demo-cratic conven-tion	Demo-cratic con-vention	Pre-Repub-lican conven-tion	Repub-lican con-vention	Labor Day	Pre-Perot	Pre-debates	Debates	Final days	Total general election
Republicans																		
Bush	69	61	49	49	43	72	77	63	75	85	77	84	80	84	90	78	89	82
Quayle	16	11	9	6	14	3	18	12	25	15	23	17	20	16	10	22	11	18
Buchanan	8	28	39	37	36	25	5	21	0	0	0	0	0	0	0	0	0	0
Duke	6	1	3	8	8	0	1	3	0	0	0	0	0	0	0	0	0	0
Democrats																		
Clinton	19	33	26	34	36	48	70	39	85	73	80	84	89	88	86	82	86	83
Gore	0	0	0	0	0	0	0	0	15	27	20	16	11	12	14	18	14	17
Brown	10	9	14	12	26	40	23	19	0	0	0	0	0	0	0	0	0	0
Tsongas	21	18	28	30	33	13	7	20	0	0	0	0	0	0	0	0	0	0
Kerrey	14	18	19	11	1	0	0	10	0	0	0	0	0	0	0	0	0	0
Harkin	19	20	13	13	5	0	0	10	0	0	0	0	0	0	0	0	0	0
Wilder	16	1	0	0	0	0	0	3	0	0	0	0	0	0	0	0	0	0
Independents																		
Perot	0	0	0	0	0	75	100	98	100	100	100	100	100	100	92	83	94	96
Stockdale	0	0	0	0	0	25	0	2	0	0	0	0	0	0	8	17	6	4
Democrats	60	59	48	69	62	83	58	62	36	64	24	11	33	36	26	33	31	35
Republicans	40	41	52	31	38	17	42	38	34	14	69	86	64	48	37	45	41	47
Perot	0	0	0	0	0	0	0	0	30	22	0	3	4	16	37	22	27	19

Note: The entries are based on the number of times each candidate appeared. Table entries give each candidate's times mentioned as a percentage of all candidate mentions within each party for each time period. Table entries for the parties indicate the coverage of each party's presidential contest as a percentage of all mentions in each time period. More precise indications of the time periods can be found in Table 2-6, this volume. Comparable data for the 1988 election can be found in Table 2-8, *Vital Statistics on American Politics,* 2nd or 3rd edition.

Source: Center for Media and Public Affairs content analysis of the ABC, CBS, and NBC evening news from January 1, 1991, through November 2, 1992.

Table 2-9 Horse Race Judgments of the Presidential Candidates in Television News Coverage, 1991-1992 (percent)

Party/candidate	1991		New Hampshire		Junior Tuesday		Super Tuesday		Midwest		New York		California	
Republicans														
Bush	60	(166)	21	(77)	45	(106)	43	(87)	76	(38)	76	(25)	44	(156)
Buchanan	62	(13)	62	(39)	73	(81)	63	(46)	48	(23)	8	(13)	—	
Duke	54	(13)	—		0	(2)	0	(5)	0	(1)	—		—	
Democrats														
Clinton	100	(11)	53	(101)	70	(63)	93	(102)	93	(84)	63	(162)	64	(259)
Brown	43	(7)	9	(22)	77	(43)	63	(27)	75	(16)	61	(82)	41	(29)
Tsongas	40	(5)	83	(77)	77	(87)	71	(91)	25	(40)	31	(45)	55	(11)
Kerrey	75	(4)	50	(16)	60	(25)	19	(26)	0	(1)	—		—	
Harkin	75	(16)	55	(29)	36	(11)	19	(26)	0	(4)	—		—	
Wilder	0	(5)	0	(2)	—		—		—		—		—	
Independent														
Perot	—		—		—		—		—		80	(5)	88	(169)

	Pre-Democratic convention	Democratic convention	Pre-Republican convention	Republican convention	Labor Day	Pre-Perot	Pre-debates	Debates	Final days	Total 1992 election
Republicans										
Bush	22 (102)	34 (73)	14 (155)	38 (167)	29 (63)	20 (190)	19 (100)	9 (149)	35 (308)	33 (1,962)
Buchanan	—	—	—	—	—	—	—	—	—	61 (215)
Duke	—	—	—	—	—	—	—	—	—	32 (21)
Democrats										
Clinton	44 (79)	88 (157)	84 (61)	74 (66)	69 (36)	77 (129)	83 (77)	94 (120)	79 (265)	75 (1,772)
Brown	100 (1)	0 (1)	—	—	—	—	—	—	—	57 (228)
Tsongas	—	—	—	—	—	—	—	—	—	64 (356)
Kerrey	—	—	—	—	—	—	—	—	—	43 (72)
Harkin	—	—	—	—	—	—	—	—	—	43 (86)
Wilder	—	—	—	—	—	—	—	—	—	0 (7)
Independent										
Perot	71 (144)	20 (75)	56 (9)	75 (8)	100 (3)	64 (44)	18 (51)	40 (62)	56 (202)	60 (772)

Note: "—" indicates candidate was not an active presidential contender. Table entries are percent positive of all clearly positive and negative assessments by news sources about the probability the candidate will become president. This excludes positive and negative assessments of the candidate in other contexts (see Table 2-10). Total number of judgments about whether the candidate will become president are given in parentheses. More precise indications of the time periods can be found in Table 2-6, this volume. Comparable data for the 1988 election can be found in Table 2-9, *Vital Statistics on American Politics*, 2nd or 3rd edition.

Source: Center for Media and Public Affairs content analysis of the ABC, CBS, and NBC evening news from January 1, 1991, through November 2, 1992.

Table 2-10 Assessments of the Presidential Candidates in Television News Coverage, 1991-1992 (percent)

Party/candidate	1991	New Hampshire	Junior Tuesday	Super Tuesday	Midwest	New York	California
Republicans							
Bush	28 (224)	25 (210)	25 (87)	18 (66)	19 (36)	24 (63)	16 (160)
Quayle	49 (35)	38 (8)	—	—	—	—	44 (18)
Buchanan	64 (11)	50 (40)	23 (64)	44 (25)	18 (11)	40 (5)	100 (1)
Duke	24 (17)	—	100 (1)	0 (1)	0 (1)	—	—
Democrats							
Clinton	56 (9)	40 (81)	36 (39)	37 (49)	28 (39)	35 (141)	58 (116)
Gore	—	—	—	—	—	—	—
Brown	40 (5)	79 (14)	100 (5)	100 (1)	50 (26)	35 (119)	31 (36)
Tsongas	71 (7)	60 (40)	63 (40)	55 (49)	41 (22)	81 (21)	100 (5)
Kerrey	67 (9)	56 (32)	75 (8)	50 (10	—	—	—
Harkin	53 (15)	56 (27)	—	—	—	—	—
Wilder	50 (10)	—	—	—	—	—	—
Independent							
Perot	—	—	—	—	—	100 (4)	63 (124)
Stockdale	—	—	—	—	—	—	—

	Pre-Democratic convention	Democratic convention	Pre-Republican convention	Republican convention	Labor Day	Pre-Perot	Pre-debates	Debates	Final days	Total 1992 election
Republicans										
Bush	32 (141)	46 (50)	34 (221)	47 (276)	33 (118)	28 (346)	36 (135)	34 (148)	34 (217)	31 (2,498)
Quayle	22 (23)	29 (7)	35 (26)	75 (8)	25 (8)	50 (16)	33 (3)	50 (18)	0 (4)	40 (174)
Buchanan	0 (2)	—	—	30 (10)	—	—	—	—	—	36 (169)
Duke	—	—	—	—	—	—	—	—	—	25 (20)
Democrats										
Clinton	50 (110)	67 (152)	32 (108)	31 (104)	36 (94)	33 (265)	37 (115)	47 (99)	36 (202)	41 (1,723)
Gore	100 (21)	79 (14)	50 (12)	50 (4)	55 (9)	70 (10)	0 (5)	45 (20)	0 (24)	51 (119)
Brown	0 (1)	0 (2)	—	—	—	—	—	—	—	41 (209)
Tsongas	—	—	—	—	—	—	—	—	—	61 (184)
Kerrey	—	—	—	—	—	—	—	—	—	41 (59)
Harkin	—	—	—	—	—	—	—	—	—	55 (42)
Wilder	—	—	—	—	—	—	—	—	—	50 (10)
Independents										
Perot	42 (170)	33 (89)	60 (10)	75 (4)	0 (2)	41 (66)	28 (72)	62 (79)	49 (134)	47 (754)
Stockdale	—	—	—	—	—	—	100 (5)	53 (17)	—	64 (22)

Note: " —" indicates candidate was not an active presidential contender. Table entries are percent positive of all clearly positive and negative assessments by news sources, excluding horse race judgments (see Table 2-9). Total number of assessments about the candidate are given in parentheses. More precise indications of the time periods can be found in Table 2-6, this volume. Comparable data for the 1988 election can be found in Table 2-10, *Vital Statistics on American Politics,* 2nd or 3rd edition.

Source: Center for Media and Public Affairs content analysis of the ABC, CBS, and NBC evening news from January 1, 1991, through November 2, 1992.

Table 2-11 Public Use of Media to Follow Presidential Campaigns, 1952-1992 (percent)

Media	1952	1956	1960	1964	1968	1972	1976	1980	1984	1988	1992
Read newspaper articles about the election											
regularly	—	—	44	40	37	26	28	—	—	—	—
often[a]	39	69	12	14	12	14	17	27	24	—	—
from time to time[b]	40	—	16	18	19	16	24	29	34	—	—
once in a great while[c]	—	—	7	6	7	4	10	17	19	—	—
no	21	31	21	22	25	40	22	27	23	—	—
Attention paid to newspaper articles about the presidential campaign											
great deal	—	—	—	—	—	—	—	—	8	6	9
quite a bit	—	—	—	—	—	—	—	—	14	12	15
some	—	—	—	—	—	—	—	—	28	22	20
very little	—	—	—	—	—	—	—	—	20	9	6
none	—	—	—	—	—	—	—	—	31	52	50
Listen to speeches or discussions on radio											
good many[d]	34	—	15	12	12	8	12	14	10	5	7
several[e]	—	45	17	23	16	21	20	22	20	10	11
one or two[f]	35	—	10	12	12	13	16	15	16	17	18
no	30	55	58	52	59	59	52	50	55	69	64
Watched programs about the campaign on television											
good many[d]	32	—	47	41	42	33	37	28	25	—	31
several[e]	—	74	29	34	34	41	38	37	37	—	39
one or two[f]	19	—	11	13	13	16	15	22	24	—	19
no	49	26	13	11	11	9	10	13	14	—	11

Attention paid to television news about the presidential campaign

great deal	—	—	—	—	—	—	—	—	17	15	20
quite a bit	—	—	—	—	—	—	—	—	24	26	29
some	—	—	—	—	—	—	—	—	28	29	28
very little	—	—	—	—	—	—	—	—	11	13	11
none	—	—	—	—	—	—	—	—	20	17	13

Read about the campaign in magazines

good many[d]	15	—	12	10	9	7	12	7	7	—	—
several[e]	—	31	15	16	12	15	24	19	16	—	—
one or two[f]	26	—	13	13	15	14	15	12	11	—	—
no	60	69	59	61	64	64	49	62	66	—	—

Attention paid to magazine articles about the presidential campaign

great deal	—	—	—	—	—	—	—	—	3	3	4
quite a bit	—	—	—	—	—	—	—	—	4	6	7
some	—	—	—	—	—	—	—	—	7	11	10
very little	—	—	—	—	—	—	—	—	2	3	3
none	—	—	—	—	—	—	—	—	84	76	77

Note: "—" indicates question not asked or response category not offered.

[a] "Quite a lot, pretty much" in 1952; "yes" in 1956; "good many" in 1980-1984.
[b] "Not very much" in 1952; "several" in 1980-1984.
[c] "One or two" in 1980-1984.
[d] "Quite a lot, pretty much" in 1952.
[e] "Yes" in 1956.
[f] "Not very much" in 1952.

Source: Calculated by the editors from the National Election Studies codebooks and data sets (Ann Arbor, Mich.: Center for Political Studies, University of Michigan).

Table 2-12 Use and Trustworthiness of Media, 1959-1994

	1959	1961	1963	1964	1967	1968	1971	1972	1974	1976	1978	1980	1982	1984	1986	1988	1990	1991	1992	1994
Source of most news[a]																				
Television	51	52	55	58	64	59	60	64	65	64	67	64	64	64	66	65	69	81	69	72
Newspapers	57	57	53	56	55	49	48	50	47	49	49	44	44	40	36	42	43	35	43	38
Radio	34	34	29	26	28	25	23	21	21	19	20	18	18	14	14	14	15	14	16	18
Magazines	8	9	6	8	7	7	5	6	4	7	5	5	5	4	4	4	3	4	4	8
People	4	5	4	5	4	5	4	4	4	5	5	4	4	4	4	5	7	6	6	—
Most believable[b]																				
Television	29	39	36	41	41	44	49	48	51	51	47	51	53	53	55	49	54	58	56	51
Newspapers	32	24	24	23	24	21	20	21	20	22	23	22	22	24	21	26	22	20	22	21
Radio	12	12	12	8	7	8	10	8	8	7	9	8	6	8	6	7	7	6	7	8
Magazines	10	10	10	10	8	11	9	10	8	9	9	9	8	7	7	5	4	5	4	5
Don't know/no answer	17	17	18	18	20	16	12	13	13	11	12	10	11	9	12	13	13	13	12	15

Note: " — " indicates not available.

[a] Question: "First, I'd like to ask you where you usually get most of your news about what's going on in the world today—from the newspapers or radio or television or magazines or talking to people or where?" (more than one answer permitted).

[b] Question: "If you got conflicting or different reports of the same news story from radio, television, the magazines, and the newspapers, which of the four versions would you be most inclined to believe—the one on the radio or television or magazines or newspapers?" (only one answer permitted).

Source: "America's Watching—Public Attitudes Toward Television 1993" (New York: The Network Television Association and the National Association of Broadcasters, 1993), 29, 31, "1995," 17, 35.

Table 2-13   National Nominating Conventions: Television Coverage
and Viewership, 1952-1992

Year/party	Audience rating[a] (percent)	Average hours viewed by household	Network hours telecast[b]
1952			
Republicans	—	10.5	57.5
Democrats	—	13.1	61.1
1956			
Republicans	—	6.4	22.8
Democrats	—	8.4	37.6
1960			
Republicans	—	6.2	25.5
Democrats	—	8.3	29.3
1964			
Republicans	—	7.0	36.5
Democrats	—	6.4	23.5
1968			
Republicans	28.5	6.5	34.0
Democrats	26.4	8.5	39.1
1972			
Republicans	18.3	3.5	19.8
Democrats	23.4	5.8	36.7
1976			
Republicans	25.2	6.3	29.5
Democrats	31.5	5.2	30.4
1980			
Republicans	27.0	3.8	22.7
Democrats	21.6	4.4	24.1
1984			
Republicans	23.4	1.9	11.9
Democrats	19.2	2.5	12.9
1988			
Republicans	19.8	2.2	12.6
Democrats	18.3	2.3	12.8
1992			
Republicans	22.0	—	7.3
Democrats	20.5	—	8.0

Note: "—" indicates not available.

[a] Percentage of television households viewing the convention during an average minute. Through 1988, based on viewing of ABC, CBS, and NBC; for 1992, based on viewing the three networks plus PBS and CNN. C-SPAN viewing not included.

[b] Number of hours during which one or more of ABC, CBS, or NBC was broadcasting the convention. In 1988, CNN broadcast 30.0 hours of the Democratic convention and 14.5 hours of the Republican convention. In 1992, CNN broadcast 8.0 hours of each convention.

Sources: 1952-1964: *Network Television Audiences to Primaries, Conventions, Elections* (Northbrook, Ill.: A. C. Nielsen, 1976), 8, 9, 21; audience rating: *Nielsen Tunes in to Politics: Tracking the Presidential Years (1960-1992)*, 1; hours viewed, hours telecast, 1968-1988: data supplied by A. C. Nielsen Co; hours telecast, 1992: calculated by the editors from television listings and *Nielsen Tunes in to Politics*, 2-3.

Table 2-14 Television Viewership of Presidential and Vice-Presidential Debates, 1960-1992

Year	Candidates	Date	Audience rating[a] (percent)	Persons (in millions)
1960	Nixon-Kennedy	Sept. 26	59.5	—
		Oct. 7	59.1	—
		Oct. 13	61.0	—
		Oct. 21	57.8	—
1976	Ford-Carter	Sept. 23	53.5	69.7
		Oct. 6	52.4	63.9
		Oct. 22	47.8	62.7
	Dole-Mondale	Oct. 15	35.5	43.2
1980	Carter-Reagan	Oct. 28	58.9	80.6
1984	Reagan-Mondale	Oct. 7	45.3	65.1
		Oct. 21	46.0	67.3
	Bush-Ferraro	Oct. 11	43.6	56.7
1988	Bush-Dukakis	Sept. 25	36.8	65.1
		Oct. 13	35.9	67.3
	Quayle-Bentsen	Oct. 5	33.6	46.9
1992	Bush-Clinton-Perot	Oct. 11[b]	38.3	62.4
		Oct. 15	46.3	69.9
		Oct. 19	45.2	66.9
	Quayle-Gore-Stockdale	Oct. 13	35.9	51.2

Note: 1976-1988 debates include ABC, CBS, and NBC only; 1992 includes CNN. PBS data not included. Combined audience estimates are based on comparable durations.

[a] Percentage of television households viewing the debates during an average minute.
[b] Does not include CBS.

Source: *Nielsen Tunes in to Politics: Tracking the Presidential Election Years (1960-1992)* (New York: Nielsen Media Research, 1993), 4-5.

Table 2-15   Newspaper Endorsements of Presidential Candidates, 1932-1992

Year/endorsement	Papers		Circulation	
	Number	Percentage	Number	Percentage
1932				
Hoover (R)	656	52	—	—
Roosevelt (D)	511	41	—	—
Uncommitted	94	7	—	—
1936				
Landon (R)	727	57	—	—
Roosevelt (D)	459	36	—	—
Uncommitted	87	7	—	—
1940				
Willkie (R)	813	64	—	—
Roosevelt (D)	289	23	—	—
Uncommitted	171	13	—	—
1944				
Dewey (R)	796	60	26,654,996	69
Roosevelt (D)	291	22	6,902,243	18
Uncommitted	237	18	5,356,807	14
1948				
Dewey (R)	771	65	35,152,807	79
Truman (D)	182	15	4,489,851	10
Thurmond	45	4	537,730	1
Wallace	3	0	60,233	0
Uncommitted	182	15	4,454,557	10
1952				
Eisenhower (R)	933	67	40,129,237	80
Stevenson (D)	202	15	5,466,781	11
Uncommitted	250	18	4,417,102	9
1956				
Eisenhower (R)	740	62	34,538,755	72
Stevenson (D)	189	15	6,122,491	13
Uncommitted	270	23	7,079,846	15
1960				
Nixon (R)	731	58	38,006,203	71
Kennedy (D)	208	16	8,448,677	16
Uncommitted	328	26	7,135,954	13
1964				
Goldwater (R)	359	35	8,977,214	21
Johnson (D)	440	42	26,997,400	62
Uncommitted	237	23	7,638,727	18

(*Table continues*)

Table 2-15   *(Continued)*

Year/endorsement	Papers		Circulation	
	Number	Percentage	Number	Percentage
1968				
Nixon (R)	634	61	34,559,385	70
Humphrey (D)	146	14	9,572,948	19
Wallace	12	1	159,524	0
Uncommitted	250	24	5,201,845	11
1972				
Nixon (R)	753	71	30,560,535	77
McGovern (D)	56	5	3,044,534	8
Uncommitted	245	23	5,864,548	15
1976				
Ford (R)	411	62	20,951,798	62
Carter (D)	80	12	7,607,739	23
Uncommitted	168	26	5,074,069	15
1980				
Reagan (R)	443	42	17,561,333	49
Carter (D)	126	12	7,782,078	22
Anderson	40	4	1,614,740	4
Uncommitted	439	42	9,131,940	25
1984				
Reagan (R)	381	58	18,357,512	52
Mondale (D)	62	9	7,568,639	21
Uncommitted	216	33	9,611,058	27
1988				
Bush (R)	241	31	18,186,225	40
Dukakis (D)	103	13	11,644,600	25
Uncommitted	428	55	16,224,807	35
1992[a]				
Bush (R)	121	15	7,134,599	18
Clinton (D)	149	18	10,961,415	27
Uncommitted	542	67	22,225,342	55

Note: "—" indicates not available.

[a] One newspaper—circulation 9,075—endorsed Ross Perot.

Sources: Editor & Publisher, October 26, 1940, 7; November 4, 1944, 9; October 30, 1948, 11; November 1, 1952, 9; November 3, 1956, 11; November 5, 1960, 10; October 31, 1964, 10; November 2, 1968, 9; November 7, 1972, 9; October 30, 1976, 5; November 1, 1980, 10; November 3, 1984, 9; November 5, 1988, 9; October 24, 1992, 9.

Figure 2-2   Newspaper Endorsements of Presidential Candidates: Democratic, Republican, and Neutral, 1932-1992

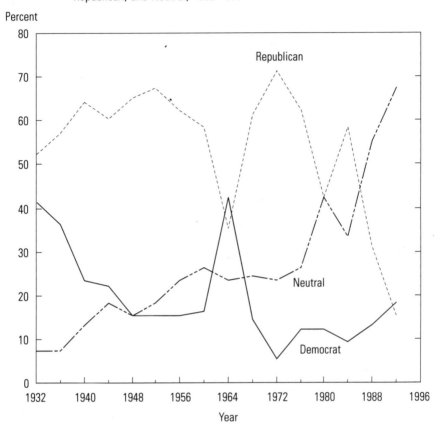

Source: This volume, Table 2-15.

3

Elections and Campaigns

Elections and campaigns provide an abundance of numbers. Indeed, if asked for examples of political statistics, most people would think first of election results. But votes are only part of the numbers election campaigns generate: opinion surveys and exit polls, for example, offer a wealth of information about who the voters are and why they chose as they did; summary statistics show which party and which types of candidates won and lost; financial disclosure requirements furnish detailed information about campaign costs and contributions.

Not only are there a great many electoral statistics, but they extend back to the early years of the country. Consider the much-researched topic of partisan realignment. Long time series on voter turnout and the partisan breakdown of the vote have allowed researchers to comb the nation's past for realignments—fundamental shifts in support for parties and the coalitions supporting them. Election returns from localities dominated by different ethnic or economic groups also have been used to reveal the links between those groups and the parties. Thus, periods of realignment and the length of time between them—scholarly consensus holds that realignments occurred in the 1850s, 1890s, and between 1928 and 1932—are important for understanding our political history and the role of electoral statistics in uncovering that history. Realignment years are useful groupings for presenting data on partisan changes (Tables 3-14 and 3-15).

Available data also document more recent trends in campaigns and elections: the decline in presidential voter turnout after 1960 (Figure 3-1), the electoral advantages of incumbency (Table 3-18), the increasingly long quests (until 1992) for the presidential nominations (Figure 3-3), the greater emphasis on primaries (Tables 3-6 and 4-9), the growing contributions from political action committees (Table 6-7), and the expense of political campaigns (Tables 7-7 and 8-5).

75

Added to the arsenal of statistics about elections in the past fifty years have been surveys of representative national, state, and local populations. These data have enlivened research on the identification and timing of electoral realignments. The partisan changes that have occurred since the mid-1960s are of particular interest. Most scholars see the period since the mid-1960s as one of "dealignment" rather than realignment—with voters more willing to vote for some nominees of both parties (Table 4-7) and with more frequent outcomes in which different parties carry the presidential and congressional vote in a district (Table 4-8). Public opinion surveys also allow researchers to move beyond reliance on the simple shape of overall election results. Extensive data on individual behavior and attitudes reveal patterns of voting turnout and support (Tables 3-1 and 3-10) and voters' opinions about the candidates, parties, and issues (for example, Tables 3-9 and 4-4) that are much more detailed than previously available.

Despite this volume of data there are some gaps: survey data is nonexistent before the mid-1930s, and reliable, consistent surveys date principally from the 1950s; until 1980, presidential primary surveys were limited; even official election returns below the state level are only now being made readily available (by the Inter-university Consortium for Political and Social Research); surveys emphasizing nonpresidential voting are very limited prior to the mid-1970s; and campaign finance data are unavailable or uninformative in some states and systematically available for the federal level only since the mid-1970s.

These are serious gaps, and they impose limits on what we know about campaigns, elections, and parties. The lack of survey data on earlier realignments, for example, is troublesome because it robs researchers of helpful historical comparisons. Nonetheless, in the area of campaigns and elections, more than anywhere, there is almost an embarrassment of riches.

Figure 3-1   Voter Turnout, Presidential and Midterm Elections, 1789-1994

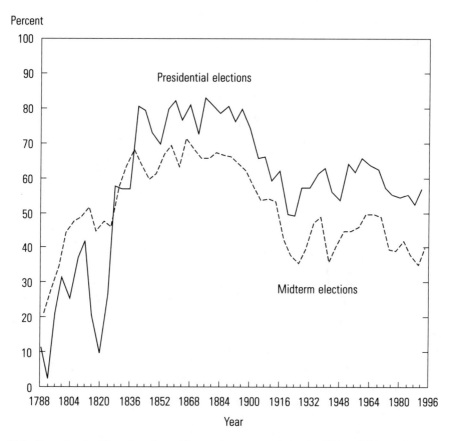

Note: Turnout calculations based on citizen voting-age population in 1924 and later; prior to 1924 the eligible voting-age population reflects various state restrictions as to citizenship, race, and sex.

Sources: 1790-1986: Walter Dean Burnham, "The Turnout Problem," in *Elections American Style,* ed. A. James Reichley (Washington, D.C.: Brookings, 1987), 113-114; 1988-1994: Walter Dean Burnham, personal communication.

Figure 3-2 Voter Turnout, Presidential Elections, South and Nonsouth, 1800-1992

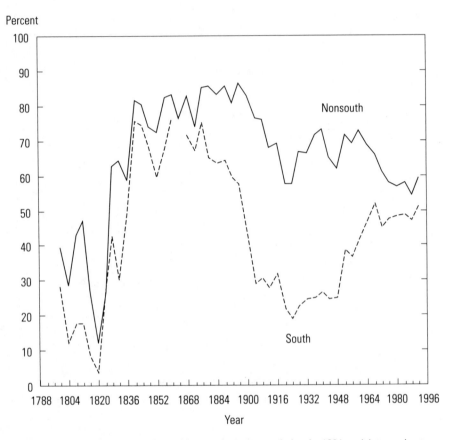

Note: Turnout calculations based on citizen voting-age population in 1924 and later; prior to 1924 the eligible voting-age population reflects various state restrictions as to citizenship, race, and sex.

Sources: 1800-1984: Walter Dean Burnham, "The Turnout Problem," in *Elections American Style,* ed. A. James Reichley (Washington, D.C.: Brookings, 1987), 113-114; 1988-1992: Walter Dean Burnham, personal communication.

Table 3-1 Voting-Age Population Registered and Voting, Cross-Sections, 1976-1994[a] (percent)

| | Percentage reporting they registered | | | | | | | | | | Percentage reporting they voted | | | | | | | | | |
| | Presidential election years | | | | | Congressional election years | | | | | Presidential election years | | | | | Congressional election years | | | | |
	1976	1980	1984	1988	1992	1978	1982	1986	1990	1994	1976	1980	1984	1988	1992	1978	1982	1986	1990	1994
Race/ethnicity																				
White	68	68	70	68	70	64	66	65	64	64	61	61	61	59	64	47	50	47	47	47
Black	59	60	66	65	64	57	59	64	59	58	49	51	56	52	54	37	43	43	39	37
Hispanic origin[b]	38	36	40	36	35	33	35	36	32	30	32	30	33	29	29	24	25	24	21	19
Hispanic citizen[b]	51	54	59	57	59	48	52	54	52	53	43	44	48	46	48	34	37	36	34	34
Sex																				
Male	67	67	67	65	67	63	64	63	61	61	60	59	59	56	60	47	49	46	45	44
Female	66	67	69	68	69	63	64	65	63	63	59	59	61	58	62	45	48	46	45	45
Region[c]																				
Northeast	66	65	67	65	67	62	63	62	61	61	60	59	60	57	61	48	50	44	45	45
Midwest	72	74	75	73	75	68	71	71	68	69	65	66	66	63	67	51	55	50	49	49
South	68	64	64	66	67	60	62	63	61	61	55	56	57	55	59	40	42	43	42	41
West	63	63	65	63	64	59	61	61	58	58	58	57	59	56	59	48	51	48	45	46
Age																				
18-20	47	45	47	45	48	35	35	35	35	37	38	36	37	33	38	20	20	19	18	17
21-24	55	53	54	51	55	45	48	47	43	46	46	43	44	38	46	26	28	24	22	22
25-34	62	62	63	58	61	56	57	56	52	52	55	55	55	48	53	38	40	35	34	32
35-44	70	71	71	69	69	67	68	68	66	63	63	64	64	61	64	50	52	49	48	46
45-64	76	76	77	76	75	74	76	75	71	71	69	69	70	68	70	59	62	59	56	56
65 and older	71	75	77	78	78	73	75	77	80	76	62	65	68	69	70	56	60	61	66	61

(Table continues)

Table 3-1 (Continued)

| | Percentage reporting they registered | | | | | | | | | | Percentage reporting they voted | | | | | | | | | |
| | Presidential election years | | | | | Congressional election years | | | | | Presidential election years | | | | | Congressional election years | | | | |
	1976	1980	1984	1988	1992	1978	1982	1986	1990	1994	1976	1980	1984	1988	1992	1978	1982	1986	1990	1994
Employment																				
Employed	69	69	69	67	70	63	66	64	63	63	62	62	62	58	64	47	50	46	45	45
Unemployed	52	50	54	50	54	44	50	49	45	46	44	41	44	39	46	27	34	30	28	28
Not in labor force	65	66	68	67	67	63	64	66	63	62	57	57	59	57	59	46	49	48	47	45
Education (years)																				
8 or less	54	53	53	48	44	53	52	51	44	40	44	43	43	37	35	35	36	33	28	23
1–3 of high school	56	55	55	53	50	53	53	52	48	45	47	46	44	41	41	35	38	34	31	27
4 of high school	67	66	67	65	65	62	63	63	60	59	59	59	59	55	58	45	47	44	42	40
1–3 of college	75	74	76	74	75	69	70	70	69	68	68	67	68	65	69	52	53	50	50	49
4 or more college	84	84	84	83	85	77	78	78	77	76	80	80	79	78	81	64	67	63	63	63
Total	67	67	68	67	68	62	64	64	62	62	59	59	60	57	61	46	49	46	45	45

a Data for earlier years can be found in previous editions of *Vital Statistics on American Politics*.
b Persons of Hispanic origin may be of any race.
c For composition of regions, see Appendix Table A-1.

Sources: U.S. Bureau of the Census, Current Population Reports, *Voting and Registration in the Election of November 1976* (Washington, D.C.: U.S. Government Printing Office, 1993), Series P-20, no. 322, 11-12, 14-21, 57, 61; *November 1978*, no. 344, 8, 11-19, 60, 65; *November 1980*, no. 370, 10-20, 50, 56; *November 1982*, no. 383, 1-12, 46, 49; *November 1984*, no. 405, 13-24, 59; *November 1986*, no. 414, 11-22, 29, 31; *November 1988*, no. 440, 13-24, 48, 50; *November 1990*, no. 453, 1-2, 4, 13-14, 17; *November, 1992*, no. 466, v-vii, 1, 5; "Voter Turnout in November 1994 Election," press release, 8 June 1995, from the November 1994 Current Population Survey on Internet (http://www.census.gov/org/pop).

Table 3-2 Presidential General Election Returns, by State, 1992

State	Clinton (Democrat) Vote	%	Bush (Republican) Vote	%	Perot (Independent) Vote	%	Other Vote	%	Total Vote	Plurality Vote	%	Electoral vote D	R
Alabama	690,080	40.9	804,283	47.6	183,109	10.8	10,588	0.6	1,688,060	114,203	6.8		9
Alaska	78,294	30.3	102,000	39.5	73,481	28.4	4,731	1.8	258,506	23,706	9.2		3
Arizona	543,050	36.5	572,086	38.5	353,741	23.8	18,098	1.2	1,486,975	29,036	2.0		8
Arkansas	505,823	53.2	337,324	35.5	99,132	10.4	8,374	0.9	950,653	168,499	17.7	6	
California	5,121,325	46.0	3,630,575	32.6	2,296,006	20.6	83,816	0.8	11,131,722	1,490,750	13.4	54	
Colorado	629,681	40.1	562,850	35.9	366,010	23.3	10,639	0.7	1,569,180	66,831	4.3	8	
Connecticut	682,318	42.2	578,313	35.8	348,771	21.6	6,930	0.4	1,616,332	104,005	6.4	8	
D.C.	192,619	84.6	20,698	9.1	9,681	4.3	4,574	2.0	227,572	171,921	75.6	3	
Delaware	126,054	43.5	102,313	35.3	59,213	20.4	2,155	0.7	289,735	23,741	8.2	3	
Florida	2,071,651	39.0	2,171,781	40.9	1,052,481	19.8	15,306	0.3	5,311,219	100,130	1.9		25
Georgia	1,008,966	43.5	995,252	42.9	309,657	13.3	7,250	0.3	2,321,125	13,714	0.6	13	
Hawaii	179,310	48.1	136,822	36.7	53,003	14.2	3,707	1.0	372,842	42,488	11.4	4	
Idaho	137,013	28.4	202,645	42.0	130,395	27.0	12,089	2.5	482,142	65,632	13.6		4
Illinois	2,453,350	48.6	1,734,096	34.3	840,515	16.6	22,196	0.4	5,050,157	719,254	14.2	22	
Indiana	848,420	36.8	989,375	42.9	455,934	19.8	12,142	0.5	2,305,871	140,955	6.1		12
Iowa	586,353	43.3	504,891	37.3	253,468	18.7	9,895	0.7	1,354,607	81,462	6.0	7	
Kansas	390,434	33.7	449,951	38.9	312,358	27.0	4,493	0.4	1,157,236	59,517	5.1		6
Kentucky	665,104	44.6	617,178	41.3	203,944	13.7	6,674	0.4	1,492,900	47,926	3.2	8	
Louisiana	815,971	45.6	733,386	41.0	211,478	11.8	29,182	1.6	1,790,017	82,585	4.6	9	
Maine	263,420	38.8	206,504	30.4	206,820	30.4	2,755	0.4	679,499	56,600	8.3	4	
Maryland	988,571	49.8	707,094	35.6	281,414	14.2	7,799	0.4	1,984,878	281,477	14.2	10	
Massachusetts	1,318,639	47.5	805,039	29.0	630,731	22.7	19,255	0.7	2,773,664	513,600	18.5	12	
Michigan	1,871,182	43.8	1,554,940	36.4	824,813	19.3	23,738	0.6	4,274,673	316,242	7.4	18	
Minnesota	1,020,997	43.5	747,841	31.9	562,506	24.0	16,603	0.7	2,347,947	273,156	11.6	10	
Mississippi	400,258	40.8	487,793	49.7	85,626	8.7	8,116	0.8	981,793	87,535	8.9		7
Missouri	1,053,873	44.1	811,159	33.9	518,741	21.7	7,792	0.3	2,391,565	242,714	10.2	11	
Montana	154,507	37.6	144,207	35.1	107,225	26.1	4,672	1.1	410,611	10,300	2.5	3	

(Table continues)

Table 3-2 (*Continued*)

| | Popular vote | | | | | | | | | Electoral vote | |
| | Clinton (Democrat) | | Bush (Republican) | | Perot (Independent) | | Other | | Total Vote | Plurality | | | |
State	Vote	%	Vote	%	Vote	%	Vote	%		Vote	%	D	R
Nebraska	216,864	29.4	343,678	46.6	174,104	23.6	2,900	0.4	737,546	126,814	17.2		5
Nevada	189,148	37.4	175,828	34.7	132,580	26.2	8,762	1.7	506,318	13,320	2.6	4	
New Hampshire	209,040	38.9	202,484	37.6	121,337	22.6	5,082	0.9	537,943	6,556	1.2	4	
New Jersey	1,436,206	43.0	1,356,865	40.6	521,829	15.6	28,694	0.9	3,343,594	79,341	2.4	15	
New Mexico	261,617	45.9	212,824	37.3	91,895	16.1	3,650	0.6	569,986	48,793	8.6	5	
New York	3,444,450	49.7	2,346,649	33.9	1,090,721	15.7	44,740	0.6	6,926,560	1,097,801	15.9	33	
North Carolina	1,114,042	42.7	1,134,661	43.4	357,864	13.7	5,283	0.2	2,611,850	20,619	0.8		14
North Dakota	99,168	32.2	136,244	44.2	71,084	23.1	1,637	0.5	308,133	37,076	12.0		3
Ohio	1,984,919	40.7	1,894,248	38.3	1,036,403	21.0	24,289	0.5	4,939,859	90,671	1.8	21	
Oklahoma	473,066	34.0	592,929	42.6	319,878	23.0	4,486	0.3	1,390,359	119,863	8.6		8
Oregon	621,314	42.5	475,757	32.5	354,091	24.2	11,481	0.8	1,462,643	145,557	10.0	7	
Pennsylvania	2,239,164	45.1	1,791,841	36.1	902,667	18.2	26,138	0.5	4,959,810	447,323	9.0	23	
Rhode Island	213,299	47.0	131,601	29.0	105,045	23.2	3,420	0.8	453,365	81,698	18.0	4	
South Carolina	479,514	39.9	577,507	48.0	138,872	11.5	6,634	0.6	1,202,527	97,993	8.2		8
South Dakota	124,888	37.1	136,718	40.7	73,295	21.8	1,353	0.4	336,254	11,830	3.5		3
Tennessee	933,521	47.1	841,300	42.4	199,968	10.1	7,849	0.4	1,982,638	92,221	4.7	11	
Texas	2,281,815	37.1	2,496,071	40.6	1,354,781	22.0	21,351	0.3	6,154,018	214,256	3.5		32
Utah	183,429	24.7	322,632	43.4	203,400	27.3	34,538	4.6	743,999	119,232	16.0		5
Vermont	133,592	46.1	88,122	30.4	65,991	22.8	1,996	0.7	289,701	45,470	15.7	3	
Virginia	1,038,650	40.6	1,150,517	45.0	348,639	13.6	20,859	0.8	2,558,665	111,867	4.4		13
Washington	993,037	43.4	731,234	32.0	541,780	23.7	22,179	1.0	2,288,230	261,803	11.4	11	
West Virginia	331,001	48.4	241,974	35.4	108,829	15.9	1,873	0.3	683,677	89,027	13.0	5	
Wisconsin	1,041,066	41.1	930,855	36.8	544,479	21.5	14,714	0.6	2,531,114	110,211	4.4	11	
Wyoming	68,160	34.0	79,347	39.6	51,263	25.6	1,847	0.9	200,617	11,187	5.6		3
Total	44,908,233	43.0	39,102,282	37.4	19,741,048	18.9	669,324	0.6	104,420,887	5,805,951	5.6	370	168

[a] "Plurality" indicates the vote margin between the leader and the second-place finisher.

Source: Congressional Quarterly Weekly Report (1993), 233.

Table 3-3 Democratic Presidential Primary Returns, 1992

State (date)	Turnout	Brown	Clinton	Harkin	Kerrey	Tsongas	Others	Uncommitted
New Hampshire (2/18)	167,819	8.1%	24.7%	10.2%	11.1%	33.2%	12.7%	—
South Dakota (2/25)	59,503	3.9	19.1	25.2	40.2	9.6	2.0	—
Colorado (3/3)	239,643	28.8	26.9	2.4	12.3	25.6	1.6	2.2%
Georgia (3/3)	454,631	8.1	57.2	2.1	4.8	24.0	—	3.8
Maryland (3/3)	567,224	8.2	33.5	5.8	4.8	40.6	0.8	6.4
South Carolina (3/7)	116,414	6.0	62.9	6.6	0.5	18.3	2.6	3.1
Florida (3/10)	1,123,857	12.4	50.8	1.2	1.1	34.5	—	—
Louisiana (3/10)	384,417	6.6	69.5	1.0	0.8	11.1	11.0	—
Massachusetts (3/10)	794,093	14.6	10.9	0.5	0.7	66.3	5.5	1.5
Mississippi (3/10)	191,357	9.6	73.1	1.3	0.9	8.1	0.8	6.2
Oklahoma (3/10)	416,129	16.7	70.5	3.4	3.2	—	11.9	1.4
Rhode Island (3/10)	50,709	18.8	21.2	0.6	0.9	52.9	4.1	3.9
Tennessee (3/10)	318,482	8.0	67.3	0.7	0.5	19.4	0.1	—
Texas (3/10)	1,482,975	8.0	65.6	1.3	1.4	19.2	4.5	4.5
Illinois (3/17)	1,504,130	14.6	51.6	2.0	0.7	25.8	0.7	4.8
Michigan (3/17)	585,972	25.8	50.7	1.1	0.5	16.6	0.5	3.1
Connecticut (3/24)	173,119	37.2	35.6	1.1	0.7	19.5	2.7	3.1
Puerto Rico (4/5)	63,398	1.6	95.6	0.0	1.3	0.1	1.0	0.3
Kansas (4/7)	160,251	13.0	51.3	0.6	1.4	15.2	4.7	13.8
Minnesota (4/7)	104,170	30.6	31.1	2.0	0.6	21.3	8.8	5.6
New York (4/7)	1,007,726	26.2	40.9	1.1	1.1	28.6	2.0	—
Wisconsin (4/7)	772,596	34.5	37.2	0.7	0.4	21.8	3.4	2.0
Pennsylvania (4/28)	1,265,495	25.7	56.5	1.7	1.6	12.8	1.7	—
District of Columbia (5/5)	61,904	7.2	73.8	—	—	10.4	—	8.5
Indiana (5/5)	476,850	21.5	63.3	—	3.0	12.2	—	—
North Carolina (5/5)	691,875	10.4	64.1	0.9	0.9	8.3	—	15.4

(Table continues)

Table 3-3 (Continued)

State (date)	Turnout	Brown	Clinton	Harkin	Kerrey	Tsongas	Others	Uncommitted
Nebraska (5/12)	150,587	21.0%	45.5%	2.8%	—	7.1%	7.1%	16.4%
West Virginia (5/12)	306,866	11.9	74.2	0.9	1.0%	6.9	5.0	—
Oregon (5/19)	347,968	31.4	45.3	—	—	10.5	12.7	—
Washington (5/19)	147,981	23.1	42.0	1.3	1.0	12.8	19.8	—
Arkansas (5/26)	502,617	11.0	68.0	—	—	—	2.9	18.0
Idaho (5/26)	55,124	16.7	49.0	—	—	—	5.2	29.1
Kentucky (5/26)	369,438	8.3	56.0	1.9	0.9	4.9	—	28.0
Alabama (6/2)	450,899	6.8	68.2	—	—	—	—	20.2
California (6/2)	2,752,029	40.2	47.5	—	1.2	7.4	4.8	—
Montana (6/2)	116,899	18.5	46.9	—	—	10.8	3.8	23.9
New Jersey (6/2)	399,913	19.5	59.2	—	—	11.1	2.9	7.3
New Mexico (6/2)	180,770	16.9	52.8	1.9	—	6.3	2.8	19.4
Ohio (6/2)	1,032,851	19.0	61.2	2.4	2.2	10.6	4.6	—
North Dakota (6/9)	31,562	—	12.6	—	—	—	87.4	—
Total	20,179,973	19.9	51.9	1.4	1.6	18.1	3.3	3.9

Note: "—" indicates that the candidate or the uncommitted line was not listed on the ballot. Clinton's vote in North Dakota came on write-in votes. Perot write-in votes totaled 2.1 percent in Minnesota, 19.1 percent in Washington, and 28.4 percent in North Dakota. Kerrey withdrew from the race on March 5; Harkin on March 9; Tsongas on March 19. Five states have both caucus and primary results (see also Table 3-5, this volume). In Minnesota, Washington, Idaho, and North Dakota, primaries were nonbinding ("beauty contests") and delegates were selected through caucuses; Texas selected delegates through caucuses, but those delegates were bound to reflect voter preferences as revealed in the primary vote.

Source: Congressional Quarterly, *Guide to the 1992 Democratic National Convention* (Washington, D.C.: Congressional Quarterly, 1992), 69, 71.

Table 3-4 Republican Presidential Primary Returns, 1992

State (date)	Turnout	Buchanan	Bush	Duke	Others	Uncommitted
New Hampshire (2/18)	174,165	37.4%	53.0%	—	9.7%	—
South Dakota (2/25)	44,671	—	69.3	—	—	30.7%
Colorado (3/3)	195,690	30.0	67.5	—	2.5	—
Georgia (3/3)	453,987	35.7	64.3	—	—	—
Maryland (3/3)	240,021	29.9	70.1	—	—	—
South Carolina (3/7)	148,840	25.7	66.9	7.1%	0.3	—
Florida (3/10)	893,463	31.9	68.1	—	—	—
Louisiana (3/10)	135,109	27.0	62.0	8.8	2.1	—
Massachusetts (3/10)	269,701	27.7	65.6	2.1	0.9	3.8
Mississippi (3/10)	154,708	16.7	72.3	10.6	0.4	—
Oklahoma (3/10)	217,721	26.6	69.6	2.6	1.2	—
Rhode Island (3/10)	15,636	31.8	63.0	2.1	0.3	2.8
Tennessee (3/10)	245,653	22.2	72.5	3.1	—	2.0
Texas (3/10)	797,146	23.9	69.8	2.5	0.3	3.5
Illinois (3/17)	831,140	22.5	76.4	—	1.2	—
Michigan (3/17)	449,133	25.0	67.2	2.4	0.1	5.3
Connecticut (3/24)	99,473	21.9	66.7	2.3	—	9.1
Puerto Rico (4/5)	262,426	0.4	99.2	0.3	0.1	—
Kansas (4/7)	213,196	14.8	62.0	1.8	4.8	16.6
Minnesota (4/7)	132,756	24.2	63.9	—	8.8	3.1
Wisconsin (4/7)	482,248	16.3	75.6	2.7	3.7	1.8
Pennsylvania (4/28)	1,008,777	23.2	76.8	—	—	—
District of Columbia (5/5)	5,235	18.5	81.5	—	—	—
Indiana (5/5)	467,615	19.9	80.1	—	—	—
North Carolina (5/5)	283,571	19.5	70.7	—	—	9.8
Nebraska (5/12)	192,098	13.5	81.4	1.5	3.7	—

(Table continues)

Table 3-4 (Continued)

State (date)	Turnout	Buchanan	Bush	Duke	Others	Uncommitted
West Virginia (5/12)	124,157	14.6%	80.5%	—	4.9%	—
Oregon (5/19)	304,159	19.0	67.1	2.2%	11.8	—
Washington (5/19)	129,655	10.2	67.0	1.2	21.6	—
Arkansas (5/26)	54,876	11.9	83.1	—	—	5.0%
Idaho (5/26)	115,502	13.1	63.5	—	—	23.4
Kentucky (5/26)	101,119	—	74.5	—	—	25.5
Alabama (6/2)	165,121	7.6	74.3	—	—	18.1
California (6/2)	2,156,464	26.4	73.6	—	—	—
Montana (6/2)	90,975	11.8	71.6	—	—	16.6
New Jersey (6/2)	310,270	15.0	77.5	—	7.5	—
New Mexico (6/2)	86,967	9.1	63.8	—	—	27.1
Ohio (6/2)	924,572	16.8	83.2	—	—	27.1
North Dakota (6/9)	47,808	—	83.4	—	16.6	—
Total	13,025,824	22.4	73.0	0.9	1.5	2.2

Note: "—" indicates that the candidate or the uncommitted line was not listed on the ballot. Results are based on official returns except for Ohio, where results are nearly complete but unofficial. Duke withdrew from the race April 22. Write-in votes for Ross Perot totaled 2.7 percent of the Republican primary vote in Minnesota, 19.6 percent in Washington, 7.5 percent in New Jersey, and 8.1 percent in North Dakota.

Source: Congressional Quarterly, *Guide to the 1992 Republican National Convention* (Washington, D.C.: Congressional Quarterly, 1992), 63.

Table 3-5 Democratic Presidential Caucus Results, 1992

State (date)	Turnout	Brown	Clinton	Harkin	Kerrey	Tsongas	Others	Uncommitted
Iowa (2/10)	30,000	1.6%	2.8%	76.4%	2.5%	4.1%	0.6%	12.0%
Maine (2/23)	13,500	30.3	14.8	5.2	3.0	29.0	1.7	16.1
Idaho (3/3)	3,090	4.5	11.4	29.7	8.0	28.4	0.8	17.2
Minnesota (3/3)	50,000-60,000	8.2	10.3	26.7	7.6	19.2	3.9	24.3
Utah (3/3)	31,638	28.4	18.3	4.0	10.9	33.4	2.7	2.3
Washington (3/3)	60,000	18.6	12.6	8.2	3.4	32.3	1.5	23.2
American Samoa (3/3)	—	—	4.3	—	8.7	—	—	87.0
North Dakota (3/5-19)	5,000	7.5	46.0	6.8	1.2	10.3	2.4	25.9
Arizona (3/7)	36,326	27.5	29.2	7.6	—	34.4	—	1.3
Wyoming (3/7)	1,500	23.0	28.5	14.2	—	11.7	0.4	22.3
Democrats Abroad (3/7-9)	4,000	12.2	26.6	6.9	—	36.8	17.5	—
Nevada (3/8)	6,000-7,000	34.4	26.6	—	—	19.6	—	19.4
Delaware (3/10)	2,500	19.5	20.8	—	—	30.2	—	29.6
Hawaii (3/10)	3,014	13.6	51.5	12.7	0.4	14.3	—	7.5
Missouri (3/10)	20,000-25,000	5.7	45.1	—	—	10.2	—	39.0
Texas (3/10)	—	—	—	—	—	—	—	—
Virgin Islands (3/28)	343	4.1	39.7	—	—	—	—	56.3
Vermont (3/31)	6,000	46.7	16.8	—	—	9.3	2.2	25.0
Alaska (4/2)	1,100	33.1	30.9	—	—	1.3	—	34.7
Virginia (4/11,13)	—	11.6	52.1	—	—	—	—	36.3
Guam (5/3)	1,000	20.0	49.0	—	—	—	—	31.0

Note: "—" indicates not available: the candidate was not listed on the caucus ballot or his votes were not tabulated separately (except for Texas where no results were available). Caucus results were mostly compiled by the state parties and reflect either the share won of delegates to the next stage of the caucus process or a tally of the presidential preferences of caucus participants. Most turnout figures are estimates. Kerry withdrew from the race March 5. Harkin withdrew from the race March 9. Tsongas suspended his campaign March 19.

Source: Congressional Quarterly, *Guide to the 1992 Democratic National Convention* (Washington, D.C.: Congressional Quarterly, 1992), 70.

Figure 3-3 Democratic and Republican Presidential Nominations, Campaign Lengths, 1968-1992

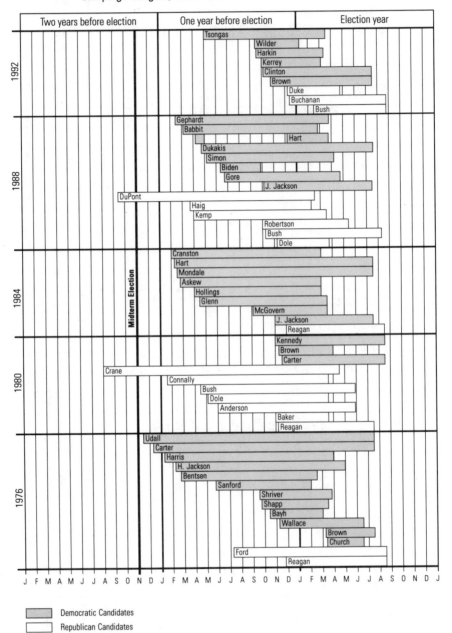

Democratic Candidates

Republican Candidates

Figure 3-3   *(Continued)*

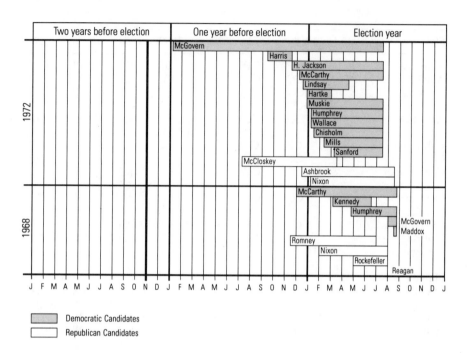

Democratic Candidates
Republican Candidates

Note: Beginning of campaigns is determined by date of the formal announcement.

Sources: 1968-1984: Congressional Quarterly, *Elections '80* (Washington, D.C.: Congressional Quarterly, 1980), and Congressional Quarterly, *Congressional Quarterly's Guide to U.S. Elections,* 2d ed. (Washington, D.C.: Congressional Quarterly, 1985), 387; 1988 and 1992: *Congressional Quarterly Weekly Report* (1987), 2732, (1988), 1894, 1896, 1899, (1991), 3735, (1992), 66, 361, 556, 633, 1086.

Table 3-6 State Methods for Choosing National Convention Delegates, 1968-1992

State	1968	1972	1976	1980	1984	1988	1992
Alabama	DP	DP	OP	OP	CPI	CPI	CPI
Alaska	CC	CC	CC	CC	CC	CC	CC
Arizona	(D)CO (R)CC	CC	CC	CC	CC	CC	CC
Arkansas	CO	CC	OP	(D)OP (R)CC	CC	OP	OP
California	CP	CP	CP	CP	CP	CP	CP
Colorado	CC	CC	CC	CC	CC	CC	OP
Connecticut	CC	CC	CC	CP	(D)CP (R)CC	CP	CP
Delaware	CC	CC	CC	CC	CC	CC	CC
District of Columbia	CP	CP	CP	CP	CP	CP	CP
Florida	CP	CP	CP	CP	CP	CP	CP
Georgia	(D)CO (R)CC	CC	OP	OP	CPI	CPI	CPI
Hawaii	CC	CC	CC	CC	CC	CC	CC
Idaho	CC	CC	OP	(D)CC (R)OP	(D)CPI	(D)X (R)OP	(D)X (R)OP
Illinois	DP,CC	CP	OP	OP	DP	DP	DP
Indiana	OP	OP	OP	OP	CPI	CPI	CPI
Iowa	CC	CC	CC	CC	CC	CC	CC
Kansas	CC	CC	CC	CPI	CC	CC	OP
Kentucky	C	CC	CP	CP	CC	CP	CP
Louisiana	CO	CC	CC	CP	CP	CP	CP
Maine	CC	CC	CC	CC	CC	CC	CC
Maryland	(D)CO (R)CC	CP	CP	CP	DP	CP	CP
Massachusetts	CPI	CPI	CPI	CPI	CPI	CPI	CPI
Michigan	CC	OP	OP	(D)CC (R)OP	CC	(D)CC (R)X	CP
Minnesota	CC	CC	CC	CC	CC	CC	CC
Mississippi	CC	CC	CC	(D)CC (R)DP	CC	CPI	CPI
Missouri	(D)CC,CO (R)CC	CC	CC	CC	CC	CPI	CC
Montana	CC	CC	OP	OP	DP	(D)CPI (R)X	(D)OP (R)X
Nebraska	OP	OP	OP	OP	CP	CP	CP
Nevada	CC	CC	CP	CP	CC	CC	CC
New Hampshire	CPI	CPI	CPI	CPI	CPI	CPI	CPI
New Jersey	CPI	CPI	CPI	CPI	DP	DP	DP
New Mexico	CC	CP	CC	CP (R)CP	CP	CP	CP
New York	DP,CO	DP,CO	DP	(D)CP	DP	CP	CP
North Carolina	CC	CP	CP	CP	CP	CP	CP
North Dakota	CC	CC	CC	CC	DP	(D)X (R)OP	(D)X (R)OP

Table 3-6   (*Continued*)

State	1968	1972	1976	1980	1984	1988	1992
Ohio	OP	OP	OP	OP	CPI	CPI	CPI
Oklahoma	CC	CC	CC	CC	CC	CP	CP
Oregon	CP	CP	CP	CP	CP	CP	CP
Pennsylvania	CP,CO	CP	CP	CP	DP	DP	DP
Rhode Island	(D)CO (R)CC	CPI	CPI	CPI	CPI	CPI	CPI
South Carolina	CC	CC	CC (R)OP	(D)CC	CC (R)OP	(D)CC (R)CC	(D)OP
South Dakota	CP	CP	CP	CP	CP	CP	CP
Tennessee	CC	OP	OP	OP	CPI	CPI	CPI
Texas	CC	CC	OP	CP	(D)CC (R)OP	CPI	CPI
Utah	CC	CC	CC	CC	CC	CC	CC
Vermont	CC	CC	X	X	X	X	X
Virginia	CC	CC	CC	CC	CC	(D)CPI (R)X	CC
Washington	(D)CC,CO (R)CC	CC CP	CC CP	CC CP	CC	CC	CP
West Virginia	CP	CP	CP	CP	CP	CP	(D)CP (R)CPI
Wisconsin	OP	OP	OP	OP	(D)X (R)OP	(D)CPI (R)OP	(D)CPI (R)OP
Wyoming	CC	CC	CC	CC	CC	CC	CC
(Puerto Rico)	(D)C	CC	CC	OP	(D)CPI (R)CC	CPI	CPI

Notes: "CC" indicates delegates chosen by state and local caucuses and conventions; "CO" indicates delegates chosen by state party committee; "CP" indicates delegates chosen or bound by presidential preference primaries open only to voters preregistered as members of the particular parties; "CPI" indicates delegates chosen or bound by presidential preference primaries open only to voters preregistered or considered as members of the particular parties or as independents; "(D)" indicates Democrats; "DP" indicates delegates chosen directly by voters in primaries—no binding presidential preference poll; "OP" indicates delegates chosen or bound by presidential preference primaries open to all registered voters without regard to party preregistration; "(R)" indicates epublicans; "X" indicates having nonbinding presidential preference primaries, but delegates are chosen by party caucuses and conventions.

Sources: 1968-1984: Austin Ranney, ed., *The American Elections of 1984* (Durham, N.C.: Duke University Press, 1985), 330-332 (copyright © American Enterprise Institute for Public Policy Research, reprinted by permission); 1988: derived by the editors from Kevin Coleman, "A Summary of National and State Party Rules and State Laws Concerning the Election of Delegates to the 1988 Democratic and Republican National Conventions" (Washington, D.C.: Congressional Research Service, 1988), Report no. 88-102 GOV; 1992: derived by the editors from *The First Hurrah: A 1992 Guide to the Nomination of the President* (Washington, D.C.: Congressional Quarterly, 1991); *Congressional Quarterly Weekly Report* (1991), 3478; and Thomas M. Durbin and L. Paige Whitaker, *Nomination and Election of the President and Vice President of the United States, 1992: Including the Manner of Selecting Delegates to National Party Conventions* (Washington, D.C.: U.S. Government Printing Office, 1992).

Table 3-7 Vote in Democratic Presidential Primaries, by Groups, 1984-1992 (percent)

Group	1984				1988				1992			
	Percentage of primary voters	Mondale	Hart	Jackson	Percentage of primary voters	Dukakis	Jackson	Others	Percentage of primary voters	Clinton	Brown	Tsongas
Sex												
Men	46	38	36	17	47	41	29	30	47	50	21	20
Women	54	39	35	20	53	43	30	26	53	51	20	21
Race/ethnicity												
White	78	42	43	5	75	54	12	35	80	47	23	25
Black	18	19	3	77	21	4	92	4	14	70	15	8
Hispanic	—	—	—	—	3	48	30	20	4	51	30	15
Age												
Under 30	17	26	39	26	14	35	38	27	12	47	24	19
30-44	30	30	38	23	31	37	36	26	33	45	26	22
45-59	24	41	34	18	25	42	30	28	25	51	19	20
60 and older	28	52	31	10	30	53	19	29	30	59	15	18
Religion												
Catholic	—	—	—	—	30	60	18	22	50	55	14	21
White Protestant	—	—	—	—	36	43	10	47	30	44	24	24
Jewish	—	—	—	—	7	75	8	17	6	75	15	33
Party												
Democrat	74	42	33	20	72	43	33	24	67	57	19	17
Independent	20	28	44	16	20	44	20	34	29	36	25	27

Ideology												
Liberal	27	34	36	25	27	41	41	19	35	47	26	20
Moderate	47	41	37	15	47	47	25	28	45	54	18	19
Conservative	21	37	34	16	22	38	23	38	20	48	17	23
Union household	33	45	31	19	—	—	—	—	—	—	—	—
Total	100	38	36	19	100	43	29	28	100	50	21	20

Note: "—" indicates not available. Entries are derived from exit poll data in twenty-four contested delegate selection primaries in 1984, thirty-three in 1988, and twenty-nine in 1992. No exit poll in Louisiana in 1984 or in Montana, Oregon, or Washington, D.C., in 1988.

Sources: Adam Clymer, "The 1984 National Primary," *Public Opinion* (August/September 1984): 52–53 (reprinted with permission of the American Enterprise Institute for Public Policy Research); *New York Times*, June 13, 1988, B7, July 12, 1992, section 1, 18 (copyright © 1988, 1992 by the New York Times Company, reprinted by permission).

Table 3-8 Convention Votes Presidential Candidates Received from Caucus State Delegates and Primary State Delegates, 1964-1992

Year/candidate	Caucus states	Primary states	Number of convention votes	Percentage of convention
1964 Republican convention				
Goldwater	74.5%	60.5%	883	67.5
Scranton	10.7	22.1	214	16.4
Rockefeller	0.6	16.8	114	8.7
Others	14.2	0.6	97	7.4
Total	N=655	N=653	1,308	100.0
1968 Democratic convention				
Humphrey	80.2	53.4	1,760.25	67.1
McCarthy	12.1	34.4	601	22.9
McGovern	3.8	7.5	146.5	5.6
Others	4.0	4.7	114.25	4.4
Total	N=1,346	N=1,276	2,622	100.0
1968 Republican convention				
Nixon	59.6	43.2	692	51.9
Rockefeller	14.4	27.9	277	20.8
Reagan	11.2	16.4	182	13.7
Others	14.7	12.4	182	13.7
Total	N=706	N=627	1,333	100.0
1972 Democratic convention				
McGovern	41.0	64.9	1,715.4	56.9
Jackson	30.0	11.5	534	17.7
Wallace	7.3	15.5	385.7	12.8
Others	21.7	8.1	380.9	12.6
Total	N=1,009	N=2,007	3,016	100.0
1976 Republican convention				
Ford	44.9	55.9	1,187	52.5
Reagan	55.1	43.9	1,070	47.4
Others	0.0	0.1	2	0.1
Total	N=693	N=1,566	2,259	100.0
1980 Democratic convention				
Carter	71.0	60.8	2,123	63.7
Kennedy	24.3	38.6	1,150.5	34.5
Others	4.7	0.5	57.5	1.7
Total	N=953	N=2,378	3,331	100.0

Table 3-8 *(Continued)*

Year/candidate	Caucus states	Primary states	Number of convention votes	Percentage of convention
1984 Democratic convention				
Mondale	56.3%	55.6%	2,191	55.9
Hart	29.6	31.2	1,200.5	30.6
Jackson	11.9	11.9	465.5	11.9
Others	2.3	1.3	66	1.7
Total	N=1,460	N=2,463	3,923	100.0
1988 Democratic convention				
Dukakis	62.6	71.5	2,876.25	69.9
Jackson	36.2	28.1	1,218.50	29.6
Others	1.2	0.4	23	0.6
Total	N=766.75	N=3,351.00	4,117.75	100.0
1992 Democratic convention				
Brown	10.9	14.2	596	13.9
Clinton	84.4	77.8	3,372	78.6
Tsongas	3.7	5.5	209	4.9
Others	1.0	2.5	111	2.6
Total	N=514	N=3,774	4,288	100.0

Note: Shown are major presidential candidates with substantial opposition. The table is based on first-ballot votes before switches. For 1984-1992, votes of Democratic superdelegates not chosen through caucuses or primaries are counted as if they were chosen by the delegate selection method in their state. States holding both primaries and caucuses are counted among primary states in these calculations. ("States" include all jurisdictions having delegates.)

Sources: 1964-1980: Congressional Quarterly, *Elections '84* (Washington, D.C.: Congressional Quarterly, 1984), 50; 1984: compiled by the editors from Congressional Quarterly, *Congressional Quarterly Almanac, 1984* (Washington, D.C.: Congressional Quarterly, 1985), B68; 1988: *Congressional Quarterly Weekly Report* (1988), 2033, 1872-1892, 1894-1895, (1992), 2220.

Table 3-9   Election Year Presidential Preferences, 1948-1992 (percent)

Year/candidate	First poll of year	First poll after conventions	Early October	Final survey	Election results
1948					
Truman (D)[a]	46 (+5)	37	40	45	50 (+5)
Dewey (R)	41	48 (+11)	46 (+6)	50 (+5)	45
1952					
Eisenhower (R)	59 (+28)	50 (+7)	53 (+12)	51 (+2)	55 (+11)
Stevenson (D)	31	43	41	49	44
1956					
Eisenhower (R)[a]	61 (+26)	52 (+11)	51 (+10)	60 (+19)	57 (+15)
Stevenson (D)	35	41	41	41	42
1960					
Kennedy (D)	43	44	49 (+3)	51 (+2)	50 (+0.2)
Nixon (R)	48 (+5)	50 (+6)	46	49	50
1964					
Johnson (D)[a]	75 (+57)	65 (+36)	64 (+35)	64 (+28)	61 (+23)
Goldwater (R)	18	29	29	36	38
1968					
Nixon (R)	43 (+9)	43 (+12)	43 (+12)	43 (+1)	43 (+0.7)
Humphrey (D)	34	31	31	42	43
Wallace (AIP)[b]	9	19	20	15	14
1972					
Nixon (R)[a]	53 (+19)	64 (+34)	60 (+26)	62 (+24)	61 (+23)
McGovern (D)	34	30	34	38	38
1976					
Carter (D)	47 (+5)	51 (+15)	47 (+2)	48	50 (+2)
Ford (R)[a]	42	36	45	49 (+1)	48
1980					
Reagan (R)	33	38	40	47 (+3)	51 (+10)
Carter (D)[a]	62 (+29)	39 (+1)	44 (+4)	44	41
Anderson (I)		13	9	8	7
1984					
Reagan (R)[a]	48 (+1)	55 (+15)	56 (+17)	59 (+18)	59 (+18)
Mondale (D)	47	40	39	41	41
1988					
Bush (R)	52 (+12)	48 (+4)	49 (+6)	53 (+11)	54 (+8)
Dukakis (D)	40	44	43	42	46
1992					
Bush (R)[a]	53 (+15)	42	35	37	37
Clinton (D)	38	52 (+10)	52 (+17)	49 (+12)	43 (+6)
Perot	—	—	7	14	19

Note: "—" indicates not included in survey question.

[a] Incumbent.
[b] American Independent Party.

Sources: Congressional Quarterly Weekly Report (1984), 2648, (1988), 3245; 1984 final survey: *The Gallup Report*, November 1984, 31; 1988-1992: The Gallup Poll, various press releases.

Table 3-10 Presidential Vote in General Elections, by Groups, Gallup Poll, 1952-1992 (percent)

	1952		1956		1960		1964		1968			1972		1976			1980			1984		1988		1992		
	D	R	D	R	D	R	D	R	D	R	Iᵃ	D	R	D	R	Iᵃ	D	R	Iᵃ	D	R	D	R	D	R	Iᵃ
Sex																										
Male	47	53	45	55	52	48	60	40	41	43	16	37	63	53	45	1	38	53	7	36	64	44	56	41	37	22
Female	42	58	39	61	49	51	62	38	45	43	12	38	62	48	51	-	44	49	6	45	55	48	52	46	38	16
Race/ethnicity																										
White	43	57	41	59	49	51	59	41	38	47	15	32	68	46	52	1	36	56	7	34	66	41	59	39	41	20
Nonwhite	79	21	61	39	68	32	94	6	85	12	3	87	13	85	15	-	86	10	2	87	13	82	18	77	11	12
Education																										
Grade school	52	48	50	50	55	45	66	34	52	33	15	49	51	58	41	1	54	42	3	51	49	55	45	56	28	16
High school	45	55	42	58	52	48	62	38	42	43	15	34	66	54	46	-	43	51	5	43	57	46	54	40	38	22
College	34	66	31	69	39	61	52	48	37	54	9	37	63	42	55	2	35	53	10	39	61	42	58	43	40	17
Employment																										
Manual	55	45	50	50	60	40	71	29	50	35	15	43	57	58	41	1	48	48	5	46	54	—	—	—	—	—
White collar	40	60	37	63	48	52	57	43	41	47	12	36	64	50	48	2	40	51	9	47	53	—	—	—	—	—
Professional and business	36	64	32	68	42	58	54	46	34	56	10	31	69	42	56	1	33	55	10	34	66	—	—	—	—	—
Age																										
Under 30	51	49	43	57	54	45	64	36	47	38	15	48	52	53	45	1	47	41	11	40	60	37	63	40	37	23
30-49	47	53	45	55	54	46	63	37	44	41	15	33	67	48	49	2	38	52	8	40	60	45	55	42	37	21
50 and older	39	61	39	61	46	54	59	41	41	47	12	36	64	52	48	-	41	54	4	41	59	49	51	46	39	15

(Table continues)

Table 3-10 (Continued)

	1952		1956		1960		1964		1968			1972		1976			1980			1984		1988		1992		
	D	R	D	R	D	R	D	R	D	R	I[a]	D	R	D	R	I[a]	D	R	I[a]	D	R	D	R	D	R	I[a]
Religion																										
Protestant	37	63	37	63	38	62	55	45	35	49	16	30	70	46	53	-	39	54	6	39	61	42	58	41	41	18
Catholic	56	44	51	49	78	22	76	24	59	33	8	48	52	57	41	1	46	47	6	39	61	51	49	47	35	18
Political affiliation																										
Democrat	77	23	85	15	84	16	87	13	74	12	14	67	33	82	18	-	69	26	4	79	21	85	15	82	8	10
Independent	35	65	30	70	43	57	56	44	31	44	25	31	69	38	57	4	29	55	14	33	67	43	57	39	30	31
Republican	8	92	4	96	5	95	20	80	9	86	5	5	95	9	91	-	8	86	5	4	96	7	93	7	77	16
Region[b]																										
East	45	55	40	60	53	47	68	32	50	43	7	42	58	51	47	1	43	47	9	46	54	51	49	47	35	18
Midwest	42	58	41	59	48	52	61	39	44	47	9	40	60	48	50	1	41	51	7	42	58	47	53	44	34	22
South	51	49	49	51	51	49	52	48	31	36	33	29	71	54	45	-	44	52	3	37	63	40	60	38	45	17
West	42	58	43	57	49	51	60	40	44	49	7	41	59	46	51	1	35	54	9	40	60	46	54	45	35	20
Union family	61	39	57	43	65	35	73	27	56	29	15	46	54	63	36	1	50	43	5	52	48	63	37	—	—	—
Total	45	55	42	58	50	50	61	39	43	43	14	38	62	50	48	1	41	51	7	41	59	46	54	43	38	19

Note: "D" indicates Democrat; "R" indicates Republican; "I" indicates less than 0.5 percent; "—" indicates not available.

[a] "I" indicates the vote for George Wallace in 1968, for Eugene McCarthy in 1976, for John Anderson in 1980, and for Ross Perot in 1992. Table does not include votes for minor-party candidates other than those shown for 1968, 1976, 1980, and 1992.
[b] For composition of regions, see Appendix Table A-2.

Sources: 1952–1988: *The Gallup Report,* November 1988, 6-7; 1992: unpublished data from the Gallup Poll.

Table 3-11 Presidential Vote in General Elections, by Groups, Network Exit Polls, 1976-1992 (percent)

	1976		1980				1984			1988			1992			
Group	D	R	D	R	I	Percentage of voters	D	R	Percentage of voters	D	R	Percentage of voters	D	R	I	Percentage of voters
Sex																
Men	50	48	36	55	7	51	37	62	47	41	54	48	41	38	21	46
Women	50	48	45	47	7	49	44	56	53	49	50	52	46	37	17	54
Race/ethnicity																
White	47	52	36	55	7	88	35	64	86	40	59	85	39	41	20	87
Black	83	16	85	11	3	10	89	9	10	86	12	10	82	11	7	8
Hispanic	76	24	56	35	8	2	61	37	3	69	30	3	62	25	14	3
Age																
Under 30	51	47	44	43	11	23	40	59	24	47	52	20	44	34	22	22
30-44	49	49	36	54	8	31	42	57	34	45	54	35	42	38	20	38
45-59	47	52	39	55	5	23	39	59	23	42	57	22	41	40	19	24
60 and older	47	52	41	54	4	18	39	60	19	49	50	22	50	38	12	16
Education																
Not high school graduate	—	—	51	46	2	—	50	49	8	56	43	8	55	28	17	6
High school graduate	—	—	43	51	4	—	39	60	30	49	50	27	43	36	20	25
College incomplete	—	—	35	55	8	28	37	61	30	42	57	30	42	37	21	29
College graduate	—	—	35	52	11	27	41	58	29	43	56	35	40	41	19	40
Religion																
White Protestant	41	58	31	63	6	46	27	72	51	33	66	48	33	46	21	49
Catholic	54	44	42	49	7	25	45	54	26	47	52	28	44	36	20	27
Jewish	64	34	45	39	15	5	67	31	3	64	35	4	78	12	10	4
White fundamentalist	—	—	33	63	3	17	22	78	15	18	81	9	23	61	15	17
Region																
East	51	47	42	47	9	32	47	52	24	49	50	25	47	35	18	24
Midwest	48	50	40	51	7	20	40	58	28	47	52	28	42	37	21	27
South	54	45	44	52	3	27	36	64	29	41	58	28	42	43	16	30
West	48	51	34	53	10	11	38	61	18	46	52	19	44	34	22	20

(Table continues)

Table 3-11 (*Continued*)

Group	1976		1980				1984			1988			1992			
	D	R	D	R	I	Percentage of voters	D	R	Percentage of voters	D	R	Percentage of voters	D	R	I	Percentage of voters
Union household	59	39	48	43	6	26	53	46	26	57	42	25	55	24	21	19
Income																
Under $12,500	58	40	51	42	6	13	54	45	15	62	37	12	59	23	18	14
$12,500-24,999	55	43	46	44	7	14	42	57	27	50	49	20	45	35	20	24
$25,000-34,999	48	50	39	52	7	30	40	59	21	44	56	20	41	38	21	30
$35,000-49,999	36	63	32	59	8	24	33	66	18	42	56	20	40	42	18	20
$50,000 and over	—	—	26	63	9	—	30	69	13	37	62	24	36	48	16	13
Party																
Republican	9	90	8	86	4	28	6	93	35	8	91	35	10	73	17	35
Independent	43	54	30	55	12	23	35	63	26	43	55	26	38	32	30	27
Democrat	77	22	67	26	6	43	75	24	38	82	17	37	77	10	13	38
Ideology																
Liberal	71	28	60	25	11	17	70	28	17	81	18	18	68	14	18	21
Moderate	51	48	42	48	8	46	47	53	44	50	49	45	48	31	21	49
Conservative	29	70	23	72	4	28	17	82	35	19	80	33	18	65	17	29
1984 vote																
Reagan voter	—	—	9	75	2	—	0	100	56	19	80	56	—	—	—	—
Democrat for Reagan	—	—	23	57	2	—	0	100	9	51	48	9	—	—	—	—
Mondale voter	—	—	63	14	8	—	100	0	28	92	7	28	—	—	—	—
Total	50	48	41	51	7	100	40	59	100	45	53	100	43	38	19	100

Note: "—" indicates not available. Income categories in 1976 were: less than $8,000; $8,000-11,999; $12,000-19,999; and $20,000 and over; in 1980: less than $10,000; $10,000-14,999; $15,000-24,999; $25,000-49,999; and $50,000 and over; in 1992: under $15,000; $15,000-29,999; $30,000-49,999; $50,000-74,999; $75,000 and over. The number of respondents in 1976 was 15,300; in 1980, 15,201; in 1984, 9,174; in 1988, 11,645; and in 1992, 15,490.

Sources: New York Times, November 8, 1984, A19; November 10, 1988, B6; November 5, 1992, B9 (copyright © 1984, 1988, and 1992 by the New York Times Company, reprinted by permission); 1992 data collected by Voter Research and Surveys.

Table 3-12 Congressional Vote in General Elections, by Groups, 1980-1994 (percent)

Group	1980 D	1980 R	1982 D	1982 R	1984 D	1984 R	1986 D	1986 R	1988 D	1988 R	1990 D	1990 R	1992 D	1992 R	1994 D	1994 R
Gender																
Men	49	51	55	45	48	52	51	49	52	48	51	49	52	48	45	55
Women	55	45	58	42	54	46	54	46	57	43	54	46	55	45	53	47
Race/ethnicity																
Whites	48	52	54	46	46	54	49	51	50	50	50	50	50	50	44	56
Blacks	87	13	89	11	92	8	86	14	85	15	79	21	89	11	89	11
Hispanics	72	28	75	25	69	31	75	25	76	24	72	28	72	28	61	39
Age																
Under 30	55	45	59	41	51	49	51	49	54	46	52	48	55	45	50	50
30-44	49	51	54	46	54	46	52	48	54	46	53	47	53	47	48	52
45-59	53	47	56	44	50	50	54	46	54	46	51	49	52	48	49	51
60 and over	51	49	58	42	48	52	52	48	55	45	53	47	56	44	52	48
Education																
Not a high school graduate	60	40	—	—	60	40	57	43	63	37	60	40	67	33	61	39
High school graduate	55	45	—	—	51	49	55	45	57	43	56	44	58	42	53	47
Some college	47	53	—	—	49	51	50	50	53	47	52	48	53	47	47	53
College graduate or more	48	52	—	—	50	50	51	49	50	50	51	49	50	50	47	53
Region																
East	52	48	65	35	54	46	52	48	54	46	54	46	55	45	54	46
Midwest	50	50	49	51	50	50	53	47	55	45	49	51	52	48	45	55
South	54	46	59	41	52	48	56	44	54	46	54	46	53	47	46	54
West	49	51	53	47	48	52	51	49	53	47	54	46	56	44	55	45
Religion																
Catholic	59	41	63	37	58	42	55	45	55	45	54	46	57	43	51	49
Jewish	69	31	82	18	70	30	70	30	68	32	73	27	79	21	69	31
White Protestant	41	59	43	57	38	62	43	57	44	56	45	55	43	57	38	62
White born-again[a]	43	57	46	54	35	65	31	69	34	66	34	66	34	66	29	71

(Table continues)

Table 3-12 *(Continued)*

Group	1980 D	1980 R	1982 D	1982 R	1984 D	1984 R	1986 D	1986 R	1988 D	1988 R	1990 D	1990 R	1992 D	1992 R	1994 D	1994 R
Union household	63	37	68	32	64	36	63	37	63	37	—	—	67	33	64	36
Family income[b]																
Under $15,000	56	44	73	27	63	37	56	44	67	33	63	37	69	31	57	43
$15,000 to 29,999	53	47	60	40	54	46	53	47	57	43	55	45	57	43	53	47
$30,000 to 49,999	47	53	52	48	49	51	53	47	53	47	52	48	52	48	51	49
Over $50,000	38	62	37	63	39	61	47	53	45	55	49	51	47	53	43	57
Party																
Democrat	83	17	90	10	85	15	81	19	83	17	79	21	89	11	88	12
Independent	44	56	51	49	49	51	52	48	54	46	52	48	44	56	45	55
Republican	10	90	12	88	14	86	20	80	21	79	23	77	15	85	9	91
Ideology																
Liberal	72	28	80	20	76	24	71	29	80	20	73	27	81	19	83	17
Moderate	57	43	60	40	57	43	58	42	57	43	56	44	57	43	58	42
Conservative	33	67	35	65	31	69	35	65	34	66	37	63	28	72	21	79
Vote history																
Reagan or Bush	23	77	31	69	21	79	35	65	28	72	37	63	15	85	12	88
Carter, Mondale, Dukakis or Clinton	87	13	89	11	93	7	83	17	84	16	81	19	89	11	84	16
Total	52	48	57	43	51	49	52	48	54	46	52	48	54	46	49	51

Notes: "D" indicates Democrat; "R" Republican; "—" indicates not available. Data based on questionnaires completed by voters leaving polling places around the nation on election day. Those who gave no answer are excluded in the above percentages. Data for 1990 collected by Voter Research and Surveys, other years collected by the *New York Times*/CBS News Poll. The number of respondents in 1982 was 7,855; in 1984, 9,174; in 1986, 8,994; in 1988, 11,645; in 1990, 19,888.

[a] Christians only. Born-again/Evangelical (1994); Born-again Fundamentalist (1992); Fundamentalist/Evangelical (1990, 1988, 1986); Born-again (1984, 1982, 1980).

[b] Family income categories in 1980: under $15,000, $15,000-$24,999, $25,000-$50,000 and over $50,000; 1982: under $10,000, $10,000-19,999, $20,000-29,999, $30,000-50,000, and over $50,000; 1984, 1986, and 1988: under $12,500, $12,500-24,999, $25,000-34,999, $35,000-49,999, and over $50,000; 1990 and 1992: under $15,000, $15,000-29,000 $30,000-49,000, and over $50,000.

Source: New York Times, "Portrait of the Electorate: Who Voted for Whom in the House," press release; March 1, 1995 (copyright © 1995 by the New York Times Company, reprinted by permission).

Table 3-13 Popular and Electoral Votes for President, 1789-1992

Year	Number of states	Candidates	Electoral vote (number and percent)	Popular vote (number and percent)
1789[a]	10	*(Federalist)* Washington	*(Federalist)* 69 / 100%	
1792[a]	15	Washington	132 / 98%	
1796[a]	16	*(Democrat-Republican)* Jefferson	*(Democrat-Republican)* 68 / 49%	
		(Federalist) Adams	*(Federalist)* 71 / 51%	
1800[a]	16	Jefferson	73 / 53%	
		Adams	65 / 47%	
1804	17	Jefferson / Clinton	162 / 92%	
		Pinckney / King	14 / 8%	
1808	17	Madison / Clinton	122 / 69%	
		Pinckney / King	47 / 27%	
1812	18	Madison / Gerry	128 / 59%	
		Clinton (Fusionist) / Ingersoll	89 / 41%	
1816	19	Monroe / Tompkins	183 / 83%	
		King / Howard	34 / 15%	
1820	24	*(Democrat-Republican)* Monroe / Tompkins	*(Democrat-Republican)* 231 / 98%	
		(Independent Democrat-Republican) Adams / Stockton	*(Independent Democrat-Republican)* 1 / 0%	
1824[b]	24	Jackson / Calhoun	99 / 38%	
		Adams / Sanford	84 / 32%	

(Table continues)

Table 3-13 (Continued)

Year	Number of states	Candidates (Democrat-Republican)	(National Republican)	Electoral vote (number and percent) (Democrat-Republican)	(National Republican)	Popular vote (number and percent) (Democrat-Republican)	(Republican)
(National)							
1828	24	Jackson	Adams	178	83	642,553	500,897
				68%	32%	56.1%	43.6%
		Calhoun	Rush				
1832	24	Jackson	Clay	219	49	701,780	484,205
				76%	17%	54.2%	37.4%
		Van Buren	Sergeant				
		(Democrat)	(Whig)			(Democrat)	(Whig)
1836	26	Van Buren	Harrison	170	73[c]	764,176	550,816
				58%	25%	50.8%	36.6%
		Johnson	Granger				
1840	26	Van Buren	Harrison	60	234	1,128,854	1,275,390
				20%	80%	46.8%	52.9%
		Johnson	Tyler				
1844	26	Polk	Clay	170	105	1,339,494	1,300,004
				62%	38%	49.5%	48.1%
		Dallas	Frelinghuysen				
1848	30	Cass	Taylor	127	163	1,223,460	1,361,393
				44%	56%	42.5%	47.3%
		Butler	Fillmore				
1852	31	Pierce	Scott	254	42	1,607,510	1,386,942
				86%	14%	50.8%	43.9%
		King	Graham				
		(Democrat)	(Republican)	(Democrat)	(Republican)	(Democrat)	(Republican)
1856	31	Buchanan	Fremont	174	114	1,836,072	1,342,345
				59%	39%	45.3%	33.1%
		Breckinridge	Dayton				
1860	33	Douglas	Lincoln	12	180	1,380,202	1,865,908
				4%	59%	29.5%	39.8%
		Johnson	Hamlin				
1864	36	McClellan	Lincoln	21	212	1,812,807	2,218,388
				9%	91%	45.0%	55.0%
		Pendleton	Johnson				
1868	37	Seymour	Grant	80	214	2,708,744	3,013,650
				27%	73%	47.3%	52.7%
		Blair	Colfax				
1872	37	Greeley	Grant	[d]	286	2,834,761	3,598,235
					78%	43.8%	55.6%
		Brown	Wilson				

Year	States	Candidate		Electoral	Popular		Candidate		Electoral	Popular	
1876	38	Tilden		184 / 50%	4,288,546	51.0%	Hayes		185 / 50%	4,034,311	47.9%
		Hendricks					Wheeler				
1880	38	Hancock		155 / 42%	4,444,260	48.2%	Garfield		214 / 58%	4,446,158	48.3%
		English					Arthur				
1884	38	Cleveland		219 / 55%	4,874,621	48.5%	Blaine		182 / 45%	4,848,936	48.2%
		Hendricks					Logan				
1888	38	Cleveland		168 / 42%	5,534,488	48.6%	Harrison		233 / 58%	5,443,892	47.8%
		Thurman					Morton				
1892	44	Cleveland		277 / 62%	5,551,883	46.1%	Harrison		145 / 33%	5,179,244	43.0%
		Stevenson					Reid				
1896	45	Bryan		176 / 39%	6,511,495	46.7%	McKinley		271 / 61%	7,108,480	51.0%
		Sewall					Hobart				
1900	45	Bryan		155 / 35%	6,358,345	45.5%	McKinley		292 / 65%	7,218,039	51.7%
		Stevenson					Roosevelt				
1904	45	Parker		140 / 29%	5,028,898	37.6%	Roosevelt		336 / 71%	7,626,593	56.4%
		Davis					Fairbanks				
1908	46	Bryan		162 / 34%	6,406,801	43.0%	Taft		321 / 66%	7,676,258	51.6%
		Kern					Sherman				
1912	48	Wilson		435 / 82%	6,293,152	41.8%	Taft		8 / 2%	3,486,333	23.2%
		Marshall					Sherman				
1916	48	Wilson		277 / 52%	9,126,300	49.2%	Hughes		254 / 48%	8,546,789	46.1%
		Marshall					Fairbanks				
1920	48	Cox		127 / 24%	9,140,884	34.2%	Harding		404 / 76%	16,133,314	60.3%
		Roosevelt					Coolidge				
1924	48	Davis		136 / 26%	8,386,169	28.8%	Coolidge		382 / 72%	15,717,553	54.1%
		Bryant					Dawes				
1928	48	Smith		87 / 16%	15,000,185	40.8%	Hoover		444 / 84%	21,411,991	58.2%
		Robinson					Curtis				
1932	48	Roosevelt		472 / 89%	22,825,016	57.4%	Hoover		59 / 11%	15,758,397	39.6%
		Garner					Curtis				

(Table continues)

Table 3-13 (Continued)

Year	Number of states	Candidates	Electoral vote (number and percent)		Popular vote (number and percent)	
1936	48	Roosevelt	523	90%	27,747,636	60.8%
		Garner				
		Landon	8	2%	16,679,543	36.5%
		Knox				
1940	48	Roosevelt	449	85%	27,263,448	54.7%
		Wallace				
		Willkie	82	15%	22,336,260	44.8%
		McNary				
1944	48	Roosevelt	432	81%	25,611,936	53.4%
		Truman				
		Dewey	99	19%	22,013,372	45.9%
		Bricker				
1948	48	Truman	303	57%	24,105,587	49.5%
		Barkley				
		Dewey	189	36%	21,970,017	45.1%
		Warren				
1952	48	Stevenson	89	17%	27,314,649	44.4%
		Sparkman				
		Eisenhower	442	83%	33,936,137	55.1%
		Nixon				
1956	48	Stevenson	73	14%	26,030,172	42.0%
		Kefauver				
		Eisenhower	457	86%	35,585,245	57.4%
		Nixon				
1960	50	Kennedy	303	56%	34,221,344	49.7%
		Johnson				
		Nixon	219	41%	34,106,671	49.5%
		Lodge				
1964	50	Johnson	486	90%	43,126,584	61.1%
		Humphrey				
		Goldwater	52	10%	27,177,838	38.5%
		Miller				
1968	50	Humphrey	191	36%	31,274,503	42.7%
		Muskie				
		Nixon	301	56%	31,785,148	43.4%
		Agnew				
1972	50	McGovern	17	3%	29,171,791	37.5%
		Shriver				
		Nixon	520	97%	47,170,179	60.7%
		Agnew				
1976	50	Carter	297	55%	40,830,763	50.1%
		Mondale				
		Ford	240	45%	39,147,793	48.0%
		Dole				
1980	50	Carter	49	9%	35,483,883	41.0%
		Mondale				
		Reagan	489	91%	43,904,153	50.7%
		Bush				
1984	50	Mondale	13	2%	37,577,137	40.6%
		Ferraro				
		Reagan	525	98%	54,455,074	58.8%
		Bush				

Year	States	Candidates	Electoral Vote	Popular Vote
1988	50	Dukakis Bentsen	111 21%	41,805,374 45.6%
		Bush Quayle	426 79%	48,881,278 53.4%
1992	50	Clinton Gore	370 69%	44,908,233 43.0%
		Bush Quayle	168 31%	39,102,282 37.4%

Note: For details of the electoral system as well as popular and electoral votes polled by minor candidates, see source. Popular vote returns are shown since 1824 because of availability and because by that time most electors were chosen by popular vote.

[a] The elections of 1789-1800 were held under different rules, which did not include separate voting for president and vice president. Scattered electoral votes are not shown.

[b] All candidates in 1824 represented factions of the Democratic-Republican party. Figures are for the two candidates with the highest electoral votes. The two other candidates were Crawford and Clay with 41 and 37 electoral votes, respectively.

[c] Three Whig candidates ran in 1836. Their electoral votes totalled 113.

[d] The Democratic presidential nominee, Horace Greeley, died between the popular vote and the meeting of presidential electors. Democratic electors split 63 votes among several candidates, Congress refused to count the three Georgians who insisted on casting their votes for Greeley, and an additional 14 electoral votes were not cast.

Sources: Congressional Quarterly's Guide to U.S. Elections, 2d ed. (Washington, D.C.: Congressional Quarterly, 1985), 269ff, 329ff, 1220ff; *Congressional Quarterly Weekly Report* (1988), 3595; (1989), 139; (1992), 3552; Table 3-2, this volume.

Table 3-14 Party Winning Presidential Election, by State, 1789-1992

State	1789-1824			1828-1856			1860-1892			1896-1928			1932-1964			1968-1992		
	D	F	O	D	R	O	D	R	O	D	R	O	D	R	O	D	R	O
Alabama	2	0	0	8	0	0	6	2	0	9	0	0	7	1	1	1	5	1
Alaska	—	—	—	—	—	—	—	—	—	—	—	—	1	1	0	0	7	0
Arizona	—	—	—	—	—	—	—	—	—	2	3	0	5	4	0	0	7	0
Arkansas	—	—	—	6	0	0	6	1	0	9	0	0	9	0	0	2	4	1
California	—	—	—	2	0	0	2	7	0	1	7	1	6	3	0	1	6	0
Colorado	—	—	—	—	—	—	0	4	1	5	4	0	4	5	0	1	6	0
Connecticut	2	8	0	2	6	0	4	5	0	1	8	0	5	4	0	2	5	0
Delaware	2	8	0	2	6	0	7	1	1	1	8	0	5	4	0	2	5	0
District of Columbia[a]	—	—	—	—	—	—	—	—	—	—	—	—	1	0	0	7	0	0
Florida	—	—	—	2	1	0	4	3	1	8	1	0	6	3	0	1	6	0
Georgia	8	2	0	5	3	0	7	0	1	9	0	0	8	1	0	3	3	1
Hawaii	—	—	—	—	—	—	—	—	—	—	—	—	2	0	0	5	2	0
Idaho	—	—	—	—	—	—	0	0	1	4	5	0	6	3	0	0	7	0
Illinois	2	0	0	8	0	0	1	8	0	1	8	0	7	2	0	1	6	0
Indiana	3	0	0	6	2	0	3	6	0	1	8	0	3	6	0	0	7	0
Iowa	—	—	—	2	1	0	0	9	0	1	8	0	4	5	0	2	5	0
Kansas	—	—	—	—	—	—	0	7	1	3	6	0	3	6	0	0	7	0
Kentucky	8	1	0	2	6	0	8	0	1	6	3	0	7	2	0	2	5	0
Louisiana	4	0	0	6	2	0	5	1	1	9	0	0	6	2	1	2	4	1
Maine	2	0	0	5	3	0	0	9	0	1	8	0	1	8	0	2	5	0
Maryland	4	6	0	1	6	1	7	1	1	4	5	0	6	3	0	4	3	0
Massachusetts	3	7	0	0	8	0	0	9	0	2	7	0	7	2	0	5	2	0
Michigan	—	—	—	4	2	0	0	9	0	0	8	1	5	4	0	5	2	0
Minnesota	—	—	—	—	—	—	0	9	0	0	8	1	7	2	0	6	1	0
Mississippi	2	0	0	7	1	0	5	1	1	9	0	0	6	1	2	1	5	1
Missouri	—	—	—	8	0	0	7	2	0	4	5	0	8	1	0	2	5	0

	D	F	R	D	F	R	D	F	R	D	F	R	D	F	R	D	F	R
Montana	—	—	—	—	—	—	0	0	0	4	5	0	6	3	0	1	6	0
Nebraska	—	—	—	—	—	—	0	0	0	4	5	0	3	6	0	0	7	0
Nevada	—	—	—	—	—	—	1	1	1	5	4	0	7	2	0	1	6	0
New Hampshire	4	6	0	6	2	0	0	6	0	2	7	0	4	5	0	1	6	0
New Jersey	5	5	0	3	5	0	7	9	0	1	8	0	6	3	0	1	6	0
New Mexico	—	—	—	—	—	—	—	2	0	2	3	0	7	2	0	1	6	0
New York	6	3	0	5	3	0	4	5	0	1	8	0	6	3	0	4	3	0
North Carolina	8	1	0	5	3	0	5	2	1	8	1	0	9	0	0	1	6	0
North Dakota	—	—	—	—	—	—	—	—	—	2	7	0	3	6	0	0	7	0
Ohio	6	0	0	4	4	0	0	9	0	2	7	0	5	4	0	2	5	0
Oklahoma	—	—	—	—	—	—	—	—	—	4	2	0	6	3	0	0	7	0
Oregon	—	—	—	—	—	—	1	8	0	1	8	1	5	4	0	2	5	0
Pennsylvania	8	2	0	6	2	0	0	9	0	0	8	0	5	4	0	3	4	0
Rhode Island	4	5	0	2	6	0	0	9	0	2	7	0	7	2	0	5	2	0
South Carolina	8	2	0	6	0	2	4	3	1	9	0	0	7	1	1	1	6	0
South Dakota	—	—	—	—	—	—	0	1	0	1	7	1	3	6	0	0	7	0
Tennessee	8	0	0	3	5	0	6	1	1	7	2	0	6	3	0	2	5	0
Texas	—	—	—	3	0	0	7	0	0	8	1	0	7	2	0	2	5	0
Utah	—	—	—	—	—	—	—	—	—	2	7	0	6	3	0	0	7	0
Vermont	6	3	0	7	1	0	0	9	0	0	9	0	1	8	0	1	6	0
Virginia	8	2	0	8	0	0	5	1	1	8	1	0	6	3	0	0	7	0
Washington	—	—	—	—	—	—	0	1	0	2	6	0	6	3	0	3	4	0
West Virginia	—	—	—	—	—	—	5	3	0	1	8	1	8	1	0	5	2	0
Wisconsin	—	—	—	2	1	0	1	8	0	1	7	1	5	4	0	3	4	0
Wyoming	—	—	—	—	—	—	0	1	0	3	6	0	5	4	0	0	7	0
Total[b]	113	61	0	136	79	3	118	189	15	170	244	7	274	158	5	96	256	5

Note: "D" indicates the Democratic-Republican party from 1796 to 1820 and in 1828, the Jackson faction in 1824, and the Democratic party from 1832 and later; "F" indicates is the Federalists from 1792 to 1816, Independent Democrat-Republicans in 1820, and the Adams faction in 1824; "R" indicates the National Republicans

(Notes continue)

Table 3-14 (*Continued*)

in 1828 and 1832, Whigs from 1836 to 1852, and the Republican party in 1856 and later. The "O" column refers to other (third-party) parties. Southern Democrats in 1860 are counted as Democratic. "—" indicates that the state was not yet admitted to the Union.

[a] Residents of the District of Columbia received the presidential vote in 1961.

[b] Fewer total votes for a given state within a party system indicate admission of the state during the party system or nonvoting in certain southern states in 1864, 1868, and 1872.

Sources: Compiled by the editors from *Congressional Quarterly's Guide to U.S. Elections*, 2d ed. (Washington, D.C.: Congressional Quarterly, 1985), 269ff, 327; *Congressional Quarterly Weekly Report* (1988), 3245; (1992), 3552.

Table 3-15 Party Victories in U.S. House Elections, by State, 1860-1994

State	Total 1860-1895			Total 1896-1931			Total 1932-1965			Total 1966-1994		
	Dem.	Rep.	Other	Dem.	Rep.	Other	Dem.	Rep.	Other	Dem.	Rep.	Other
Alabama	92	19	8	170	0	8	146	5	0	68	40	0
Alaska	—	—	—	—	—	—	4	0	0	2	14	0
Arizona	—	—	—	11	0	0	26	7	0	22	44	0
Arkansas	54	5	6	124	0	0	109	0	0	40	19	0
California[a]	29	46	8	30	133	15	234	212	0	383	281	0
Colorado	1	9	3	21	34	6	43	26	0	40	39	0
Connecticut	33	36	5	11	77	0	58	44	0	55	35	0
Delaware	15	3	2	5	14	0	9	8	0	5	10	0
Florida	18	8	1	57	4	0	111	8	0	155	97	0
Georgia	111	11	12	207	0	1	170	1	0	126	27	1
Hawaii	—	—	—	0	0	1	6	0	0	28	2	0
Idaho	0	4	0	5	42	2	20	14	0	6	24	0
Illinois	118	191	20	136	333	1	220	221	0	184	162	0
Indiana	104	105	17	97	139	0	85	108	0	80	69	0
Iowa	16	131	11	10	193	0	35	105	0	36	55	0
Kansas	0	62	12	30	114	0	16	90	0	19	54	0
Kentucky	133	20	38	151	54	0	122	25	0	63	41	0
Louisiana	69	20	2	136	0	2	139	0	2	88	32	0
Maine	3	76	7	4	71	0	8	41	0	12	18	0
Maryland	74	15	18	63	49	0	87	25	0	80	43	0
Massachusetts	31	165	17	60	211	2	103	136	0	138	34	0
Michigan	33	118	13	12	214	2	112	187	0	156	119	0
Minnesota	11	51	5	8	146	12	44	91	16	69	51	1

(Table continues)

Table 3-15 (Continued)

State	Total 1860-1895			Total 1896-1931			Total 1932-1965			Total 1966-1994		
	Dem.	Rep.	Other	Dem.	Rep.	Other	Dem.	Rep.	Other	Dem.	Rep.	Other
Mississippi	70	17	3	142	0	0	110	1	0	59	17	0
Missouri	143	43	38	202	88	0	157	49	0	106	37	0
Montana	1	3	0	13	14	1	23	12	0	17	12	0
Nebraska	3	28	5	36	63	9	21	50	0	5	40	0
Nevada	4	9	4	5	10	4	14	3	0	13	8	0
New Hampshire	11	33	3	3	33	0	3	31	0	7	23	0
New Jersey	53	58	5	66	137	0	84	158	0	130	87	0
New Mexico	—	—	—	7	5	0	29	0	0	14	23	0
New York	236	312	66	328	397	6	387	368	1	339	213	0
North Carolina	78	32	19	157	11	9	189	9	0	113	54	0
North Dakota	0	4	0	0	44	0	2	33	0	9	9	0
Ohio	146	186	39	123	264	0	163	238	0	134	197	0
Oklahoma	—	—	—	70	27	0	112	14	0	65	25	0
Oregon	7	13	2	2	44	0	22	41	0	46	21	0
Pennsylvania	158	300	38	83	522	17	255	291	0	197	168	0
Rhode Island	8	32	2	13	34	0	32	2	0	23	8	0
South Carolina	62	30	6	127	0	0	97	2	0	59	32	0
South Dakota	6	11	0	3	42	2	7	27	0	12	11	0
Tennessee	83	52	13	139	39	4	121	37	1	77	52	0
Texas	110	1	3	295	7	0	365	8	0	297	88	0
Utah	—	—	—	7	23	0	23	11	0	14	23	0
Vermont	0	42	5	0	36	0	1	16	0	0	12	3
Virginia	81	23	23	167	15	0	147	15	0	75	74	0
Washington	0	6	0	8	61	2	54	55	0	80	35	0

West Virginia	37	15	6	23	75	0	84	16	0	58	3	0
Wisconsin	40	94	9	18	176	4	46	105	21	73	67	0
Wyoming	1	2	0	1	17	0	3	14	0	4	11	0

Note: " — " indicates that the state was not yet admitted to the Union. The 1966-1992 period does not include special elections; candidates endorsed by both major and minor parties are counted as major party candidates.

[a] When it could be determined, candidates who ran as both Republican and Democrat were classified by their usual party affiliation.

Sources: Congressional Quarterly's Guide to U.S. Elections, 2d ed. (Washington, D.C.: Congressional Quarterly, 1985), 1118-1119; 1986-1994: *Congressional Quarterly Weekly Report* (1986), 2843, (1988), 3269, (1990), 3802, (1992), 3571, (1994), 3236.

Table 3-16 House and Senate Election Results, by Congress, 1788-1994

Year	Congress	House Dem.[a]	House Rep.[b]	House Other	House Gains/losses[c] Dem.	House Gains/losses[c] Rep.	Senate Dem.[a]	Senate Rep.[b]	Senate Other	Senate Gains/losses[c] Dem.	Senate Gains/losses[c] Rep.	President[d]
1788	1st	26	38				9	17				Washington (F)
1790	2d	33	37				13	16				
1792	3d	57	48				13	17				Washington (F)
1794	4th	52	54				13	19				
1796	5th	48	58				12	20				John Adams (F)
1798	6th	42	64				13	19				
1800	7th	69	36				18	13				Jefferson (DR)
1802	8th	102	39				25	9				
1804	9th	116	25				27	7				Jefferson (DR)
1806	10th	118	24				28	6				
1808	11th	94	48				28	6				Madison (DR)
1810	12th	108	36				30	6				
1812	13th	112	68				27	9				Madison (DR)
1814	14th	117	65				25	11				
1816	15th	141	42				34	10				Monroe (DR)
1818	16th	156	27				35	7				
1820	17th	158	25				44	4				Monroe (DR)
1822	18th	187	26				44	4				
1824	19th	105	97				26	20				John Q.Adams (DR)
1826	20th	94	119				20	28				
1828	21st	139	74				26	22				Jackson (D)
1830	22d	141	58				25	21				
1832	23d	147	53				20	20				Jackson (D)
1834	24th	145	98				27	25				
1836	25th	108	107	24			30	18	4			Van Buren (D)
1838	26th	124	118				28	22				
1840	27th	102	133	6			28	22				Harrison (W)

Year	Congress	House					Senate					President
1842	28th	142	79	1	+48	-16	25	28	1	-3	+5	Tyler (W)
1844	29th	143	77	6	-30	+21	31	25	2	-1	+6	Polk (D)
1846	30th	108	115	4	-59	-7	36	21	3	-27	+5	Taylor (W)
1848	31st	112	109	9	+38	-3	35	25	2	+1	+8	Fillmore (W)
1850	32d	140	88	5	-34	+42	35	24	5	-2	+3	Pierce (D)
1852	33d	159	71	4	+3	-2	38	22	5	+1	0	
1854	34th	83	108	43	+24	+27	42	15	2	0	+19	Buchanan (D)
1856	35th	131	92	14	+31	-31	39	20	7	+6	-4	
1858	36th	101	113	23	-16	+64	38	26		+2	-3	Lincoln (R)
1860	37th	42	106	28	+93	-96	11	31		+10	-8	
1862	38th	80	103		-25	+30	12	39		+7	-7	Lincoln (R)
1864	39th	46	145		-6	-9	10	42		+7	-6	A. Johnson (R)
1866	40th	49	143		-20	+24	11	42		-6	+4	Grant (R)
1868	41st	73	170		+70	-33	11	61		-1	+3	
1870	42d	104	139		-18	+21	17	57		-2	+2	Grant (R)
1872	43d	88	203	3	-12	+11	19	54		+3	-2	
1874	44th	181	107		-14	+22	29	46	1	0	+8	Hayes (R)
1876	45th	156	137		+75	-85	36	39		+2	0	
1878	46th	150	128	14	-11	+38	43	33		+5	-9	Garfield (R)
1880	47th	130	152	11	-116	+120	37	37	2	-5	+6	Arthur (R)
1882	48th	200	119	6	+30	-40	36	40		-5	+2	Cleveland (D)
1884	49th	182	140	2	+29	-21	34	41		-8	+7	
1886	50th	170	151	4	-10	+13	37	39		+3	+3	Harrison (R)
1888	51st	156	173	1	+25	+9	37	47		+3	+2	
1890	52d	231	88	14			39	47	2			Cleveland (D)
1892	53d	220	126	8			44	38	3			
1894	54th	104	246	7			39	44	5			McKinley (R)
1896	55th	134	206	16			34	46	10			
1898	56th	163	185	9			26	53	11			McKinley (R)
1900	57th	153	198	5			29	56	3			Roosevelt (R)
1902	58th	178	207				32	58				

(Table continues)

Table 3-16 (*Continued*)

Year	Congress	House Dem.[a]	House Rep.[b]	House Other	House Gains/losses[c] Dem.	House Gains/losses[c] Rep.	Senate Dem.[a]	Senate Rep.[b]	Senate Other	Senate Gains/losses[c] Dem.	Senate Gains/losses[c] Rep.	President[d]
1904	59th	136	250		−42	+43	32	58		0	0	Roosevelt (R)
1906	60th	164	222		+28	−28	29	61		−3	−3	
1908	61st	172	219		+8	−3	32	59		+3	−2	Taft (R)
1910	62d	228	162	1	+56	−57	42	49	1	+10	−10	
1912	63d	290	127	18	+62	−35	51	44	1	+9	−5	Wilson (D)
1914	64th	231	193	8	−59	+66	56	39	1	+5	−5	
1916	65th	210	216	9	−21	+23	53	42	1	−3	+3	Wilson (D)
1918	66th	191	237	7	−19	+21	47	48	1	−6	+6	
1920	67th	132	300	1	−59	+63	37	59		−10	+11	Harding (R)
1922	68th	207	225	3	+75	−75	43	51	2	+6	−8	
1924	69th	183	247	5	−24	+22	40	54	1	−3	+3	Coolidge (R)
1926	70th	195	237	3	+12	−10	47	48	1	+7	−6	
1928	71st	163	267	1	−32	+30	39	56	1	−8	+8	Hoover (R)
1930	72d	216	218	1	+53	−49	47	48	1	+8	−8	
1932	73d	313	117	5	+97	−101	59	36	1	+12	−12	Roosevelt (D)
1934	74th	322	103	10	+9	−14	69	25	2	+10	−11	
1936	75th	333	89	13	+11	−14	75	17	4	+6	−8	Roosevelt (D)
1938	76th	262	169	4	−71	+80	69	23	4	−6	+6	
1940	77th	267	162	6	+5	−7	66	28	2	−3	+5	Roosevelt (D)
1942	78th	222	209	4	−45	+47	57	38	1	−9	+10	
1944	79th	243	190	2	+21	−19	57	38	1	0	0	Roosevelt (D)
1946	80th	188	246	1	−55	+56	45	51		−12	+13	Truman (D)
1948	81st	263	171	1	+75	−75	54	42		+9	−9	Truman (D)
1950	82d	234	199	2	−29	+28	48	47		−6	+5	
1952	83d	213	221	1	−21	+22	47	48	1	−1	+1	Eisenhower (R)
1954	84th	232	203		+19	−18	48	47	1	+1	−1	
1956	85th	234	201		+2	−2	49	47	1	+1	0	Eisenhower (R)
1958	86th	283	154		+49	−47	64	34		+17	−13	

Year	Congress	House Dem[a]	Other	House Rep[b]	Dem +/−	Rep +/−	Senate Dem[a]	Senate Rep[b]	Dem +/−	Rep +/−	President[d]
1960	87th	263		174	−20	+20	64	36	−2	+2	Kennedy (D)
1962	88th	258	1	176	−4	+2	67	33	+4	−4	
1964	89th	295		140	+38	−38	68	32	+2	−2	L. Johnson (D)
1966	90th	248		187	−47	+47	64	36	−3	+3	
1968	91st	243		192	−4	+4	58	42	−5	+5	Nixon (R)
1970	92d	255		180	+12	−12	55	45	−4	+2	
1972	93d	243		192	−12	+12	57	43	+2	−2	Nixon (R)
1974	94th	291		144	+43	−43	61	38	+3	−3	Ford (R)
1976	95th	292		143	+1	−1	62	38	0	0	Carter (D)
1978	96th	277		158	−11	+11	59	41	−3	+3	
1980	97th	243		192	−33	+33	47	53	−12	+12	Reagan (R)
1982	98th	269		166	+26	−26	46	54	0	0	
1984	99th	253		182	−14	+14	47	53	+2	−2	Reagan (R)
1986	100th	258		177	+5	−5	55	45	+8	−8	Bush (R)
1988	101st	260		175	+3	−3	55	45	+1	−1	
1990	102d	267	1	167	+9	−8	56	44	+1	−1	Clinton (D)
1992	103d	258	1	176	−10	+10	57	43	0	0	
1994	104th	203	1	231	−53	+53	48[e]	52[e]	+7[e]	−7[e]	

[a] "Democratic" column indicates Democratic partisans in 1828 and later, "Administration" in 1824 and 1826, "Democratic Republicans" from 1790 to 1822, and "Opposition" in 1788.

[b] The "Republican" column indicates Republican partisans in 1854 and later, "Whigs" from 1834 to 1852, "Anti-Masons" in 1832, "National Republicans" in 1828 and 1830, "Jacksonians" in 1824 and 1826, "Federalists" from 1790 to 1822, and "Administration" in 1788.

[c] Because of changes in the overall number of seats in the Senate and House, in the number of seats won by third parties, and in the number of vacancies, a Republican loss is not always matched precisely by a Democratic gain, or vice versa. Gains/losses reflect preelection/postelection changes. Deaths, resignations, and special elections can cause further changes in party make-up. In the 1930 election, for example, Republicans won majority control, but when Congress organized, special elections held to fill fourteen vacancies resulted in a Democratic majority.

[d] President elected in the year indicated or, if a midterm election year, nonelected president in office at the time of the midterm election.

[e] In 1994 U.S. Senator Richard Shelby switched from Democrat to Republican the day after the election. With his switch the partisan balance became 53-47 and the Republican gain 8 seats.

Sources: 1788–1852: Bureau of the Census, Historical Statistics of the United States, Colonial Times to 1970 (Washington, D.C.: U.S. Government Printing Office, 1975), 1083–1084; 1854: Congressional Quarterly, Elections '84 (Washington, D.C.: Congressional Quarterly, 1984), 106; 1856–1984: Congressional Quarterly's Guide to U.S. Elections, 2d ed. (Washington, D.C.: Congressional Quarterly, 1985), 1124; 1986–1990: Congressional Quarterly Weekly Report (1986), 2811, 2843; (1988), 3249, 3264, 3269; (1990), 3796; (1992), 3557, 3570, 3719, 3821; (1994), 3232, 3240.

Table 3-17 Popular Vote and Seats in House Elections, by Party, 1896-1994

Year	Democratic candidates		Republican candidates		Change from last election[a]		Difference between Democratic percentage of all seats and all votes[a]
	Percentage of all votes	Percentage of all seats	Percentage of all votes	Percentage of all seats	Percentage of major party votes	Percentage of major party seats	
1896	43.3	37.6	46.7	57.9	—	—	-5.6
1898	46.7	45.7	45.7	51.8	2.5D	7.4D	-1.0
1900	44.7	43.0	51.2	55.6	3.9R	3.2R	-1.7
1902	46.7	46.2	49.3	53.8	2.1D	2.6D	-0.5
1904	41.7	35.2	53.8	64.8	5.0R	11.0R	-6.5
1906	44.2	42.5	50.7	57.5	2.9D	7.3D	-1.7
1908	46.1	44.0	49.7	56.0	1.6D	1.5D	-2.1
1910	47.4	58.3	46.5	41.4	2.4D	14.5D	10.9
1912	45.3	66.7	34.0	29.2	6.6D	11.1D	21.3
1914	43.1	53.5	42.6	44.7	6.8R	15.1R	10.3
1916	46.3	48.3	48.4	49.7	1.5R	5.2R	2.0
1918	43.1	43.9	52.5	54.5	3.8R	4.7R	0.8
1920	35.8	30.5	58.6	69.3	7.1R	14.1R	-5.4
1922	44.7	47.6	51.7	51.7	8.4D	17.4D	2.8
1924	40.4	42.1	55.5	56.8	4.3R	5.4R	1.7
1926	40.5	44.8	57.0	54.5	0.5R	2.6D	4.3
1928	42.4	37.8	56.5	61.9	1.3D	7.2R	-4.5
1930	44.6	49.7	52.6	50.1	3.0D	11.9D	5.1
1932	54.5	72.0	41.4	26.9	11.0D	23.0D	17.4
1934	53.9	74.0	42.0	23.7	0.7R	3.0D	20.1
1936	55.8	76.6	39.6	20.5	2.3D	3.1D	20.7
1938	48.6	60.2	47.0	38.9	7.7R	18.1R	11.6
1940	51.3	61.4	45.6	37.2	2.2D	1.4D	10.1
1942	46.1	51.0	50.6	48.0	5.3R	10.7R	5.0

1944	55.9	47.2	43.7	4.0D	4.6D	5.3
1946	43.2	53.5	56.6	6.4R	12.8R	-1.0
1948	60.5	45.5	39.3	8.0D	17.3D	8.6
1950	53.8	49.0	45.7	3.2R	6.6R	4.7
1952	49.0	49.3	50.8	0.2D	5.0R	-0.8
1954	53.3	47.0	46.7	2.6D	4.3D	0.8
1956	53.8	48.7	46.2	1.6R	0.5D	2.7
1958	64.8	43.5	35.2	5.2D	11.0D	8.5
1960	60.2	45.4	39.8	1.9R	4.6R	6.0
1962	59.3	47.4	40.5	2.0R	0.7R	7.0
1964	67.8	42.1	32.2	5.3D	8.4D	10.4
1966	57.0	48.2	43.0	6.3R	10.8R	6.1
1968	55.9	48.5	44.1	0.5R	1.1R	5.7
1970	58.6	45.1	41.4	3.4D	2.8R	5.2
1972	55.9	46.4	44.1	1.5R	2.7R	4.2
1974	66.9	40.6	33.1	5.9D	11.0D	9.9
1976	67.1	42.1	32.9	1.4R	0.2D	10.9
1978	63.7	44.7	36.3	2.8R	3.4R	10.3
1980	55.9	48.0	44.1	3.2R	7.8R	5.5
1982	61.8	42.9	38.2	5.3D	5.9D	6.2
1984	58.2	47.0	41.8	3.9R	3.6R	6.0
1986	59.3	44.6	40.7	2.4D	1.1D	4.8
1988	59.8	45.5	40.2	1.0R	0.5D	6.5
1990	61.4	45.0	38.4	0.1D	1.8D	8.5
1992	59.3	45.6	40.5	1.4R	2.1R	8.5
1994	46.7	52.4	53.1	6.3R	12.7R	1.3

Note: "—" indicates not available.

a Calculated before rounding.

Source: Votes, 1896-1970: U.S. Bureau of the Census, *Historical Statistics of the United States, Colonial Times to 1970*, Bicentennial ed. (Washington, D.C.: U.S. Government Printing Office, 1975), Part 2, 1084; votes, 1972-1974: U.S. Bureau of the Census, *Statistical Abstract of the United States, 1976* (Washington, D.C.: U.S. Government Printing Office, 1976), 460; votes, 1976-1994: Congressional Quarterly Weekly Report (1977), 488; (1979), 571; (1981), 713; (1983), 387; (1985), 687; (1987), 484; (1989) 1063; (1991), 487; (1993), 965 (1995), 1079; seats: this volume, Table 3-16.

Table 3-18 Incumbent Reelection Rates: Representatives, Senators, and Governors, General Elections, 1960-1994

Year/Office	Number of incumbents			Incumbents winning election	Incumbents reelected with 60+ percent of the major-party vote
	Ran	Won	Lost		
1960					
House	400	374	26	93.5%	58.9%
Senate	29	28	1	96.6	41.3
Governor	13	7	6	53.8	15.4
1962					
House	396	381	15	94.3	63.6
Senate	34	29	5	85.3	26.4
Governor	24	15	9	62.5	12.5
1964					
House	389	344	45	88.4	58.5
Senate	32	28	4	87.5	46.8
Governor	14	12	2	85.7	42.9
1966					
House	402	362	40	90.1	67.7
Senate	29	28	1	96.6	41.3
Governor	21	14	7	66.7	23.8
1968					
House	401	396	5	98.8	72.2
Senate	24	20	4	83.3	37.5
Governor	13	9	4	69.2	15.4
1970					
House	391	379	12	96.9	77.3
Senate	29	23	6	79.3	31.0
Governor	24	17	7	70.8	4.2
1972					
House	380	367	13	95.6	77.8
Senate	25	20	5	80.0	52.0
Governor	9	7	2	77.8	44.5
1974					
House	383	343	40	89.6	66.4
Senate	25	23	2	92.0	40.0
Governor	22	17	5	77.3	36.4
1976					
House	381	368	13	96.6	69.2
Senate	25	16	9	64.0	40.0
Governor	7	5	2	71.4	28.6
1978					
House	378	359	19	95.0	76.6
Senate	22	15	7	68.1	31.8
Governor	21	16	5	76.2	28.6
1980					
House	392	361	31	90.7	72.9
Senate	25	16	9	55.2	40.0
Governor	10	7	3	70.0	30.0

Table 3-18   *(Continued)*

Year/Office	Number of incumbents			Incumbents winning election	Incumbents reelected with 60+ percent of the major-party vote
	Ran	Won	Lost		
1982					
House	381	352	29	92.4%	68.9%
Senate	30	28	2	93.3	56.7
Governor	24	19	5	79.2	41.7
1984					
House	407	391	16	96.1	78.9
Senate	29	26	3	89.7	65.5
Governor	6	4	2	66.7	50.0
1986					
House	391	385	6	98.5	84.5
Senate	28	21	7	75.0	50.0
Governor	17	15	2	88.2	52.9
1988					
House	409	402	6	98.3	87.3
Senate	27	23	4	85.0	60.9
Governor	9	8	1	89.0	37.5
1990					
House	406	391	15	96.3	79.5
Senate	32	31	1	96.9	66.7
Governor	23	17	6	73.9	64.7
1992					
House	349	325	24	93.1	65.0
Senate	28	24	4	85.7	46.4
Governor	4	4	0	100.0	100.0
1994					
House	384	349	35	90.9	63.0
Senate	25	23	2	92.0	48.0
Governor	20	18	2	90.0	50.0

Note: Percentage gaining more than 60 percent of the vote is calculated on the basis of the vote for the two major parties. "Off-off" year gubernatorial elections, held in Kentucky, Louisiana, Mississippi, New Jersey, and Virginia, are not included in the above totals. For these gubernatorial election outcomes, see *Congressional Quarterly's Guide to U.S. Elections.*

Sources: House and Senate, 1960-1978: Congressional Quarterly, *Elections '80* (Washington, D.C.: Congressional Quarterly, 1980), 14; House and Senate, 1980-1982, and governor, 1960-1966: Richard M. Scammon and Alice V. McGillivray, comps. and eds., *America Votes 16: A Handbook of Contemporary American Election Statistics* (Washington, D.C.: Elections Research Center, Congressional Quarterly, 1985); 1984: *Congressional Quarterly Almanac 1984* (Washington, D.C.: Congressional Quarterly, 1985), B7, B13, B19; House and Senate, 1986-1990, and governor, 1968-1992: *Congressional Quarterly Weekly Report* (1988), 3249, 3266, 3296-3298, 3301-3307; (1989), 1074-1080, 1149; (1990), 3797, 3801, 3838, 3847-3854; (1991), 493-500; (1992), 3557, 3570, 3579, 3596, 3719, 3821; (1993), 973-980; (1995), 1090-1097.

4

Political Parties

Political parties live and die by the numbers—numbers of supporters, candidates, contributors, and especially voters. Therefore, it is not surprising that a book of statistics on American politics contains a great deal of data about parties or that these data appear throughout the volume.

Parties can be profitably viewed from three different perspectives: parties in the electorate, parties in government, and parties as organizations. As Chapter 3 is devoted entirely to elections and campaigns, and Chapter 5 includes considerable data about elements of voting (partisanship and party evaluations), in this chapter only a portion of the material is devoted to parties in the electorate, despite the overwhelming importance to parties of gathering votes. Although no sharp distinction is possible or intended, the emphasis here is on aspects of voting that relate more closely to parties as organizations. Thus, for example, a number of tables concern the topics of party-line versus split-ticket voting and partisan versus split outcomes (Tables 4-4 through 4-8). Such topics are useful for assessing the strength of parties and of partisanship.

The party-line voting tables draw on two kinds of data—aggregate data (about collectivities such as states and congressional districts) and individual data (about individual voters, chiefly drawn from sample surveys). Although the two are likely to indicate the same sort of conclusions, they are independent of one another and each tells something distinct. It is possible, for example, for there to be a large amount of split-ticket voting by individuals and yet a small number of split district outcomes. For example, a very large majority may support the Democratic candidate for governor and a much narrower majority support the Democratic candidate for president. Likewise, it is possible for many individuals to split their tickets and still have winning candidates from the same party; if those who split their tickets do so in opposite ways, they will offset each others' votes.

123

Many of the tables in Chapters 7 and 8 concern parties in government. Voting in Congress frequently takes on partisan tones, as does support for or opposition to the president. Party unity and presidential support scores therefore offer important perspectives on the continuing or changing significance of political parties. Like voting by the electorate, congressional voting is viewed from both individual and aggregate perspectives. How individual representatives and senators vote is important to their constituents and to organized interests, so publications and tabulations showing individual voting behavior have become widespread (see Tables 7-15 and 7-16). How unified party members are in their voting, the degree to which the parties oppose each other, and the extent to which there are other cohesive groups—such as the so-called Conservative Coalition of Republicans and southern Democrats—are all important analytically for understanding congressional behavior and practically for those who wish to influence congressional action (Tables 7-9 through 7-11 and Figure 7-2).

In this chapter the emphasis is on parties as organizations, beginning simply with their organizational identities (Figure 4-1). The growth of presidential primaries is also documented (Table 4-9). Two additional topics are covered principally since the 1970s when data collection began in earnest. First, as is discussed further in Chapter 6, the establishment of the Federal Election Commission in 1973 has led to more extensive and more revealing data about expenditures (Table 4-12). Second, just as surveys have expanded the kind of material available about voters, they have been used to provide insight into party elites, especially national convention delegates. The data that have been systematically collected are largely limited to demographic information (Table 4-10). Nevertheless, data about national convention delegates are now available over an increasingly long period.

It is fortunate, in any event, that some information is available about party elites. In part because of the decentralized nature of American parties, scholars only recently have begun systematically to study parties as organizations.[1] Consequently, data are scarce and available from limited time periods and a restricted range of localities. This systematic study has occurred just as Republican and Democratic national party organizations have responded to the declining importance of parties in the electorate by stepping up the services they provide to local and state party organizations in areas such as candidate recruitment, media consulting, polling information, and fund raising.

How parties fare in the altered context of American politics depends partially on how parties as organizations respond to changes such as the growth of political action committees, increased campaign costs, and the pervasive reach and use of media, particularly television. In doing so, the parties may add to scholarly efforts to increase available information about their activities and organizational efforts. Ironically, the much-heralded decline of parties in the electorate may make parties as organizations a growth area of data collection over the next decade.

Notes

1. Cornelius P. Cotter, James L. Gibson, John F. Bibby, and Robert J. Huckshorn, *Party Organizations in American Politics* (New York: Praeger, 1984).

Figure 4-1   American Political Parties Since 1789

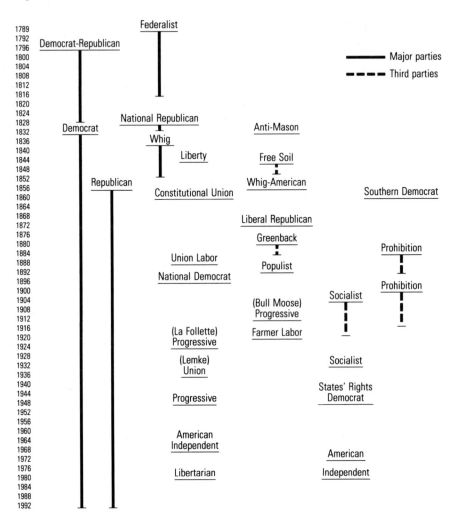

Note: The chart indicates the years in which the presidential candidate of a political party received 1.0 percent or more of the popular vote. Minor parties are not included if the minor party candidate is also the candidate of one of the two major parties (as happened in 1896 when the Populists endorsed Bryan, the Democratic candidate). Party candidates sometimes run under different designations in different states (in 1968 George C. Wallace ran for president under at least ten party labels). In such cases the vote totals for the candidate were aggregated under a single party designation. Sometimes candidates run under no party label as H. Ross Perot did in 1992.

Table 4-1 Party Competition: The Presidency, 1968-1992

Number of times Republican presidential candidate carried the state

0	1	2	3	4	5	6	7
District of Columbia (3)	Minnesota (10)	Hawaii (4) Massachusetts (12) Rhode Island (4) West Virginia (5)	Georgia (13) Maryland (10) New York (33)	Arkansas (6) Louisiana (9) Pennsylvania (23) Washington (11) Wisconsin (11)	Alabama (9) Connecticut (8) Delaware (3) Iowa (7) Kentucky (8) Maine (4) Michigan (18) Mississippi (7) Missouri (11) Ohio (21) Oregon (7) Tennessee (11) Texas (32)	California (54) Colorado (8) Florida (25) Illinois (22) Montana (3) Nevada (4) New Hampshire (4) New Jersey (15) New Mexico (5) North Carolina (14) South Carolina (8) Vermont (3)	Alaska (3) Arizona (8) Idaho (4) Indiana (12) Kansas (6) Nebraska (5) North Dakota (3) Oklahoma (8) South Dakota (3) Utah (5) Virginia (13) Wyoming (3)

Note: Number of electoral votes for 1992, 1996, and 2000 are shown in parentheses.

Sources: Compiled by the editors from Richard M. Scammon and Alice V. McGillivray, comps. and eds., *America Votes 16: A Handbook of Contemporary American Election Statistics* (Washington, D.C.: Elections Research Center, Congressional Quarterly, 1985), 31, 33, 35, 37, 41; Congressional Quarterly Weekly Report (1988), 3245; (1992), 3552.

Table 4-2   Party Competition in the States, 1968-1994

Percentage of Republican wins[a]				
0-20	21-40	41-60	61-80	81-100
Alabama	Maine	Alaska	Arizona	New
Arkansas	Michigan	Delaware	Colorado	Hampshire
California	Montana	Illinois	Idaho	South Dakota
Connecticut	Nebraska[d]	Iowa	Indiana	Wyoming
Florida	Nevada	New York	Kansas	
Georgia	New Jersey	Ohio	North Dakota	
Hawaii	Oregon	Pennsylvania	Utah	
Kentucky	Washington		Vermont	
Louisiana	Wisconsin			
Maryland				
Massachusetts				
Minnesota				
Mississippi				
Missouri				
New Mexico				
North				
Carolina				
Oklahoma				
Rhode Island				
South				
Carolina				
Tennessee				
Texas				
Virginia				
West Virginia				

[a] The governorship, control of the lower chamber, and control of the upper chamber are figured separately. That is, if in a given year the Republicans won the governorship and control of one chamber, they had 66.7 percent of the wins.

[b] Results are for the governorship only because the legislature is nonpartisan.

Sources: Calculated by the editors. 1968-1986: Republican National Committee, *Republican Almanac, 1987: State Political Profiles* (Washington, D.C.: Republican National Committee, 1987); 1987-1994: *Congressional Quarterly Weekly Report* (1988), 3298; (1990), 3840; (1992), 3599; (1994), 3250; National Conference of State Legislatures, unpublished data.

Table 4-3   Party Competition, by Region, 1860-1994 (percent)

Region/office	1860-1895	1896-1931	1932-1965	1966-1994
New England				
President	85.2	85.5	53.7	61.9
Governor	74.3	85.5	63.1	51.7
U.S. representative	86.8	82.8	60.6	35.6
U.S. senator	[a]	83.3	65.1	48.2
Middle Atlantic				
President	38.9	88.9	47.2	60.7
Governor	34.9	66.7	51.4	51.6
U.S. representative	59.3	68.9	52.9	41.6
U.S. senator	[a]	76.9	57.7	59.0
Midwest				
President	77.8	84.4	44.4	77.1
Governor	78.8	78.9	46.9	75.0
U.S. representative	61.1	74.5	57.8	49.5
U.S. senator	[a]	83.3	50.8	38.5
Plains				
President	88.9	77.8	57.4	85.7
Governor	94.4	71.3	70.4	47.8
U.S. representative	88.6	84.2	76.4	59.5
U.S. senator	[a]	83.9	79.7	52.0
South				
President	18.4	6.1	15.8	71.4
Governor	21.2	4.2	0.0	43.5
U.S. representative	25.0	7.5	7.2	31.5
U.S. senator	[a]	0.0	1.5	52.6
Border South				
President	8.6	56.8	22.2	54.3
Governor	22.2	38.6	16.7	32.4
U.S. representative	19.4	36.5	18.7	28.6
U.S. senator	[a]	42.4	23.4	41.2
Rocky Mountain				
President	73.3	57.8	35.2	89.3
Governor	58.3	51.1	38.5	40.5
U.S. representative	70.0	67.6	30.3	58.6
U.S. senator	[a]	32.4	20.6	56.6
Pacific Coast				
President	75.0	75.0	37.5	68.6
Governor	47.4	70.8	59.4	44.7
U.S. representative	64.4	85.6	49.0	39.6
U.S. senator	[a]	73.7	44.4	50.0

Note: Table entries are the percentages of all elections won by Republicans. For composition of regions, see Appendix Table A-3.

[a] Direct election of U.S. senators began after passage of the Seventeenth Amendment in 1913.

Sources: Congressional Quarterly's Guide to U.S. Elections, 2d ed. (Washington, D.C.: Congressional Quarterly, 1985), 1118-1119; *Congressional Quarterly Weekly Report* (1988), 3245, 3264, 3269, 3298, (1990), 3802, 3828, 3840, (1992), 3557, 3571, 3599, (1994), 3236, 3232, 3250.

Table 4-4 Strength of Party Identification and the Presidential Vote, 1952-1992 (percent)

Year/candidate	Strong Democrat	Weak Democrat	Independent Democrat	Independent	Independent Republican	Weak Republican	Strong Republican	Total
1952								
Stevenson (D)	84	62	61	20	7	6	2	42
Eisenhower (R)	16	38	39	80	93	94	98	58
1956								
Stevenson (D)	85	63	67	17	6	7	0	40
Eisenhower (R)	15	37	33	83	94	93	100	60
1960								
Kennedy (D)	91	72	90	46	12	13	2	49
Nixon (R)	9	28	10	54	88	87	98	51
1964								
Johnson (D)	95	82	90	77	25	43	10	68
Goldwater (R)	5	18	10	23	75	57	90	32
1968								
Humphrey (D)	92	68	64	30	5	11	3	46
Nixon (R)	8	32	36	70	95	89	97	54
1972								
McGovern (D)	73	48	61	30	13	9	3	36
Nixon (R)	27	52	39	70	87	91	97	64
1976								
Carter (D)	92	75	76	44	14	22	3	51
Ford (R)	8	25	24	56	86	78	97	49
1980								
Carter (D)	89	65	60	26	13	5	5	44
Reagan (R)	11	35	40	74	87	95	95	56
1984								
Mondale (D)	89	68	79	28	7	6	3	42
Reagan (R)	11	32	21	72	93	94	97	58

1988								
Dukakis (D)	94	72	88	35	15	17	2	47
Bush (R)	6	28	12	65	85	83	98	53
1992								
Clinton (D)	97	84	92	65	15	20	3	58
Bush (R)	3	16	8	35	85	80	98	42

Note: "D" indicates Democrat; "R" indicates Republican. Results are from surveys in which voters are asked which party they identify with and who they voted for. The exact question is as follows: "Generally speaking, do you consider yourself a Republican, a Democrat, an Independent, or what?" If Republican or Democrat: "Would you consider yourself a strong (R/D) or a not very strong (R/D)?" If Independent or other: "Do you think of yourself as closer to the Republican or Democratic party?" Votes for candidates other than the Democrat or Republican were excluded.

Source: Calculated by the editors from National Election Studies data (Ann Arbor, Mich. Center for Political Studies, University of Michigan).

Table 4-5 Party-Line Voting in Presidential and Congressional Elections, 1952-1994 (percent)

Year	Presidential elections			U.S. Senate elections			U.S. House elections		
	Party-line voters[a]	Defectors[b]	Independents	Party-line voters[a]	Defectors[b]	Independents	Party-line voters[a]	Defectors[b]	Independents
1952	77	18	5	79	16	5	80	15	5
1956	76	15	9	80	12	8	82	9	9
1958				84	11	5	84	11	5
1960	79	13	8	79	12	9	80	11	8
1962				—	—	—	83	11	6
1964	79	15	5	78	16	6	79	15	5
1966				76	17	7	76	17	7
1968	69	24	7	73	20	7	74	19	7
1970				77	13	10	76	16	9
1972	67	25	8	69	22	9	74	17	8
1974				74	18	8	74	18	8
1976	73	16	11	69	19	12	72	19	9
1978				71	20	9	67	23	10
1980	68	24	8	71	21	8	69	23	8
1982				77	17	6	76	17	6
1984	79	13	8	72	20	9	70	23	7
1986				76	20	4	72	22	6
1988	81	12	7	72	20	7	74	19	7
1990				73	23	6	76	19	5
1992	68	24	9	74	20	7	71	21	7
1994				77	17	6	77	17	6

Note: "—" indicates not available. In presidential elections the base for percentages is all voters. In Senate and House elections the base for percentages is all voters supporting Democratic or Republican candidates.

[a] Democratic or Republican identifiers who vote for the candidate of their party. Party identification is based on surveys in which voters are asked which party they identify with. See Table 4-4 for question. "Independent partisans," or so-called "leaners," are included here as party-line voters or defectors.

[b] Democratic or Republican identifiers who do not vote for the candidate of their party.

Source: Calculated by the editors from National Election Studies data (Ann Arbor, Mich.: Center for Political Studies, University of Michigan).

Table 4-6 Partisan Division of Governors and State Legislatures

| | Governor | | | Legislature | | | | |
| | | | | Upper House | | Lower House | | |
State	Name	Party	Next up for election	Democrats	Republicans	Democrats	Republicans	Next up for election[a]
Alabama	Fob James Jr.	R[b]	1998	23	12	74	31	1995
Alaska	Tony Knowles	D[b]	1998	8	12	17	22[c]	1996
Arizona	Fife Symington	R	1998	11	19	22	38	1996
Arkansas	Jim Guy Tucker	D	1998	28	7	88	12	1996
California	Pete Wilson	R	1998	21	17[d]	39	40[c]	1996
Colorado	Roy Romer	D[b]	1998	16	19	24	41	1996
Connecticut	John G. Rowland	R[b]	1998	17	19	90	61	1996
Delaware	Thomas R. Carper	D	1996	12	9	14	27	1996
Florida	Lawton Chiles	D	1998	19	21	63	57	1996
Georgia	Zell Miller	D	1998	36	20	114	65	1996
Hawaii	Benjamin J. Cayetano	D	1998	23	2	44	7	1996
Idaho	Phil Batt	R[b]	1998	8	27	13	5	1996
Illinois	Jim Edgar	R	1998	26	33	54	6	1996
Indiana	Evan Bayh	D	1996	20	30	44	56	1996
Iowa	Terry E. Branstad	R	1998	27	23	36	64	1996
Kansas	Bill Graves	R[b]	1998	13	27	45	80	1996
Kentucky	Brereton Jones	D	1998	21	17	64	36	1996
Louisiana	Edwin Edwards	D	1995	33	6	86	17	1995
Maine	Angus King	I[b]	1998	16	18[c]	77	74	1996
Maryland	Parris Glendening	D	1998	32	15	100	41	1998
Massachusetts	William F. Weld	R	1998	30	10	125	34	1996
Michigan	John Engler	R	1998	16	22	53	55	1996

(Table continues)

Table 4-6 (Continued)

| | Governor | | | Legislature | | | | |
| | | | | Upper House | | Lower House | | |
State	Name	Party	Next up for election	Democrats	Republicans	Democrats	Republicans	Next up for election[a]
Minnesota	Arne Carlson	R	1998	43	21	71	63	1996
Mississippi	Kirk Fordice	R	1995	36	14	89	31[d]	1995
Missouri	Mel Carnahan	D	1996	19	15	87	76	1996
Montana	Mark Racicot	R	1996	19	31	33	67	1996
Nebraska	Ben Nelson	D	1998	e	e	e	e	1996
Nevada	Bob Miller	D	1998	8	13	21	21	1996
New Hampshire	Stephen Merrill	R	1996	6	18	112	288[d]	1996
New Jersey	Christine Todd Whitman	R[b]	1997	16	24	28	52	1995
New Mexico	Gary E. Johnson	R[b]	1998	27	15	46	24	1996
New York	George E. Pataki	R[b]	1998	25	36	94	56	1996
North Carolina	James B. Hunt Jr.	D	1996	26	24	52	68	1996
North Dakota	Edward T. Schafer	R	1996	20	29	23	75	1996
Ohio	George V. Voinovich	R	1998	13	20	43	56	1996
Oklahoma	Frank Keating	R[b]	1998	35	13	65	36	1996
Oregon	John Kitzhaber	D	1998	11	19	26	34	1996
Pennsylvania	Tom Ridge	R[b]	1998	21	29	101	102	1996
Rhode Island	Lincoln C. Almond	R[b]	1998	40	10	84	16	1996
South Carolina	David Beasley	R	1998	29	17	58	62[f]	1996
South Dakota	William J. Janklow	R	1998	16	19	24	46	1996
Tennessee	Don Sundquist	R[b]	1998	18	15	59	40	1996
Texas	George W. Bush	R[b]	1998	17	14	89	61	1996
Utah	Michael O. Leavitt	R	1996	10	19	20	55	1996
Vermont	Howard Dean	D	1996	12	18	86	61[g]	1996
Virginia	George F. Allen	R[b]	1997	22	18	52	47[c]	1995

Washington	Mike Lowry	D	1996	25	24	38	60	1996
West Virginia	Gaston Caperton	D	1996	26	8	69	30	1996
Wisconsin	Tommy G. Thompson	R	1998	16	17	48	51	1996
Wyoming	Jim Geringer	R[b]	1998	10	20	13	47	1996
Total				1,022	905	2,817	2,604	

Note: As of December 7, 1994. Legislative divisions reflect seated members; some vacancies exist.

[a] Only some members may be up for reelection.
[b] Change in party control from previous election
[c] One independent.
[d] Two independents
[e] Nebraska's forty-nine member state legislature is nonpartisan and unicameral.
[f] Four independents.
[G] Three independents.

Sources: Governors: Congressional Quarterly Weekly Report (1994), 3250; state legislative divisions: National Conference of State Legislatures; legislature next up for reelection: Council of State Governments, *Book of the States, 1994-1995* (Lexington, Ky: Council of State Governments, 1994), 269-272.

Table 4-7   Split-Ticket Voting, 1952-1994 (percent)

Year	President-House	Senate-House	State-local
1952	13	9	26
1956	16	10	29
1958		10	31
1960	14	9	27
1962		—	42
1964	14	18	41
1966		21	50
1968	17	21	47
1970		20	51
1972	30	22	58
1974		24	61
1976	25	23	—
1978		35	—
1980	28	31	59
1982		24	55
1984	25	20	52
1986		28	—
1988	25	27	—
1990		25	—
1992	22	25	—
1994		24	—

Note: "—" indicates not available. Entries are the percentages of voters who "split" their ticket by supporting candidates of different parties for the offices indicated. Those who cast ballots for other than Democratic and Republican candidates are excluded in presidential and congressional calculations. The state-local figure is based on a general question: "Did you vote for other state and local offices? Did you vote a straight ticket, or did you vote for candidates from different parties?"

Source: Calculated by the editors from National Election Studies data (Ann Arbor, Mich.: Center for Political Studies, University of Michigan).

Table 4-8   Split District Outcomes: Presidential and House Voting,
1900-1992

Year	Total number of districts[a]	Number of districts with split results[b]	Percentage of total
1900	295	10	3.4
1904	310	5	1.6
1908	314	21	6.7
1912	333	84	25.2
1916	333	35	10.5
1920	344	11	3.2
1924	356	42	11.8
1928	359	68	18.9
1932	355	50	14.1
1936	361	51	14.1
1940	362	53	14.6
1944	367	41	11.2
1948	422	90	21.3
1952	435	84	19.3
1956	435	130	29.9
1960	437	114	26.1
1964	435	145	33.3
1968	435	139	32.0
1972	435	192	44.1
1976	435	124	28.5
1980	435	143	32.8
1984	435	196	45.0
1988	435	148	34.0
1992	435	100	23.0

[a] Before 1952 complete data are not available on every congressional district.
[b] Congressional districts carried by a presidential candidate of one party and a House candidate of another party.

Source: Norman J. Ornstein et al., eds., *Vital Statistics on Congress, 1993-1994* (Washington, D.C.: Congressional Quarterly, 1994), 64.

Table 4-9   Presidential Primaries, 1912-1992

	Democratic party			Republican party		
Year	Number of primaries	Votes cast	Percentage of delegates from primary "states"[a]	Number of primaries	Votes cast	Percentage of delegates from primary "states"[a]
1912	12	974,775	32.9	13	2,261,240	41.7
1916	20	1,187,691	53.5	20	1,923,374	58.9
1920	16	571,671	44.6	20	3,186,248	57.8
1924	14	763,858	35.5	17	3,525,185	45.3
1928	17	1,264,220	42.2	16	4,110,288	44.9
1932	16	2,952,933	40.0	14	2,346,996	37.7
1936	14	5,181,808	36.5	12	3,319,810	37.5
1940	13	4,468,631	35.8	13	3,227,875	38.8
1944	14	1,867,609	36.7	13	2,271,605	38.7
1948	14	2,151,865	36.3	12	2,635,255	36.0
1952	16	4,928,006	39.2	13	7,801,413	39.0
1956	19	5,832,592	41.3	19	5,828,272	43.5
1960	16	5,686,664	38.4	15	5,537,967	38.6
1964	16	6,247,435	41.4	17	5,935,339	45.6
1968	17	7,535,069	48.7	17	4,473,551	47.0
1972	23	15,993,965	66.5	22	6,188,281	58.2
1976	30	16,052,652	76.1	29	10,374,125	70.4
1980	35	18,747,825	81.1	36	12,690,451	78.0
1984	30	18,009,217	67.1	29	6,575,651	66.6
1988	37	23,230,525	81.4	38	12,169,003	80.7
1992	40	20,179,973	88.0	39	13,025,824	85.4

Note: Primaries include binding and nonbinding presidential preference primaries as well as primaries selecting national convention delegates only without indication of presidential preference. Prior to 1980, votes cast in the delegate-only primaries are not included in the total votes cast.

[a] "States" include all jurisdictions having delegates.

Sources: 1936 Democratic delegates: Democratic National Committee; 1964 Democratic delegates: *Congressional Quarterly Weekly Report* (1964), 1140; votes cast, number of primaries, and remaining delegates: Congressional Quarterly, *Congressional Quarterly's Guide to U.S. Elections*, 2d ed. (Washington, D.C.: Congressional Quarterly, 1985), 188-221, 387-441; 1988: *Congressional Quarterly Weekly Report* (1987), 1988, (1988), 1892, 1894-1897, 2033, 2254-2255; 1992: Congressional Quarterly, *Guide to the 1992 Democratic National Convention* (Washington, D.C.: Congressional Quarterly, 1992), 69-71, 82, and *Guide to the 1992 Republican National Convention* (Washington, D.C.: Congressional Quarterly, 1992), 63, 67, 78.

Table 4-10 Profile of National Convention Delegates, 1944-1992 (percent)

	1944 D	1944 R	1968 D	1968 R	1972 D	1972 R	1976 D	1976 R	1980 D	1980 R	1984 D	1984 R	1988 D	1988 R	1992 D	1992 R
Women	11	9	13	16	40	29	33	31	49	29	49	44	48	33	50	43
Black	—	—	5	2	15	4	11	3	15	3	18	4	23	4	18	5
Under thirty	—	—	3	4	22	8	15	7	11	5	8	4	4	3	5	—
Lawyer	38	37	28	22	12	—	16	15	13	15	17	14	16	17	12	—
Teacher	—	—	8	2	11	—	12	4	15	4	16	6	14	5	9	—
Union member	—	—	—	—	16	—	21	3	27	4	25	4	25	3	28	—
Attending first convention	63	63	67	66	83	78	80	78	87	84	78	69	65	68	62	—
Protestant	—	—	—	—	42	—	47	73	47	72	49	71	50	69	49	—
Catholic	—	—	—	—	26	—	34	18	37	22	29	22	30	22	31	32
Jewish	—	—	—	—	9	—	9	3	8	3	8	2	7	2	9	—
Liberal	—	—	—	—	—	—	40	3	46	2	48	1	43	0	47	1
Moderate	—	—	—	—	—	—	47	45	42	36	42	35	43	35	44	32
Conservative	—	—	—	—	—	—	8	48	6	58	4	60	5	58	5	63
Median age	—	—	49	49	42	—	43	48	44	49	43	51	46	51	46	—

Note: "D" indicates Democrat; "R" indicates Republican; "—" indicates not available.

Sources: 1944: Barbara Farah, "Delegate Polls: 1944-1984," *Public Opinion* (August/September 1984): 43-45; 1968-1988: Martin Plissner and Warren J. Mitofsky, "The Making of the Delegates, 1968-1988," *Public Opinion* (September/October 1988): 47 (reprinted with permission of the American Enterprise Institute for Public Policy Research); 1992 (ideology, Democratic): *"The New York Times* Democratic Delegate Poll"; 1992 (other Democratic): *"New York Newsday* Democratic Delegate Survey"; 1992 (Republican): Martin Plissner, "The 1992 Republican Convention Delegates," CBS News.

Table 4-11   Location and Size of National Party Conventions, 1932-1992

	Democrats		Republicans	
Year	Location	Delegate votes	Location	Delegate votes
1932	Chicago	1,154	Chicago	1,154
1936	Philadelphia	1,100	Cleveland	1,003
1940	Chicago	1,100	Philadelphia	1,000
1944	Chicago	1,176	Chicago	1,056
1948	Philadelphia	1,234	Philadelphia	1,094
1952	Chicago	1,230	Chicago	1,206
1956	Chicago	1,372	San Francisco	1,323
1960	Los Angeles	1,521	Chicago	1,331
1964	Atlantic City	2,316	San Francisco	1,308
1968	Chicago	2,622	Miami Beach	1,333
1972	Miami Beach	3,016	Miami Beach	1,348
1976	New York	3,008	Kansas City	2,259
1980	New York	3,331	Detroit	1,994
1984	San Francisco	3,933	Dallas	2,235
1988	Atlanta	4,161	New Orleans	2,277
1992	New York	4,288	Houston	2,210

Note: The number of delegates (persons attending) may be larger because of fractional votes.

Sources: Location (1932-1984), delegate votes (Democrats, 1932, 1940-1984): Congressional Quarterly, *Congressional Quarterly's Guide to U.S. Elections,* 2d ed. (Washington, D.C.: Congressional Quarterly, 1985), 16-17, 115, 198-221; location (Democrats, 1988, 1992), delegate votes (Democrats, 1936, 1988): Democratic National Committee; delegate votes (Democrats, 1992): *Congressional Quarterly Weekly Report* (1992), 2220; location (Republicans, 1988, 1992), delegate votes (Republicans, 1932-1988): Republican National Committee; delegate votes (Republicans, 1992): *Congressional Quarterly Weekly Report* (1992), 2582.

Table 4-12 Financial Activity of the National Political Parties, 1983-1994 (millions of current dollars)

Party	1983-1984	1985-1986	1987-1988	1989-1990	1991-1992	1993-1994
Democrat						
Raised	$84.4	$57.0	$116.1	$76.9	$162.2	$131.3
Spent	83.7	57.8	109.9	81.6	156.8	129.7
Contributions	2.6	1.7	1.8	1.5	2.0	2.2
Coordinated expenditures[a]	9.0	9.0	17.9	8.7	28.0	21.1
Republican						
Raised	289.0	255.2	257.5	206.4	254.8	245.6
Spent	291.9	255.8	251.4	213.5	246.4	234.7
Contributions	4.9	3.4	3.4	2.9	3.0	2.8
Coordinated expenditures[a]	20.1	14.3	22.7	10.7	33.8	20.4

Note: Building funds and state and local election spending are not reported to the Federal Election Commission.

[a] Party committees are also allowed to spend money on behalf of federal candidates, in addition to the money party committees may contribute directly. This spending may be coordinated with a candidate.

Source: Federal Election Commission, "FEC Reports on Political Party Activity for 1993-94," April 1995, 6-7.

Table 4-13   Party Contributions and Coordinated Expenditures, by
Office and Party, 1975-1994

Year/party	Senate		House	
	Contributions	Expenditures	Contributions	Expenditures
1975-1976				
Democrats	$468,795	$4,359	$1,465,629	$500
Republicans	930,034	113,976	3,658,310	329,583
1977-1978				
Democrats	466,683	229,218	1,262,298	72,892
Republicans	703,204	2,723,880	3,621,104	1,297,079
1979-1980				
Democrats	480,464	1,132,912	1,025,989	256,346
Republicans	677,004	5,434,758	3,498,323	2,203,748
1981-1982				
Democrats	579,337	2,265,197	1,052,286	694,321
Republicans	600,221	8,715,761	4,720,959	5,293,260
1983-1984				
Democrats	441,467	3,947,731	1,280,672	1,774,452
Republicans	590,922	6,518,415	4,060,120	6,190,309
1985-1986				
Democrats	583,305	6,066,372	610,840	1,545,376
Republicans	629,472	9,959,330	1,655,250	4,098,389
1987-1988				
Democrats	488,899	6,592,264	1,197,537	2,880,301
Republicans	721,237	10,260,600	2,650,569	4,162,644
1989-1990				
Democrats	515,332	5,210,002	943,135	3,401,579
Republicans	862,621	7,725,853	2,019,279	3,012,313
1991-1992				
Democrats	689,953	11,915,878	1,234,593	5,883,678
Republicans	807,397	16,509,940	2,197,611	6,906,729
1993-1994				
Democrats	638,618	13,204,309	1,501,220	8,455,070
Republicans	748,011	11,561,866	2,036,712	8,851,875

Note: Includes direct contributions made by party committees to congressional candidates and coordinated expenditures made on their behalf. In current dollars.

Sources: 1975-1984: Norman J. Ornstein et al., eds., *Vital Statistics on Congress, 1987-1988,* (Washington, D.C.: Congressional Quarterly, 1987), 102; 1985-1994: Federal Election Commission, press releases.

5

Public Opinion

Public opinion data are everywhere. They are perhaps most prominent in preelection polls showing who is ahead and who is behind, but they are more important and more often used as guides by candidates and officeholders about what the public thinks and how it would react to changes in public policies. Surveys are also used, in a more partisan way, by politicians, journalists, and interest groups to support their positions. And, in a slightly different form, they are even more widely used by advertisers and manufacturers to gauge consumer reactions to new products and services. Reflecting this frequent and varied use, this book is interspersed with public opinion data. The present chapter includes what might be called general perspectives on public opinion.

Figures 5-1 through 5-3 and Tables 5-1 through 5-3 cover two of the most frequently cited components of public opinion—partisanship and political ideology. These characteristics merit emphasis due to their practical political significance. They are of interest not only to those who wish to understand scientifically why people behave as they do. They also attract the attention of those who analyze long-term political and social trends, and are of intense interest to those who track day-to-day politics.

From another perspective, these results are important because they illustrate the reliability and validity of public opinion polling as well as the hazards of gauging personal opinions. Figures 5-1 and 5-2, showing self-proclaimed party identification, are reasonably similar for the period they jointly cover. If public opinion data were totally unreliable, as some contend, such similarity would be unlikely. Moreover, these figures illustrate two aspects of reliability and validity. First, polling as few as fifteen hundred people tells something very real about the entire population; two separate organizations, as represented in Figures 5-1 and 5-2, would not obtain such similarity over several decades of interviewing if the **143** results represented only those actually interviewed. (Of course, one must choose the fifteen hundred respondents according to scientific sampling procedures, as do all the major polling organizations.) Second, poll results are not completely dependent on exact question wording. The Gallup question focuses on the immediate situation ("In politics, as of today. . . ."), while the National Election Studies question is broader ("Generally speaking. . . ."), suggesting that the Gallup question might pick up more short-term fluctuations in partisanship. Yet the results are somewhat similar.

At the same time, differences between the two series indicate that we cannot consider one a mere clone of the other. The National Election Studies surveys probe those who claim to be independents to determine whether they lean toward one party or the other. The responses to this probe as well as other evidence (Table 4-4) raise the question of whether independents are really closet partisans. How we answer that question, as the contrast between the two plots in Figure 5-1 shows, has major implications for conclusions about the relative strengths of the parties. As has been emphasized in earlier introductions, even simple data descriptions involve interpretation.

Because surveys are not exact counts of the whole population, "sampling error" is often reported to convey the range within which the true population result lies. For example, results are said to be accurate to within plus or minus 3 percent. Yet even with greater precision (achieved by increasing the size of the sample), survey results still require interpretation. Suppose one could ask every American adult simultaneously whether he or she was a Democrat, an independent, or a Republican. There would then be no sampling error; because everyone was asked, the information would describe the entire U.S. population at that particular time. But that returns us to an equally vexing question: What does it mean to be an independent?

The "don't know" and "no opinion" responses to the ideology question about liberal or conservative self-identification in Table 5-3—and in the other public opinion tables—illustrate a similar point. Whether pollsters ask about a general position or a specific issue, some proportion of the sample—often as many as 15 percent and sometimes many more—respond "don't know." It is not immediately apparent how to interpret such responses; some people have information about the subject matter but no opinion, some have no information and no opinion, and a few have no information but have an opinion anyway—and the pollster's decision about how to treat such responses can make a large difference. For example, in a preelection poll, should a pollster assume that those who have not yet chosen whom to support will eventually (1) split votes between candidates in similar proportions as those who have already decided, (2) not vote, (3) divide evenly between the candidates, or (4) overwhelmingly support a particular candidate?

For public officials seeking guidance on public sentiment, no simple reading suffices because they must assess intensity as well as direction. Those seeking a theoretical understanding of politics face the same problem. For example, although more than public opinion accounted for the outcome, consider the Senate rejection of Judge Robert Bork's nomination to the Supreme Court (Table 9-4). Polls showed the public almost evenly divided on the matter, with a slight edge to those opposing the nomination. Such a close balance was misleading. Deeper political meaning turned on the intensity of those views. One senator said, "If you vote against Bork, those in favor of him will be mad at you for a week. But if you vote for him, those who don't like him will be mad at you for the rest of their lives." Understanding the importance of public opinion in politics requires more than a simple nose count. The salience of an opinion to the person holding it also counts.

In addition, a particular survey result usually tells little in isolation. The soundest interpretations depend upon several surveys stretching over time, often over a period of years. Consider the decline and partial recovery in public confidence in government (Figure 5-9). The confidence level at a particular time is a mere point, difficult or impossible to interpret. That point, when viewed with comparable points from similar surveys over the years, indicates a trend—decline, upsurge, constancy, whatever. Consequently, reports of public opinion increasingly emphasize long time series, as we do here and in other chapters (Figures 5-4 through 5-8). Such time series data can be usefully supplemented by cross-sections (Table 5-2); such within-survey contrasts convey whether and how groups differ in attitudes.

A final note. Even a firm understanding of public opinion can be contradicted by events, as one cannot blindly equate opinion with behavior. The growth of racial tolerance in the South, such as it is, is a telling counterpoint to a political atmosphere formerly committed to white supremacy. As one respondent, a segregationist, told a pollster in the mid-1960s: "You asked me what I favored, not what I will accept graciously, not what I thought was right."[1]

Notes

1. Donald R. Matthews and James W. Prothro, *Negroes and the New Southern Politics* (New York: Harcourt, Brace & World, 1966), 363.

Table 5-1 Partisan Identification, National Election Studies, 1952-1994 (percent)

Year	Democrat			Inde-pen-dent	Republican			Apo-litical	Total	Number of inter-views
	Strong	Weak	Inde-pendent		Inde-pendent	Weak	Strong			
1952	22	25	10	6	7	14	14	3	101	1,784
1954	22	25	9	7	6	14	13	4	100	1,130
1956	21	23	6	9	8	14	15	4	100	1,757
1958	27	22	7	7	5	17	11	4	100	1,808
1960	20	25	6	10	7	14	16	2	100	1,911
1962	23	23	7	8	6	16	12	4	99	1,287
1964	27	25	9	8	6	14	11	1	101	1,550
1966	18	28	9	12	7	15	10	1	100	1,278
1968	20	25	10	11	9	15	10	1	101	1,553
1970	20	24	10	13	8	15	9	1	100	1,501
1972	15	26	11	13	10	13	10	1	99	2,694
1974	17	21	13	15	9	14	8	3	100	2,505
1976	15	25	12	15	10	14	9	1	101	2,850
1978	15	24	14	14	10	13	8	3	101	2,283
1980	18	23	11	13	10	14	9	2	100	1,613
1982	20	24	11	11	8	14	10	2	100	1,418
1984	17	20	11	11	12	15	12	2	100	2,236
1986	18	22	10	12	11	15	10	2	100	2,166
1988	17	18	12	11	13	14	14	2	101	2,032
1990	20	19	12	11	12	15	10	2	101	1,991
1992	17	18	14	12	13	15	11	1	101	2,487
1994	15	19	13	10	12	15	16	1	101	1,795

Note: Question: "Generally speaking, do you consider yourself a Republican, a Democrat, an Independent, or what?" If Republican or Democrat: "Would you call yourself a strong (R/D) or a not very strong (R/D)?" If Independent or other: "Do you think of yourself as closer to the Republican or Democratic party?"

Source: Calculated by the editors from National Election Studies data (Ann Arbor, Mich.: Center for Political Studies, University of Michigan).

Figure 5-1   Partisan Identification, National Election Studies, 1952-1994

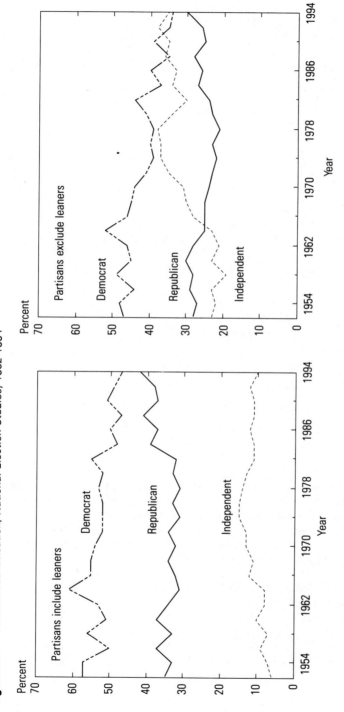

Note: See Table 5-1 for question. "Leaners" are independents who consider themselves closer to one party.

Source: Calculated by the editors from National Election Studies codebooks and data sets.

Figure 5-2   Partisan Identification, Gallup Poll, 1937-1995

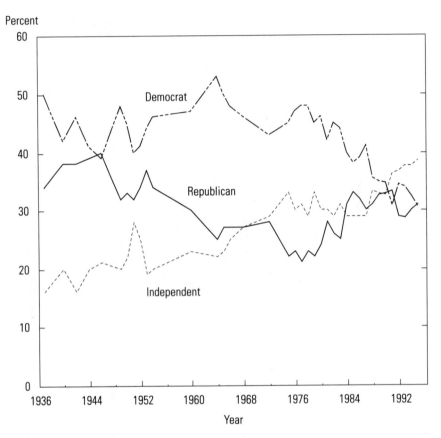

Note: Respondents who gave replies other than Democrat, Republican, or Independent are excluded. Question: "In politics, as of today, do you consider yourself a Republican, a Democrat, or an Independent?" Data from 1988 and later are from telephone surveys, which tend to report more Republican and fewer Democratic partisans than in-person interviews. See Larry Hugick, "Party Identification: The Disparity between Gallup's In-person and Telephone Interview Findings," *Public Perspective,* September/October 1991, 23-24.

Sources: The Gallup Organization, "The Gallup Poll Party ID Trend to 1937," no date; and unpublished data from the Gallup Poll.

Table 5-2   Partisan Identification, Gallup Poll, Cross-Section, 1995 (percent)

	Republican	Independent	Democrat
Gender			
Men	35	37	28
Women	30	34	36
Age			
18-29	34	42	24
30-49	33	35	33
50 and over	31	33	36
Race			
White	37	35	29
Black	5	38	57
Education			
No college	28	39	33
College incomplete	35	34	31
College graduate	38	31	31
Post graduate	34	35	31
Household income			
Under $20,000	17	45	38
$20,000-29,999	36	29	35
$30,000-49,999	33	36	31
$50,000 and over	44	31	25
Religious preference			
Protestant	40	33	27
Catholic	25	41	34
Jewish	29	21	50
None	23	52	26
Region[a]			
East	32	40	29
Midwest	30	39	32
South	34	34	32
West	34	30	36
National	32	36	32

Note: Question: "In politics, as of today, do you consider yourself a Republican, a Democrat, or an Independent?" Data on partisanship by religious preference are from a December 1994 Gallup survey. The other data are from an April 1995 Gallup Survey.

[a] For composition of regions, see the Appendix, Table A-2.

Sources: Unpublished data from the Gallup Poll.

Table 5-3   Liberal or Conservative Self-Identification, 1973-1994 (percent)

Date	Extremely liberal	Liberal	Slightly liberal	Moderate	Slightly conservative	Conservative	Extremely conservative	Don't know	Number of interviews
March 1973	4	14	13	36	13	13	3	6	1,484
March 1974	1	14	14	38	15	11	2	5	1,480
March 1975	3	12	13	38	16	10	2	5	1,478
March 1976	2	13	12	37	15	13	2	6	1,494
March 1977	2	11	14	37	16	12	3	5	1,524
March 1978	1	9	16	36	17	12	2	5	1,505
March 1980	2	8	14	40	18	12	3	2	1,451
March 1982	2	9	15	39	14	13	4	4	1,495
March 1983	2	8	12	40	18	13	2	4	801
March 1984	2	9	12	39	19	13	3	4	1,462
March 1985	2	11	11	37	18	14	3	4	1,525
March 1986	2	9	12	39	16	14	3	5	1,468
March 1987	2	12	13	37	16	12	2	4	1,437
March 1988	2	12	13	35	17	15	2	4	1,472
March 1989	3	12	12	37	16	13	2	6	1,530
March 1990	3	10	13	35	18	14	4	4	1,368
March 1991	2	10	14	39	14	14	3	4	1,513
March 1993	2	11	13	36	17	16	3	3	1,597
March 1994	2	11	13	35	16	16	3	3	2,980

Note: Question: "We hear a lot of talk these days about liberals and conservatives. I'm going to show you a seven-point scale on which the political views that people might hold are arranged from extremely liberal—point 1—to extremely conservative—point 7. Where would you place yourself on this scale?"

Source: General Social Survey, National Opinion Research Center, University of Chicago.

Figure 5-3   Ideological Self-Identification of College Freshmen, 1970-1994

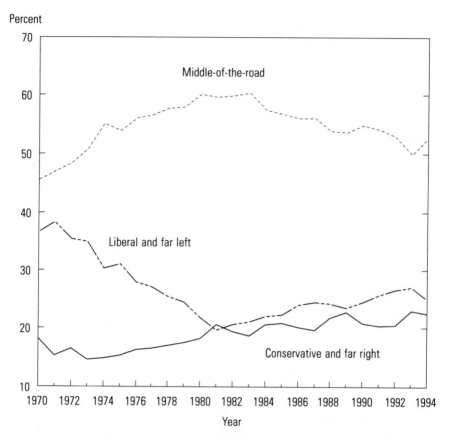

Note: Question: "How would you characterize your political views? Mark one: Far left, liberal, middle-of-the-road, conservative, far right."

Sources: Eric Dey, Alexander Astin, and William Korn, *The American Freshman: Twenty-five Year Trends* (Los Angeles: Higher Education Research Institute, University of California, Los Angeles, 1991); *The American Freshman: National Norms for Fall 1991* (Los Angeles: Higher Education Research Institute, University of California, Los Angeles, 1991); *Fall 1992* (1992); Fall 1993 (1993); *Fall 1994* (1994).

Figure 5-4 The Most Important Problem: Domestic or Foreign, 1947-1995

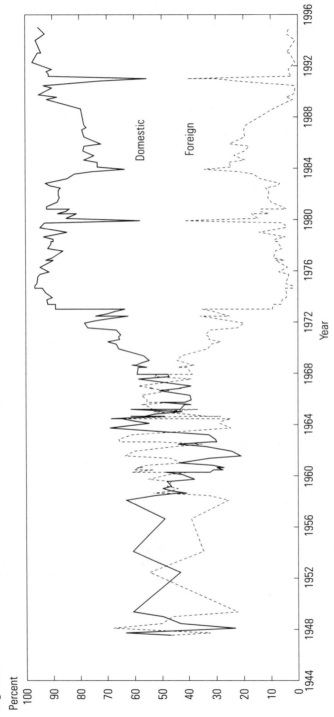

Note: Typical question: "What do you think is the most important problem facing this country today?"

Sources: Gallup polls as reported in Tom W. Smith, "The Polls: America's Most Important Problems," *Public Opinion Quarterly* 49 (1985): 268-274; data updated by the editors from *The Gallup Report,* July 1984, 17, December 1985, 13, September 1986, 29, May 1987, 7; The Gallup Poll, "Republicans Gain on Issue Barometers," press release, September 28, 1988, 1; *The Gallup Poll News Service,* July 25, 1990; and unpublished data from the Gallup Poll.

153

Figure 5-5 The Most Important Problem: Civil Rights, Drugs, Economics, and Vietnam, 1947-1995

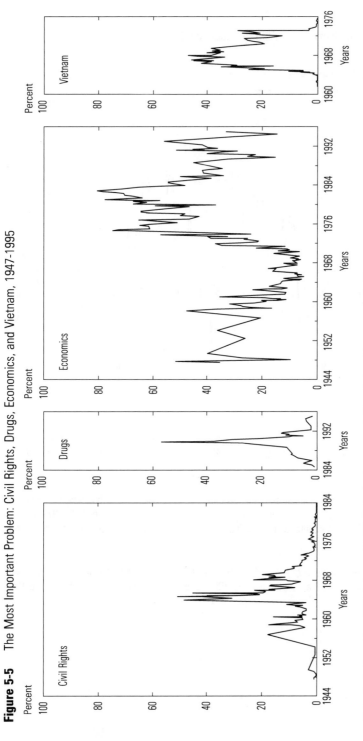

Note: Typical question: "What do you think is the most important problem facing this country today?"

Sources: Gallup polls as reported in Tom W. Smith, "The Polls: America's Most Important Problems," *Public Opinion Quarterly* 49 (1985): 268-274; data calculated by the editors from *The Gallup Report,* July 1984, 17, December 1985, 13, September 1986, 29, May 1987, 7; The Gallup Poll, "Republicans Gain on Issue Barometers," press release, September 28, 1988, 1; *The Gallup Poll Newsletter,* July 25, 1990, 2; and unpublished data from the Gallup Poll.

Figure 5-6 The Party Better Able to Handle the Most Important Problem, 1945-1995

Democratic advantage (percent)

Year

Note: Question: "Which political party do you think can do a better job of handling the problems you have just mentioned—the Republican party or the Democratic party?" "Democratic advantage" is the percentage responding Democratic minus the percentage responding Republican.

Sources: The Gallup Report, May 1987, 9; The Gallup Poll, "Republicans Gain on Issue Barometers," press release, September 28, 1988; and unpublished data from the Gallup Poll.

Figure 5-7   The Party More Likely to Keep the United States Out of War, 1951-1994

Democratic advantage (percent)

Note: Question: "Looking ahead for the next few years, which political party would be more likely to keep the United States out of World War III—the Republican or the Democratic party?" In 1992 and subsequent years the question phrasing was "keep the country out of war." "Democratic advantage" is the percentage responding Democratic minus the percentage responding Republican.

Sources: The Gallup Report, October 1988, 5; *The Gallup Poll News Service,* vol. 55, no. 18, September 12, 1990, 2; *The Gallup Poll Monthly,* July 1992, 47; and unpublished data from the Gallup Poll.

Figure 5-8   The Party Better Able to Keep the United States Prosperous, 1951-1994

Democratic advantage (percent)

Year

Note: Question: "Which political party—the Republican or the Democratic party—would do a better job of keeping the country prosperous?" "Democratic advantage" is the percentage responding Democratic minus the percentage responding Republican.

Sources: The Gallup Report, October 1988, 5; *The Gallup Poll News Service,* vol. 55, no. 18, September 12, 1990, 1; and unpublished data from the Gallup Poll.

Figure 5-9   Individual Confidence in Government, 1952-1994

Percentage difference index

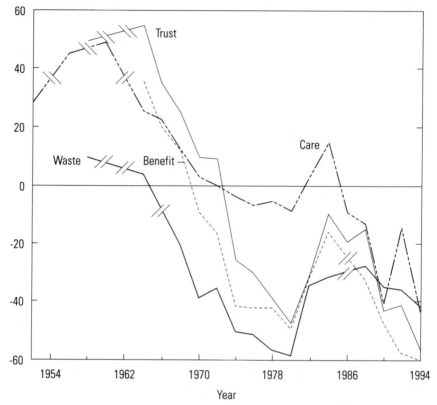

Note: Broken line indicates question not asked that year in the biennial National Election Study. Questions: (Care) "I don't think public officials care much about what people like me think." (Trust) "How much of the time do you think you can trust the government in Washington to do what is right—just about always, most of the time, or only some of the time?" (Benefit) "Would you say the government is pretty much run by a few big interests looking out for themselves or that it is run for the benefit of all people?" (Waste) "Do you think that people in the government waste a lot of money we pay in taxes, waste some of it, or don't waste very much of it?" The percentage difference index is calculated by subtracting the percentage giving a trusting response from the percentage giving a cynical response.

Source: Calculated by the editors from National Election Studies codebooks and data sets.

Figure 5-10   Satisfaction with "The Way Things Are," 1979-1995

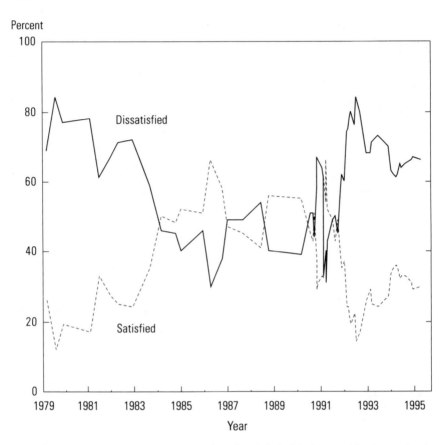

Note: Question: "In general, are you satisfied or dissatisfied with the way things are going in the United States at this time?"

Sources: The Gallup Poll News Service, vol. 55, no. 12, July 25, 1990, 3; and unpublished data from the Gallup Poll.

6

Interest Groups

When people think about interest groups, they think about dollars. Not surprisingly, then, most of the information in this chapter and in related tables in other chapters is about money—who gives it, who spends it, who regulates it, and what effect it has. Even more surprising is the huge quantity of information available, which results chiefly from the large number of elections in the United States and the collection and publication of data about them. For example, the most recent campaign expenditures are shown for all 435 representatives and 100 senators (Tables 7-15 and 7-16), as well as the amounts of money spent by individual presidential candidates (Table 8-5), and more aggregated information about expenditures by congressional candidates (Table 7-7). The present chapter concentrates on the sources of these funds, especially on funds derived from organized groups.

One could, in fact, easily be inundated by numbers relating to organized interests. The publications of the Federal Election Commission (FEC) alone run to multiple volumes every two years, with detailed accountings of receipts and expenditures of candidates in federal elections. More volumes are produced, though inconsistently and much less systematically, by various state agencies. Because such information is so voluminous, it is often summarized as it is here: how much money was contributed to incumbents versus challengers in congressional campaigns (Table 7-7), how much was spent by various types of political action committees (PACs) (Table 6-4), which are the biggest interest organizations (Table 6-12), and so on.

However, this wealth of information has not been collected for many U.S. elections. The FEC only began operations in the mid-1970s. Although there were studies of campaign costs before then, present time series are often limited to a span of no more than twenty years. In addition, laws **159** regulating campaign contributions, expenditures, and interest groups' activities change so frequently that long time series are often unobtainable and would be misleading if they could be compiled. For example, the growth of PACs dates from 1974 because changes in the laws at that time allowed their establishment (Table 6-1).

Concern about money is not limited to the sums spent by candidates. Indeed, there is probably more concern over interest group spending and about where candidates' funds come from and what, if anything, that money buys. Fortunately, data are increasingly available on interest group finances and on candidates' fund raising as well as expenditures. Much of the data concern PACs, the dominant organizations through which interest groups raise and spend money. The primary information is about general categories of PACs (Tables 6-1, 6-4, 6-5, and 6-7); a list of PACs illustrates the variety of organizations that fall into these categories (Table 6-2).

Because money is at the heart of interest group activities, matters of campaign finance law are directly relevant in this chapter. At the federal level these regulations consist mainly of fairly straightforward contribution limits (Table 6-8). At the state level, there is a myriad of contribution and expenditure limits (Tables 6-9 and 6-10).

Not all questions about interest groups involve money. Some other aspects of interest group activity that can be quantified are reflected in this volume, such as the growth and decline of labor unions (Table 6-11). For example, several interest groups rate members of Congress on how favorable their votes were to the groups' interests. A number of recent ratings of each representative and senator are provided in Tables 7-15 and 7-16.

Another perennial question about interest groups concerns those that work in the presumed "public interest." A listing of the types of such groups and of information about specific organizations (Table 6-12) provides some insight into the variety of organized interests and of their support throughout the country.

For obvious reasons no one is able to collect systematically what would surely be the most captivating data on the activities of organized interests, that is, bribes, threats, blackmail, and so forth. But political analysts now have a larger body of material on interest groups than ever before. Although much of this information is buried in hard-to-digest volumes on campaign contributions and spending or in seemingly bland lists showing what interests are represented, the data provide more knowledge and more research capabilities than ever before about the scope and potential influence of organized interests.

Table 6-1   Number of Political Action Committees (PACs), 1974-1995

Date	Corpor-ate	Labor	Trade/member-ship/health	Cooper-ative	Corpor-ation without stock	Noncon-nected[b]	Total
			Connected[a]				
December 31, 1974	89	201	318	—	—	—	608
November 24, 1975	139	226	357	—	—	—	722
May 10, 1976	294	246	452	—	—	—	992
December 31, 1976	433	224	489	—	—	—	1,146
December 31, 1977	550	234	438	8	20	110	1,360
December 31, 1978	785	217	453	12	24	162	1,653
August, 1979	885	226	483	13	27	206	1,840
December 31, 1979	950	240	514	17	32	247	2,000
July 1, 1980	1,107	255	544	23	41	309	2,279
December 31, 1980	1,206	297	576	42	56	374	2,551
July 1, 1981	1,253	303	579	38	64	441	2,678
December 31, 1981	1,329	318	614	41	68	531	2,901
July 1, 1982	1,417	350	627	45	82	628	3,149
December 31, 1982	1,469	380	649	47	103	723	3,371
July 1, 1983	1,514	379	664	50	114	740	3,461
December 31, 1983	1,538	378	643	51	122	793	3,525
July 1, 1984	1,642	381	662	53	125	940	3,803
December 31, 1984	1,682	394	698	52	130	1,053	4,009
July 1, 1985	1,687	393	694	54	133	1,039	4,000
December 31, 1985	1,710	388	695	54	142	1,003	3,992
July 1, 1986	1,734	386	707	56	146	1,063	4,092
December 31, 1986	1,744	384	745	56	151	1,077	4,157
July 1, 1987	1,762	377	795	56	152	967	4,109
December 31, 1987	1,775	364	865	59	145	957	4,165
July 1, 1988	1,806	355	766	60	143	1,066	4,196
December 31, 1988	1,816	354	786	59	138	1,115	4,268
July 1, 1989	1,802	349	831	58	143	1,051	4,234
December 31, 1989	1,796	349	777	59	137	1,060	4,178
July 1, 1990	1,782	346	753	58	139	1,115	4,192
December 31, 1990	1,795	346	774	59	136	1,062	4,172
July 1, 1991	1,745	339	749	57	137	1,096	4,123
December 31, 1991	1,738	338	742	57	136	1,083	4,094
July 1, 1992	1,731	344	759	56	144	1,091	4,125
December 31, 1992	1,735	347	770	56	142	1,145	4,195
July 1, 1993	1,715	338	767	55	139	1,011	4,025
December 31, 1993	1,789	337	761	56	146	1,121	4,210
July 1, 1994	1,666	336	777	53	138	963	3,933
December 31, 1994	1,660	333	792	53	136	980	3,954
July 1, 1995	1,670	334	804	43	129	1,002	3,982

Note: "—" indicates not available. The counts above reflect federally registered PACs. Registration does not necessarily imply financial activity. Trade/membership/health category for 1974-1976 includes all PACs except corporate and labor; no further breakdown available.

[a] Connected PACs are associated with a sponsoring organization that may pay operating and fund-raising expenses. They are typically subdivided by the type of sponsor: corporate (with stockholders), labor (unions), membership/trade/health (professional groups and associations of corporations), cooperatives (primarily agricultural), and corporations without stock.
[b] Nonconnected PACs do not have a sponsoring organization.

Source: Federal Election Commission, "FEC Releases Semi-Annual Federal PAC Count," press release, July 19, 1995; media advisory, August 2, 1995.

Table 6-2 The Largest Washington-Based PACs

Type of PAC/name

Labor PACs
    Active Ballot Club (United Food and Commercial Workers International Union)
    AFL-CIO Committee on Political Education (COPE)
    Air Line Pilots Association Political Action Committee
    American Federation of State, County, and Municipal Employees--PEOPLE, Qualified,
    American Federation of Teachers Committee on Political Education
    Carpenters' Legislative Improvement Committee
    Committee on Letter Carriers Political Education
    CWA-COPE Political Contributions Committee (Communications Workers of America, AFL-CIO)
    Democratic Republican Independent Voter Education Committee (International Brotherhood of Teamsters, Chauffeurs, Warehousemen, and Helpers of America)
    District No. 1-MEBA/NMU (AFL-CIO) Political Action Fund
    International Brotherhood of Electrical Workers Committee on Political Education
    Ironworkers Political Action League
    Laborers' Political League of Laborers' International Union of North America
    Machinists Non-Partisan Political League
    National Education Association Political Action Committee
    Political Fund Committee of the American Postal Workers Union, AFL-CIO
    Seafarers Political Activity Donation
    Service Employees International Union Committee on Political Education Political Campaign Committee
    Sheet Metal Workers' International Association Political Action League
    United Association Political Education Committee

Nonconnected PACs
    Americans for Free International Trade
    Campaign America
    Conservative Campaign Fund
    Council for a Livable World
    Effective Government Committee
    Emily's List
    English Language PAC
    Ernst & Young PAC
    GOPAC Inc.
    The House Leadership Fund
    Independent Action Inc.
    National Abortion Rights Action League PAC
    National Committee for an Effective Congress
    National PAC
    National Right to Life PAC
    Republicans for Choice
    Ruff-PAC
    United Conservatives of America
    Voters for Choice/Friends of Family Planning
    Women's Pro-Israel National PAC

Table 6-2   (*Continued*)

Type of PAC/name

Trade/membership/health PACs
  Action Committee for Rural Electrification
  American Bankers Association PAC
  American Chiropractic Association
  American Dental Political Action Committee
  American Medical Association Political Action Committee
  American Optometric Association PAC
  Association of Trial Lawyers of America Political Action Committee
  Build Political Action Committee of the National Association of Home
    Builders
  Dealers Election Action Committee of the National Automobile Dealers
    Association
  Independent Insurance Agents of America Inc. Political Action Committee
  National Association of Broadcasters Television and Radio PAC
  National Association of Life Underwriters Political Action Committee
  National Association of Retired Federal Employees Political Action Committee
  National Association of Social Workers Political Action for Candidate Election
  National Beer Wholesalers' Association Political Action Committee
  National Cable Television Association's PAC
  National Committee to Preserve Social Security and Medicare PAC
  NRA Political Victory Fund
  Veterans of Foreign Wars Political Action Committee
  Woman's Campaign Fund

Note: The listed political action committees are among the top twenty Washington-based PACs in each of the categories indicated. This list is based on disbursements reported under the Federal Election Campaign Act of 1971, as amended.

Source: Congressional Quarterly, *Washington Information Directory, 1994-1995* (Washington, D.C.: Congressional Quarterly, 1994), 764-767.

Table 6-3 PACs: Receipts, Expenditures, Contributions, 1975-1994

Election cycle[a]	Receipts[b] (millions)	Expenditures[b] (millions)	Contributions to congressional candidates (millions)[c]	Percentage contributed to congressional candidates
1975-1976	$54.0	$52.9	$22.6	42
1977-1978	80.0	77.4	34.1	43
1979-1980	137.7	131.2	55.2	40
1981-1982	199.5	190.2	83.6	42
1983-1984	288.7	266.8	105.3	36
1985-1986	353.4	340.0	132.7	38
1987-1988	384.6	364.2	151.2	39
1989-1990	372.1	357.6	149.8	40
1991-1992	385.3	394.1	178.4	46
1993-1994	391.0	387.4	178.8	46

Note: Figures are in current dollars.

[a] Data cover January 1 of the odd-numbered year to December 31 of the even-numbered year.
[b] 1975-1984 receipts and expenditures exclude funds transferred between affiliated committees.
[c] Contributions to candidates for election in the even-numbered year, made during the two-year election cycle.

Sources: 1975-1976: Joseph E. Cantor, "Political Action Committees: Their Evolution and Growth and Their Implications for the Political System" (Washington, D.C.: Congressional Research Service, 1982), report no. 83, 87-88; 1977-1978: Federal Election Commission, "FEC Releases First PAC Figures for 1985-86," press release, May 21, 1987, 1; 1979-1990 (contributions): "PAC Activity Falls in 1990 Elections," press release, March 31, 1991, 9; 1979-1992 (receipts, expenditures), 1992 (contributions): "PAC Activity Rebounds in 1991-1992 Election Cycle," press release, April 29, 1993, 5, 9; 1993-1994: "PAC Activity in 1994 Election Remains at 1992 Levels," press release, March 31, 1995, 5, 12.

Table 6-4 Spending, by Type of PAC, 1977-1994 (millions)

Election cycle	Corporate	Labor	Trade membership/ health	Non-connected	Other connected[a]	Total
1977-1978	$15.2	$18.6	$23.8	$17.4	$2.4	$77.4
1979-1980	31.4	25.1	32.0	38.6	4.0	131.2
1981-1982	43.3	34.8	41.9	64.3	5.8	190.2
1983-1984	59.2	47.5	54.0	97.4	8.7	266.8
1985-1986	79.3	57.9	73.3	118.4	11.1	340.0
1987-1988	89.9	74.1	83.7	104.9	11.7	364.2
1989-1990	101.1	84.6	88.1	71.4	12.5	357.6
1991-1992	112.2	94.3	97.4	76.1	14.1	394.1
1993-1994	116.9	88.2	94.1	74.6	13.7	387.4

Note: Figures are in current dollars. Expenditures exclude transfers of funds between affiliated committees for 1975-1984. Detail may not add to totals because of rounding.

[a] This category combines the FEC categories of cooperatives and corporations without stock.

Sources: 1977-1978: Norman J. Ornstein et al., eds., *Vital Statistics on Congress, 1987-1988* (Washington, D.C.: Congressional Quarterly, 1987), 105; 1979-1994: Federal Election Commission, "PAC Activity in 1994 Elections Remains at 1992 Levels," press release, March 31, 1995, 12.

Table 6-5 Contributions and Independent Expenditures, by Type of PAC, 1991-1994[a]

Type of PAC	Number[b]	Receipts[c]	Contributed to candidates[d] Amount	Percentage	Independent expenditures[e] Amount	Percentage
1991-1992						
Corporate	1,501	$112,359,989	$68,442,883	61	$47,883	0.0
Labor	254	89,863,124	41,339,090	46	298,497	0.3
Trade/membership/health	625	95,729,703	53,746,146	56	3,422,300	3.6
Cooperative	48	4,798,441	2,981,390	62	0	0.0
Corporations without stock	112	8,713,184	3,983,452	46	385,300	4.4
Nonconnected	531	73,851,846	18,183,052	25	6,276,696	8.5
Total	3,071	385,316,287	188,676,013	49	10,430,676	2.7
1993-1994						
Corporate	1,461	114,978,803	69,581,799	61	31,214	0.0
Labor	255	89,898,089	41,825,927	47	103,743	0.1
Trade/membership/health	628	96,370,335	52,799,649	55	1,767,450	1.8
Cooperative	50	4,377,763	3,042,328	69	0	0.0
Corporations without stock	112	8,848,760	4,071,108	46	509,901	5.8
Nonconnected	500	76,535,445	18,049,730	24	2,307,490	3.0
Total	3,006	391,009,195	189,370,541	48	4,719,848	1.2

Note: Figures are in current dollars and reflect preliminary rather than final reports for the election cycles.

[a] Data for earlier years can be found in previous editions of *Vital Statistics on American Politics*.
[b] The numbers shown are those PACs that actually made contributions.
[c] Not adjusted for money transferred between affiliated committees.
[d] Figures include contributions to all federal candidates, including those who did not run for office during the years indicated.
[e] Independent expenditures include money spent on behalf of candidates and against candidates.

Sources: Federal Election Commission, "PAC Activity Rebounds in 1991-1992 Election Cycle," press release, April 29, 1993, 3, 8-9, "PAC Activity in 1994 Elections Remains at 1992 Levels," press release, March 31, 1995, 3, 11-12.

Table 6-6   Top Twenty PACs in Overall Spending and in
Contributions to Federal Candidates, 1993-1994[a]

PAC	Overall Spending
1. Democratic Republican Independent Voter Education Committee	$8,455,641
2. Emily's List	7,481,360
3. Campaign America	6,701,622
4. American Federation of State County & Municipal Employees—PEOPLE, Qualified	6,414,368
5. NRA Political Victory Fund	5,948,803
6. Association of Trial Lawyers of America Political Action Committee	4,568,788
7. National Education Association Political Action Committee	4,434,084
8. American Medical Association Political Action Committee	3,924,057
9. Machinists Non-Partisan Political League	3,684,825
10. UAW-V-CAP (UAW Voluntary Community Action Program)	3,595,504
11. United Parcel Service Political Action Committee (UPSPAC)	3,350,884
12. Dealers Election Action Committee of the National Automobile Dealers Association (NADA)	2,751,789
13. American Telephone & Telegraph Company Political Action Committee (AT&T PAC)	2,667,973
14. Realtors Political Action Committee	2,572,473
15. Transportation Political Education League	2,547,886
16. International Brotherhood of Electrical Workers Committee on Political Education	2,376,812
17. National Conservative Club (FKA) National Congressional Club	2,372,999
18. National Committee to Preserve Social Security and Medicare—PAC	2,208,721
19. Active Ballot Club, A Department of United Food & Commercial Workers International Union	2,152,005
20. CWA-COPE Political Contributions Committee	2,131,112

Name	Contributions to federal candidates
1. United Parcel Service Political Action Committee (UPSPAC)	$2,647,113
2. American Federation of State County & Municipal Employees—PEOPLE, Qualified	2,529,682
3. Democratic Republican Independent Voter Education Committee	2,487,152
4. American Medical Association Political Action Committee	2,386,947
5. National Education Association Political Action Committee	2,260,850
6. Association of Trial Lawyers Of America Political Action Committee	2,164,035
7. UAW-V-CAP (UAW Voluntary Community Action Program)	2,147,190
8. NRA Political Victory Fund	1,853,038
9. Realtors Political Action Committee	1,851,978
10. Dealers Election Action Committee of The National Automobile Dealers Association (NADA)	1,832,570

Table 6-6   (*Continued*)

Name	Contributions to federal candidates
11. American Institute of Certified Public Accountants Effective Legislation Committee (AICPA)	$1,737,520
12. Machinists Non-Partisan Political League	1,702,081
13. International Brotherhood of Electrical Workers Committee On Political Education	1,610,025
14. Active Ballot Club, A Department of United Food & Commercial Workers International Union	1,460,639
15. Committee of Letter Carriers Political Education (Letter Carriers Political Action Fund)	1,428,290
16. Carpenters Legislative Improvement Commmittee United Brotherhood of Carpenters & Joiners of AME	1,423,200
17. American Bankers Association BANKPAC	1,343,150
18. National Association of Life Underwriters Political Action Committee	1,338,890
19. Build Political Action Committee of The National Association Of Home Builders	1,329,599
20. American Telephone & Telegraph Company Political Action Committee (AT&T PAC)	1,294,244

Note: Figures are in current dollars.

[a] Information for previous years can be found in previous editions of *Vital Statistics on American Politics*.

Source: Federal Election Commission, "PAC Activity in 1994 Elections Remains at 1992 Levels," press release, March 31, 1995, 19, 20.

Table 6-7 Political Action Committee (PAC) Congressional Campaign Contributions, by Type of PAC and Incumbency Status of Candidate, 1981-1994[a] (millions)

Election cycle/ PAC type	House						Senate					
	Dem.	Rep.	Incum- bent	Chal- lenger	Open seat[b]	Total	Dem.	Rep.	Incum- bent	Chal- lenger	Open seat[b]	Total
1981-1982												
Corporate	7.0	12.0	14.4	2.0	2.6	18.9	2.4	6.2	5.5	1.7	1.4	8.6
Trade/membership/health	7.2	9.7	12.4	2.1	2.3	16.8	2.2	2.8	3.7	0.8	0.5	5.0
Labor	14.7	0.7	8.5	4.3	2.6	15.4	4.5	0.4	3.0	1.3	0.5	4.9
Nonconnected	3.9	3.5	3.4	2.5	1.6	7.4	1.6	1.7	1.5	1.3	0.5	3.3
Total[c]	34.2	26.8	40.8	10.9	9.4	61.1	11.2	11.4	14.3	5.2	3.0	22.6
1983-1984												
Corporate	10.4	13.1	18.8	2.6	2.0	23.4	3.2	8.8	8.8	1.1	2.2	12.0
Trade/membership/health	10.5	9.9	16.5	2.1	1.7	20.4	2.7	3.7	4.5	0.9	1.0	6.3
Labor	18.8	1.0	14.3	3.5	2.0	19.8	4.7	0.3	1.6	2.3	1.2	5.0
Nonconnected	4.7	4.4	4.9	2.9	1.3	9.1	3.0	2.4	2.4	2.0	1.0	5.4
Total[c]	46.3	29.3	57.2	11.3	7.2	75.7	14.0	15.6	17.9	6.3	5.4	29.7
1985-1986												
Corporate	12.9	14.0	22.9	1.0	3.0	26.9	4.8	14.4	11.7	2.7	4.9	19.2
Trade/membership/health	12.3	11.2	19.3	1.3	2.8	23.4	3.8	5.7	5.7	1.6	2.1	9.5
Labor	21.1	1.6	14.7	4.3	3.6	22.6	6.6	0.6	2.2	3.2	1.9	7.2
Nonconnected	6.6	4.5	6.1	2.4	2.6	11.1	4.2	3.4	3.1	2.4	2.2	7.7
Total[c]	54.7	32.6	65.9	9.1	12.4	87.4	20.2	25.1	23.7	10.2	11.4	45.3
1987-1988												
Corporate	16.3	15.3	28.7	1.1	1.9	31.7	7.2	11.6	12.9	2.4	3.7	18.8
Trade/membership/health	16.6	12.0	24.6	1.5	2.5	28.6	4.8	5.6	7.1	1.2	2.0	10.3
Labor	24.9	2.0	18.4	5.1	3.4	26.9	6.5	0.5	3.6	2.2	1.3	7.1
Nonconnected	7.4	3.9	7.3	2.1	1.9	11.3	4.8	3.0	4.2	2.0	1.6	7.7
Total[c]	67.6	34.6	82.4	10.0	9.9	102.3	24.1	21.5	28.7	8.0	8.9	45.6

1989-1990												
Corporate	19.1	17.1	31.4	1.5	3.2	36.2	8.4	13.5	16.8	3.6	1.5	22.0
Trade/membership/health	19.3	13.4	27.7	1.4	3.6	32.7	5.2	6.5	9.0	1.8	0.9	11.7
Labor	26.1	1.8	20.1	3.3	4.5	28.0	6.2	0.6	4.6	1.7	0.4	6.8
Nonconnected	6.0	3.1	5.8	1.2	2.0	9.1	4.0	2.5	4.9	1.0	0.5	6.5
Total[c]	73.4	36.9	89.0	7.7	13.6	110.4	24.9	23.9	36.9	8.4	3.4	48.8
1991-1992												
Corporate	24.3	20.5	36.9	2.9	5.0	44.9	9.9	13.5	16.8	2.4	4.2	23.4
Trade/membership/health	23.9	16.2	30.5	3.0	6.5	40.2	7.1	6.3	9.3	1.7	2.4	13.5
Labor	29.8	1.7	20.7	4.5	6.2	31.7	8.9	0.4	4.2	2.9	2.2	9.3
Nonconnected	6.9	3.7	6.5	1.6	2.4	10.6	4.6	2.9	4.4	1.5	1.5	7.4
Total[c]	88.1	43.7	98.7	12.4	20.7	132.2	31.8	23.9	36.3	8.7	10.7	55.7
1993-1994												
Corporate	24.8	20.4	37.9	3.1	4.3	45.3	9.2	15.1	15.2	2.0	7.1	24.2
Trade/membership/health	22.7	17.1	31.0	3.4	5.4	39.9	5.6	7.4	8.3	1.1	3.5	12.9
Labor	32.5	1.4	24.2	4.2	5.6	34.1	7.4	0.3	4.0	1.7	1.9	7.7
Nonconnected	7.5	4.4	7.6	1.9	2.4	11.9	3.3	2.8	3.6	0.8	1.7	6.1
Total[c]	90.9	45.0	104.9	13.0	18.2	136.2	26.6	26.5	32.6	5.8	14.7	53.1

Note: Figures are current dollar amounts given during the two-year calendar period indicated to candidates in primary, general, run-off, and special elections.

[a] Data for earlier years can be found in previous editions of *Vital Statistics on American Politics*.

[b] Open seat refers to candidates in elections in which an incumbent did not seek reelection.

[c] Includes PACs classified by the Federal Election Commission as cooperatives and corporations without stock.

Sources: 1979-1984: *Statistical Abstract of the United* States, 1987 (Washington, D.C.: U.S. Government Printing Office, 1986), 246; 1985-1988: *Statistical Abstract of the United States,* 1990, 269; 1989-1990: Federal Election Commission, "PAC Activity Falls in 1990 Elections," press release, March 31, 1991, 3; 1991-1992: "PAC Activity Rebounds in 1991-1992 Election Cycle," press release, April 29, 1993, 4-5, "PAC Activity in 1994 Elections Remains at 1992 Levels," press release, March 31, 1995, 4, 5.

Table 6-8   Contribution Limits Under Federal Election Commission Act

Source	Candidate or his/her authorized committee	National party committee[a]	Any other committee	Total contributions
Individual	$1,000 per election[b]	$20,000	$5,000	$25,000
Multicandidate committee[c]	$5,000 per election	$15,000	$5,000	NL
Party committee	$1,000-5,000 per election[d]	NL	$5,000	NL
Republican or Democratic Senatorial Campaign Committee,[e] or the National Party Committee, or a combination of both	$17,500 to Senate candidate per calendar year in which candidate seeks election	NA	NA	NA
Any other committee or group[f]	$1,000 per election	$20,000	$5,000	NL

Note: "NL" indicates no limit; "NA" indicates not applicable. Limits on contributions to national party committees and other committees and on total contributions are per calendar year.

[a] The following are considered national party committees: a party's national committee, the Senate campaign committees, and the national congressional committees, provided they are not authorized by any candidate. Individual contributions made or earmarked to influence a specific election of a clearly identified candidate are counted as if made during the year in which the election is held.

[b] The following are considered separate elections: primary election, general election, runoff election, special election, and party caucus or convention that has authority to select the nominee.

[c] A multicandidate committee is any committee with more than fifty contributors that has been registered for at least six months and, with the exception of state party committees, has made contributions to five or more federal candidates. Most PACs qualify as a multicandidate committee.

[d] Limit depends on whether party committee is a multicandidate committee.

[e] Republican and Democratic Senatorial Campaign committees are subject to all other limits applicable to a multicandidate committee.

[f] Group includes an organization, partnership, or group of persons.

Source: Federal Election Commission.

Table 6-9 Contribution Limits for Funding of State Election Campaigns

State	Individual	Candidate	Candidate's family members	Corporations	Labor unions	PACs	Regulated industries	Parties
Alabama	no	no	no	yes	no	no	yes	no
Alaska	yes	no	yes	yes	yes	yes	yes	no
Arizona	yes	no	no	prohibited	prohibited	yes	prohibited	—
Arkansas	yes	no	yes	yes	yes	yes	yes	yes
California	yes	no	yes	yes	yes	yes	yes	yes
Colorado	no	no	no	no	no	no	no	no
Connecticut	yes	no	yes	prohibited	prohibited	yes	prohibited	no
Delaware	yes	yes	yes	yes	yes	yes	yes	yes
District of Columbia	yes	yes	yes	yes	yes	yes	yes	—
Florida	yes	yes	yes	yes	yes	yes	yes	no[a]
Georgia	yes	yes	yes	yes	yes	yes	yes	yes
Hawaii	yes	yes	yes	yes	yes	yes	yes	yes
Idaho	no[a]	no	no	no	no	no	no	no
Illinois	no[a]	no[a]	no	no	no	no	no	no
Indiana	no	no	no	yes	no	no	yes	no
Iowa	no	no	no	prohibited	no	no	prohibited	no
Kansas	yes	no	yes	yes	yes	yes	yes	no
Kentucky	yes	no	yes	prohibited	yes	yes	prohibited	no
Louisiana	yes	no	yes	yes	yes	yes	prohibited	no
Maine	yes	no	yes / unlimited for spouse	yes	yes	yes	—	yes
Maryland	yes	no	unlimited for spouse	yes	yes	yes	yes	no
Massachusetts	yes	no	yes	prohibited	no	yes	prohibited	yes

(Table continues)

Table 6-9 (Continued)

State	Individual	Candidate	Candidate's family members	Corporations	Labor unions	PACs	Regulated industries	Parties
Michigan	yes	no[b]	no[b]	prohibited	yes	yes	prohibited	yes
Minnesota	yes	no	yes	prohibited	yes	yes	prohibited	yes
Mississippi	no	no	no	yes	no	no	prohibited	no
Missouri	no	no	no	no	no	no	no	no
Montana	yes	no	yes	prohibited	yes	yes	prohibited	yes
Nebraska	no	no	no	no	no	no	no	no
Nevada	yes	yes	yes	yes	yes	yes	yes	yes
New Hampshire	yes	no[b]	yes	prohibited	prohibited	yes	prohibited	no[b]
New Jersey	yes	no[b]	no[b]	yes	yes	yes	prohibited	no
New Mexico	no	no	no	no	no	no	no	no
New York	yes	no	unlimited for spouse	yes	yes	yes	yes	no[c]
North Carolina	yes	no	no	prohibited	prohibited	yes	prohibited	no
North Dakota	no	no	no	prohibited	prohibited	no	prohibited	no
Ohio	no	no	no	prohibited	no	no	prohibited	no
Oklahoma	yes	yes	yes	prohibited	yes	yes	prohibited	yes
Oregon	no	no	no	no	no	no	no	no
Pennsylvania	no	no[d]	no	prohibited	prohibited	yes	prohibited	no
Rhode Island	yes	no	yes	prohibited	prohibited	yes	yes	yes
South Carolina	yes	no	yes	yes	yes	no	yes	yes
South Dakota	yes	no	no	prohibited	no	no	prohibited	no
Tennessee	no	no	no	no	no	no	prohibited	no
Texas	no	no	no	no	yes	no	yes	no
Utah	no	no	no	no	no	no	yes	no
Vermont	yes	yes	no	yes	yes	yes	yes	no
Virginia	no	no	no	no	no	no	no	no
Washington	yes	yes	yes	yes	yes	yes	yes	yes

West Virginia	yes	yes	yes	prohibited	yes	yes	prohibited	yes
Wisconsin	yes	no[d]	no[d]	prohibited	prohibited	yes	prohibited	yes
Wyoming	yes	no	no	prohibited	prohibited	no	prohibited	no[c]

Note: "—" indicates not available. Limits on sizes of contributions and other restrictions (e.g., from government employees, regulated industries) vary widely across states. For details see source.

[a] Prohibited for judges.
[b] Limited for governor only.
[c] Prohibited in primaries.
[d] Limited if candidate receives public funds.

Source: Campaign Finance Law 94 (Washington, D.C.: National Clearinghouse Election Administration, Federal Election Commission, 1994), Charts 2A–2B.

Table 6-10   State Campaign Finance: Tax Provisions, Public Funding, and Expenditure Limits

State	Tax provisions[a]	Public financing Source of funds	Public financing Distribution of funds[b]	Expenditure limits[c]
Alabama	surcharge	surcharge	parties	no
Arizona	deduction, surcharge	surcharge, donations	parties	no
California	surcharge	surcharge, direct appropriation	parties	no
District of Columbia	credit	—	—	no
Florida	surcharge	direct appropriation	candidates	yes
Hawaii	deduction, checkoff	checkoff, direct appropriation	candidates	voluntary
Idaho	checkoff	checkoff	parties	no
Indiana	none	revenues from personalized license plates	parties	no
Iowa	checkoff	checkoff	parties	no
Kentucky	checkoff	checkoff	parties	yes
Maine	surcharge	surcharge	parties	yes
Maryland	none	direct appropriation	candidates	yes
Massachusetts	surcharge	surcharge	candidates	no
Michigan	checkoff	checkoff	candidates	yes
Minnesota	checkoff, credit	checkoff, contributions	candidates	yes
Montana	deduction	—	—	no
Nebraska	surcharge	direct appropriation	candidates	no
New Hampshire	—	—	—	voluntary
New Jersey	checkoff	checkoff, direct appropriation	candidates	yes
New Mexico	checkoff	checkoff	parties	no
North Carolina	deduction, checkoff, surcharge	checkoff, surcharge	parties, candidates	yes
Ohio	checkoff	checkoff	parties	no

(Table continues)

Table 6-10   (*Continued*)

State	Tax provisions[a]	Public financing		Expenditure limits[c]
		Source of funds	Distribution of funds[b]	
Oklahoma	deduction	—	—	no
Oregon	credit	—	—	no
Rhode Island	checkoff	checkoff	parties, candidates	yes
Utah	checkoff	checkoff	parties	no
Virginia	surcharge	surcharge	parties	no
Wisconsin	checkoff	checkoff	candidates	yes[d]

Note: "—" indicates no such provision. Omitted states have no tax provisions or public funding for campaign finance.

[a] Credits and deductions reduce the taxes paid by an individual; checkoffs neither raise nor lower an individual's taxes; surcharges add to an individual's taxes. Checkoffs and surcharges are usually limited to $1.00-$5.00; deductions and credits are for larger amounts. For details, see source.

[b] Funds distributed to parties are usually given to a party designated by the taxpayer, often for party activities and distribution to candidates. Funds distributed to candidates are given to nonfederal candidates; states vary as to which candidates and whether for primary or general election. For details, see source.

[c] "Yes" indicates a limit on total expenditures. (Only states that provide public funding of candidates or political parties are permitted expenditure limits. See *Buckley v. Valeo*, 424 U.S. 1 [1976].) Most states have some provisions governing the use of campaign funds (e.g., who may make expenditures, how postelection surpluses are handled). For details, see source.

[d] Unless opponents who have not accepted public financing exceed limits.

Source: *Campaign Finance Law 94* (Washington, D.C.: National Clearinghouse on Election Administration, Federal Election Commission, 1994), Chart 3A, 4.

Table 6-11 Membership in Labor Unions, 1900-1993

Year	Membership (in thousands)	Percent in unions Nonagricultural employment	Labor force
1900	932.4	6.5	3.3
1905	1,947.1	10.8	6.0
1910	2,168.5	10.3	5.9
1915	2,597.6	11.5	6.6
1920	4,823.3	17.6	11.7
1925	3,685.1	12.8	8.2
1930	3,749.6	12.7	7.5
1935	3,649.6	13.5	6.9
1940	7,296.7	22.5	13.1
1945	12,254.2	30.4	22.8
1950	14,294.2	31.6	23.0
1955	16,126.9	31.8	24.8
1960	15,516.1	28.6	22.3
1965	18,268.9	30.1	24.5
1970	20,990.3	29.6	25.4
1971	20,711.1	29.1	24.5
1972	21,205.8	28.8	24.4
1973	21,881.3	28.5	24.5
1974	22,165.4	28.3	24.1
1975	22,207.0	28.9	23.7
1976	22,153.0	27.9	23.0
1977	21,632.1	26.2	21.8
1978	21,756.5	25.1	21.3
1979	22,025.4	24.5	21.0
1980	20,968.2	23.2	19.6
1981	20,646.8	22.6	19.0
1982	19,571.4	21.9	17.8
1983	18,633.6	20.7	16.6
1984	18,306.0	19.4	16.1
1985	16,996.0	18.0	14.5
1986	16,975.0	17.5	14.2
1987	16,913.0	17.0	13.9
1988	17,002.0	16.8	13.8
1989	16,960.0	16.4	13.5
1990	16,740.0	16.1	13.2
1991	16,568.0	16.1	13.1
1992	16,390.0	15.8	12.8
1993	16,389.0	15.8	12.8

Note: Comparisons of two years in which both sources reported union membership show that the counts by Troy and Sheflin are about one million members higher per year than the counts based on the Current Population Surveys reported by the Bureau of Labor Statistics in *Employment and Earnings*. In 1985-1993, self-employed workers whose businesses are incorporated are excluded from calculations for the percent in unions in nonagricultural employment.

Sources: 1900-1984: Leo Troy and Neil Sheflin, *U.S. Union Sourcebook* (West Orange, N.J.: Industrial Relations Data and Information Services, 1985), A-1, A-2, 3-10; 1985-1993: U.S. Department of Labor, Bureau of Labor Statistics, *Employment and Earnings*, January 1987 (Washington, D.C.: U.S. Government Printing Office, 1987), 219; (1988), 222; (1990), 232; (1992), 228; (1994), 248; size of the labor force from *Employment and Earnings*, January 1994, 13.

Table 6-12 Selected Public Interest Groups

Name (founded)	Staff size[a]	1990 budget (millions)	Members (individuals or as noted)	PAC
Business/Economic				
Business Roundtable (1972)	16	—	200 corporations	No
The Conference Board, Inc. (1916)	310	$19.6	3,000 labor unions, colleges & universities, etc.	No
National Association of Manufacturers (1895)	185	15.0	12,500 companies	No
U.S. Chamber of Commerce (1912)	1,700	70.0	180,000 companies, state & local chambers of commerce, etc.	National Chamber Alliance for Politics
Civil/Constitutional Rights				
Aids Coalition to Unleash Power (Act-Up-New York) (1987)	volunteer	1.2	4,000 (NYC) + national branches	No
American Association of Retired Persons (1958)	1,585	—	32,000,000	No
American Civil Liberties Union (1920)	162	18.7	280,000	No
Amnesty International USA (1961)	91	21.3	386,000	No
Handgun Control, Inc. (1974)	28	6.5	360,000	Handgun Control Voter Education Fund
Leadership Conference on Civil Rights, Inc. (1950)	8	.5	180 national organizations	No
League of United Latin American Citizens (LULAC) (1929)	5	—	110,000	No
Mexican-American Legal Defense and Educational Fund (1968)	63	3.8	—	No
NAACP Legal Defense and Educational Fund, Inc. (1940)	79	8.9	—	No

(Table continues)

Table 6-12 *(Continued)*

Name *(founded)*	Staff size[a]	1990 budget *(millions)*	Members *(individuals or as noted)*	PAC
National Abortion Rights Action League (1969)	45	$9.3	450,000	NARAL PAC
National Association for the Advancement of Colored People (1909)	100	12.0	345,000	No
National Gay and Lesbian Task Force (1973)	15	1.0	17,000	No
National Organization for Women, Inc. (1966)	32	7.0	25,000	National NOW PAC & National Equality PAC
National Rifle Association of America (1871)	550	86.9	2,650,000	Political Victory Fund
National Right to Life Committee, Inc. (1973)	55	10.9	3,000 local chapters	National Right to Life PAC
National Urban League (1910)	185	24.6	1,600,000	No
Planned Parenthood Federation of America, Inc. (1916)	253	368.4	172 U.S. affiliates	No
Women's Legal Defense Fund (1971)	24	—	1,500	No
Community/Grassroots				
The American Society for the Prevention of Cruelty to Animals (1866)	203	17.8	400,000	No
Association of Community Organizations for Reform Now (ACORN) (1970)	200	3.0	80,000	No
Mothers Against Drunk Driving (1980)	260	43.5	2,950,000	No
National Anti-Vivisection Society (1929)	15	—	—	No
Environmental				
Environmental Defense Fund (1967)	110	15.1	150,000	No
Greenpeace USA (1971)	250	35.0	2,100,000	No
Izaak Walton League of America (1922)	23	1.8	52,700	No

Organization	Staff[a]	Budget ($ millions)	Membership	PAC
League of Conservation Voters (1970)	67	$1.3	60,000	LCV is a political committee
National Audubon Society (1905)	315	35.8	600,000	No
National Wildlife Federation (1936)	608	87.2	5,600,000	No
The Nature Conservancy (1951)	1,150	68.0	580,000 industries	No
Sierra Club (1892)	325	35.0	650,000	Sierra Club Political Committee
The Wilderness Society (1935)	136	17.9	383,000	No
World Wildlife Fund (1948)	244	54.0	1,000,000	No
International Affairs				
American Israel Public Affairs Committee (1954)	100+	—	55,000	No
Human Rights Watch (1978)	60	4.2	—	No
Accuracy in Media (1969)	15	1.6	25,000	No
Political/Governmental Process				
The American Conservative Union (1964)	8	2.8	100,000	American Conservation Union PAC
Americans for Democratic Action, Inc. (1947)	6	.6	20,000	ADA PAC
Common Cause (1970)	70	11.3	270,000	No
Public Citizen, Inc. (1971)	50	6.2	100,000	No
Religious				
American Jewish Committee (1906)	214	17.9	50,000	No
American Jewish Congress (1918)	100	6.6	50,000	No
Anti-Defamation League of B'nai B'rith (1913)	400	30.0	—	No

Note: "—" indicates not available.

[a] Professional and support staff; often supplemented by interns or part-time workers.

Source: Selected by the editors from Foundation for Public Affairs, *Public Interest Profiles 1992-1993* (Washington, D.C.: Congressional Quarterly, 1992.)

7

Congress

Statistics about Congress abound. Capsule descriptions of senators and representatives and their districts run to more than a thousand pages for each Congress (see, for example, *Politics in America* and the *Almanac of American Politics*). Elections are held every two years, generating mounds of electoral and financial data. Recorded votes annually number more than four hundred in the House and more than three hundred in the Senate. It is thus hardly surprising that votes for Congress, votes in Congress, those who work for Congress, and those who gain from (or are hurt by) congressional activities have been subject to extensive statistical scrutiny.

Congressional elections and roll call votes in Congress constitute the largest areas of research. Elections are covered in several other chapters, and the nature of electoral data is discussed in the introductions to Chapters 3 and 4. What is added here are a number of tables that pertain to hypotheses about congressional elections. Losses by the president's party in midterm elections (Table 7-4) have long been of interest because of a strong regularity and because the pattern has a variety of implications for the way voters evaluate their representatives. The same is true of incumbency; the results are interesting in and of themselves (Table 7-5) and because of what they suggest about how voters make choices. The electoral vulnerability of incumbents is reduced by their considerably greater ability to raise campaign funds (Table 7-7); PACs have been a large source of those funds in recent years (Table 7-8).

Congress generates other kinds of statistics. Simply apportioning members among the states (Table 7-1 and Figure 7-1) has led to a surprising amount of controversy and statistical calculation, which resulted in a fascinating, book-length treatment.[1] As the composition of Congress changes to include more women and minorities, these and other characteristics have also been tabulated and analyzed (Tables 7-2 and 7-3).

Cohesion within and contrasts between the political parties were the topics of some of the first statistical treatments of political subjects.[2] Increased numbers of roll calls and other recorded votes (Table 7-13) have done nothing to dampen this tradition. Party unity and presidential support by individual representatives and senators (Tables 7-15 and 7-16) and for groups (Tables 7-9 through 7-11, Figure 7-2) have become a standard part of congressional analyses.

As Congress becomes a larger and more complex operation, more interest has been expressed in its workload and structure. These aspects of Congress are represented here with information about staff size (Figure 7-3), numbers of measures considered and passed (Table 7-12 and Figure 7-4), numbers of votes (Table 7-13), and numbers of committees and their leadership (Table 7-14). Although these, too, at first might be considered insignificant or analytically useless tabulations, analyses of the relationships among committee staffs, congressional voting, voter behavior, and legislative output suggest otherwise.

For the statistically minded, the study of Congress has long been an inviting prospect. The traditional topics are still interesting because the turnover of personnel, the constant change in congressional leadership and of the president, changes in regional strength, and so on make Congress anything but static. In addition, reforms of congressional procedures and of campaign finance since Watergate, technological changes that have resulted in electronic voting and the televising of proceedings in both chambers, and changes in the size and scope of the government bureaucracy Congress must deal with are adequate reasons to scrutinize anew the data underlying one's understanding of Congress.

Notes

1. Michel Balinski and H. P. Young, *Fair Representation* (New Haven, Conn.: Yale University Press, 1982).
2. Stuart Rice, *Quantitative Methods in Politics* (New York: Knopf, 1928).

Table 7-1 Apportionment of Membership in the House of Representatives, 1789-1990

State	1789[a]	1790	1800	1810	1820	1830	1840	1850	1860	1870	1880	1890	1900	1910	1930[b]	1940	1950	1960	1970	1980	1990
Alabama	—	—	—	1[c]	3	5	7	7	6	8	8	9	9	10	9	9	9	8	7	7	7
Alaska	—	—	—	—	—	—	—	—	—	—	—	—	—	—	—	—	1[c]	1	1	1	1
Arizona	—	—	—	—	—	—	—	—	—	—	—	—	—	1[c]	1	2	2	3	4	5	6
Arkansas	—	—	—	—	—	1[c]	1	2	3	4	5	6	7	7	7	7	6	4	4	4	4
California	—	—	—	—	—	—	2[c]	2	3	4	6	7	8	11	20	23	30	38	43	45	52
Colorado	—	—	—	—	—	—	—	—	—	1[c]	1	2	3	4	4	4	4	4	5	6	6
Connecticut	5	7	7	7	6	6	4	4	4	4	4	4	5	5	6	6	6	6	6	6	6
Delaware	1	1	1	2	1	1	1	1	1	1	1	1	1	1	1	1	1	1	1	1	1
Florida	—	—	—	—	—	—	1[c]	1	1	2	2	2	3	4	5	6	8	12	15	19	23
Georgia	3	2	4	6	7	9	8	8	7	9	10	11	11	12	10	10	10	10	10	10	11
Hawaii	—	—	—	—	—	—	—	—	—	—	—	—	—	—	—	—	1[c]	2	2	2	2
Idaho	—	—	—	—	—	—	—	—	—	—	1[c]	1	1	2	2	2	2	2	2	2	2
Illinois	—	—	—	1[c]	1	3	7	9	14	19	20	22	25	27	27	26	25	24	24	22	20
Indiana	—	—	—	1[c]	3	7	10	11	11	13	13	13	13	13	12	11	11	11	11	10	10
Iowa	—	—	—	—	—	—	2[c]	2	6	9	11	11	11	11	9	8	8	7	6	6	5
Kansas	—	—	—	—	—	—	—	—	1[c]	3	7	8	8	8	7	6	6	5	5	5	4
Kentucky	—	2	6	10	12	13	10	10	9	10	11	11	11	11	9	9	8	7	7	7	6
Louisiana	—	—	—	1[c]	3	3	4	4	5	6	6	6	7	8	8	8	8	8	8	8	7
Maine	—	—	—	7[c]	7	8	7	6	5	5	4	4	4	4	3	3	3	2	2	2	2
Maryland	6	8	9	9	9	8	6	6	5	6	6	6	6	6	6	6	7	8	8	8	8
Massachusetts	8	14	17	13[d]	13	12	10	11	10	11	12	13	14	16	15	14	14	12	12	11	10
Michigan	—	—	—	—	—	1[c]	3	4	6	9	11	12	12	13	17	17	18	19	19	18	16
Minnesota	—	—	—	—	—	—	—	2[c]	2	3	5	7	9	10	9	9	9	8	8	8	8

(Table continues)

Table 7-1 (Continued)

State	1789[a]	1790	1800	1810	1820	1830	1840	1850	1860	1870	1880	1890	1900	1910	1930[b]	1940	1950	1960	1970	1980	1990
Mississippi	—	—	—	1[c]	2	2	4	5	5	6	7	7	8	8	7	7	6	5	5	5	5
Missouri	—	—	—	1	1	2	5	7	9	13	14	15	16	16	13	13	11	10	10	9	9
Montana	—	—	—	—	—	—	—	—	—	—	1[c]	1	1	2	2	2	2	2	2	2	1
Nebraska	—	—	—	—	—	—	—	—	1[c]	1	3	6	6	6	5	4	4	3	3	3	3
Nevada	—	—	—	—	—	—	—	—	1[c]	1	1	1	1	1	1	1	1	1	1	2	2
New Hampshire	3	4	5	6	6	5	4	3	3	3	2	2	2	2	2	2	2	2	2	2	2
New Jersey	4	5	6	6	6	6	5	5	5	7	7	8	10	12	14	14	14	15	15	14	13
New Mexico	—	—	—	—	—	—	—	—	—	—	—	—	—	1[c]	1	2	2	2	2	3	3
New York	6	10	17	27	34	40	34	33	31	33	34	34	37	43	45	45	43	41	39	34	31
North Carolina	5	10	12	13	13	13	9	8	7	8	9	9	10	10	11	12	12	11	11	11	12
North Dakota	—	—	—	—	—	—	—	—	—	—	1[c]	1	2	3	2	2	2	2	1	1	1
Ohio	—	—	1[c]	6	14	19	21	21	19	20	21	21	21	22	24	23	23	24	23	21	19
Oklahoma	—	—	—	—	—	—	—	—	—	—	—	—	5[c]	8	9	8	6	6	6	6	6
Oregon	—	—	—	—	—	—	—	1[c]	1	1	1	2	2	3	3	4	4	4	4	5	5
Pennsylvania	8	13	18	23	26	28	24	25	24	27	28	30	32	36	34	33	30	27	25	23	21
Rhode Island	1	2	2	2	2	2	2	2	2	2	2	2	2	3	2	2	2	2	2	2	2
South Carolina	5	6	8	9	9	9	7	6	4	5	7	7	7	7	6	6	6	6	6	6	6
South Dakota	—	—	—	—	—	—	—	—	—	—	2[c]	2	2	3	2	2	2	2	2	1	1
Tennessee	—	1	3	6	9	13	11	10	8	10	10	10	10	10	9	10	9	9	8	9	9
Texas	—	—	—	—	—	—	2[c]	2	4	6	11	13	16	18	21	21	22	23	24	27	30
Utah	—	—	—	—	—	—	—	—	—	—	—	1[c]	1	2	2	1	2	2	2	3	3
Vermont	—	2	4	6	5	5	4	3	3	3	2	2	2	2	2	1	1	1	1	1	1
Virginia	10	19	22	23	22	21	15	13	11	9	10	10	10	10	9	9	10	10	10	10	11
Washington	—	—	—	—	—	—	—	—	—	—	1[c]	2	3	5	6	6	7	7	7	8	9

West Virginia	—	—	—	—	—	—	—	—	—	3	4	4	5	6	6	6	6	5	4	4	3
Wisconsin	—	—	—	—	—	—	2ᶜ	3	6	8	9	10	11	11	10	10	10	10	9	9	9
Wyoming	—	—	—	—	—	—	—	—	—	—	1ᶜ	1	1	1	1	1	1	1	1	1	1
Total	65	106	142	186	213	242	232	237	243	293	332	357	391	435	435	435	437ᵉ	435	435	435	435
Apportion-ment ratioᶠ	30	33	33	35	40	48	71	93	127	131	152	174	194	211	281	301	345	410	469	521	574

Note: "—" indicates state not yet admitted to Union. Apportionment effective with congressional election two years after census.

[a] Original apportionment made in Constitution, pending first census.
[b] No apportionment was made in 1920.
[c] Representation accorded newly admitted states by Congress, pending the next census.
[d] Twenty members were assigned to Massachusetts, but seven of these were credited to Maine when that area became a state.
[e] Normally 435, but temporarily increased two seats by Congress when Alaska and Hawaii became states.
[f] In thousands.

Sources: *Congressional Quarterly Weekly Report* (1990), 4240; Congressional Quarterly, *Congressional Quarterly's Guide to Congress*, 3d ed. (Washington, D.C.: Congressional Quarterly, 1982), 699; U.S. Bureau of the Census, *Historical Statistics of the United States* (Washington, D.C.: U.S. Government Printing Office, 1975), 1085.

Figure 7-1 Apportionment of Membership in the House of Representatives, by Region, 1910 and 1990

New England
23
32

Mid-Atlantic
66
92

Midwest
74
86

South
125
104

Border
32
47

Plains
22
41

Rocky Mountain
24
14

Pacific Coast
69
19

■ 1990
□ 1910

Source: This volume, Table 7-1.

Table 7-2   Members of Congress: Female, Black, Hispanic, Marital Status, and Age, 1971-1995

				His-	Not	Age					
						Under	40-	50-	60-	70-	80 and
Congress		Female	Black	panic	married[a]	40	49	59	69	79	over
Representatives											
92d	(1971)	12	12	5	26	40	133	152	86	19	3
93d	(1973)	14	15	5	34	45	132	154	80	20	2
94th	(1975)	18	16	5	54	69	138	137	75	14	2
95th	(1977)	18	16	5	56	81	121	147	71	15	0
96th	(1979)	16	16	6	69	86	125	145	63	14	0
97th	(1981)	19	16	6	86	94	142	132	54	12	1
98th	(1983)	21	20	10	68	86	145	132	57	13	1
99th	(1985)	22	19	11	69	71	154	131	59	17	2
100th	(1987)	23	22	11	64	63	153	137	56	24	2
101st	(1989)	25	23	11	—	41	163	133	74	20	2
102d	(1991)	29	25	10	—	39	153	133	86	20	4
103d	(1993)	48	38	17	—	47	152	129	91	13	3
104th	(1995)	49	39	18	—	53	153	136	80	12	1
Senators											
92d	(1971)	1	1	1	3	4	24	32	23	16	1
93d	(1973)	0	1	1	4	3	25	37	23	11	1
94th	(1975)[b]	0	1	1	6	5	21	35	24	15	0
95th	(1977)	0	1	0	9	6	26	35	21	10	2
96th	(1979)	1	0	0	5	10	31	33	17	8	1
97th	(1981)	2	0	0	7	9	35	36	14	6	0
98th	(1983)	2	0	0	10	7	28	39	20	3	3
99th	(1985)	2	0	0	8	4	27	38	25	4	2
100th	(1987)	2	0	0	11	5	30	36	22	5	2
101st	(1989)	2	0	0	—	0	30	40	22	6	2
102d	(1991)	2	0	0	—	0	22	47	24	5	2
103d	(1993)	6	1	0	—	1	16	49	22	11	1
104th	(1995)	8	1	0	—	1	14	41	27	16	1

Note: "—" indicates not available. As of beginning of first session of each Congress. Figures for representatives exclude vacancies. The counts above exclude nonvoting delegates and commissioners from American Samoa, Guam, Puerto Rico, the Virgin Islands, and Washington, D.C.

[a] Single, widowed, or divorced.
[b] Includes Sen. John Durkin (D-N.H.), seated September 1975.

Sources: Hispanic (1971-1985): Congressional Quarterly, *American Leaders, 1789-1987* (Washington, D.C.: Congressional Quarterly, 1987), 55; female and black (1971-1995) and Hispanic (1987-1995), *Congressional Quarterly Weekly Report* (1970), 2756; (1972), 2991; (1974), 3104; (1976), 3155; (1978), 3252; (1980), 3318; (1982), 2805; (November 12, 1994, Supplement), 10; (1984), 2921; (1986), 2863; (1988), 3294; (1990), 3835-3836; (January 16, 1993, Supplement), 12; not married and age (1971-1989): U.S. Bureau of the Census, *Statistical Abstract of the United States, 1988* (Washington, D.C.: U.S. Government Printing Office, 1987), 244; *1990*, 257; age (1991-1995): calculated by the editors from *Congressional Quarterly Weekly Report* (1991), 118-127; (January 16, 1993, Supplement), 12, 160-168; (1995), 541-549.

Table 7-3 Members of Congress: Seniority and Occupation, 1985-1995[a]

Seniority and occupation	Representatives					104th (1995)			Senators					104th (1995)[b]		
	99th (1985)	100th (1987)	101st (1989)	102d (1991)	103d (1993)	Dem.	Rep.	Total	99th (1985)	100th (1987)	101st (1989)	102d (1991)	103d (1993)	Dem.	Rep.	Total
Seniority[c]																
Under 2 years	49	51	38	55	115	15	77	92	8	14	11	6	15	0	12	12
2-9 years	237	221	230	176	139	101	87	189[d]	56	41	34	33	31	19	18	37
10-19 years	104	114	117	149	134	57	52	109	27	36	43	47	38	15	16	31
20-29 years	34	37	35	42	34	24	12	36	7	7	10	10	11	8	7	15
30 years or more	10	12	13	13	13	7	2	9	2	2	2	4	5	4	1	5
Total	435	435	435[e]	435	435	204	230	435	100	100	100	100	100	46	54	100
Occupation																
Agriculture	24	20	19	20	19	5	14	19	7	5	4	8	9	4	5	9
Business or banking	144	142	138	157	131	46	117	163[d]	30	28	28	31	27	11	13	24
Education	37	38	42	57	66	39	36	76[d]	10	12	11	10	12	5	5	10
Journalism	21	20	17	25	24	4	10	15[d]	8	8	8	10	8	5	3	8
Law	190	184	184	183	181	92	78	170	61	62	63	61	58	26	28	54
Public service/ politics	65	94	94	61	86	53	49	102	11	20	20	4	12	7	5	12

Note: Members of Congress may state more than one occupation; therefore, sum may be greater than total. Not all occupations reported are listed.

[a] Data for earlier years can be found in previous editions of *Vital Statistics on American Politics.*
[b] Data have been adjusted for the post-election switch to the Republicans by Senators Richard Shelby of Alabama and Ben Nighthorse Campbell of Colorado.
[c] Represents consecutive years of service.
[d] Includes Rep. Bernard Sanders (I-Vt).
[e] Includes two vacancies.

Sources: U.S. Bureau of the Census, *Statistical Abstract of the United States, 1988* (Washington, D.C.: U.S. Government Printing Office, 1987), 244; *Congressional Quarterly Weekly Report* (1988), 3295; (1989), 41-44; (1990), 3837; (1991), 127-130; (January 16, 1993, Supplement), 13, 170-173; (November 12, 1994, Supplement), 11; (1995), 550-553.

Table 7-4   Losses by President's Party in Midterm Elections, 1862-1994

Year	Party holding presidency	President's party: gain/loss of seats in House	President's party: gain/loss of seats in Senate
1862	R	−3	8
1866	R	−2	0
1870	R	−31	−4
1874	R	−96	−8
1878	R	−9	−6
1882	R	−33	3
1886	D	−12	3
1890	R	−85	0
1894	D	−116	−5
1898	R	−21	7
1902	R	9[a]	2
1906	R	−28	3
1910	R	−57	−10
1914	D	−59	5
1918	D	−19	−6
1922	R	−75	−8
1926	R	−10	−6
1930	R	−49	−8
1934	D	9	10
1938	D	−71	−6
1942	D	−55	−9
1946	D	−55	−12
1950	D	−29	−6
1954	R	−18	−1
1958	R	−48	−13
1962	D	−4	3
1966	D	−47	−4
1970	R	−12	2
1974	R	−48	−5
1978	D	−15	−3
1982	R	−26	1
1986	R	−5	−8
1990	R	−8	−1
1994	D	−53	−8

Note: Each entry is the difference between the number of seats won by the president's party in that midterm election and the number of seats won by that party in the preceding general election. Because of changes in the overall number of seats in the Senate and House, in the number of seats won by third parties, and in the number of vacancies, a Republican loss is not always matched precisely by a Democratic gain, or vice versa.

[a] Although the Republicans gained nine seats in the 1902 elections, they actually lost ground to the Democrats, who gained twenty-five seats after the increase in the overall number of representatives after the 1900 census.

Sources: 1862-1990: Norman J. Ornstein et al., eds., *Vital Statistics on Congress, 1993-1994* (Washington, D.C.: Congressional Quarterly, 1994), 53; 1994: *Congressional Quarterly Weekly Report* (1994), 3232, 3240, and this volume, Table 3-16.

Table 7-5 House and Senate Incumbents Reelected, Defeated, or Retired, 1946-1994

Chamber/ years	Retired[a]	Number seeking reelection	Defeated		Reelected	
			Primaries	General election	Total	Percentage of those seeking reelection
House						
1946	32	398	18	52	328	82.4
1948	29	400	15	68	317	79.3
1950	29	400	6	32	362	90.5
1952	42	389	9	26	354	91.0
1954	24	407	6	22	379	93.1
1956	21	411	6	16	389	94.6
1958	33	396	3	37	356	89.9
1960	26	405	5	25	375	92.6
1962	24	402	12	22	368	91.5
1964	33	397	8	45	344	86.6
1966	22	411	8	41	362	88.1
1968	23	409	4	9	396	96.8
1970	29	401	10	12	379	94.5
1972	40	390	12	13	365	93.6
1974	43	391	8	40	343	87.7
1976	47	384	3	13	368	95.8
1978	49	382	5	19	358	93.7
1980	34	398	6	31	361	90.7
1982	40	393	10	29	354	90.1
1984	22	411	3	16	392	95.4
1986	40	394	3	6	385	97.7
1988	23	409	1	6	402	98.3
1990	27	406	1	15	390	96.0
1992	65	368	19	24	325	88.3
1994	48	382	4	35	347	90.8
Senate						
1946	9	30	6	7	17	56.7
1948	8	25	2	8	15	60.0
1950	4	32	5	5	22	68.8
1952	4	31	2	9	20	64.5
1954	6	32	2	6	24	75.0
1956	6	29	0	4	25	86.2
1958	6	28	0	10	18	64.3
1960	5	29	0	1	28	96.6
1962	4	35	1	5	29	82.9
1964	2	33	1	4	28	84.8
1966	3	32	3	1	28	87.5
1968	6	28	4	4	20	71.4
1970	4	31	1	6	24	77.4
1972	6	27	2	5	20	74.1
1974	7	27	2	2	23	85.2
1976	8	25	0	9	16	64.0
1978	10	25	3	7	15	60.0
1980	5	29	4	9	16	55.2

Table 7-5   (*Continued*)

Chamber/ years	Retired[a]	Number seeking reelection	Defeated		Reelected	
			Primaries	General election	Total	Percentage of those seeking reelection
1982	3	30	0	2	28	93.3
1984	4	29	0	3	26	89.6
1986	6	28	0	7	21	75.0
1988	6	27	0	4	23	85.2
1990	3	32	0	1	31	96.9
1992	7	28	1	4	23	82.1
1994	8	26	0	2	24	92.2

[a] Does not include persons who died or resigned from office before the election.

Sources: 1946-1992: Norman J. Ornstein et al., eds., *Vital Statistics on Congress, 1993-1994* (Washington, D.C.: Congressional Quarterly, 1994), 58, 59; *Congressional Quarterly Weekly Report* (1994), 2945, 3232, 3240.

Table 7-6 House and Senate Seats That Changed Party, 1954-1994

Chamber/ year	Total changes	Incumbent defeated		Open seat	
		Democrat to Republican	Republican to Democrat	Democrat to Republican	Republican to Democrat
House					
1954	26	3	18	2	3
1956	20	7	7	2	4
1958	50	1	35	0	14
1960	37	23	2	6	6
1962	19	9	5	2	3
1964	57	5	39	5	8
1966	47	39	1	4	3
1968	11	5	0	2	4
1970	25	2	9	6	8
1972	23	6	3	9	5
1974	55	4	36	2	13
1976	22	7	5	3	7
1978	33	14	5	8	6
1980	41	27	3	10	1
1982	31	1	22	3	5
1984	22	13	3	5	1
1986	21	1	5	7	8
1988	9	2	4	1	2
1990	21	6	9	0	6
1992	43	16	8	11	8
1994	61	35	0	22	4
Senate					
1954	8	2	4	1	1
1956	8	1	3	3	1
1958	13	0	11	0	2
1960	2	1	0	1	0
1962	8	2	3	0	3
1964	4	1	3	0	0
1966	3	1	0	2	0
1968	9	4	0	3	2
1970	6	3	2	1	0
1972	10	1	4	3	2
1974	6	0	2	1	3
1976	14	5	4	2	3
1978	13	5	2	3	3
1980	12	9	0	3	0
1982	4	1	1	1	1
1984	4	1	2	0	1
1986	10	0	7	1	2
1988	7	1	3	2	1
1990	1	0	1	0	0
1992	4	2	2	0	0
1994	8	2	0	6	0

Note: This table reflects shifts in party control from before to after the November elections. It does not include shifts from the creation of districts or the reduction of two districts to one.

Sources: 1954-1992: Norman J. Ornstein et al., eds., *Vital Statistics on Congress, 1993-1994* (Washington, D.C.: Congressional Quarterly, 1994), 54, 56; 1994: *Congressional Quarterly Weekly Report* (1994), 3232-3233, 3240.

Table 7-7 Congressional Campaign Costs, by Party and Incumbency Status, 1987-1994[a]

Year/party/status	House					Senate				
	Number of candidates	Receipts[b]	Percentage individual contributions	Percentage committee[c] contributions	Expenditures[b]	Number of candidates	Receipts[b]	Percentage individual contributions	Percentage committee[c] contributions	Expenditures[b]
1987-1988										
Democrats	429	137.38	40.88	47.57	123.06	33	96.52	61.84	24.04	96.97
Incumbents	248	102.53	39.46	52.04	88.85	15	51.00	63.84	29.94	51.86
Challengers	154	22.50	47.96	32.62	22.14	12	26.18	73.87	17.38	25.93
Open seats	27	12.35	39.76	37.65	12.07	6	19.34	40.28	17.48	19.18
Republicans	384	105.08	54.43	32.12	99.19	33	86.09	68.15	24.63	88.01
Incumbents	164	72.46	52.40	39.58	67.11	12	47.25	66.94	28.40	49.34
Challengers	194	19.83	59.61	10.94	19.48	15	23.13	75.53	13.49	23.21
Open seats	26	12.79	57.94	22.67	12.60	6	15.71	60.92	29.66	15.45
Other	188	0.81	85.84	0.11	0.81	42	0.24	77.70	1.35	0.23
Total	1,001	243.28	46.88	40.73	223.07	108	182.86	64.83	24.28	185.21
1989-1990										
Democrats	413	142.83	39.61	48.33	130.70	34	85.67	66.49	23.74	83.78
Incumbents	249	111.35	37.98	52.63	99.70	17	63.58	67.82	26.74	61.51
Challengers	132	14.61	47.78	30.25	14.35	14	19.26	63.76	14.54	19.47
Open seats	32	16.87	43.27	35.63	16.65	3	2.83	55.12	18.73	2.81
Republicans	394	105.95	52.43	32.87	98.70	33	92.65	63.69	21.89	88.73
Incumbents	159	70.00	50.86	41.14	63.22	15	55.18	69.50	22.07	52.01
Challengers	206	22.95	56.38	11.29	22.62	15	30.04	57.36	17.44	29.93
Open seats	26	13.00	53.92	26.46	12.86	3	7.42	46.09	38.54	6.80
Other	164	0.96	61.39	8.72	0.97	11	[d]	[d]	[d]	[d]
Total	971	249.74	45.13	41.62	230.37	78	178.33	65.03	22.78	172.52

(Table continues)

Table 7-7 (Continued)

Year/party/status	House					Senate				
	Number of candidates	Receipts[b]	Percentage individual contributions	Percentage committee[c] contributions	Expenditures[b]	Number of candidates	Receipts[b]	Percentage individual contributions	Percentage committee[c] contributions	Expenditures[b]
1991-1992										
Democrats	426	178.57	44.19	44.36	186.53	35	97.65	67.13	25.47	98.63
Incumbents	213	119.35	41.12	51.57	128.44	15	41.43	55.35	37.82	42.71
Challengers	139	22.80	52.73	28.49	22.39	13	37.45	78.82	13.70	37.29
Open seats	74	36.42	48.86	30.69	35.70	7	18.76	69.82	21.70	18.63
Republicans	417	139.55	52.95	28.29	140.30	34	91.87	64.19	21.88	96.70
Incumbents	137	73.06	52.57	40.20	74.59	12	51.90	66.55	27.20	57.37
Challengers	210	41.06	51.03	10.19	40.56	15	19.38	67.63	11.97	19.20
Open seats	70	25.42	57.13	23.28	25.15	7	20.59	54.68	17.79	20.13
Other	294	3.29	58.40	9.17	3.23	43	1.27	31.34	0.75	1.27
Total	1,137	321.40	48.14	37.02	330.05	112	190.79	65.44	23.58	196.60
1993-1994										
Democrats	832	216.87	46.26	40.61	213.23	106	133.51	60.21	17.75	135.87
Incumbents	232	140.62	43.62	50.54	138.79	16	79.94	58.78	19.85	82.46
Challengers	379	29.17	53.88	21.22	28.71	50	15.74	53.97	15.69	15.56
Open Seats	221	47.08	49.41	22.98	45.73	40	37.84	65.84	14.17	37.86
Republicans	871	201.83	56.76	21.66	190.47	118	183.52	57.11	12.52	180.53
Incumbents	159	82.15	59.18	36.37	72.77	10	33.39	63.39	31.31	32.63
Challengers	498	69.77	55.57	9.25	68.62	70	102.30	48.38	30.93	101.60
Open seats	214	49.91	54.45	14.79	49.08	38	47.82	71.40	19.58	46.30
Other	342	2.82	41.34	10.01	1.95	109	2.03	63.31	1.33	1.99
Total	2,045	421.53	51.26	31.33	405.7	333	319.06	58.45	14.64	318.39

Note: Figures are for general election candidates (primary and general election activity included) for the calendar years indicated. Numbers of candidates are determined from election ballots in the states; financial activity determined from reports filed with the Federal Election Commission. Federal candidates raising or spending less than $5,000 are not required to file with the Federal Election Commission.

[a] Data for earlier years can be found in previous editions of *Vital Statistics on American Politics*.
[b] In millions of current dollars.
[c] Prior to 1993-1994, "Committee" refers to contributions received mostly from PACs but also from other candidates' committees and some bodies not registered with the Federal Election Commission. In 1993-1994 "Committee" refers to PACs.
[d] Neither receipts nor expenditures exceeded $5,000.

Sources: 1987-1988 (Other and Total): Federal Election Commission, ''FEC Final Report on 1988 Campaign Shows $459 Million Spent,'' press release, October 31, 1989, 7-8; 1987-1988 (all except Other and Total) and 1989-1990: ''1990 Congressional Election Spending Drops to Low Point,'' press release, February 22, 1991, 7-9; 1991-1992: Federal Election Commission, ''1992 Congressional Election Spending Jumps 52% to $678 Million,'' press release, March 4, 1993, 7; 1993-1994: ''1994 Congressional Fundraising Climbs to New High,'' press release, April 28, 1995, 4-5.

Table 7-8   Campaign Spending for Winning Congressional
Candidates, 1975-1994

Chamber/years	Receipts[a]	Expenditures[a]	Political action committee contributions	
			Total[a]	Percentage of receipts
House				
1975-1976	$42.5	$38.0	$10.9	25.6
1977-1978	60.0	55.6	17.0	28.3
1979-1980	86.0	78.0	27.0	31.4
1981-1982	123.1	114.7	42.7	34.7
1983-1984	144.8	127.0	59.5	41.1
1985-1986	172.7	154.9	72.8	42.2
1987-1988	191.0	171.0	86.4	45.2
1989-1990	198.3	179.1	91.5	46.1
1991-1992	235.9	243.6	97.7	41.4
1993-1994	245.8	230.6	97.6	39.7
Senate				
1975-1976	21.0	20.1	3.1	14.8
1977-1978	43.0	42.3	6.0	14.0
1979-1980	41.7	40.0	10.2	24.5
1981-1982	70.7	68.2	15.6	22.1
1983-1984	100.9	97.5	20.0	19.8
1985-1986	106.8	104.3	28.4	26.6
1987-1988	121.7	123.6	31.8	26.1
1989-1990	121.5	115.4	31.1	25.6
1991-1992	118.5	123.7	32.2	27.2
1993-1994	151.0	150.7	32.7	21.7

[a] In millions of current dollars.

Source: Federal Election Commission, "1994 Congressional Fundraising Climbs to New High," press release, April 28, 1995, 2; percentages calculated by the editors.

Table 7-9   Party Unity and Polarization in Congressional Voting,
1953-1994 (percent)

Year	House	Senate		Year	House	Senate
1953	52	—		1974	29	44
1954	38	47		1975	48	48
1955	41	30		1976	36	37
1956	44	53		1977	42	42
1957	59	36		1978	33	45
1958	40	44		1979	47	47
1959	55	48		1980	38	46
1960	53	37		1981	37	48
1961	50	62		1982	36	43
1962	46	41		1983	56	44
1963	49	47		1984	47	40
1964	55	36		1985	61	50
1965	52	42		1986	57	52
1966	41	50		1987	64	41
1967	36	35		1988	47	42
1968	35	32		1989	55	35
1969	31	36		1990	49	54
1970	27	35		1991	55	49
1971	38	42		1992	64	53
1972	27	36		1993	65	67
1973	42	40		1994	62	52

Note: "—" indicates not available. Data indicate the percentage of all recorded votes on which
a majority of voting Democrats opposed a majority of voting Republicans.

Sources: 1953-1992: Norman J. Ornstein et al., eds., *Vital Statistics on Congress, 1993-1994*
(Washington, D.C.: Congressional Quarterly, 1994), 200; 1993-1994: *Congressional Quarterly
Weekly Report* (1994), 3658.

Table 7-10 Party Unity in Congressional Voting, 1954-1994 (percent)

	House			Senate		
Year	All Democrats	Southern Democrats	Republicans	All Democrats	Southern Democrats	Republicans
1954	80	—	84	77	—	89
1955	84	68	78	82	78	82
1956	80	79	78	80	75	80
1957	79	71	75	79	81	81
1958	77	67	73	82	76	74
1959	85	77	85	76	63	80
1960	75	62	77	73	60	74
1961	—	—	—	—	—	—
1962	81	—	80	80	—	81
1963	85	—	84	79	—	79
1964	82	—	81	73	—	75
1965	80	55	81	75	55	78
1966	78	55	82	73	52	78
1967	77	53	82	75	59	73
1968	73	48	76	71	57	74
1969	71	47	71	74	53	72
1970	71	52	72	71	49	71
1971	72	48	76	74	56	75
1972	70	44	76	72	43	73
1973	75	55	74	79	52	74
1974	72	51	71	72	41	68
1975	75	53	78	76	48	71
1976	75	52	75	74	46	72
1977	74	55	77	72	48	75
1978	71	53	77	75	54	66
1979	75	60	79	76	62	73
1980	78	64	79	76	64	74
1981	75	57	80	77	64	85
1982	77	62	76	76	62	80
1983	82	67	80	76	70	79
1984	81	68	77	75	61	83
1985	86	76	80	79	68	81
1986	86	76	76	74	59	80
1987	88	78	79	85	80	78
1988	88	81	80	85	78	74
1989	86	77	76	79	69	79
1990	86	78	78	82	75	77
1991	86	78	81	83	73	83
1992	86	79	84	82	70	83
1993	89	83	88	87	78	86
1994	88	83	88	86	77	81

Note: "—" indicates not available. Data show percentage of members voting with a majority of their party on party unity votes. Party unity votes are those roll calls on which a majority of Democrats vote against a majority of Republicans. Percentages are calculated to eliminate the impact of absences as follows: unity = (unity)/(unity + opposition).

Sources: 1954-1992: Norman J. Ornstein et al., eds., *Vital Statistics on Congress, 1993-1994* (Washington, D.C.: Congressional Quarterly, 1994), 201-202; 1993-1994: *Congressional Quarterly Weekly Report* (1993), 3479; (1994), 3659.

Figure 7-2   Party Votes in the House, 1877-1994

Percent

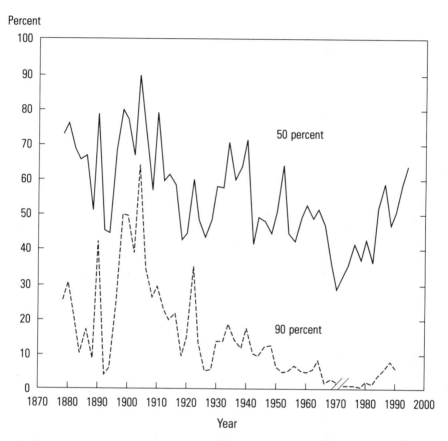

Note: Figures shown by Congress. A party vote occurs when the specified percentage (or more) of one party votes against the specified percentage (or more) of the other party.

Sources: 1877-1886 and 90 percent vote from 1972-1990: Brinck Kerr, "Structural Determinants of Party Voting in the U.S. Congress, 1877-1990," Ph.D. dissertation, Texas A&M University, 1993; 1887-1969: Joseph Cooper, David William Brady, and Patricia A. Hurley, "The Electoral Basis of Party Voting: Patterns and Trends in the U.S. House of Representatives, 1887-1969," in *The Impact of the Electoral Process,* ed. Louis Maisel and Joseph Cooper (Beverly Hills: Sage, 1977), 139; 1970-1990: Congressional Quarterly, *Congressional Quarterly Almanac* (Washington, D.C.: Congressional Quarterly, annual volumes); 1991-1994: *Congressional Quarterly Weekly Report* (1992), 3906, (1993), 3480, (1994), 3658.

Table 7-11 Conservative Coalition Votes and Victories, 1957-1994 (percent)

	House		Senate	
Year	Votes	Victories	Votes	Victories
1957	16	81	11	100
1958	15	64	19	86
1959	13	91	19	65
1960	20	35	22	67
1961	30	74	32	48
1962	13	44	15	71
1963	13	67	19	44
1964	11	67	17	47
1965	25	25	24	39
1966	19	32	30	51
1967	22	73	18	54
1968	22	63	25	80
1969	25	71	28	67
1970	17	70	26	64
1971	31	79	28	86
1972	25	79	29	63
1973	25	67	21	54
1974	22	67	30	54
1975	28	52	28	48
1976	17	59	26	58
1977	22	60	29	74
1978	20	57	23	46
1979	121	73	18	65
1980	16	67	20	75
1981	21	88	21	95
1982	16	78	20	90
1983	18	71	12	89
1984	14	75	17	94
1985	13	84	16	93
1986	11	78	20	93
1987	9	88	8	100
1988	8	82	10	97
1989	11	80	12	95
1990	10	74	11	95
1991	9	86	14	95
1992	10	88	14	87
1993	7	98	10	90
1994	7	42	10	72

Note: "Votes" is the percentage of all roll call votes on which a majority of voting southern Democrats and a majority of voting Republicans—the Conservative Coalition—opposed the stand taken by a majority of voting northern Democrats. "Victories" is the percentage of Conservative Coalition votes won.

Sources: 1957-1992: Norman J. Ornstein et al., eds., *Vital Statistics on Congress, 1993-1994* (Washington, D.C.: Congressional Quarterly, 1994), 203; 1993-1994: *Congressional Quarterly Weekly Report* (1993), 3435; (1994), 3627.

Figure 7-3   Congressional Staff, 1930-1993

Number of employees

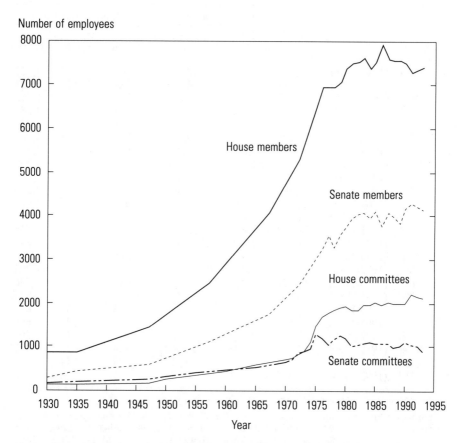

Year

Source: Norman Ornstein et al., eds., *Vital Statistics on Congress, 1995-1996* (Washington, D.C.: Congressional Quarterly, 1995), Tables 5-2 and 5-5.

Table 7-12   Bills, Acts, and Resolutions, 1947-1994

		Measures introduced			Measures enacted		
Congress		Bills	Joint resolutions	Total	Public	Private	Total
80th	(1947-1948)	10,108	689	10,797	906	457	1,363
81st	(1949-1951)	14,219	769	14,988	921	1,103	2,024
82d	(1951-1952)	12,062	668	12,730	594	1,023	1,617
83d	(1953-1954)	14,181	771	14,952	781	1,002	1,783
84th	(1955-1956)	16,782	905	17,687	1,028	893	1,921
85th	(1957-1958)	18,205	907	19,112	936	784	1,720
86th	(1959-1960)	17,230	1,031	18,261	800	492	1,292
87th	(1961-1962)	17,230	1,146	18,376	885	684	1,569
88th	(1963-1964)	16,079	1,401	17,480	666	360	1,026
89th	(1965-1966)	22,483	1,520	24,003	810	473	1,283
90th	(1967-1968)	24,786	1,674	26,460	640	362	1,002
91st	(1969-1970)	24,631	1,672	26,303	695	246	941
92d	(1971-1972)	21,363	1,606	22,969	607	161	768
93d	(1973-1974)	21,950	1,446	23,396	651	123	774
94th	(1975-1976)	19,762	1,334	21,096	588	141	729
95th	(1977-1978)	18,045	1,342	19,387	633	170	803
96th	(1979-1980)	11,722	861	12,583	613	123	736
97th	(1981-1982)	10,582	908	11,490	473	56	529
98th	(1983-1984)	10,134	1,022	11,156	623	54	677
99th	(1985-1986)	8,697	1,188	9,885	664	24	688
100th	(1987-1988)	8,515	1,073	9,588	713	48	761
101st	(1989-1990)	9,257	1,095	10,352	404	7	411
102d	(1991-1992)	9,601	909	10,510	589	14	603
103d	(1993-1994)	7,883	661	8,544	465	8	473

Note: Measures exclude simple and concurrent resolutions.

Sources: 80th-99th: United States Congress, *Calendars of the U.S. House of Representatives and History of Legislation*, 99th Cong., Final ed., 19-57 through 19-68; 100th-102d: *Congressional Record*, Daily Digest, "Resume of Congressional Activity," 100th Cong. (2d sess., D1399), 101st (1st sess., D1431; 2d sess., D1449), 102d (2d sess., D1335), 103d (2d sess., D1275).

Figure 7-4   Proportion of Measures Introduced That Were Passed, 1789-1994

Proportion

Note: Measures include acts, bills, and joint resolutions. Prior to 1824 only bills and acts are included. Figures are for each Congress.

Sources: 1789-1968: U.S. Bureau of the Census, *Historical Statistics of the United States,* Series Y189-198 (Washington, D.C.: U.S. Government Printing Office, 1975), 1081-1082; 1969-1994: Table 7-12, this volume.

Table 7-13 Recorded Votes in the House and the Senate, 1947-1994

Year	House	Senate		Year	House	Senate
1947	84	138		1971	320	423
1948	75	110		1972	329	532
1949	121	226		1973	541	594
1950	154	229		1974	537	544
1951	109	202		1975	612	602
1952	72	129		1976	661	688
1953	71	89		1977	706	635
1954	76	181		1978	834	516
1955	73	88		1979	672	497
1956	74	136		1980	681	546
1957	100	111		1981	371	497
1958	93	202		1982	488	469
1959	87	215		1983	533	381
1960	93	207		1984	463	292
1961	116	207		1985	482	381
1962	124	227		1986	488	359
1963	119	229		1987	511	420
1964	113	312		1988	465	379
1965	201	259		1989	379	312
1966	193	238		1990	536	326
1967	245	315		1991	444	280
1968[a]	233	280		1992	488	270
1969	177	245		1993	615	395
1970	266	422		1994	507	329

Note: The count of recorded votes prior to 1980 excludes quorum calls.

[a] The Senate recorded vote total does not include one "yea-and-nay" vote that was ruled invalid for lack of a quorum.

Sources: 1947-1979: Norman J. Ornstein et al., eds., *Vital Statistics on Congress, 1989-1990*, (Washington, D.C.: Congressional Quarterly, 1990), 158; 1980-1994: Congressional Quarterly Weekly Report (1994), 3623.

Table 7-14 Number of Committees and Majority Party Chairmanships, 1955-1996

Congress		Number of committees[a]	Party in majority	Number of majority party members	Number of majority party members chairing standing committees and subcommittees	Percentage of majority party members chairing standing committees and subcommittees	Number of majority party members chairing all committees and subcommittees	Percentage of majority party members chairing all committees and subcommittees
House								
84th	(1955-1956)	130	D	232	63	27.2	75	32.3
90th	(1967-1968)	185	D	247	111	44.9	117	47.4
92d	(1971-1972)	175	D	254	120	47.2	131	51.6
94th	(1975-1976)	204	D	289	142	49.1	150	51.9
96th	(1979-1980)	193	D	276	144	52.2	149	54.0
97th	(1981-1982)	174	D	243	121	49.8	125	51.4
98th	(1983-1984)	172	D	267	124	46.4	127	47.6
99th	(1985-1986)	191	D	253	129	51.0	131	51.8
100th	(1987-1988)	192	D	258	128	49.6	132	51.2
101st	(1989-1990)	189	D	260	134	51.5	137	52.7
102d	(1991-1992)	185	D	267	130	48.7	135	50.6
103d	(1993-1994)	146	D	258	113	43.8	116	45.0
104th	(1995-1996)	110	R	230	86	37.4	86	37.4

(Table continues)

Table 7-14 (*Continued*)

Congress		Number of committees[a]	Party in majority	Number of majority party members	Number of majority party members chairing standing committees and subcommittees	Percentage of majority party members chairing standing committees and subcommittees	Number of majority party members chairing all committees and subcommittees	Percentage of majority party members chairing all committees and subcommittees
Senate								
84th	(1955-1956)	133	D	48	42	87.5	42	87.5
90th	(1967-1968)	155	D	64	55	85.9	58	90.6
92d	(1971-1972)	181	D	55[b]	51	92.7	52	94.5
94th	(1975-1976)	205	D	62[b]	57	91.9	57	91.9
96th	(1979-1980)	130	D	59[b]	58	98.3	58	98.3
97th	(1981-1982)	136	R	53	51	96.2	52	98.1
98th	(1983-1984)	137	R	54	52	96.3	52	96.3
99th	(1985-1986)	120	R	53	49	92.4	49	92.4
100th	(1987-1988)	118	D	54	47	87.0	47	87.0
101st	(1989-1990)	118	D	55	46	83.6	46	83.6
102d	(1991-1992)	119	D	56	50	89.3	50	89.3
103d	(1993-1994)	111	D	57	46	80.7	46	80.7
104th	(1995-1996)	92	R	54	46	81.5	44	81.5

[a] Includes standing committees, subcommittees of standing committees, select and special committees, subcommittees of select and special committees, joint committees, and subcommittees of joint committees.
[b] Includes Harry Byrd, Jr. (I-Va.), elected as independent.

Sources: 84th-103d: Norman J. Ornstein et al., eds., *Vital Statistics on Congress, 1993-1994* (Washington, D.C.: Congressional Quarterly, 1994), 113, 117-118; 104th calculated by the editors from *Congressional Quarterly Weekly Report*, supplement to vol. 53, no. 12 (March 25, 1995).

Table 7-15 The 104th Congress: The House of Representatives

State/district/representative	Party	Year born	Year first elected	% vote in 1994 Primary	General	Campaign expenditures (1993-94)	VP	PS	PU	CC	ADA	AFL-CIO	CCUS	ACU
Alabama														
1. Callahan	R	1932	1984	U	67	$416,080	94	41	88	100	5	13	92	100
2. Everett	R	1937	1992	U	74	224,606	99	44	80	97	0	33	75	100
3. Browder	D	1943	1989	85	64	171,912	97	77	76	94	25	78	75	62
4. Bevill	D	1921	1966	U	98	274,164	95	88	85	94	35	56	50	50
5. Cramer	D	1947	1990	U	50	565,457	97	86	81	97	40	78	58	38
6. Bachus	R	1947	1992	U	79	332,233	96	44	94	97	15	22	82	95
7. Hilliard	D	1942	1992	U	77	337,772	86	75	94	39	80	100	25	29
Alaska														
AL Young	R	1933	1973	U	57	930,513	97	45	83	97	10	33	92	100
Arizona														
1. Salmon	R	1958	1994	39	56	508,421	-	-	-	-	-	-	-	-
2. Pastor	D	1943	1991	74	62	349,627	98	84	95	42	80	78	42	14
3. Stump	R	1927	1976	U	70	152,718	99	27	99	94	0	11	75	100
4. Shadegg	R	1949	1994	43	60	590,725	-	-	-	-	-	-	-	-
5. Kolbe	R	1942	1984	80	68	478,730	99	51	83	82	15	11	100	80
6. Hayworth	R	1958	1994	45	55	538,650	-	-	-	-	-	-	-	-
Arkansas														
1. Lincoln	D	1960	1992	U	53	505,453	99	73	79	67	60	33	83	10
2. Thornton	D	1928	1990	U	57	423,597	97	90	93	71	75	78	50	19

(Table continues)

Table 7-15 (*Continued*)

State/ district/ representative	Party	Year born	Year first elected	% vote in 1994 Primary	% vote in 1994 General	Campaign expenditures (1993-94)	Voting ratings[a] VP	PS	PU	CC	ADA	AFL-CIO	CCUS	ACU
3. Hutchinson	R	1949	1992	U	68	$288,412	98	38	95	86	5	22	75	95
4. Dickey	R	1939	1992	U	52	832,117	97	42	93	91	0	22	75	95
California														
1. Riggs	R	1950	1990	63	53	605,185	—	62	71	79	25	36	88	75
2. Herger	R	1945	1986	U	64	572,629	94	39	97	94	5	0	91	100
3. Fazio	D	1942	1978	75	50	1,972,033	98	87	95	50	75	78	42	14
4. Doolittle	R	1950	1990	U	61	664,109	97	36	99	97	5	13	82	100
5. Matsui	D	1941	1978	U	68	929,895	95	93	98	32	75	67	42	11
6. Woolsey	D	1937	1992	U	58	649,388	99	77	99	8	100	100	25	0
7. Miller	D	1945	1974	U	70	442,581	93	79	98	3	90	100	25	0
8. Pelosi	D	1940	1987	91	82	370,000	94	79	99	0	90	89	25	0
9. Dellums	D	1935	1970	U	72	482,877	94	74	99	0	100	100	17	5
10. Baker	R	1940	1992	77	59	909,065	98	41	98	97	0	11	83	100
11. Pombo	R	1961	1992	U	62	657,627	95	40	87	100	5	25	92	100
12. Lantos	D	1928	1980	U	67	322,016	91	84	95	46	70	88	50	24
13. Stark	D	1931	1972	77	65	391,319	93	78	98	0	95	100	27	0
14. Eshoo	D	1942	1992	87	61	487,660	100	81	98	11	95	89	33	0
15. Mineta	D	1931	1974	U	60	1,009,947	98	90	98	15	90	75	33	10
16. Lofgren	D	1947	1994	45	65	646,764	—	—	—	—	—	—	—	—
17. Farr	D	1941	1993	81	52	387,872	96	84	99	13	90	88	45	0
18. Condit	D	1948	1989	U	66	387,494	97	66	59	66	45	67	92	38
19. Radanovich	R	1955	1994	51	57	468,818	—	—	—	—	—	—	—	—
20. Dooley	D	1954	1990	U	57	275,544	96	74	82	71	55	22	92	22
21. Thomas	R	1941	1978	70	68	434,146	96	51	90	94	10	29	100	84

#	Name	Party	Born	Elected		%	Expenditures								
22.	Seastrand	R	1941	1994	59	49	630,933	'	'	'	'	'	'	'	'
23.	Gallegly	R	1944	1986	U	66	300,846	92	54	94	100	10	25	92	95
24.	Beilenson	D	1932	1976	87	49	587,641	99	85	97	19	95	89	33	0
25.	McKeon	R	1939	1992	82	65	474,945	98	48	96	100	5	11	100	95
26.	Berman	D	1941	1982	76	63	432,535	92	84	98	15	90	88	30	0
27.	Moorhead	R	1922	1972	77	53	968,212	99	41	97	97	0	11	83	100
28.	Dreier	R	1952	1980	U	67	279,050	98	38	99	100	5	0	92	100
29.	Waxman	D	1939	1974	80	68	186,127	95	77	98	3	90	100	25	0
30.	Becerra	D	1958	1992	82	66	234,096	89	78	98	13	100	78	36	0
31.	Martinez	D	1929	1982	55	59	123,767	96	86	94	63	70	67	58	15
32.	Dixon	D	1934	1978	90	78	141,941	96	91	99	15	75	88	33	10
33.	Roybal-Allard	D	1941	1992	79	81	124,271	99	87	99	14	100	78	33	0
34.	Torres	D	1930	1982	U	62	178,972	94	93	98	27	75	75	42	10
35.	Waters	D	1938	1990	U	78	177,791	95	75	97	6	100	89	25	10
36.	Harman	D	1945	1992	U	48	1,300,855	96	88	83	74	60	67	83	10
37.	Tucker	D	1957	1992	84	77	269,976	76	77	97	25	90	89	42	19
38.	Horn	R	1931	1992	76	58	442,982	95	69	69	85	30	33	91	11
39.	Royce	R	1951	1992	U	66	403,335	96	34	97	82	10	11	83	57
40.	Lewis	R	1934	1978	69	71	209,763	95	55	81	91	0	13	82	95
41.	Kim	R	1939	1992	41	62	810,211	100	44	96	100	5	0	100	88
42.	Brown	D	1920	1962	U	51	485,455	87	89	96	27	80	78	33	95
43.	Calvert	R	1953	1992	51	55	768,290	93	58	91	100	5	13	100	10
44.	Bono	R	1935	1994	49	56	731,238	'	'	'	'	'	'	'	90
45.	Rohrabacher	R	1947	1988	U	69	187,656	99	29	97	69	10	22	75	86
46.	Dornan	R	1933	1976	U	57	2,261,696	92	36	97	97	0	33	75	100
47.	Cox	R	1952	1988	86	72	246,400	94	37	98	89	0	11	82	100
48.	Packard	R	1931	1982	81	73	210,125	99	45	91	97	0	0	92	95
49.	Bilbray	R	1951	1994	51	49	750,654	'	'	'	'	'	'	'	'
50.	Filner	D	1942	1992	U	57	818,051	100	79	98	17	100	78	50	0

(Table continues)

Table 7-15 (*Continued*)

State/ district/ representative	Party	Year born	Year first elected	% vote in 1994 Primary	General	Campaign expenditures (1993-94)	VP	PS	PU	CC	ADA	AFL-CIO	CCUS	ACU
51. Cunningham	R	1941	1990	86	67	$395,144	98	55	91	94	15	22	100	95
52. Hunter	R	1948	1980	U	64	559,926	96	33	93	94	0	33	73	100
Colorado														
1. Schroeder	D	1940	1972	85	60	502,466	99	74	83	14	100	78	42	5
2. Skaggs	D	1943	1986	U	57	576,719	99	90	97	20	80	67	50	10
3. McInnis	R	1953	1992	U	70	387,210	99	43	86	88	15	11	83	81
4. Allard	R	1943	1990	U	72	267,997	99	40	97	94	5	0	83	95
5. Hefley	R	1935	1986	U	U	137,960	99	33	96	89	0	22	75	100
6. Schaefer	R	1936	1983	U	70	495,506	96	35	96	92	10	22	83	90
Connecticut														
1. Kennelly	D	1936	1982	U	73	579,121	98	90	96	42	85	67	50	10
2. Gejdenson	D	1948	1980	U	43	1,422,126	96	87	99	17	80	89	36	10
3. DeLauro	D	1943	1990	U	63	655,245	99	86	97	31	90	78	42	5
4. Shays	R	1945	1987	U	74	438,259	100	56	67	42	55	22	100	38
5. Franks	R	1953	1990	U	52	574,024	98	71	74	86	20	38	91	70
6. Johnson	R	1935	1982	U	64	597,703	97	68	62	66	30	22	100	52
Delaware														
AL Castle	R	1939	1992	U	71	400,083	99	71	82	92	20	33	100	67
Florida														
1. Scarborough	R	1963	1994	54	62	345,687	-	-	-	-	-	-	-	-
2. Peterson	D	1935	1990	U	61	334,740	96	84	87	85	50	67	67	38

Note: The column header "Voting ratings" spans VP, PS, PU, CC, ADA, AFL-CIO, CCUS, ACU. Footnote marker: *Voting ratings*[a]. "AFL-CIO" appears above the CIO column.

3.	Brown	D	1946	1992	67	58	383,017	94	90	95	47	85	78	50	24
4.	Fowler	R	1942	1992	U	U*	103,233	97	62	89	94	15	22	92	90
5.	Thurman	D	1951	1992	U	57	564,265	99	73	81	69	65	89	67	19
6.	Stearns	R	1941	1988	U	99	189,905	99	35	99	89	0	22	75	100
7.	Mica	R	1943	1992	U	73	300,058	98	42	94	97	10	22	83	95
8.	McCollum	R	1944	1980	U	100	448,334	91	44	91	93	0	13	91	95
9.	Bilirakis	R	1930	1982	U	100	191,717	95	50	89	94	20	56	75	86
10.	Young	R	1930	1970	U	U*	146,246	97	55	87	85	25	33	83	81
11.	Gibbons	D	1920	1962	U	52	1,155,373	93	90	94	51	70	63	42	16
12.	Canady	R	1954	1992	U	65	333,623	99	54	94	100	5	0	92	90
13.	Miller	R	1942	1992	81	U*	278,042	98	42	96	82	20	11	100	90
14.	Goss	R	1938	1988	U	U*	142,940	100	51	94	89	10	22	92	86
15.	Weldon	R	1953	1994	54	54	478,303	-	-	-	-	-	-	-	-
16.	Foley	R	1954	1994	61	58	629,406	-	-	-	-	-	-	-	-
17.	Meek	D	1926	1992	U	100	166,452	95	86	97	32	95	78	50	10
18.	Ros-Lehtinen	R	1952	1989	U	U*	148,381	94	61	78	72	25	67	82	65
19.	Johnston	D	1931	1988	U	66	288,073	92	83	97	14	90	63	67	5
20.	Deutsch	D	1957	1992	U	61	1,011,936	99	84	92	49	60	67	75	19
21.	Diaz-Balart	R	1954	1992	U	100	125,082	99	61	71	80	25	78	83	71
22.	Shaw	R	1939	1980	78	63	808,984	96	64	89	94	15	13	92	74
23.	Hastings	D	1936	1992	U	U*	217,742	78	78	97	21	80	88	36	7
Georgia															
1.	Kingston	R	1955	1992	U	77	296,202	99	43	89	97	5	11	83	100
2.	Bishop	D	1947	1992	67	66	473,931	95	90	92	70	75	56	64	25
3.	Collins	R	1944	1992	U	66	503,867	98	36	92	86	0	22	75	95
4.	Linder	R	1942	1992	U	58	671,801	99	46	96	100	0	11	92	95
5.	Lewis	D	1940	1986	U	69	323,725	96	73	97	6	100	100	25	5
6.	Gingrich	R	1943	1978	77	64	1,817,792	95	45	95	100	5	13	91	100
7.	Barr	R	1948	1994	57	52	622,336	-	-	-	-	-	-	-	-

(Table continues)

Table 7-15 (*Continued*)

State/ district/ representative	Party	Year born	Year first elected	% vote in 1994 Primary	% vote in 1994 General	Campaign expenditures (1993-94)	VP	PS	PU	CC	ADA	AFL- CIO	CCUS	ACU
8. Chambliss	R	1943	1994	U	63	$680,079	–	–	–	–	–	–	–	–
9. Deal	R	1942	1992	53	58	368,648	98	64	63	91	15	33	92	67
10. Norwood	R	1941	1994	51	65	787,441	–	–	–	–	–	–	–	–
11. McKinney	D	1955	1992	U	66	274,232	99	77	99	3	100	100	33	0
Hawaii														
1. Abercrombie	D	1938	1990	66	54	391,451	97	72	98	17	100	89	25	0
2. Mink	D	1927	1990	85	70	157,523	98	74	99	3	100	100	17	0
Idaho														
1. Chenoweth	R	1938	1994	48	55	796,149	–	–	–	–	–	–	–	–
2. Crapo	R	1951	1992	U	75	352,461	99	40	96	97	5	11	83	90
Illinois														
1. Rush	D	1946	1992	U	76	195,833	90	74	97	6	100	89	33	5
2. Reynolds	D	1952	1992	56	98	427,562	77	86	99	21	85	63	50	0
3. Lipinski	D	1937	1982	U	54	366,804	95	74	77	71	45	88	42	38
4. Gutierrez	D	1954	1992	64	75	367,811	93	69	96	6	90	100	33	0
5. Flanagan	R	1962	1994	38	54	112,638	–	–	–	–	–	–	–	–
6. Hyde	R	1924	1974	82	73	423,027	98	54	87	86	5	11	96	90
7. Collins	D	1931	1973	U	80	200,544	85	70	96	3	95	89	25	6
8. Crane	R	1930	1969	40	65	722,267	91	29	98	81	5	0	83	100
9. Yates	D	1909	1948	75	66	217,952	95	72	98	0	100	89	25	0
10. Porter	R	1935	1980	66	75	538,716	97	55	73	61	30	33	83	52
11. Weller	R	1957	1994	32	61	877,429	–	–	–	–	–	–	–	–

12.	Costello	D	1949	1988	U	66	499,844	98	73	76	72	50	78	50	38
13.	Fawell	R	1929	1984	U	73	278,469	99	51	85	78	25	11	92	81
14.	Hastert	R	1942	1986	80	76	696,217	97	47	95	94	5	0	92	95
15.	Ewing	R	1935	1991	U	68	511,926	96	43	94	94	10	0	92	90
16.	Manzullo	R	1944	1992	U	71	579,059	99	46	94	94	5	0	92	95
17.	Evans	D	1951	1982	U	55	270,939	99	77	99	6	100	100	25	0
18.	LaHood	R	1945	1994	50	60	697,727	–	–	–	–	–	–	–	–
19.	Poshard	D	1945	1988	U	58	164,541	100	63	65	69	55	56	83	38
20.	Durbin	D	1944	1982	U	55	692,886	99	78	98	22	95	78	25	0
Indiana															
1.	Visclosky	D	1949	1984	77	56	290,049	98	91	96	36	75	78	50	19
2.	McIntosh	R	1958	1994	43	54	973,209	–	–	–	–	–	–	–	–
3.	Roemer	D	1956	1990	86	55	350,594	99	83	86	69	65	56	92	14
4.	Souder	R	1950	1994	40	55	422,161	–	–	–	–	–	–	–	–
5.	Buyer	R	1958	1992	U	70	501,287	98	50	94	97	0	11	100	100
6.	Burton	R	1938	1982	87	77	455,095	97	29	99	97	0	22	73	100
7.	Myers	R	1927	1966	54	65	543,967	99	42	75	92	5	33	83	100
8.	Hostettler	R	1961	1994	35	52	309,484	–	–	–	–	–	–	–	–
9.	Hamilton	D	1931	1964	82	52	578,468	99	82	78	69	60	44	67	38
10.	Jacobs	D	1932	1964	61	53	27,554	98	71	62	40	85	56	83	30
Iowa															
1.	Leach	R	1942	1976	U	60	268,937	99	64	69	69	40	22	100	33
2.	Nussle	R	1960	1990	U	56	876,142	99	43	94	81	25	22	100	70
3.	Lightfoot	R	1938	1984	U	58	709,487	98	51	89	94	5	0	92	95
4.	Ganske	R	1949	1994	78	53	1,195,525	–	–	–	–	–	–	–	–
5.	Latham	R	1948	1994	62	61	742,308	–	–	–	–	–	–	–	–

(Table continues)

Table 7-15 (Continued)

State/ district/ representative	Party	Year born	Year first elected	% vote in 1994 Primary	General	Campaign expenditures (1993-94)	VP	PS	PU	CC	ADA	AFL-CIO	CCUS	ACU
Kansas														
1. Roberts	R	1936	1980	U	77	$309,950	98	40	96	97	0	0	92	100
2. Brownback	R	1956	1994	48	66	749,330	-	-	75	78	30	22	100	57
3. Meyers	R	1928	1984	59	57	376,484	99	70	75	-	-	-	-	-
4. Tiahrt	R	1951	1994	54	53	199,973	-	-	-	-	-	-	-	-
Kentucky														
1. Whitfield	R	1943	1994	53	51	349,472	-	-	-	-	-	-	-	-
2. Lewis	R	1946	1994	U	60	393,266	100	40	96	89	0	40	75	86
3. Ward	D	1951	1994	27	44	565,022	-	-	-	-	-	-	-	-
4. Bunning	R	1931	1986	U	74	560,590	99	31	96	83	5	11	83	95
5. Rogers	R	1937	1980	U	79	348,253	98	49	81	86	15	56	75	89
6. Baesler	D	1941	1992	U	59	223,327	99	85	83	83	45	56	92	33
Louisiana														
1. Livingston	R	1943	1977	81	+	348,081	93	43	84	94	0	25	83	95
2. Jefferson	D	1947	1990	75	+	608,567	92	89	97	29	90	78	33	15
3. Tauzin	D	1943	1980	76	+	680,211	97	56	51	92	15	33	100	76
4. Fields	D	1962	1992	70	+	271,463	97	76	97	25	90	100	30	5
5. McCrery	R	1949	1988	80	+	459,098	95	56	86	92	5	13	100	90
6. Baker	R	1948	1986	81	+	518,945	93	47	94	100	0	13	100	100
7. Hayes	D	1946	1986	53	+	436,254	90	60	57	94	20	38	91	83

District	Member	Party													
Maine															
1.	Longley	R	1951	1994	43	52	196,048	–	–	–	–	–	–	–	–
2.	Baldacci	D	1955	1994	27	46	442,226	–	–	–	–	–	–	–	–
Maryland															
1.	Gilchrest	R	1946	1990	65	68	153,133	99	64	72	78	30	22	100	62
2.	Ehrlich	R	1957	1994	57	63	562,892	–	–	–	–	–	–	–	–
3.	Cardin	D	1943	1986	87	71	550,172	97	79	96	31	75	89	50	10
4.	Wynn	D	1951	1992	84	75	358,607	97	82	97	26	95	89	42	0
5.	Hoyer	D	1939	1981	82	59	1,295,542	97	86	95	57	70	78	42	24
6.	Bartlett	R	1926	1992	84	66	369,904	99	40	99	100	0	0	92	100
7.	Mfume	D	1948	1986	U	82	161,285	94	73	96	9	95	100	33	0
8.	Morella	R	1931	1986	70	70	306,968	98	78	46	51	70	56	83	29
Massachusetts															
1.	Olver	D	1936	1991	100	99	317,317	99	78	99	3	100	89	33	0
2.	Neal	D	1949	1988	100	59	318,582	96	79	98	26	95	89	42	0
3.	Blute	R	1956	1992	99	55	977,107	99	68	72	78	20	56	92	67
4.	Frank	D	1940	1980	86	99	208,936	97	69	98	0	100	100	25	0
5.	Meehan	D	1956	1992	76	70	803,523	93	70	91	12	85	67	83	16
6.	Torkildsen	R	1958	1992	99	51	768,072	98	73	69	78	15	33	100	67
7.	Markey	D	1946	1976	100	64	757,993	97	76	99	3	85	88	33	0
8.	Kennedy	D	1952	1986	99	99	839,275	96	78	98	20	90	75	58	5
9.	Moakley	D	1927	1972	86	70	981,247	98	78	99	25	95	100	25	0
10.	Studds	D	1937	1972	76	69	639,313	97	82	99	0	95	89	33	0
Michigan															
1.	Stupak	D	1952	1992	U	57	678,925	99	72	85	67	70	100	42	24
2.	Hoekstra	R	1953	1992	U	75	134,979	99	40	94	81	20	0	100	86
3.	Ehlers	R	1934	1993	U	74	531,562	99	47	77	81	25	0	100	81

(Table continues)

Table 7-15 (Continued)

State/ district/ representative	Party	Year born	Year first elected	% vote in 1994 Primary	General	Campaign expenditures (1993-94)	VP	PS	PU	CC	ADA	AFL-CIO	CCUS	ACU
4. Camp	R	1953	1990	U	73	$444,419	98	51	92	89	20	11	100	95
5. Barcia	D	1952	1992	U	65	205,769	98	64	70	75	50	78	67	43
6. Upton	R	1953	1986	U	73	575,406	100	49	83	64	35	33	92	67
7. Smith	R	1934	1992	68	65	289,573	97	47	93	91	5	13	100	95
8. Chrysler	R	1942	1994	U	52	356,924	-	-	-	-	-	-	-	-
9. Kildee	D	1929	1976	U	51	963,249	100	77	93	25	90	100	42	5
10. Bonior	D	1945	1976	U	62	1,123,472	97	79	99	11	95	100	25	5
11. Knollenberg	R	1933	1992	U	68	507,622	99	44	96	94	0	0	92	100
12. Levin	D	1931	1982	80	52	1,536,445	99	84	95	28	85	89	50	5
13. Rivers	D	1956	1994	56	52	610,394	-	-	-	-	-	-	-	-
14. Conyers	D	1929	1964	51	81	575,696	95	74	98	13	100	100	25	5
15. Collins	D	1939	1990	100	84	177,120	91	69	99	3	100	100	25	0
16. Dingell	D	1926	1955	U	59	1,075,063	93	82	94	41	70	75	33	15
Minnesota														
1. Gutknecht	R	1951	1994	57	55	581,099	-	-	-	-	-	-	-	-
2. Minge	D	1942	1992	U	52	622,920	99	68	72	61	60	33	92	14
3. Ramstad	R	1946	1990	U	73	498,146	99	55	82	72	30	11	100	62
4. Vento	D	1940	1976	U	55	339,703	98	78	98	6	100	89	27	0
5. Sabo	D	1938	1978	57	62	333,075	98	83	99	6	95	89	25	10
6. Luther	D	1945	1994	U	50	1,133,977	-	-	-	-	-	-	-	-
7. Peterson	D	1944	1990	U	51	584,092	99	58	59	74	45	44	83	52
8. Oberstar	D	1934	1974	U	66	488,411	98	74	96	14	80	89	25	15

Voting ratings[a]

	Party													
Mississippi														
1. Wicker	R	1951	1994	53	63	729,704	-	-	-	-	-	-	-	-
2. Thompson	D	1948	1993	U	54	396,502	94	88	96	37	80	88	36	20
3. Montgomery	D	1920	1966	U	68	571,635	98	79	76	97	35	50	58	57
4. Parker	D	1949	1988	58	68	672,593	96	68	62	100	20	50	83	67
5. Taylor	D	1953	1989	U	60	182,381	98	60	37	97	15	56	50	67
Missouri														
1. Clay	D	1931	1968	53	63	349,528	86	71	86	9	85	100	18	14
2. Talent	R	1956	1992	U	67	773,953	99	51	95	97	5	0	100	95
3. Gephardt	D	1941	1976	77	58	2,621,479	95	91	99	21	80	89	33	5
4. Skelton	D	1931	1976	82	68	427,184	96	78	70	100	35	56	67	62
5. McCarthy	D	1947	1994	41	57	866,808	-	-	-	-	-	-	-	-
6. Danner	D	1934	1992	77	66	474,038	98	70	81	77	70	78	58	29
7. Hancock	R	1929	1988	U	57	218,098	99	29	98	89	10	11	75	95
8. Emerson	R	1938	1980	U	70	396,967	96	47	88	100	0	0	100	100
9. Volkmer	D	1931	1976	67	50	473,716	98	74	78	83	50	78	58	48
Montana														
AL. Williams	D	1937	1978	U	49	734,121	91	74	88	54	75	78	64	19
Nebraska														
1. Bereuter	R	1939	1978	U	63	334,598	99	55	78	83	15	11	100	71
2. Christensen	R	1963	1994	53	50	953,163	-	-	-	-	-	-	-	-
3. Barrett	R	1929	1990	U	79	232,013	99	47	95	97	5	11	92	95
Nevada														
1. Ensign	R	1958	1994	83	48	687,194	-	-	-	-	-	-	-	-
2. Vucanovich	R	1921	1982	78	64	692,936	98	53	88	100	0	22	100	95

(Table continues)

Table 7-15 (Continued)

State/district/representative	Party	Year born	Year first elected	% vote in 1994 Primary	% vote in 1994 General	Campaign expenditures (1993-94)	VP	PS	PU	CC	ADA	AFL-CIO	CCUS	ACU
New Hampshire														
1. Zeliff	R	1936	1990	U	66	$786,042	95	50	93	94	5	0	100	86
2. Bass	R	1952	1994	29	51	448,431	-	-	-	-	-	-	-	-
New Jersey														
1. Andrews	D	1957	1990	U	72	674,366	95	71	69	72	45	67	83	26
2. LoBiondo	R	1946	1994	55	65	757,681	-	-	-	-	-	-	-	-
3. Saxton	R	1943	1984	U	66	356,108	98	63	83	89	15	22	100	67
4. Smith	R	1953	1980	U	68	271,108	98	54	66	74	30	56	83	70
5. Roukema	R	1929	1980	77	74	497,345	92	67	69	67	35	17	100	50
6. Pallone	D	1951	1988	U	60	672,626	100	71	89	39	70	78	67	14
7. Franks	R	1951	1992	U	60	542,564	99	55	77	69	25	0	91	62
8. Martini	R	1947	1994	U	50	851,781	-	-	-	-	-	-	-	-
9. Torricelli	D	1951	1982	91	63	744,648	91	78	90	50	65	78	58	6
10. Payne	D	1934	1988	U	76	309,623	96	74	98	3	95	100	18	5
11. Frelinghuysen	R	1946	1994	—	—	—	-	-	-	-	-	-	-	-
12. Zimmer	R	1944	1990	U	68	612,178	99	44	81	67	25	0	92	57
13. Menendez	D	1954	1992	U	71	488,448	99	79	96	31	90	89	50	5
New Mexico														
1. Schiff	R	1947	1988	U	74	458,653	97	53	81	89	15	44	83	80
2. Skeen	R	1927	1980	U	63	384,687	99	53	83	100	0	11	75	95
3. Richardson	D	1947	1982	U	64	579,737	96	89	94	57	55	78	55	26

a Voting ratings

New York

1.	Forbes	R	1952	1994	55	53	265,930	–	–	–	–	–	–	–	–
2.	Lazio	R	1958	1992	U	68	484,133	100	72	77	83	20	33	100	57
3.	King	R	1944	1992	73	59	516,548	99	45	92	83	5	22	83	81
4.	Frisa	R	1955	1994	50	50	231,931	–	–	–	–	–	–	–	–
5.	Ackerman	D	1942	1983	U	55	1,376,467	93	81	96	28	90	71	50	0
6.	Flake	D	1945	1986	U	80	227,256	88	84	99	16	95	78	45	0
7.	Manton	D	1932	1984	U	87	360,940	94	86	94	49	70	75	45	15
8.	Nadler	D	1947	1992	62	82	791,767	93	74	96	6	100	100	17	5
9.	Schumer	D	1950	1980	U	73	157,108	93	83	94	31	90	75	58	5
10.	Towns	D	1934	1982	U	89	453,427	83	81	98	16	85	100	25	0
11.	Owens	D	1936	1982	82	89	295,986	81	73	97	4	90	100	18	0
12.	Velazquez	D	1953	1992	U	92	605,787	96	71	98	6	100	100	17	71
13.	Molinari	R	1958	1990	79	71	481,588	99	60	84	83	20	44	92	0
14.	Maloney	D	1948	1992	61	64	1,032,181	95	76	94	22	100	78	58	5
15.	Rangel	D	1930	1970	U	97	1,437,297	82	80	98	12	95	100	18	0
16.	Serrano	D	1943	1990	62	96	125,441	96	73	98	9	95	78	42	0
17.	Engel	D	1947	1988	U	78	464,001	93	80	97	11	100	100	18	0
18.	Lowey	D	1937	1988	23	57	1,343,347	97	82	98	11	85	89	42	10
19.	Kelly	R	1936	1994	U	52	570,821	–	–	–	–	–	–	–	–
20.	Gilman	R	1922	1972	U	67	547,731	99	71	45	69	35	89	67	52
21.	McNulty	D	1947	1988	U	67	217,642	93	75	84	60	55	63	60	42
22.	Solomon	R	1930	1978	U	73	444,067	95	35	97	88	0	38	67	95
23.	Boehlert	R	1936	1982	U	71	336,183	98	71	58	63	50	67	75	38
24.	McHugh	R	1948	1992	U	79	53,187	99	51	94	89	10	33	92	90
25.	Walsh	R	1947	1988	U	58	415,314	98	70	74	86	20	44	91	67
26.	Hinchey	D	1938	1992	U	49	738,098	98	79	99	14	95	100	33	5
27.	Paxon	R	1954	1988	U	75	642,531	99	35	98	92	0	0	92	100
28.	Slaughter	D	1929	1986	U	57	790,778	98	82	99	14	95	75	50	0
29.	LaFalce	D	1939	1974	81	55	825,314	97	88	89	53	80	78	58	15

(Table continues)

Table 7-15 (*Continued*)

State/district/representative	Party	Year born	Year first elected	% vote in 1994 Primary	% vote in 1994 General	Campaign expenditures (1993-94)	Voting ratings[a] VP	PS	PU	CC	ADA	AFL-CIO	CCUS	ACU
30. Quinn	R	1951	1992	U	67	$488,083	95	64	82	83	30	56	91	76
31. Houghton	R	1926	1986	U	85	356,525	93	72	61	82	20	11	100	68
North Carolina														
1. Clayton	D	1934	1992	U	61	417,700	97	82	98	22	100	89	42	0
2. Funderburk	R	1944	1994	54	56	725,357	-	-	-	-	-	-	-	-
3. Jones	R	1943	1994	U	53	477,463	-	-	-	-	-	-	-	-
4. Heineman	R	1929	1994	51	50	264,869	-	-	-	-	-	-	-	-
5. Burr	R	1955	1994	U	57	741,986	-	-	-	-	-	-	-	-
6. Coble	R	1931	1984	U	U	350,981	100	28	97	83	5	22	83	95
7. Rose	D	1939	1972	U	52	823,282	91	81	94	57	75	100	50	14
8. Hefner	D	1930	1974	65	52	669,622	97	79	93	71	65	89	45	19
9. Myrick	R	1941	1994	68	65	663,405	-	-	-	-	-	-	-	-
10. Ballenger	R	1926	1986	U	72	221,536	97	36	98	91	5	0	92	90
11. Taylor	R	1941	1990	U	60	999,467	97	36	94	94	5	33	75	100
12. Watt	D	1945	1992	U	66	253,715	98	73	98	3	100	100	17	10
North Dakota														
AL Pomeroy	D	1952	1992	U	52	813,900	98	79	86	72	65	38	75	14
Ohio														
1. Chabot	R	1953	1994	U	56	542,829	-	-	-	-	-	-	-	-
2. Portman	R	1955	1993	U	77	250,860	96	45	94	88	10	0	100	86
3. Hall	D	1942	1978	U	59	292,838	94	81	91	46	85	78	33	19
4. Oxley	R	1944	1981	74	U	279,829	96	48	92	91	0	0	92	95

District	Name	Party													
5.	Gillmor	R	1939	1988	U	73	210,789	98	64	68	89	15	33	100	86
6.	Cremeans	R	1943	1994	50	51	862,015	–	–	–	–	–	–	–	–
7.	Hobson	R	1936	1990	U	U	191,660	99	58	82	83	20	22	83	67
8.	Boehner	R	1949	1990	U	100	713,223	96	38	98	97	5	0	83	100
9.	Kaptur	D	1946	1982	U	75	309,247	94	80	89	58	60	100	40	20
10.	Hoke	R	1952	1992	80	52	675,825	95	45	88	88	15	13	91	80
11.	Stokes	D	1925	1968	92	77	382,332	93	72	98	9	100	100	18	10
12.	Kasich	R	1952	1982	U	66	560,117	99	47	81	86	10	11	92	76
13.	Brown	D	1952	1992	69	49	974,225	99	64	92	36	75	78	67	14
14.	Sawyer	D	1945	1986	U	52	595,448	99	92	98	30	90	78	50	5
15.	Pryce	R	1951	1992	86	71	443,007	94	55	90	88	15	11	100	67
16.	Regula	R	1924	1972	U	75	120,279	100	59	76	89	15	11	92	86
17.	Traficant	D	1941	1984	U	77	145,793	99	68	80	67	65	100	42	33
18.	Ney	R	1954	1994	69	54	600,426	–	–	–	–	–	–	–	–
19.	LaTourette	R	1954	1994	54	48	712,925	–	–	–	–	–	–	–	–
Oklahoma															
1.	Largent	R	1955	1994	51	63	610,211	–	–	–	–	–	–	–	–
2.	Coburn	R	1948	1994	64	52	604,924	–	–	–	–	–	–	–	–
3.	Brewster	D	1941	1990	71	74	833,456	95	75	73	91	30	33	80	60
4.	Watts	R	1957	1994	52	52	568,942	–	–	–	–	–	–	–	–
5.	Istook	R	1950	1992	U	78	274,179	95	38	96	91	5	11	83	95
6.	Lucas	R	1960	1994	U	70	146,806	99	49	93	100	0	17	89	100
Oregon															
1.	Furse	D	1936	1992	U	48	1,132,394	98	81	96	22	95	78	67	5
2.	Cooley	R	1932	1994	23	57	298,053	–	–	–	–	–	–	–	–
3.	Wyden	D	1949	1980	U	73	437,586	99	81	96	33	80	78	58	0
4.	DeFazio	D	1947	1986	U	67	221,718	91	62	90	34	70	75	75	29
5.	Bunn	R	1956	1994	42	50	362,620	–	–	–	–	–	–	–	–

(Table continues)

Table 7-15 (Continued)

State/ district/ representative	Party	Year born	Year first elected	% vote in 1994 Primary	General	Campaign expenditures (1993-94)	VP	PS	PU	CC	ADA	AFL-CIO	CCUS	ACU
Pennsylvania														
1. Foglietta	D	1928	1980	69	82	$486,812	92	81	99	9	95	89	25	0
2. Fattah	D	1956	1994	58	86	492,348	-	-	-	-	-	-	-	-
3. Borski	D	1948	1982	86	63	323,957	96	86	95	46	65	89	33	29
4. Klink	D	1951	1992	U	64	467,285	99	72	83	53	50	100	33	43
5. Clinger	R	1929	1978	80	100	340,709	96	59	73	97	15	33	100	95
6. Holden	D	1957	1992	U	57	675,274	100	68	75	72	45	100	58	43
7. Weldon	R	1947	1986	80	70	349,639	96	65	81	81	10	33	92	74
8. Greenwood	R	1951	1992	U	66	360,600	97	69	71	78	20	11	100	70
9. Shuster	R	1932	1972	U	100	776,175	98	45	93	94	0	0	92	100
10. McDade	R	1931	1962	U	66	415,387	83	69	73	94	20	38	89	83
11. Kanjorski	D	1937	1984	U	67	304,520	99	82	88	47	55	89	42	29
12. Murtha	D	1932	1974	U	69	913,004	92	85	88	78	50	78	55	38
13. Fox	R	1947	1994	37	49	1,015,330	-	-	-	-	-	-	-	-
14. Coyne	D	1936	1980	U	64	185,539	98	75	99	3	100	89	25	0
15. McHale	D	1950	1992	U	48	284,930	100	78	84	69	45	67	83	24
16. Walker	R	1942	1976	U	70	242,192	100	31	98	94	0	0	92	100
17. Gekas	R	1930	1982	U	100	86,839	99	41	93	97	10	11	92	95
18. Doyle	D	1953	1994	20	55	381,733	-	-	-	-	-	-	-	-
19. Goodling	R	1927	1974	U	100	50,718	97	46	90	85	10	33	92	90
20. Mascara	D	1930	1994	54	53	489,508	-	-	-	-	-	-	-	-
21. English	R	1956	1994	66	49	450,795	-	-	-	-	-	-	-	-

Voting ratings[a]

	Party													
Rhode Island														
1. Kennedy	D	1967	1994	78	54	1,065,597	–	–	–	–	–	–	–	–
2. Reed	D	1949	1990	U	68	604,267	99	91	97	28	85	78	50	5
South Carolina														
1. Sanford	R	1960	1994	52	66	544,574	–	–	–	–	–	–	–	–
2. Spence	R	1928	1970	U	100	149,321	98	53	89	92	5	33	82	95
3. Graham	R	1955	1994	52	60	551,212	–	–	–	–	–	–	–	–
4. Inglis	R	1959	1992	U	73	184,079	99	38	86	92	5	22	67	100
5. Spratt	D	1942	1982	U	52	643,947	98	82	91	78	65	88	50	24
6. Clyburn	D	1940	1992	86	64	445,461	96	89	96	37	75	88	45	15
South Dakota														
AL Johnson	D	1946	1986	U	60	480,230	99	82	90	62	55	67	75	24
Tennessee														
1. Quillen	R	1916	1962	79	73	1,117,126	93	49	77	94	5	43	100	95
2. Duncan	R	1947	1988	100	90	200,332	99	25	95	67	20	22	75	76
3. Wamp	R	1957	1994	67	52	704,220	–	–	–	–	–	–	–	–
4. Hilleary	R	1959	1994	58	57	613,648	–	–	–	–	–	–	–	–
5. Clement	D	1943	1988	U	60	486,214	94	83	84	82	35	56	92	35
6. Gordon	D	1949	1984	68	51	1,385,995	98	76	85	79	55	25	83	24
7. Bryant	R	1948	1994	35	60	493,712	–	–	–	–	–	–	–	–
8. Tanner	D	1944	1988	100	64	251,431	99	74	69	94	30	44	83	67
9. Ford	D	1945	1974	79	58	366,683	77	83	96	24	75	88	45	0
Texas														
1. Chapman	D	1945	1985	U	55	752,189	89	73	74	94	45	75	67	45
2. Wilson	D	1933	1972	68	57	848,019	89	75	82	86	55	67	67	53
3. Johnson	R	1930	1991	89	91	417,039	98	37	98	97	0	11	83	100

(Table continues)

223

Table 7-15 (*Continued*)

State/district/representative	Party	Year born	Year first elected	% vote in 1994 Primary	General	Campaign expenditures (1993-94)	VP	PS	PU	CC	ADA	AFL-CIO	CCUS	ACU
4. Hall	D	1923	1980	79	59	$559,157	98	54	37	97	10	44	92	95
5. Bryant	D	1947	1982	U	50	799,511	96	82	95	50	80	67	67	5
6. Barton	R	1949	1984	89	76	574,897	94	38	95	97	0	13	90	100
7. Archer	R	1928	1970	U	U	215,637	99	33	99	94	0	0	92	100
8. Fields	R	1952	1980	U	92	709,896	90	39	97	100	0	11	91	100
9. Stockman	R	1956	1994	73	52	245,547	-	-	-	-	-	-	-	-
10. Doggett	D	1946	1994	83	56	567,552	-	-	-	-	-	-	-	-
11. Edwards	D	1951	1990	U	59	420,832	98	82	76	94	45	44	75	38
12. Geren	D	1952	1989	U	69	345,739	98	69	58	97	15	33	92	67
13. Thornberry	R	1958	1994	75	55	442,237	-	-	-	-	-	-	-	-
14. Laughlin	R	1942	1988	U	56	789,201	84	77	74	87	50	63	83	60
15. de la Garza	D	1927	1964	60	59	701,528	91	78	81	86	50	56	67	45
16. Coleman	D	1941	1982	62	57	704,186	95	88	96	62	80	78	58	19
17. Stenholm	D	1938	1978	U	54	712,156	99	53	42	97	5	0	100	90
18. Jackson-Lee	D	1950	1994	63	73	593,740	-	-	-	-	-	-	-	-
19. Combest	R	1945	1984	U	U	148,894	99	40	86	97	0	11	83	100
20. Gonzalez	D	1916	1961	U	63	55,382	99	80	96	22	75	100	25	15
21. Smith	R	1947	1986	82	90	538,347	97	43	96	94	5	11	92	95
22. DeLay	R	1947	1984	U	74	701,245	95	31	98	94	0	0	92	100
23. Bonilla	R	1954	1992	U	63	758,591	99	44	93	100	0	0	100	95
24. Frost	D	1942	1978	U	53	1,589,612	93	86	89	82	55	67	75	25
25. Bentsen	D	1959	1994	64	52	972,688	-	-	-	-	-	-	-	-
26. Armey	R	1940	1984	U	76	900,871	98	38	99	94	0	0	83	100
27. Ortiz	D	1937	1982	U	59	469,694	96	79	79	82	45	56	55	48
28. Tejeda	D	1945	1992	U	71	224,124	99	78	81	86	50	67	50	43

	Name	Party	Born	Elected		%	Receipts								
29.	Green	D	1947	1992	55	73	594,375	90	78	90	56	80	88	55	16
30.	Johnson	D	1935	1992	U	73	240,577	98	86	96	29	85	78	33	19
Utah															
1.	Hansen	R	1932	1980	U	65	348,036	98	37	95	100	0	0	92	95
2.	Waldholtz	R	1958	1994	U	46	1,976,289	-	-	-	-	-	-	-	-
3.	Orton	D	1948	1990	U	59	278,477	97	61	58	86	25	33	92	79
Vermont															
AL	Sanders	I	1941	1990	—	50	105,502	—	73	—	11	100	100	—	0
Virginia															
1.	Bateman	R	1928	1982	C	74	423,501	97	60	69	86	10	22	92	90
2.	Pickett	D	1930	1986	U	59	386,469	97	78	70	91	35	56	75	48
3.	Scott	D	1947	1992	C	79	252,350	98	82	96	28	80	89	42	24
4.	Sisisky	D	1927	1982	C	62	741,224	97	81	72	91	35	67	75	48
5.	Payne	D	1945	1988	C	53	915,224	98	77	76	89	25	33	83	62
6.	Goodlatte	R	1952	1992	C	100	211,653	99	39	96	86	10	0	92	90
7.	Bliley	R	1932	1980	C	84	572,427	98	44	92	97	0	11	100	100
8.	Moran	D	1945	1990	C	59	910,239	93	88	91	53	55	67	55	29
9.	Boucher	D	1946	1982	C	59	779,616	95	80	91	65	65	67	42	30
10.	Wolf	R	1939	1980	C	87	222,532	99	53	87	89	0	33	83	86
11.	Davis	R	1949	1994	C	53	1,430,272	-	-	-	-	-	-	-	-
Washington															
1.	White	R	1953	1994	28	52	877,570	-	-	-	-	-	-	-	-
2.	Metcalf	R	1927	1994	26	55	407,902	-	-	-	-	-	-	-	-
3.	Smith	R	1950	1994	29	52	515,316	-	-	-	-	-	-	-	-
4.	Hastings	R	1941	1994	50	53	619,963	-	-	-	-	-	-	-	-
5.	Nethercutt	R	1944	1994	29	51	1,067,185	-	-	-	-	-	-	-	-

(Table continues)

Table 7-15 (Continued)

State/district/representative	Party	Year born	Year first elected	% vote in 1994 Primary	% vote in 1994 General	Campaign expenditures (1993-94)	VP	PS	PU	CC	ADA	AFL-CIO	CCUS	ACU
6. Dicks	D	1940	1976	59	58	$629,161	97	91	94	58	65	78	58	14
7. McDermott	D	1936	1988	71	75	275,259	96	79	98	15	95	78	33	5
8. Dunn	R	1941	1992	71	76	685,083	99	55	91	97	5	11	92	86
9. Tate	R	1965	1994	52	52	617,127	—	—	—	—	—	—	—	—
West Virginia														
1. Mollohan	D	1943	1982	U	70	315,389	97	75	89	58	60	89	33	38
2. Wise	D	1948	1982	U	64	271,315	97	82	94	71	75	89	42	30
3. Rahall	D	1949	1976	U	64	389,323	99	65	87	47	75	100	25	24
Wisconsin														
1. Neumann	R	1954	1994	U	49	512,091	—	—	—	—	—	—	—	—
2. Klug	R	1953	1990	U	69	689,215	99	51	80	61	45	44	75	43
3. Gunderson	R	1951	1980	63	56	658,181	98	53	86	86	10	33	83	81
4. Kleczka	D	1943	1984	U	54	495,371	97	87	94	35	85	78	67	5
5. Barrett	D	1953	1992	U	62	239,418	98	77	90	22	90	89	58	0
6. Petri	R	1940	1979	U	99	326,635	99	41	93	81	25	11	100	76
7. Obey	D	1938	1969	U	54	607,058	95	72	97	16	80	89	18	10
8. Roth	R	1938	1978	68	64	683,149	96	35	93	77	15	11	92	81
9. Sensenbrenner	R	1943	1978	U	100	161,986	100	21	96	69	20	22	67	76
Wyoming														
AL Cubin	R	1946	1994	39	53	511,119	—	—	—	—	—	—	—	—

Note: "—" indicates not available. "." indicates a newly elected representative (no basis for voting ratings). Information as of July 15, 1995. "AL" indicates at large; "R" indicates Republican; "D" indicates Democrat; "U" indicates unopposed, name did not appear on ballot; "+" indicates lack of opposition other than write-in candidates; "U" indicates the primary is open to candidates of all parties (if a candidate wins 50 percent or more of the vote in the primary, that candidate is declared the winner and no general election is held); "C" indicates candidate nominated by party convention rather than primary.

a Voting ratings based on recorded votes in 1994. "VP" indicates voting participation score (percentage of recorded votes on which a representative voted "yea" or "nay"). "PS" indicates presidential support score (percentage of the votes on which the president took a position that the representative supported the president). "PU" indicates party unity score (percentage of the votes on which a representative supported his or her party when a majority of voting Democrats opposed a majority of voting Republicans). "CC" indicates conservative coalition score (percentage of the votes on which a representative voted in agreement with majorities of voting Republicans and southern Democrats against a majority of nonsouthern Democrats). Group ratings indicate the percentage of the time a representative supported the group-preferred position on votes the group selects. "ADA" (Americans for Democratic Action) is a liberal group. "AFL-CIO" (American Federation of Labor-Congress of Industrial Organizations) is a labor group. "CCUS" (Chamber of Commerce of the United States) is a business group, and "ACU" (American Conservative Union) is a conservative group. Voting participation and "ADA" scores are lowered by a member's failure to vote. Failure to vote does not lower the other scores.

Table 7-16 The 104th Congress: The Senate

State/ district/ representative	Party	Year born	Year first elected	% vote in last Primary	% vote in last General	Last campaign expenditures[a]	Voting ratings[b] VP	PS	PU	CC	ADA	AFL-CIO	CCUS	ACU
Alabama														
Heflin	D	1921	1978	81	61	$3,204,160	96	85	66	88	55	63	40	28
Shelby	R	1934	1986	U	65	2,451,191	83	67	50	96	30	83	50	55
Alaska														
Stevens	R	1923	1970	59	66	1,273,954	93	52	73	87	25	43	67	77
Murkowski	R	1933	1980	31	53	1,663,865	96	34	92	90	10	0	90	96
Arizona														
McCain	R	1936	1986	U	56	3,481,915	94	44	91	73	10	0	80	96
Kyl	R	1942	1994	U	54	4,138,203	-	-	-	-	-	-	-	-
Arkansas														
Bumpers	D	1925	1974	65	60	1,878,472	99	95	86	63	80	63	40	4
Pryor	D	1934	1978	U	U	368,579	93	95	84	62	80	50	44	4
California														
Feinstein	D	1933	1992	74	47	14,407,179	99	92	89	44	70	63	40	8
Boxer	D	1940	1992	44	48	10,368,600	97	87	92	19	95	88	20	0
Colorado														
Brown	R	1940	1990	U	56	3,723,911	99	21	93	77	30	13	70	92
Campbell	R	1933	1992	U	52	1,561,347	94	83	78	48	55	88	50	25
Connecticut														
Dodd	D	1944	1980	U	59	4,122,268	92	95	90	24	80	75	38	0
Lieberman	D	1942	1988	U	67	3,238,026	97	88	76	45	65	71	30	8
Delaware														
Roth	R	1921	1970	U	56	2,233,279	98	56	77	66	35	38	70	68
Biden	D	1942	1972	U	63	1,888,146	94	89	92	31	80	86	20	0

(Table continues)

227

Table 7-16 (Continued)

State/ district/ representative	Party	Year born	Year first elected	% vote in last Primary	% vote in last General	Last campaign expenditures[a]	VP	PS	PU	CC	ADA	AFL- CIO	CCUS	ACU
Florida														
Graham	D	1936	1986	84	65	2,979,552	99	92	85	53	75	75	30	8
Mack	R	1940	1988	U	70	3,735,719	99	40	89	94	10	0	90	96
Georgia														
Nunn	D	1938	1972	U	U	882,336	98	89	66	91	50	25	70	33
Coverdell	R	1939	1992	50	51	3,193,774	97	35	95	90	5	0	90	100
Hawaii														
Inouye	D	1924	1962	76	57	2,971,128	94	95	92	42	75	88	20	0
Akaka	D	1924	1990	U	72	418,630	100	97	94	31	85	88	20	0
Idaho														
Craig	R	1945	1990	59	61	1,652,532	98	30	98	94	0	13	80	100
Kempthorne	R	1951	1992	57	57	1,305,338	99	31	98	94	0	13	80	100
Illinois														
Simon	D	1928	1984	U	65	7,656,514	98	85	96	17	95	75	30	4
Moseley-Braun	D	1947	1992	38	53	6,594,570	95	86	91	13	85	75	33	4
Indiana														
Lugar	R	1932	1976	U	67	4,063,703	100	45	78	78	10	0	90	76
Coats	R	1943	1990	U	57	3,802,077	99	42	89	81	5	0	90	92
Iowa														
Grassley	R	1933	1980	U	70	2,322,262	100	34	87	69	15	0	90	92
Harkin	D	1939	1984	U	54	5,263,568	95	92	97	10	100	88	30	0
Kansas														
Dole	R	1923	1968	80	63	1,990,098	99	35	96	97	0	0	90	100
Kassebaum	R	1932	1978	87	74	407,387	97	74	61	63	45	13	70	48

Kentucky														
Ford	D	1924	1974	U*	63	2,076,069	99	92	82	61	60	75	30	24
McConnell	R	1942	1984	89	52	5,074,187	99	37	92	87	5	0	90	92
Louisiana														
Johnston	D	1932	1972	54	+	4,989,521	95	91	78	74	55	75	22	22
Breaux	D	1944	1986	73	+	1,446,199	95	85	78	78	55	63	44	17
Maine														
Cohen	R	1940	1978	U	61	1,572,195	95	63	61	65	40	29	70	45
Snowe	R	1947	1994	U	60	2,041,834	-	-	-	-	-	-	-	-
Maryland														
Sarbanes	D	1933	1976	79	59	2,698,928	100	95	98	13	95	88	20	0
Mikulski	D	1936	1986	77	71	3,161,104	96	93	90	29	85	75	33	0
Massachusetts														
Kennedy	D	1932	1962	U	58	10,540,244	95	95	94	19	90	88	20	0
Kerry	D	1943	1984	U	57	6,234,887	99	90	94	16	95	88	30	0
Michigan														
Levin	D	1934	1978	U	57	6,930,262	100	90	92	16	95	88	20	0
Abraham	R	1952	1994	52	52	4,453,648	-	-	-	-	-	-	-	-
Minnesota														
Wellstone	D	1944	1990	60	50	1,340,708	98	82	94	3	100	100	10	4
Grams	R	1948	1994	58	49	2,439,798	-	-	-	-	-	-	-	-
Mississippi														
Cochran	R	1937	1978	U	U	567,446	98	45	82	94	10	13	90	92
Lott	R	1941	1988	95	69	2,138,544	95	40	97	100	5	0	90	100
Missouri														
Bond	R	1939	1986	83	52	4,577,895	95	49	78	90	20	13	100	83
Ashcroft	R	1942	1994	83	60	4,063,927	-	-	-	-	-	-	-	-
Montana														
Baucus	D	1941	1978	83	68	2,409,262	99	89	86	50	85	100	20	0
Burns	R	1935	1988	U	62	3,157,084	98	43	84	94	0	13	70	92

(Table continues)

Table 7-16 (*Continued*)

State/ district/ representative	Party	Year born	Year first elected	% vote in last Primary	% vote in last General	Last campaign expenditures[a]	VP	PS	PU	CC	ADA	AFL-CIO	CCUS	ACU
												Voting ratings[b]		
Nebraska														
Exon	D	1921	1978	U	59	2,349,739	99	84	78	63	65	63	40	24
Kerrey	D	1943	1988	U	55	4,471,081	99	90	83	47	80	88	40	24
Nevada														
Reid	D	1939	1986	53	51	2,725,713	97	90	88	41	85	100	20	4
Bryan	D	1937	1988	U	51	3,021,834	98	85	85	48	75	88	30	12
New Hampshire														
Smith	R	1941	1990	65	65	1,420,172	99	20	96	88	5	14	80	100
Gregg	R	1947	1992	50	48	875,675	98	42	84	78	15	0	90	79
New Jersey														
Bradley	D	1943	1978	92	50	9,563,942	95	80	84	7	85	88	20	4
Lautenberg	D	1924	1982	81	50	7,278,332	99	82	84	19	95	88	30	4
New Mexico														
Domenici	R	1932	1972	U	73	1,925,057	99	53	78	94	25	13	90	84
Bingaman	D	1943	1982	U	54	3,227,352	99	89	84	53	60	75	50	16
New York														
Moynihan	D	1927	1976	75	55	5,784,736	99	84	92	16	100	88	20	0
D'Amato	R	1937	1980	U	49	9,175,533	96	34	82	84	20	38	80	92
North Carolina														
Helms	R	1921	1972	84	53	13,355,336	95	19	95	87	0	14	80	100
Faircloth	R	1928	1992	48	50	2,952,102	98	24	98	100	5	0	90	100
North Dakota														
Conrad	D	1948	1986	U	58	1,927,866	99	89	85	53	85	75	40	12
Dorgan	D	1942	1992	U	59	1,124,512	99	81	86	44	85	75	20	8

	Party													
Ohio														
Glenn	D	1921	1974	U	51	3,999,271	98	95	90	23	80	75	33	4
DeWine	R	1947	1994	52	53	6,274,663	-	-	-	-	-	-	-	-
Oklahoma														
Nickles	R	1948	1980	U	59	3,316,336	96	25	94	88	5	0	90	100
Inhofe	R	1934	1994	78	55	2,013,227	100	0	0	0	-	-	0	-
Oregon														
Hatfield	R	1922	1966	78	54	2,357,058	97	77	34	34	80	63	60	29
Packwood	R	1932	1968	59	52	6,078,359	95	55	63	47	50	38	90	67
Pennsylvania														
Specter	R	1930	1980	65	49	8,854,815	97	56	56	61	55	38	60	46
Santorum	R	1958	1994	82	49	6,732,849	-	-	-	-	-	-	-	-
Rhode Island														
Pell	D	1918	1960	U	62	2,350,128	98	98	92	28	95	75	30	0
Chafee	R	1922	1976	69	65	1,896,589	94	80	46	42	65	25	67	30
South Carolina														
Thurmond	R	1902	1954	U	64	1,916,702	98	39	93	97	5	13	80	96
Hollings	D	1922	1966	U	50	3,642,045	97	86	80	71	50	71	40	22
South Dakota														
Pressler	R	1942	1978	U	52	1,664,341	98	34	89	84	0	13	90	96
Daschle	D	1947	1986	U	65	2,878,375	100	94	91	38	80	63	40	4
Tennessee														
Thompson	R	1942	1994	64	60	3,843,813	-	-	-	-	-	-	-	-
Frist	R	1952	1994	44	56	9,517,424	-	-	-	-	-	-	-	-
Texas														
Gramm	R	1942	1984	U	60	9,799,104	90	36	94	93	5	0	100	100
Hutchison	R	1943	1993	84	61	6,114,755	93	38	94	94	10	0	100	96
Utah														
Hatch	R	1934	1976	U	69	3,456,031	98	37	95	94	5	0	90	100
Bennett	R	1933	1992	51	55	4,439,376	96	38	91	94	5	0	90	100

(Table continues)

Table 7-16 (Continued)

State/district/representative	Party	Year born	Year first elected	% vote in last Primary	General	Last campaign expenditures[a]	VP	PS	PU	CC	ADA	AFL-CIO	CCUS	ACU
												Voting ratings[b]		
Vermont														
Leahy	D	1940	1974	U	54	950,331	100	89	96	6	95	100	20	0
Jeffords	R	1934	1988	U	50	1,043,626	98	79	32	25	85	50	50	12
Virginia														
Warner	R	1927	1978	U	81	1,151,605	99	60	77	84	20	25	90	80
Robb	D	1939	1988	58	46	5,501,697	99	85	82	45	60	63	40	12
Washington														
Gorton	R	1928	1980	53	56	4,792,764	100	48	76	84	30	13	90	80
Murray	D	1950	1992	28	54	1,342,038	98	94	98	13	90	88	20	0
West Virginia														
Byrd	D	1917	1958	85	69	1,550,354	100	74	73	69	75	75	30	40
Rockefeller	D	1937	1984	85	68	2,650,320	97	97	90	34	95	75	22	0
Wisconsin														
Kohl	D	1935	1988	90	58	7,374,312	100	81	75	41	90	63	50	12
Feingold	D	1953	1992	70	53	1,979,454	100	65	84	9	100	100	10	4
Wyoming														
Simpson	R	1931	1978	84	64	1,000,462	96	40	86	100	15	14	80	88
Thomas	R	1933	1994	U	59	1,068,335	-	-	-	-	-	-	-	-

Note: "—" indicates not available. "-" indicates a newly elected senator (no basis for voting ratings). Information as of June 15, 1995. "R" indicates Republican; "D" indicates Democrat; "U" indicates lack of opposition other than write-in candidates; "U*" indicates unopposed, name did not appear on ballot; "+" indicates Louisiana where the primary is open to candidates of all parties (if a candidate wins 50 percent or more of the vote in the primary, that candidate is declared the winner and no general election is held).

[a] Figures for campaign expenditures cover from January 1 of the year preceding the last campaign (or whenever the campaign registered with the Federal Election Commission during the election cycle) through December 31 of the election year.

[b] For a description of the voting ratings, see footnote a, Table 7-15, this volume.

Source: Congressional Quarterly.

Figure 7-5   Approval of Congress, 1974-1995

Percent

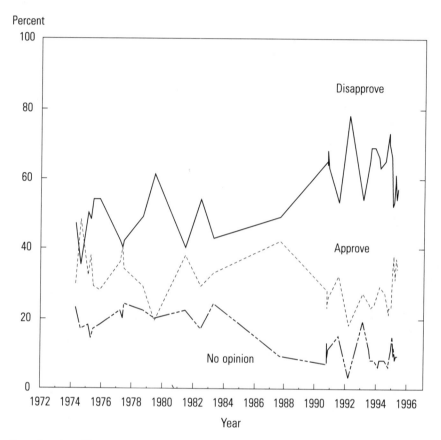

Note: Question: "Do you approve or disapprove of the way the U.S. Congress is handling its job?"

Source: Gallup Poll Monthly, July 1994, 48; and unpublished data from the Gallup Poll.

8

The Presidency and the Executive Branch

The presidency poses special problems to those interested in the collection of statistical data. The scope and the variety of data available on the presidency are limited by the singularity of the president and the difference the individual president makes on the office's organization and operation. Moreover, the modern presidency has evolved since Franklin Roosevelt took office in the 1930s. Since then the emergence of the United States as a world power, the expansion of television, the growth of government, and the alteration of the presidential selection process have further changed the demands on and expectations of the presidency. Hence, for data on many points, the recent occupants of the Oval Office are just too few to sustain statistical analysis.

In spite of these seemingly insurmountable handicaps, the visibility of the president provides a considerable amount of relevant data. Of all elected officials, for example, only presidents have public judgments about how well they are doing prominently and repeatedly displayed: the twists and turns in the public approval ratings of a president's job performance are themselves news items. Consequently, in this book a series of figures are devoted to this subject alone—showing overall presidential approval scores for ten presidents (Figure 8-1), and detailed ratings for Jimmy Carter, Ronald Reagan, George Bush, and Bill Clinton (Figure 8-2). But presidents are not judged only by the public or only while they are in office. At various times and in various ways, historians and political scientists have rated all the U.S. presidents (Table 8-2).

Apart from approval ratings (and of course presidential elections), the presidency has not been subjected to extensive statistical scrutiny. However, perhaps because the number of presidents has now reached forty-one individuals, some additional areas are beginning to receive systematic **235** study. The president's relationship with Congress is one such area. Information about presidential "victories" on votes in Congress (Table 8-11), the extent to which the president is supported by his own party and by the other party (Table 8-12), and success in having nominations approved (Table 8-14) are all regularly tabulated and increasingly analyzed.

Media coverage is also beginning to receive systematic study. In part this study results from the extreme visibility of the president and of the federal government in general (Figure 2-1); it is also due to changing relationships between the president and the press, as indicated, for example, by the considerable decline in press conferences since the 1930s (Table 2-4).

Compilations of various presidential characteristics and activities also have become more numerous or more meaningful with the larger number who have served as president. How individuals get to be president, for example, has been a subject of considerable interest (Tables 8-3 through 8-5). Presidential appointments have been checked for their partisan characteristics (Table 9-3) and increasingly for their racial and sex distributions (Table 9-2).

The executive branch, apart from the president, has been subjected even less to statistical analysis. Yet here, too, there is ample opportunity for meaningful tabulations if not for t-tests and correlations. The tremendous size of the federal government (Table 8-8) necessitates such an interest. The expanded involvement of the government in regulation (Table 8-10), at least until the Reagan administration, also compels attention. But there are other more subtle and more significant messages in these data. For example, the changing emphases of the nation and of the priorities of particular presidents can be seen in such mundane listings as the size and composition of the White House staff (Table 8-7).

Thus, while the presidency provides data for conventional statistical analyses in only a few areas, a generous and increasing amount of numerical data provides considerable insight into what has traditionally been viewed as an office of impressive singularity.

Table 8-1   Presidents and Vice Presidents of the United States

President (political party)	Born	Died	Age at inauguration	Native of . . .	Elected from . . .	Term of service	Vice president
George Washington (F)	1732	1799	57	Va.	Va.	April 30, 1789-March 4, 1793	John Adams
George Washington (F)			61			March 4, 1793-March 4, 1797	John Adams
John Adams (F)	1735	1826	61	Mass.	Mass.	March 4, 1797-March 4, 1801	Thomas Jefferson
Thomas Jefferson (D-R)	1743	1826	57	Va.	Va.	March 4, 1801-March 4, 1805	Aaron Burr
Thomas Jefferson (D-R)			61			March 4, 1805-March 4, 1809	George Clinton
James Madison (D-R)	1751	1836	57	Va.	Va.	March 4, 1809-March 4, 1813	George Clinton
James Madison (D-R)			61			March 4, 1813-March 4, 1817	Elbridge Gerry
James Monroe (D-R)	1758	1831	58	Va.	Va.	March 4, 1817-March 4, 1821	Daniel D. Tompkins
James Monroe (D-R)			62			March 4, 1821-March 4, 1825	Daniel D. Tompkins
John Q. Adams (N-R)	1767	1848	57	Mass.	Mass.	March 4, 1825-March 4, 1829	John C. Calhoun
Andrew Jackson (D)	1767	1845	61	S.C.	Tenn.	March 4, 1829-March 4, 1833	John C. Calhoun
Andrew Jackson (D)			65			March 4, 1833-March 4, 1837	Martin Van Buren
Martin Van Buren (D)	1782	1862	54	N.Y.	N.Y.	March 4, 1837-March 4, 1841	Richard M. Johnson
W. H. Harrison (W)	1773	1841	68	Va.	Ohio	March 4, 1841-April 4, 1841	John Tyler
John Tyler (W)	1790	1862	51	Va.	Va.	April 6, 1841-March 4, 1845	
James K. Polk (D)	1795	1849	49	N.C.	Tenn.	March 4, 1845-March 4, 1849	George M. Dallas
Zachary Taylor (W)	1784	1850	64	Va.	La.	March 4, 1849-July 9, 1850	Millard Fillmore
Millard Fillmore (W)	1800	1874	50	N.Y.	N.Y.	July 10, 1850-March 4, 1853	
Franklin Pierce (D)	1804	1869	48	N.H.	N.H.	March 4, 1853-March 4, 1857	William R. King
James Buchanan (D)	1791	1868	65	Pa.	Pa.	March 4, 1857-March 4, 1861	John C. Breckinridge
Abraham Lincoln (R)	1809	1865	52	Ky.	Ill.	March 4, 1861-March 4, 1865	Hannibal Hamlin
Abraham Lincoln (R)			56			March 4, 1865-April 15, 1865	Andrew Johnson
Andrew Johnson (R)	1808	1875	56	N.C.	Tenn.	April 15, 1865-March 4, 1869	
Ulysses S. Grant (R)	1822	1885	46	Ohio	Ill.	March 4, 1869-March 4, 1873	Schuyler Colfax
Ulysses S. Grant (R)			50			March 4, 1873-March 4, 1877	Henry Wilson

(Table continues)

Table 8-1 (Continued)

President (political party)	Born	Died	Age at inauguration	Native of . . .	Elected from . . .	Term of service	Vice president
Rutherford B. Hayes (R)	1822	1893	54	Ohio	Ohio	March 4, 1877-March 4, 1881	William A. Wheeler
James A. Garfield (R)	1831	1881	49	Ohio	Ohio	March 4, 1881-Sept. 19, 1881	Chester A. Arthur
Chester A. Arthur (R)	1830	1886	50	Vt.	N.Y.	Sept. 20, 1881-March 4, 1885	
Grover Cleveland (D)	1837	1908	47	N.J.	N.Y.	March 4, 1885-March 4, 1889	Thomas A. Hendricks
Benjamin Harrison (R)	1833	1901	55	Ohio	Ind.	March 4, 1889-March 4, 1893	Levi P. Morton
Grover Cleveland (D)	1837	1908	55			March 4, 1893-March 4, 1897	Adlai E. Stevenson
William McKinley (R)	1843	1901	54	Ohio	Ohio	March 4, 1897-March 4, 1901	Garret A. Hobart
William McKinley (R)			58			March 4, 1901-Sept. 14, 1901	Theodore Roosevelt
Theodore Roosevelt (R)	1858	1919	42	N.Y.	N.Y.	Sept. 14, 1901-March 4, 1905	
Theodore Roosevelt (R)			46			March 4, 1905-March 4, 1909	Charles W. Fairbanks
William H. Taft (R)	1857	1930	51	Ohio	Ohio	March 4, 1909-March 4, 1913	James S. Sherman
Woodrow Wilson (D)	1856	1924	56	Va.	N.J.	March 4, 1913-March 4, 1917	Thomas R. Marshall
Woodrow Wilson (D)			60			March 4, 1917-March 4, 1921	Thomas R. Marshall
Warren G. Harding (R)	1865	1923	55	Ohio	Ohio	March 4, 1921-Aug. 2, 1923	Calvin Coolidge
Calvin Coolidge (R)	1872	1933	51	Vt.	Mass.	Aug. 3, 1923-March 4, 1925	
Calvin Coolidge (R)			52			March 4, 1925-March 4, 1929	Charles G. Dawes
Herbert Hoover (R)	1874	1964	54	Iowa	Calif.	March 4, 1929-March 4, 1933	Charles Curtis
Franklin D. Roosevelt (D)	1882	1945	51	N.Y.	N.Y.	March 4, 1933-Jan. 20, 1937	John N. Garner
Franklin D. Roosevelt (D)			55			Jan. 20, 1937-Jan. 20, 1941	John N. Garner
Franklin D. Roosevelt (D)			59			Jan. 20, 1941-Jan. 20, 1945	Henry A. Wallace
Franklin D. Roosevelt (D)			63			Jan. 20, 1945-April 12, 1945	Harry S. Truman
Harry S. Truman (D)	1884	1972	60	Mo.	Mo.	April 12, 1945-Jan. 20, 1949	
Harry S. Truman (D)			64			Jan. 20, 1949-Jan. 20, 1953	Alben W. Barkley
Dwight D. Eisenhower (R)	1890	1969	62	Texas	N.Y.	Jan. 20, 1953-Jan. 20, 1957	Richard M. Nixon
Dwight D. Eisenhower (R)			66		Pa.	Jan. 20, 1957-Jan. 20, 1961	Richard M. Nixon
John F. Kennedy (D)	1917	1963	43	Mass.	Mass.	Jan. 20, 1961-Nov. 22, 1963	Lyndon B. Johnson
Lyndon B. Johnson (D)	1906	1973	55	Texas	Texas	Nov. 22, 1963-Jan. 20, 1965	

President (party)	Born	Died	Native of	Elected from	Age	Term of service	Vice president
Lyndon B. Johnson (D)	1908	1973	Texas	Texas	56	Jan. 20, 1965-Jan. 20, 1969	Hubert H. Humphrey
Richard M. Nixon (R)	1913	1994	Calif.	N.Y.	56	Jan. 20, 1969-Jan. 20, 1973	Spiro T. Agnew
Richard M. Nixon (R)			Calif.	Calif.	60	Jan. 20, 1973-Aug. 9, 1974	Spiro T. Agnew
							Gerald R. Ford
Gerald R. Ford (R)	1913		Neb.	Mich.	61	Aug. 9, 1974-Jan. 20, 1977	Nelson A. Rockefeller
Jimmy Carter (D)	1924		Ga.	Ga.	52	Jan. 20, 1977-Jan. 20, 1981	Walter F. Mondale
Ronald Reagan (R)	1911		Ill.	Calif.	69	Jan. 20, 1981-Jan. 20, 1985	George Bush
Ronald Reagan (R)					73	Jan. 20, 1985-Jan. 20, 1989	George Bush
George Bush (R)	1924		Conn.	Texas	64	Jan. 20, 1989-Jan. 20, 1993	J. Danforth Quayle
William Clinton (D)	1946		Ark.	Ark.	46	Jan. 20, 1993-	Albert Gore, Jr.

Note: "D" indicates Democrat, "D-R" indicates Democrat-Republican, "F" indicates Federalist, "N-R" indicates National Republican, "R" indicates Republican, and "W" indicates Whig.

Source: Congressional Quarterly, *Presidential Elections Since 1789*, 4th ed. (Washington, D.C.: Congressional Quarterly, 1987), 4; updated by the editors.

Table 8-2 Ratings of U.S Presidents

Schlesinger poll (1948)	Schlesinger poll (1962)	Maranell-Dodder poll (1970)	DiClerico poll (1977)	Tribune poll (1982)	Murray-Blessing poll[a] (1982)

Great
1. Lincoln
2. Washington
3. F. Roosevelt
4. Wilson
5. Jefferson
6. Jackson
 	
Near great
7. T. Roosevelt
8. Cleveland
9. J. Adams
10. Polk
 	
Average
11. J. Q. Adams
12. Monroe
13. Hayes
14. Madison
15. Van Buren
16. Taft
17. Arthur
18. McKinley
19. A. Johnson
20. Hoover
21. B. Harrison
	Great
	1. Lincoln
	2. Washington
	3. F. Roosevelt
	4. Wilson
	5. Jefferson
	
	Near great
	6. Jackson
	7. T. Roosevelt
	8. Cleveland
	   Truman (tie)
	9. J. Adams
	10. Cleveland
	
	Average
	11. Madison
	12. J. Q. Adams
	13. Hayes
	14. McKinley
	15. Taft
	16. Van Buren
	17. Monroe
	18. Hoover
	19. B. Harrison
	20. Eisenhower
	   Arthur (tie)
	21. A. Johnson
		Accomplishments of administration
		1. Lincoln
		2. F. Roosevelt
		3. Washington
		4. Jefferson
		5. T. Roosevelt
		6. Truman
		7. Wilson
		8. Jackson
		9. L. Johnson
		10. Polk
		11. J. Adams
		12. Kennedy
		13. Monroe
		14. Cleveland
		15. Madison
		16. Taft
		17. McKinley
		18. J. Q. Adams
		19. Hoover
		20. Eisenhower
		21. A. Johnson
		22. Van Buren
		23. Arthur
		24. Hayes
		25. Tyler
			Ten greatest presidents
			1. Lincoln
			2. Washington
			3. F. Roosevelt
			4. Jefferson
			5. T. Roosevelt
			6. Wilson
			7. Jackson
			8. Truman
			9. Polk
			10. J. Adams
				Ten best presidents
				1. Lincoln (best)
				2. Washington
				3. F. Roosevelt
				4. T. Roosevelt
				5. Jefferson
				6. Wilson
				7. Jackson
				8. Truman
				9. Eisenhower
				10. Polk (10th best)
				
				Ten worst presidents
				1. Harding (worst)
				2. Nixon
				3. Buchanan
				4. Pierce
				5. Grant
				6. Fillmore
				7. A. Johnson
				8. Coolidge
				9. Tyler
				10. Carter (10th worst)
					Great
					1. Lincoln
					2. F. Roosevelt
					3. Washington
					4. Jefferson
					
					Near great
					5. T. Roosevelt
					6. Wilson
					7. Jackson
					8. Truman
					
					Above average
					9. J. Adams
					10. L. Johnson
					11. Eisenhower
					12. Polk
					13. Kennedy
					14. Madison
					15. Monroe
					16. J. Q. Adams
					17. Cleveland
					
					Average
					18. McKinley
					19. Taft

Below average
22. Tyler
23. Coolidge
24. Fillmore
25. Taylor
26. Buchanan
27. Pierce

Failure
28. Grant
29. Harding

Below average
22. Taylor
23. Tyler
24. Fillmore
25. Coolidge
26. Pierce
27. Buchanan

Failure
28. Grant
29. Harding

26. B. Harrison
27. Taylor
28. Buchanan
29. Fillmore
30. Coolidge
31. Pierce
32. Grant
33. Harding

20. Van Buren
21. Hoover
22. Hayes
23. Arthur
24. Ford
25. Carter
26. B. Harrison

Below average
27. Taylor
28. Reagan
29. Tyler
30. Fillmore
31. Coolidge
32. Pierce

Failure
33. A. Johnson
34. Buchanan
35. Nixon
36. Grant
37. Harding

Note: These ratings result from surveys of scholars and range in number from 49 to 846.

[a] The rating of President Reagan was obtained in a separate poll conducted in 1989.

Sources: Henry J. Abraham, *Justices and Presidents: Appointments to the Supreme Court,* 2d ed. (New York: Oxford University Press, 1985), 380–383 (copyright © Henry J. Abraham, 1974, 1985, reprinted by permission of Oxford University Press, Inc.); Tim H. Blessing, "Updating the Murray-Blessing Survey: The Presidential Performance Study Ranks Reagan," unpublished paper, Pennsylvania State University, 1991.

Table 8-3 Previous Public Positions Held by Presidents

Position	Number of presidents holding position prior to presidency	
	Pre-1900 (24)	Post-1900 (17)
Vice president	7	7
Cabinet member	7	3
U.S. representative	13	5
U.S. senator	9	5
U.S. Supreme Court justice	0	0
Federal judge	0	1
Governor	11	7
State legislator	16	5
State judge	1	2
Mayor	2	1
Diplomat, ambassador	7	2
Military general	11	1

Position	Last public position held before presidency	
	Pre-1900 (24)	Post-1900 (17)
Vice president		
Succeeded to presidency	4	5
Won presidency in own right	3	2
Congress		
House	1	0
Senate	3	2
Appointive federal office		
Military general	3	1
Cabinet secretary	3	2
Ambassador	2	0
Other civilian	1	0
Governor	4	5

Source: Compiled by the editors from Robert G. Ferris, *The Presidents*, rev. ed. (Washington, D.C.: National Park Service, 1977). In the list of generals, we have included Andrew Johnson (who had the rank of general when serving as military governor of Tennessee) and Chester A. Arthur (who held the rank of general when serving as quartermaster general); listed in various sources other than Ferris. Updated through President Clinton.

Table 8-4   Latest Public Office Held by Candidates for Democratic and Republican Presidential Nominations, 1936-1992

Public office[a]	Percentage of all persons polling at least 1 percent in Gallup Poll	Percentage of all presidential nominees
President[b]	1	9
Vice president	1	26
U.S. senator	37	13
Governor	23	43
Cabinet officer	15	0
U.S. representative	8	0
Mayor	3	0
U.S. Supreme Court justice	1	0
All others	2	0
No public office	9	9
Total	100	100
	(N = 151)	(N = 23)

[a] Last or current office at time person first polled at least 1 percent support for presidential nomination among fellow partisans or was first nominated.

[b] Presidents Truman and Ford received poll support for the presidential nomination only after they had actually served in the office.

Source: William R. Keech and Donald R. Matthews, *The Party's Choice: with an Epilogue on the 1976 Nominations* (Washington, D.C.: Brookings, 1976), 18; updated by the editors.

Table 8-5 Presidential Prenomination Campaign Finance, 1992

Party/Candidate	Federal matching funds	Individual contributions minus refunds	Adjusted total receipts	Adjusted total disbursements
Democrats				
Larry Agran	$269,691	$331,631	$610,790	$601,533
Jerry Brown	4,239,345	5,176,336	9,420,374	9,069,125
Bill Clinton	12,518,130	25,106,949	37,643,304	33,516,819
Tom Harkin	2,103,351	3,069,363	5,677,833	5,208,403
Bob Kerrey	2,198,284	3,913,072	6,469,781	6,470,393
Lyndon LaRouche	0	1,570,875	1,570,875	1,554,768
Paul Tsongas	2,989,282	4,941,768	7,970,041	7,562,435
Doug Wilder	289,026	508,519	799,334	794,552
Total Democrats	24,607,109	44,618,513	70,162,332	64,778,028
Republicans				
Patrick Buchanan	4,999,963	7,147,143	12,181,131	11,374,167
George Bush	10,557,736	27,088,083	37,910,572	37,798,718
David Duke	0	220,715	271,815	354,838
Total Republicans	15,557,719	34,455,941	50,363,518	49,527,723
Other party				
Andre Marrou	0	562,770	578,067	575,795
Lenora Fulani	1,935,524	2,201,407	4,137,198	4,195,744
Total other party	1,935,524	2,764,177	4,715,265	4,771,539
Grand total	42,100,352	81,838,631	125,241,115	119,077,290

Sources: Federal Election Commission, "Adjusted Receipts (Through March 31, 1993)" and "Adjusted Disbursements (Through March 31, 1993)."

Table 8-6 The President's Cabinet, 1995

Cabinet office	Year established[a]	Current secretary[b]	Date confirmed	Number of paid civilian employees 1980[c]	1994[c]	Number of noncivil service positions[c]	Percentage of all positions
State	1789	Warren M. Christopher	1/20/93	23,644	25,866	20,532	79
Treasury	1789	Robert Rubin	1/10/95	123,754	160,220	10,354	6
War	1789[d]						
Navy	1798[d]						
Interior	1849	Bruce Babbitt	1/21/93	79,505	77,435	11,419	15
Justice	1870	Janet Reno	3/11/93	56,426	97,634	38,745	40
Post Office	1872[e]						
Agriculture	1889[f]	Dan Glickman	3/30/95	122,839	110,065	13,062	12
Commerce and Labor	1903[f]						
Commerce	1913	Ronald H. Brown	1/21/93	46,189	37,732	7,213	18
Labor	1913	Robert B. Reich	1/21/93	23,717	17,251	815	5
Defense	1947	William Perry	2/3/94	972,999	905,167	135,946	15
Health, Education and Welfare	1953[g]						
Health and Human Services	1979	Donna E. Shalala	1/21/93	158,644	129,100	16,531	13
Housing and Urban Development	1965	Henry Cisneros	1/21/93	16,890	13,161	736	5
Transportation	1966	Federico Peña	1/21/93	72,066	68,243	2,984	5
Energy	1977	Hazel R. O'Leary	1/21/93	21,729	20,171	1,804	10
Education	1979	Richard W. Riley	1/21/93	7,370	4,973	640	14
Veterans Affairs	1989	Jesse Brown	1/21/93	235,501[h]	264,689	111,008	41

Note: The Cabinet also currently includes Chief of Staff Leon F. Panetta, Chair of the Council of Economic Advisors Joseph Stiglitz, Environmental Protection Agency Administrator Carol Browner, Director of the Office of Management and Budget Alice Rivlen, Ambassador to the United Nations Madeleine Albright, Director of the Central Intelligence Agency John Deutch, U.S. Trade Representative Michael Kantor, Director of the Office of National Drug Control Policy Lee

(Notes continue)

Table 8-6 (*Continued*)

P. Brown, Director of the Small Business Administration Phillip Lader, and Counselor to the President Mack McLarty.

[a] Dates are when the department achieved cabinet status. Offices of Attorney General and Postmaster General were created in 1789, but executive departments were not created until later. A Department of Agriculture was established in 1862, but the commissioner did not achieve cabinet status until 1889.

[b] As of July 1, 1995.

[c] December 1980; January 1994. Noncivil service positions include excepted and senior executive service and are as of January 1994.

[d] Incorporated into Defense Department in 1947.

[e] Independent agency as of 1971.

[f] Split into separate departments in 1913.

[g] Split into Health and Human Services and Education in 1979.

[h] Figures are for the Veterans Administration, the agency that was upgraded on March 15, 1989 to the Department of Veterans Affairs.

Sources: Year established: Ronald C. Moe, "The Federal Executive Establishment: Evolution and Trends," prepared for the U.S. Senate Committee on Governmental Affairs by the Congressional Research Service (Washington, D.C.: U.S. Government Printing Office, 1980), 26-27; *Congressional Quarterly Weekly Report* (1988), 3059; secretary and date confirmed: *Congressional Quarterly Weekly Report;* employees and noncivil service positions: U.S. Office of Personnel Management, *Federal Civilian Workforce Statistics, Employment and Trends* (January 1981), 8-9, 11, (January 1994), 38-39; note: Office of Cabinet Secretary and *Congressional Quarterly Weekly Report* (1993), 1091.

Table 8-7 White House Staff and the Executive Office of the President, 1943-1994

Year	White House	OMB/ Bureau of Budget[a]	Council of Economic Advisers	National Security Council	Office of Economic Opportunity	Office of Science and Technology	Office of Administration	Special Representative for Trade Negotiations	Office of Policy Development/ Domestic Council	Total executive office[b]
1943[c]	51	543								703
1944[c]	58	542								683
1945[c]	64	705								820
1946[c]	216	692	26							1,034
1947[c]	228	549	26							1,077
1948[c]	209	521	38	20						1,205
1949	243	517	36	17						1,240
1950	313	509	38	17						1,408
1951	246	518	37	21						1,326
1952	248	470	31	22						1,296
1953	247	417	28	28						1,183
1954	262	430	34	26						1,078
1955	366	422	33	27						1,221
1956	392	443	38	25						1,228
1957	399	441	35	65						1,255
1958	395	424	33	61						2,605
1959	406	432	33	64						2,735
1960	423	441	31	64						2,779
1961	439	456	45	43						1,586
1962	338	465	65	39		63		30		1,492
1963	376	485	57	43		48				1,572

(Table continues)

Table 8-7 (Continued)

Year	White House	OMB/ Bureau of Budget[a]	Council of Economic Advisers	National Security Council	Office of Economic Opportunity	Office of Science and Technology	Office of Adminis- tration	Special Rep- resentative for Trade Negotiations	Office of Policy Development/ Domestic Council	Total executive office[b]
1964	328	493	46	41		57		29		1,478
1965	292	506	45	39	1,768	75		24		3,307
1966	270	592	62	40	2,319	105		26		4,050
1967	271	570	56	38	2,951	58		24		4,747
1968	261	550	74	35	3,211	62		22		4,964
1969	341	576	54	66	2,282	75		22		4,116
1970	491	636	57	82	2,633	77		26	26	4,808
1971	580	717	62	80	2,304	75		33	44	4,809
1972	583	703	58	80	2,066	76		38	53	5,721
1973	528	642	49	85	1,148			39	24	3,877
1974	560	646	46	87	1,090			45	32	2,868
1975	525	664	48	85		19		56	55	1,801
1976	534	694	39	79		44		55	43	1,796
1977	387	721	36	68		46		52	41	1,637
1978	381	617	35	76		44	197	58	55	1,679
1979	418	638	36	73		50	180	70	60	1,918
1980	426	631	38	74		13	182	131	68	2,013
1981	378	679	38	65		20	190	139	48	1,674
1982	374	617	35	59		23	196	138	46	1,608
1983	376	619	34	61		21	213	139	39	1,622
1984	371	605	28	63		17	196	147	40	1,593
1985	362	569	32	61		11	193	152	38	1,549
1986	365	537	36	69		11	200	144	40	1,526
1987	375	573	31	56		11	199	155	37	1,604

Year									
1988	357	573	35	63	10	232	162	32	1,594
1989	370	536	32	62	20	213	164	37	1,640
1990	391	568	35	60	22	215	172	37	1,729
1991	358	608	36	61	39	241	181	33	1,797
1992	392	553	34	62	47	247	185	42	1,869
1993	392	522	31	52	35	185	177	42	1,570
1994	381	544	29	49	36	182	166	38	1,577

Note: In almost all instances when no figures are shown, the office did not exist as a separate entity. Data as of December of the year indicated, except 1947 (January), 1960 (October).

[a] The Bureau of the Budget became the Office of Management and Budget in 1970.

[b] Includes offices not shown separately.

[c] Total executive office excludes personnel in war establishments or emergency war agencies.

Source: U.S. Office of Personnel Management, *Federal Manpower Statistics, Federal Civilian Workforce Statistics,* bimonthly release.

Table 8-8   Number of Civilian Federal Government Employees and Percentage Under Merit Civil Service, 1816-1995

Year	Total number of employees[a]	Percentage under merit	Year	Total number of employees[a]	Percentage under merit
1816	4,837	—	1948	2,071,009	82.4
1821	6,914	—	1949	2,102,109	84.3
1831	11,491	—	1950	1,960,708	84.5
1841	18,038	—	1951	2,482,666	86.4
1851	26,274	—	1952	2,600,612	86.4
1861	36,672	—	1953	2,558,416	83.6
1871	51,020	—	1954	2,407,676	82.7
1881	100,020	—	1955	2,397,309	83.6
1891	157,442	21.5	1956	2,398,736	85.1
1901	239,476	44.3	1957	2,417,565	85.5
1910	388,708	57.2	1958	2,382,491	85.3
1911	395,905	57.5	1959	2,382,807	85.7
1912	400,150	54.3	1960	2,398,704	85.5
1913	396,494	71.3	1961	2,435,804	86.1
1914	401,887	72.8	1962	2,514,197	85.9
1915	395,429	73.9	1963	2,527,960	85.6
1916	399,381	74.3	1964	2,500,503	86.1
1917	438,500	74.5	1965	2,527,915	85.2
1918	854,500	75.2	1966	2,759,019	85.8
1919[b]	794,271	86.6	1967	3,002,461	82.8
1920[c]	655,265	75.9	1968	3,055,212	84.1
1921[c]	561,142	79.9	1969	3,076,414	82.9
1922	543,507	77.4	1970	2,981,574	82.3
1923	536,900	76.6	1971	2,862,894	84.1
1924	543,484	76.5	1972[d]	2,779,261	61.6
1925	553,045	76.6	1973	2,732,377	62.0
1926	548,713	77.0	1974[e]	2,893,118	57.0
1927	547,127	77.3	1975[e]	2,896,944	57.4
1928	560,772	77.0	1976[e]	2,883,134	57.6
1929	579,559	88.2	1977[e]	2,893,334	57.1
1930	601,319	87.9	1978[e]	2,929,100	57.3
1931	609,746	76.8	1979[e]	2,949,630	56.6
1932	605,496	77.2	1980	3,121,769	56.1
1933	603,587	75.6	1981	2,947,428	58.7
1934	698,649	64.5	1982	2,917,095	59.2
1935	780,582	58.3	1983	2,920,514	59.2
1936	867,432	57.5	1984	2,959,317	58.7
1937	895,993	59.4	1985	3,059,987	57.2
1938	882,226	63.8	1986	3,061,210	56.6
1939	953,891	69.5	1987	3,125,635	56.2
1940	1,042,420	69.7	1988	3,126,171	56.0
1941	1,437,682	68.9	1989[f]	3,151,334	56.2
1942	2,296,384	—	1990	3,503,550	50.5
1943	3,299,414	—	1991	3,138,180	56.4
1944	3,332,356	—	1992	3,134,915	56.7
1945	3,816,310	—	1993	3,050,711	56.7
1946	2,696,529	—	1994	2,992,840	55.4
1947	2,111,001	80.2	1995[g]	2,928,402	—

Table 8-8   (*Continued*)

Note: "—"indicates not available. As of June, except where indicated.

[a] Excludes employees of the Central Intelligence Agency and the National Security Agency.
[b] As of November.
[c] As of July.
[d] Under Postal Reorganization Act of 1970, U.S. Postal Service employees were changed from competitive (merit) service to excepted service.
[e] Excludes those employees in temporary and indefinite competitive status. In June 1973, 3.6 percent of federal civilian employees were in such service. In June 1980, 2.9 percent were.
[f] As of May.
[g] As of January.

Sources: 1816-1970: U.S. Bureau of the Census, *Historical Statistics of the United States* (Washington, D.C.: U.S. Government Printing Office, 1975), 1102-1103; 1971-1995: U.S. Office of Personnel Management, *Federal Civilian Workforce Statistics, Employment and Trends,* bimonthly release.

Table 8-9   Major Regulatory Agencies

Agency	Year established	Agency head Number	Agency head Title	Number of employees[a]
Consumer Product Safety Commission	1972	3	commissioner	483
Environmental Protection Agency	1970	1	administrator	17,850
Equal Employment Opportunity Commission	1965	5	commissioner	2,910
Federal Communications Commission	1934	5	commissioner	2,129
Federal Deposit Insurance Corporation	1933	5	board of director	17,253
Federal Energy Regulatory Commission	1977	5	commissioner	1,430
Federal Reserve System	1913	7	governor	1,677
Federal Trade Commission	1914	5	commissioner	983
Food and Drug Administration	1906	1	commissioner	8,782
Interstate Commerce Commission	1887	5	commissioner	419
National Labor Relations Board	1935	5	board of director	2,050
Occupational Safety and Health Administration	1970	1	assistant secretary	2,317
Securities and Exchange Commission	1934	5	commissioner	2,718

[a] As of January 1995.

Sources: Year established, agency head: Congressional Quarterly, *Federal Regulatory Directory* (Washington, D.C.: Congressional Quarterly, 1994), passim; number of employees: U.S. Office of Personnel Management, *Federal Civilian Workforce Statistics, Employment and Trends* (January 1995), and unpublished data from the agencies.

Table 8-10   Number of Pages in the *Federal Register*, 1940-1994

Year	Pages	Year	Pages
1940	5,307	1978	61,261
1945	15,508	1979	77,497
1950	9,562	1980	87,012
1955	10,196	1981	63,554
1960	14,479	1982	58,493
1965	17,206	1983	57,703
1966	16,850	1984	50,997
1967	21,087	1985	53,479
1968	20,068	1986	47,418
1969	20,464	1987	49,653
1970	20,032	1988	53,375
1971	25,442	1989	53,821
1972	28,920	1990	53,618
1973	35,586	1991	67,716
1974	45,422	1992	62,919
1975	60,221	1993	69,684
1976	57,072	1994	68,107
1977	63,629		

Source: Compiled from successive volumes of the *Federal Register* (Washington, D.C.: U.S. Government Printing Office).

Table 8-11 Presidential Victories on Votes in Congress, 1953-1994

President (political party)/year	House and Senate victories	House Victories	House Number of votes	Senate Victories	Senate Number of votes
Eisenhower (R)					
1953	89.2%	91.2%	34	87.8%	49
1954	82.8	78.9	38	77.9	77
1955	75.3	63.4	41	84.6	52
1956	69.2	73.5	34	67.7	65
1957	68.4	58.3	60	78.9	57
1958	75.7	74.0	50	76.5	98
1959	52.9	55.6	54	50.4	121
1960	65.1	65.1	43	65.1	86
Average	69.9	68.4		70.7	
Total			354		605
Kennedy (D)					
1961	81.5	83.1	65	80.6	124
1962	85.4	85.0	60	85.6	125
1963	87.1	83.1	71	89.6	115
Average	84.6	83.7		85.2	
Total			196		364
Johnson (D)					
1964	87.9	88.5	52	87.6	97
1965	93.1	93.8	112	92.6	162
1966	78.9	91.3	103	68.8	125
1967	78.8	75.6	127	81.2	165
1968	74.5	83.5	103	68.9	164
Average	82.2	85.9		79.7	
Total			497		713
Nixon (R)					
1969	74.8	72.3	47	76.4	72
1970	76.9	84.6	65	71.4	91
1971	74.8	82.5	57	69.5	82
1972	66.3	81.1	37	54.3	46
1973	50.6	48.0	125	52.4	185
1974	59.6	67.9	53	54.2	83
Average	64.3	68.2		61.5	
Total			384		559
Ford (R)					
1974	58.2	59.3	54	57.4	68
1975	61.0	50.6	89	71.0	93
1976	53.8	43.1	51	64.2	53
Average	58.3	51.0		65.0	
Total			194		214

Table 8-11   (*Continued*)

President (political party)/year	House and Senate victories	House		Senate	
		Victories	Number of votes	Victories	Number of votes
Carter (D)					
1977	75.4%	74.7%	79	76.1%	88
1978	78.3	69.6	112	84.8	151
1979	76.8	71.7	145	81.4	161
1980	75.1	76.9	117	73.3	116
Average	76.6	73.1		79.7	
Total			453		516
Reagan (R)					
1981	82.4	72.4	76	88.3	128
1982	72.4	55.8	77	83.2	119
1983	67.1	47.6	82	85.9	85
1984	65.8	52.2	113	85.7	77
1985	59.9	45.0	80	71.6	102
1986	56.5	33.3	90	80.7	83
1987	43.5	33.3	99	56.4	78
1988	47.4	32.7	104	64.8	88
Average	62.2	45.6		77.9	
Total			721		760
Bush (R)					
1989	62.6	50.0	86	73.3	101
1990	46.8	32.4	108	63.4	93
1991	54.2	43.2	111	67.5	83
1992	43.0	37.1	105	53.3	60
Average	51.8	40.2		65.6	
Total			410		337
Clinton (D)					
1993	86.4	87.3	102	85.4	89
1994	86.4	87.2	78	85.5	62
Average	86.4	87.2		85.4	
Total			180		151

Note: "R" indicates Republican; "D" indicates Democrat. Percentages based on the number of congressional votes supporting the president divided by the total number of votes on which the president had taken a position. The percentages differ slightly from those found in *Congressional Quarterly Almanac*, *Congressional Quarterly Weekly Report*, and Ornstein et al.'s *Vital Statistics on Congress* due to corrections and consistent rounding of percentages to one decimal place.

Sources: Congressional Quarterly Almanac (Washington, D.C.: Congressional Quarterly, various years); *Congressional Quarterly Weekly Report* (1992), 3894, (1993), 3473, (1994), 3620.

Table 8-12   Congressional Voting in Support of the President's Position, 1953-1994 (percent)

President/year	House			Senate		
	All Demo-crats	Southern Demo-crats	Repub-licans	All Demo-crats	Southern Demo-crats	Repub-licans
Eisenhower						
1953	55	—	80	55	—	78
1954	54	—	80	45	—	82
1955	58	—	67	65	—	85
1956	58	—	79	44	—	80
1957	54	—	60	60	—	80
1958	63	—	65	51	—	77
1959	44	—	76	44	—	80
1960	49	—	63	52	—	76
Kennedy						
1961	81	—	41	73	—	42
1962	83	71	47	76	63	48
1963	84	71	36	77	65	52
Johnson						
1964	84	70	42	73	63	52
1965	83	65	46	75	60	55
1966	81	64	45	71	59	53
1967	80	65	51	73	69	63
1968	77	63	59	64	50	57
Nixon						
1969	56	55	65	55	56	74
1970	64	64	79	56	62	74
1971	53	69	79	48	59	76
1972	56	59	74	52	71	77
1973	39	49	67	42	55	70
1974	52	64	71	44	60	65
Ford						
1974	48	52	59	45	55	67
1975	40	48	67	53	67	76
1976	36	52	70	47	61	73
Carter						
1977	69	58	46	77	71	58
1978	67	54	40	74	61	47
1979	70	58	37	75	66	51
1980	71	63	44	71	69	50

Table 8-12   (*Continued*)

President/year	House			Senate		
	All Demo-crats	Southern Demo-crats	Repub-licans	All Demo-crats	Southern Demo-crats	Repub-licans
Reagan						
1981	46	60	72	52	63	84
1982	43	55	70	46	57	77
1983	30	45	74	45	46	77
1984	37	47	64	45	58	81
1985	31	43	69	36	46	80
1986	26	37	69	39	56	90
1987	26	37	65	38	43	67
1988	28	34	61	51	58	73
Bush						
1989	38	49	72	56	66	84
1990	26	35	65	39	49	72
1991	35	43	74	42	53	84
1992	27	38	75	33	40	75
Clinton						
1993	79	80	40	89	85	30
1994	79	79	48	89	88	44

Note: "—" indicates not available. Percentages indicate number of congressional votes supporting the president divided by the total number of votes on which the president took a position. The percentages are calculated to eliminate the effects of absences as follows: support = (support)/(support + opposition).

Sources: 1953-1954: Congressional Quarterly Almanac, 1953 (Washington, D.C.: Congressional Quarterly, 1954), 78; 1954, 48; 1955-1988: Norman J. Ornstein et al., eds., *Vital Statistics on Congress, 1989-1990* (Washington, D.C.: Congressional Quarterly, 1990), 196-197; 1989-1994: Congressional Quarterly Weekly Report (1990), 4208; (1992), 3896, (1994), 3654.

Table 8-13   Presidential Vetoes, 1789-1994

Years	President	Regular vetoes	Vetoes overridden	Pocket vetoes	Total vetoes
1789-1797	Washington	2	0	0	2
1797-1801	Adams	0	0	0	0
1801-1809	Jefferson	0	0	0	0
1809-1817	Madison	5	0	2	7
1817-1825	Monroe	1	0	0	1
1825-1829	J. Q. Adams	0	0	0	0
1829-1837	Jackson	5	0	7	12
1837-1841	Van Buren	0	0	1	1
1841-1841	Harrison	0	0	0	0
1841-1845	Tyler	6	1	4	10
1845-1849	Polk	2	0	1	3
1849-1850	Taylor	0	0	0	0
1850-1853	Fillmore	0	0	0	0
1853-1857	Pierce	9	5	0	9
1857-1861	Buchanan	4	0	3	7
1861-1865	Lincoln	2	0	5	7
1865-1869	A. Johnson	21	15	8	29
1869-1877	Grant	45	4	48	93
1877-1881	Hayes	12	1	1	13
1881-1881	Garfield	0	0	0	0
1881-1885	Arthur	4	1	8	12
1885-1889	Cleveland	304	2	110	414
1889-1893	Harrison	19	1	25	44
1893-1897	Cleveland	42	5	128	170
1897-1901	McKinley	6	0	36	42
1901-1909	T. Roosevelt	42	1	40	82
1909-1913	Taft	30	1	9	39
1913-1921	Wilson	33	6	11	44
1921-1923	Harding	5	0	1	6
1923-1929	Coolidge	20	4	30	50
1929-1933	Hoover	21	3	16	37
1933-1945	F. Roosevelt	372	9	263	635
1945-1953	Truman	180	12	70	250
1953-1961	Eisenhower	73	2	108	181
1961-1963	Kennedy	12	0	9	21
1963-1969	L. Johnson	16	0	14	30
1969-1974	Nixon	26[a]	7	17	43
1974-1977	Ford	48	12	18	66
1977-1981	Carter	13	2	18	31
1981-1989	Reagan	39	9	39	78
1989-1992	Bush	29	1	17	46
1993-1994	Clinton	0	0	0	0
Total		1,448	104	1,067	2,515

[a] Two pocket vetoes, overruled in the courts, are counted here as regular vetoes.

Sources: Congressional Quarterly Weekly Report (1989), 7; (1992), 3925-3926; (1994), 3623.

Table 8-14   Senate Action on Nominations, 1935-1994[a]

			Senate action			
Congress		Number received	Con-firmed	Withdrawn	Rejected[b]	Unconfirmed
74th	(1935-1936)	22,487	22,286	51	15	135
75th	(1937-1938)	15,330	15,193	20	27	90
76th	(1939-1941)	29,072	28,939	16	21	96
77th	(1941-1942)	24,344	24,137	33	5	169
78th	(1943-1944)	21,775	21,371	31	6	367
79th	(1945-1946)	37,022	36,550	17	3	452
80th	(1947-1948)	66,641	54,796	153	0	11,692
81st	(1949-1951)	87,266	86,562	45	6	653
82d	(1951-1952)	46,920	46,504	45	2	369
83d	(1953-1954)	69,458	68,563	43	0	852
84th	(1955-1956)	84,173	82,694	38	3	1,438
85th	(1957-1958)	104,193	103,311	54	0	828
86th	(1959-1960)	91,476	89,900	30	1	1,545
87th	(1961-1962)	102,849	100,741	1,279	0	829
88th	(1963-1964)	122,190	120,201	36	0	1,953
89th	(1965-1966)	123,019	120,865	173	0	1,981
90th	(1967-1968)	120,231	118,231	34	0	1,966
91st	(1969-1971)	134,464	133,797	487	2	178
92d	(1971-1972)	117,053	114,909	11	0	2,133
93d	(1973-1974)[c]	134,384	131,254	15	0	3,069
94th	(1975-1976)	132,151	131,378	6	0	3,801
95th	(1977-1978)	137,504	124,730	66	0	12,713
96th	(1979-1980)	154,797	154,665	18	0	1,458
97th	(1981-1982)	186,264	184,844	55	7	1,346
98th	(1983-1984)	97,893	97,262	4	0	610
99th	(1985-1986)	99,614	95,811	16	0	3,787
100th	(1987-1988)	89,193	88,721	23	1	5,922
101st	(1989-1990)	93,368	88,078	48	1	7,951
102d	(1991-1992)	76,446	75,349	24	0	756
103d	(1993-1994)	77,384	76,122	1,080	0	2,741

[a] Data for earlier years can be found in previous editions of *Vital Statistics on American Politics*.
[b] Includes only those nominations rejected outright by a vote of the Senate. Most nominations that fail to win approval of the Senate are unfavorably reported by committees and never reach the Senate floor, having been withdrawn. In some cases, the full Senate may vote to recommit a nomination to committee, in effect killing it.
[c] Forty-six nominations were returned to the president during the October-November 1974 recess in accordance with Senate Rule 38, which states: "[I]f the Senate shall adjourn or take a recess for more than thirty days, all nominations pending and not finally acted upon at the time of taking such adjournment or recess shall be returned by the Secretary to the President, and shall not again be considered unless they shall again be made to the Senate by the President."

Sources: 1929-1980: Congressional Quarterly, *Congressional Quarterly's Guide to Congress*, 3d ed. (Washington, D.C.: Congressional Quarterly, 1982), 195; 1981-1992: Congressional Record (daily ed.), Daily Digest, "Resume of Congressional Activity," 97th Cong. (1st sess., D1613; 2d sess., D1499); 98th Cong. (2d sess., D1348); 99th Cong. (1st sess., D1565; 2d sess., D1343); 100th Cong. (2d sess., D1400); 101st Cong. (1st sess., D1431; 2d sess., D1449); 102d Cong. (2d sess., D1336); 103d Cong. (2d sess., D1276).

Table 8-15   Senate Rejections of Cabinet Nominations

Nominee	Position	President	Date	Vote
Roger B. Taney	secretary of treasury	Jackson	6/23/1834	18-28
Caleb Cushing	secretary of treasury	Tyler	3/3/1843	19-27
Caleb Cushing	secretary of treasury	Tyler	3/3/1843	10-27
Caleb Cushing	secretary of treasury	Tyler	3/3/1843	2-29
David Henshaw	secretary of navy	Tyler	1/15/1844	6-34
James M. Porter	secretary of war	Tyler	1/30/1844	3-38
James S. Green	secretary of treasury	Tyler	6/15/1844	[a]
Henry Stanbery	attorney general	A. Johnson	6/2/1868	11-29
Charles B. Warren	attorney general	Coolidge	3/10/1925	39-41
Charles B. Warren	attorney general	Coolidge	3/16/1925	39-46
Lewis L. Strauss	secretary of commerce	Eisenhower	6/19/1959	46-49
John Tower	secretary of defense	Bush	3/9/1989	47-53

[a] Not recorded.

Source: Congressional Quarterly, Congressional Quarterly's Guide to Congress, 4th ed. (Washington, D.C.: Congressional Quarterly, 1991), 252.

Table 8-16   Treaties and Executive Agreements Concluded by the United States, 1789-1994

Years	Number of treaties	Number of executive agreements
1789-1839	60	27
1839-1889	215	238
1889-1929	382	763
1930-1932	49	41
1933-1944 (F. Roosevelt)	131	369
1945-1952 (Truman)	132	1,324
1953-1960 (Eisenhower)	89	1,834
1961-1963 (Kennedy)	36	813
1964-1968 (L. Johnson)	67	1,083
1969-1974 (Nixon)	93	1,317
1975-1976 (Ford)	26	666
1977-1980 (Carter)	79	1,476
1981-1988 (Reagan)	125	2,840
1989-1992 (Bush)	67	1,350
1993-1994 (Clinton)	41	594

Note: Number of treaties includes those concluded during the indicated span of years. Some of these treaties did not receive the consent of the U.S. Senate. Varying definitions of what comprises an executive agreement and their entry-into-force date make the above numbers approximate.

Sources: 1789-1980: *Congressional Quarterly's Guide to Congress,* 291; 1981-1994: Office of the Assistant Legal Adviser for Treaty Affairs, U.S. Department of State.

Figure 8-1   Presidential Approval, Gallup Poll, 1938-1995

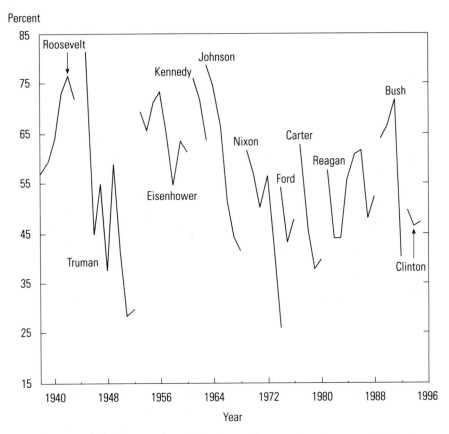

Note: Averaged by year. Question: "Do you approve or disapprove of the way ____ (last name of president) is handling his job as president?"

Sources: Calculated by the editors; 1938-1980: *The Gallup Opinion Index,* October-November 1980, 13-38; 1981-1995: *The Gallup Report,* July 1988, 19-20; The Gallup Poll, "Reagan Regaining Public Confidence," press release, October 9, 1988; and the Gallup Library.

Figure 8-2   Presidential Approval, 1977-1995

Note: Question: "Do you approve or disapprove of the way _____ (last name of president) is handling his job as president?"

Sources: 1977-1980: *The Gallup Opinion Index,* October-November 1980, 13-14; 1981-1995: *The Gallup Report,* July 1988, 19-20; The Gallup Poll, "Reagan Regaining Public Confidence," press release, October 9, 1988; and unpublished data from the Gallup Poll.

9

The Judiciary

The judiciary, although one of the three "separate but equal" branches of government, is often considered remote from the political push and pull that characterizes the other two. Preoccupation with process, precedent, and the meaning of the law gives the courts a strikingly different appearance. But grappling with the constitutionality of abortion or the death penalty and pouring practical meaning into ambiguous, generally worded statutes enacted by legislatures put the courts squarely in the midst of the political process.

But even if courts can be considered political, are statistics essential to understanding the courts? They are for two reasons. First, the courts themselves have to deal with statistics. A 1987 Supreme Court decision, for example, considered the question of racially disparate patterns in the imposition of the death penalty—Georgia defendants who killed whites were eleven times more likely to be sentenced to die as those who killed blacks.[1] The Court held that the statistics were not relevant to this particular case. Although the numbers may have been accurate and meaningful, they did not show that there was racial discrimination against this defendant. This case serves as a pointed reminder of the distinction a court draws between general patterns and the facts of the specific case before it.

But this example should not give the impression that courts disdain statistics. In fact, as one federal judge wrote, "In the problem of racial discrimination, statistics often tell much, and Courts listen."[2] Cases often turn on conclusions drawn from numerical data—voting rights (Table 1-17), reapportionment (Tables 1-15 and 1-16), and school desegregation (Table 12-13) are but three areas in which this is true.

Statistics also can promote understanding of the courts. A single case does not lend itself to statistical analysis, but the large number, the hierarchy (Figure 9-1), and the geographical spread (Figure 9-2) of the federal courts, and the even greater variety of state courts and appointment methods (Table 9-1) suggest that numerical summarization aids comprehension. In addition, precisely because of the judicial emphasis on precedents, there are perhaps better records of previous activities than in most other areas of government.

The characteristics of those on the federal bench are one area of interest. Although the nature of the courts might suggest that appointments are merely a matter of judicial qualifications, the record indicates otherwise. Federal judicial appointments have always been subject to partisan considerations (Tables 9-3 and 9-5), and other characteristics of federal judges have been shown to vary with the appointing president (Table 9-2). Partisan and ideological differences also explain part of the frustration presidents have encountered with nominations to the Supreme Court (Table 9-4). Nor are more subjective judgments ignored in characterizing court appointees. Just as historians have judged presidents, legal scholars have evaluated Supreme Court justices (Table 9-6).

The growing caseload of the courts has become a major concern in recent years, and, while individual "horror" stories may be more dramatic (when Chief Justice Warren E. Burger retired in 1986 he noted that in a recent week he had worked more than one hundred hours), statistical evidence tells an even more convincing story. The caseload of the courts has indeed climbed dramatically in recent years (Tables 9-7 through 9-10, Figure 9-3). Cases filed in the district courts rose by 59 percent between 1980 and 1985, while the number of judges rose by only 2 percent (Table 9-9).

There is also considerable information on the nature of judicial work. For example, civil rather than criminal cases account for the increased workload (Table 9-10). One can also see from the distribution of types of cases in the federal courts that a district court judge must be prepared to hear and decide cases on a wide range of topics (Table 9-11). Dramatic changes also have occurred in the kinds of cases courts must deal with and in the ways they have responded. The Supreme Court has struck down more federal, state, and local laws on constitutional grounds in this century than in the nineteenth (Table 9-12). Within this century, however, doctrinal trends have changed. For example, since the 1930s the Court has rejected far fewer economic regulatory laws and has increasingly struck down laws restricting civil liberties (Figure 9-4).

As they are with the executive and the legislature, statistics are a necessary component for understanding the courts and their decisions.

Notes

1. *McCleskey v. Kemp*, 481 U.S. 279.
2. *Alabama v. United States*, 304 F.2d 201 (1961).

Figure 9-1 The United States Federal Court System

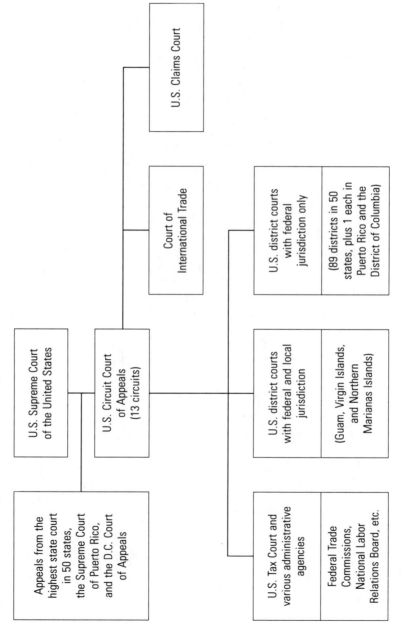

Source: Administrative Office of the United States Courts.

Figure 9-2 The Thirteen Federal Judicial Circuits and Ninety-four U.S. District Courts

Source: Administrative Office of the United States Courts (January 1983).

Table 9-1 Principal Methods of Judicial Selection for State Courts

Partisan election	Nonpartisan election	Legislative election	Gubernatorial appointment	Merit plan
Alabama[a]	Georgia[a]	Connecticut[a]	California	Alaska[a]
Arkansas	Idaho[a]	Rhode Island[c]	Delaware	Arizona[a]
Illinois[a]	Kentucky	South Carolina[a]	Maine[a]	Colorado[a]
Mississippi[a]	Louisiana	Virginia	Massachusetts	Florida[a,b]
North Carolina[b]	Michigan[a]		New Hampshire	Hawaii
Pennsylvania[a]	Minnesota		New Jersey[a]	Indiana[a]
Tennessee[a,b]	Montana		New York[a,d]	Iowa[a]
Texas[a]	Nevada			Kansas[a]
West Virginia	North Dakota			Maryland
	Ohio[a]			Missouri[a]
	Oregon[a]			Nebraska
	Washington[a]			New Mexico
	Wisconsin[a]			Oklahoma[a,b]
				South Dakota[a]
				Utah
				Vermont
				Wyoming[a]

Note: "Merit plan" typically involves appointment by governor from a list of candidates submitted by an independent or quasi-independent judiciary council or commission.

[a] Minor court judges chosen by other methods.
[b] Most but not all major judicial positions selected this way.
[c] Supreme Court justices only.
[d] Appellate judges only.

Source: Council of State Governments, *Book of the States, 1994-1995* (Lexington, Ky.: Council of State Governments, 1994), 190-192.

Table 9-2 Characteristics of Federal District and Appellate Court Appointees, Presidents Johnson to Clinton (percent)

	Johnson appointees	Nixon appointees	Ford appointees	Carter appointees	Reagan appointees	Bush appointees	Clinton appointees
District courts							
Occupation							
Politics/government	21.3	10.6	21.2	4.4	12.8	10.8	11.2
Judiciary	31.1	28.5	34.6	44.6	37.2	41.9	43.9
Large law firm	2.5	11.2	9.6	13.9	17.6	25.7	21.5
Moderate firm	18.9	27.9	25.0	19.8	19.3	14.9	11.2
Small/solo firm	23.0	19.0	9.6	13.9	10.4	4.7	8.4
Other	3.3	2.8	0.0	3.5	2.8	2.1	3.7
Experience							
Judicial	34.4	35.2	42.3	54.5	46.6	46.6	48.6
Prosecutorial	45.9	41.9	50.0	38.6	44.1	39.2	35.5
Neither	33.6	36.3	30.8	28.2	28.3	31.8	32.7
Political affiliation							
Democrat	94.3	7.3	21.2	92.6	4.8	5.4	88.8
Republican	5.7	92.7	78.8	4.4	93.1	88.5	2.8
Independent or other	0.0	0.0	0.0	2.9	2.1	6.1	7.5
Past party activism	49.2	48.6	50.0	60.9	58.6	60.8	53.3
Religion							
Protestant	58.2	73.2	73.1	60.4	60.3	64.2	—
Catholic	31.1	18.4	17.3	27.7	30.0	28.4	—
Jewish	10.7	8.4	9.6	11.9	9.3	7.4	—
Race/ethnicity							
White	93.4	95.5	88.5	78.7	92.4	89.2	64.5
Black	4.1	3.4	5.8	13.9	2.1	6.8	25.2
Asian-American	0.0	0.0	3.9	0.5	0.7	0.0	0.9
Hispanic	2.5	1.1	1.9	6.9	4.8	4.0	8.4
Sex							
Female	1.6	0.6	1.9	14.4	8.3	19.6	31.8
Number of appointees	122	179	52	202	290	148	107

Courts of Appeals

Occupation							
Politics/government	10.0	4.4	8.3	5.4	6.4	10.8	0.0
Judiciary	57.5	53.3	75.0	46.4	55.1	59.5	66.7
Large law firm	5.0	4.4	8.3	10.8	12.8	16.2	16.7
Moderate firm	17.5	22.2	8.3	16.1	10.3	10.8	5.6
Small/solo firm	7.5	6.7	0.0	5.4	1.3	0.0	0.0
Other	2.5	8.9	0.0	16.1	14.1	2.7	11.1
Experience							
Judicial	65.0	57.8	75.0	53.6	60.3	62.2	72.2
Prosecutorial	47.5	46.7	25.0	32.1	28.2	29.7	50.0
Neither	20.0	17.8	25.0	37.5	34.6	32.4	11.1
Political affiliation							
Democrat	95.0	6.7	8.3	82.1	0.0	5.4	88.9
Republican	5.0	93.3	91.7	7.1	97.4	89.2	5.6
Independent or other	0.0	0.0	0.0	10.7	2.6	5.4	5.6
Past party activism	57.5	60.0	58.3	73.2	69.2	70.3	50.0
Religion							
Protestant	60.0	75.6	58.3	60.7	55.1	59.4	—
Catholic	25.0	15.6	33.3	23.2	30.8	24.3	—
Jewish	15.0	8.9	8.3	16.1	14.1	16.3	—
Race/ethnicity							
White	95.0	97.8	100.0	78.6	97.4	89.2	72.2
Black	5.0	0.0	0.0	16.1	1.3	5.4	16.7
Asian-American	0.0	2.2	0.0	3.6	0.0	0.0	0.0
Hispanic	0.0	0.0	0.0	1.8	1.3	5.4	11.1
Sex							
Female	2.5	0.0	0.0	19.6	5.1	18.9	27.8
Number of appointees	40	45	12	56	78	37	18

Note: "—" Indicates not available. Large law firm: twenty-five or more partners and associates; moderate: five to twenty-four; small: two to four.

Source: Sheldon Goldman, "Bush's Judicial Legacy: The Final Imprint," *Judicature* 76 (April-May 1993), 287, 293; Goldman, "Judicial Selection under Clinton: A Midterm Examination," *Judicature* 78 (May-June 1995), 281, 287.

Table 9-3 Federal Judicial Appointments of Same Party as President, Presidents Cleveland to Clinton

President	Party	Percentage
Cleveland	Democrat	97.3
Harrison	Republican	87.9
McKinley	Republican	95.7
T. Roosevelt	Republican	95.8
Taft	Republican	82.2
Wilson	Democrat	98.6
Harding	Republican	97.7
Coolidge	Republican	94.1
Hoover	Republican	85.7
F. Roosevelt	Democrat	96.4
Truman	Democrat	93.1
Eisenhower	Republican	95.1
Kennedy	Democrat	90.9
Johnson	Democrat	94.3
Nixon	Republican	92.7
Ford	Republican	78.8
Carter	Democrat	92.6
Reagan	Republican	93.1
Bush	Republican	88.5
Clinton	Democrat	88.8

Source: Cleveland-Kennedy: Henry J. Abraham, *Justices and Presidents: Appointments to the Supreme Court*, 3d ed. (New York: Oxford University Press, 1991), 68, (copyright © Henry J. Abraham, 1974, 1985, 1991, reprinted by permission of Oxford University Press, Inc.); Johnson-Clinton: Table 9-2, this volume.

Table 9-4   Supreme Court Nominations That Failed

Nominee	Date of nomination	President	Action
William Paterson	1793	Washington	withdrawn
John Rutledge	1795	Washington	rejected, 10-14
Alexander Wolcott	1811	Madison	rejected, 9-24
John Crittenden	1828	J. Q. Adams	postponed
Roger B. Taney	1835	Jackson	postponed
John Spencer	1844	Tyler	rejected, 21-26
R. Walworth	1844	Tyler	withdrawn
Edward King	1844	Tyler	postponed
Edward King	1844	Tyler	withdrawn
John Read	1845	Tyler	not acted on
G. Woodward	1845	Polk	rejected, 20-29
Edward Bradford	1852	Fillmore	not acted on
George Badger	1853	Fillmore	postponed
William Micou	1853	Fillmore	not acted on
Jeremiah Black	1861	Buchanan	rejected, 25-26
Henry Stanbery	1866	A. Johnson	not acted on
Ebenezer Hoar	1869	Grant	rejected, 24-33
George Williams	1873	Grant	withdrawn
Caleb Cushing	1874	Grant	withdrawn
Stanley Matthews	1881	Hayes	not acted on
W. B. Hornblower	1893	Cleveland	rejected, 24-30
Wheeler H. Peckham	1894	Cleveland	rejected, 32-41
John J. Parker	1930	Hoover	rejected, 39-41
Abe Fortas[a]	1968	L. Johnson	withdrawn
Homer Thornberry	1968	L. Johnson	not acted on
C. Haynsworth	1969	Nixon	rejected, 45-55
G. H. Carswell	1970	Nixon	rejected, 45-51
Robert Bork	1987	Reagan	rejected, 42-58
Douglas Ginsburg	1987	Reagan	not submitted[b]

Note: Twenty-nine of the 145 presidential nominations have failed to obtain Senate confirmation. However, five nominees declined appointment after having been nominated (Harrison, 1789; W. Cushing, 1796; Jay, 1800; Lincoln, 1811; Adams, 1811) and two withdrew after being confirmed (W. Smith, 1837; Conkling, 1882).

[a] In 1968, Fortas, an associate justice, was nominated for chief justice.
[b] Publicly announced but withdrawn before the president formally submitted his nomination to the Senate.

Source: Congressional Quarterly, *Guide to the U.S. Supreme Court*, 2d ed. (Washington, D.C.: Congressional Quarterly, 1990), 652; updated by the editors.

Table 9-5 Characteristics of Supreme Court Justices

Seat number and justice	Party	Home state	Years on Court	Age at nomination	Years of previous judicial experience
Washington appointees					
1 John Jay	Federalist	New York	1789-1795	44	2
2 John Rutledge	Federalist	South Carolina	1789-1791	50	6
3 William Cushing	Federalist	Massachusetts	1789-1810[a]	57	29
4 James Wilson	Federalist	Pennsylvania	1789-1798[a]	47	0
5 John Blair, Jr.	Federalist	Virginia	1789-1796	57	11
6 James Iredell	Federalist	North Carolina	1790-1799[a]	38	0.5
2 Thomas Johnson	Federalist	Maryland	1791-1793	59	1.5
2 William Paterson	Federalist	New Jersey	1793-1806[a]	47	0
1 John Rutledge	Federalist	South Carolina	1795	55	6[b]
5 Samuel Chase	Federalist	Maryland	1796-1811[a]	55	8
1 Oliver Ellsworth	Federalist	Connecticut	1796-1800	51	5
J. Adams appointees					
4 Bushrod Washington	Federalist	Virginia	1798-1829[a]	36	0
6 Alfred Moore	Federalist	North Carolina	1799-1804	44	1
1 John Marshall	Federalist	Virginia	1801-1835[a]	45	3
Jefferson appointees					
6 William Johnson	Jeffersonian	South Carolina	1804-1834[a]	32	6
2 H. Brockholst Livingston	Jeffersonian	New York	1806-1823[a]	49	0
7 Thomas Todd	Jeffersonian	Kentucky	1807-1826[a]	42	6
Madison appointees					
5 Gabriel Duvall	Jeffersonian	Maryland	1811-1835	58	6
3 Joseph Story	Jeffersonian	Massachusetts	1811-1845[a]	32	0
Monroe appointee					
2 Smith Thompson	Jeffersonian	New York	1823-1843[a]	55	16

J. Q. Adams appointee					
7 Robert Trimble	Jeffersonian	Kentucky	1826-1828[a]	49	11
Jackson appointees					
7 John McLean	Democrat	Ohio	1829-1861[a]	44	6
4 Henry Baldwin	Democrat	Pennsylvania	1830-1844[a]	50	0
6 James Wayne	Democrat	Georgia	1835-1867[a]	45	5
1 Roger B. Taney	Democrat	Maryland	1836-1864[a]	59	0
5 Philip P. Barbour	Democrat	Virginia	1836-1841[a]	52	8
Van Buren appointees					
8 John Catron	Democrat	Tennessee	1837-1865[a]	51	10
9 John McKinley	Democrat	Alabama	1837-1852[a]	57	0
5 Peter V. Daniel	Democrat	Virginia	1841-1860[a]	57	0
Tyler appointee					
2 Samuel Nelson	Democrat	New York	1845-1872	52	22
Polk appointees					
3 Levi Woodbury	Democrat	New Hampshire	1845-1851[a]	55	6
4 Robert C. Grier	Democrat	Pennsylvania	1846-1870	52	13
Fillmore appointee					
3 Benjamin R. Curtis	Whig	Massachusetts	1851-1857	41	0
Pierce appointee					
9 John A. Campbell	Democrat	Alabama	1853-1861	41	0
Buchanan appointee					
3 Nathan Clifford	Democrat	Maine	1858-1881[a]	54	0
Lincoln appointees					
7 Noah H. Swayne	Republican	Ohio	1862-1881	57	0
5 Samuel F. Miller	Republican	Iowa	1862-1890[a]	46	0
9 David Davis	Republican	Illinois	1862-1877	47	14
10 Stephen J. Field	Democrat	California	1863-1897	46	6
1 Salmon P. Chase	Republican	Ohio	1864-1873[a]	56	0

(Table continues)

Table 9-5 (*Continued*)

Seat number and justice	Party	Home state	Years on Court	Age at nomination	Years of previous judicial experience
Grant appointees					
4 William Strong	Republican	Pennsylvania	1870-1880	61	11
6 Joseph P. Bradley	Republican	New Jersey	1870-1892[a]	56	0
2 Ward Hunt	Republican	New York	1873-1882	62	8
1 Morrison R. Waite	Republican	Ohio	1874-1888[a]	57	0
Hayes appointees					
9 John M. Harlan	Republican	Kentucky	1877-1911[a]	44	1
4 William B. Woods	Republican	Georgia	1880-1887[a]	56	12
Garfield appointee					
7 Stanley Matthews	Republican	Ohio	1881-1889[a]	56	4
Arthur appointees					
3 Horace Gray	Republican	Massachusetts	1881-1902	53	18
2 Samuel Blatchford	Republican	New York	1882-1893[a]	62	15
Cleveland appointees (first term)					
4 Lucius Q. C. Lamar	Democrat	Mississippi	1883-1893[a]	62	0
1 Melville W. Fuller	Democrat	Illinois	1888-1910[a]	55	0
Harrison appointees					
7 David J. Brewer	Republican	Kansas	1889-1910[a]	52	19
5 Henry B. Brown	Republican	Michigan	1891-1906	54	16
6 George Shiras, Jr.	Republican	Pennsylvania	1892-1903	60	0
4 Howell E. Jackson	Democrat	Tennessee	1893-1895[a]	60	7
Cleveland appointees (second term)					
2 Edward D. White	Democrat	Louisiana	1894-1910[a]	48	1.5
4 Rufus W. Peckham	Democrat	New York	1895-1909[a]	57	9

McKinley appointee					
8 Joseph McKenna	Republican	California	1898-1925	54	5
T. Roosevelt appointees					
3 Oliver W. Holmes	Republican	Massachusetts	1902-1932	61	20
6 William R. Day	Republican	Ohio	1903-1922	53	7
5 William H. Moody	Republican	Massachusetts	1906-1910	52	0
Taft appointees					
4 Horace H. Lurton	Democrat	Tennessee	1909-1914[a]	65	26
7 Charles E. Hughes	Republican	New York	1910-1916	48	0
1 Edward D. White	Democrat	Louisiana	1910-1921[a]	65	1.5[b]
2 Willis Van Devanter	Republican	Wyoming	1910-1937	51	8
5 Joseph R. Lamar	Democrat	Georgia	1910-1916[a]	53	2
9 Mahlon Pitney	Republican	New Jersey	1912-1922	54	11
Wilson appointees					
4 James C. McReynolds	Democrat	Tennessee	1914-1941	52	0
5 Louis D. Brandeis	Republican	Massachusetts	1916-1939	59	0
7 John H. Clarke	Democrat	Ohio	1916-1922	59	2
Harding appointees					
1 William H. Taft	Republican	Ohio	1921-1930	63	13
7 George Sutherland	Republican	Utah	1922-1938	60	0
6 Pierce Butler	Democrat	Minnesota	1923-1939[a]	56	0
9 Edward T. Sanford	Republican	Tennessee	1923-1930[a]	57	14
Coolidge appointee					
8 Harlan Fiske Stone	Republican	New York	1925-1941	52	0
Hoover appointees					
1 Charles E. Hughes	Republican	New York	1930-1941	67	0
9 Owens J. Roberts	Republican	Pennsylvania	1930-1945	55	0
3 Benjamin N. Cardozo	Democrat	New York	1932-1938[a]	61	18

(Table continues)

Table 9-5 *(Continued)*

Seat number and justice	Party	Home state	Years on Court	Age at nomination	Years of previous judicial experience
F. Roosevelt appointees					
2 Hugo L. Black	Democrat	Alabama	1937-1971[a]	51	1.5
7 Stanley F. Reed	Democrat	Kentucky	1938-1957	53	0
3 Felix Frankfurter	Independent	Massachusetts	1939-1962	56	0
5 William O. Douglas	Democrat	Connecticut	1939-1975	40	0
6 Frank Murphy	Democrat	Michigan	1940-1949[a]	49	7
4 James F. Byrnes	Democrat	South Carolina	1941-1942	62	0
1 Harlan Fiske Stone	Republican	New York	1941-1946[a]	68	0[b]
8 Robert H. Jackson	Democrat	New York	1941-1954[a]	49	0
4 Wiley B. Rutledge	Democrat	Iowa	1943-1949[a]	48	4
Truman appointees					
9 Harold H. Burton	Republican	Ohio	1945-1958	57	0
1 Fred M. Vinson	Democrat	Kentucky	1946-1953[a]	56	5
6 Tom C. Clark	Democrat	Texas	1949-1967	49	0
4 Sherman Minton	Democrat	Indiana	1949-1956	58	8
Eisenhower appointees					
1 Earl Warren	Republican	California	1953-1969	62	0
8 John M. Harlan	Republican	New York	1955-1971	55	1
4 William J. Brennan	Democrat	New Jersey	1956-1990	50	7
7 Charles E. Whittaker	Republican	Missouri	1957-1962	56	3
9 Potter Stewart	Republican	Ohio	1958-1981	43	4
Kennedy appointees					
7 Byron R. White	Democrat	Colorado	1962-1993	44	0
3 Arthur J. Goldberg	Democrat	Illinois	1962-1965	54	0
L. Johnson appointees					
3 Abe Fortas	Democrat	Tennessee	1965-1969	55	0
6 Thurgood Marshall	Democrat	New York	1967-1991	59	4

	Party	State	Term	Age	Prior judicial experience
Nixon appointees					
1 Warren E. Burger	Republican	Minnesota	1969-1986	61	13
3 Harry A. Blackmun	Republican	Minnesota	1970-1994	61	11
2 Lewis F. Powell, Jr.	Democrat	Virginia	1971-1987	64	0
8 William H. Rehnquist	Republican	Arizona	1971-1986	47	0
Ford appointee					
5 John Paul Stevens	Republican	Illinois	1976-	55	5
Reagan appointees					
9 Sandra Day O'Connor	Republican	Arizona	1981-	51	6.5
1 William H. Rehnquist	Republican	Arizona	1986-	61	0[b]
8 Antonin Scalia	Republican	Illinois	1986-	50	4
2 Anthony Kennedy	Republican	California	1988-	51	12
Bush appointees					
4 David H. Souter	Republican	New Hampshire	1990-	50	13
6 Clarence Thomas	Republican	Georgia	1991-	43	1
Clinton appointee					
7 Ruth Bader Ginsburg	Democrat	New York	1993-	60	13
3 Stephen B. Breyer	Democrat	Massachusetts	1994-	55	15

Note: Seat number 1 is always held by the chief justice of the United States.

[a] Died in office.
[b] Prior to appointment to associate justice.

Sources: Sheldon Goldman, *Constitutional Law: Cases and Essays* (New York: Harper and Row, 1987); previous judicial experience: Abraham, *Justices and Presidents,* 56-58 (copyright © Henry J. Abraham, 1974, 1985, reprinted by permission of Oxford University Press, Inc.); *Congressional Quarterly's Guide to Congress,* 786-788; updated by the editors.

Table 9-6 Ratings of Supreme Court Justices

Great	Near great	Average			Below average	Failure
J. Marshall	W. Johnson	Jay	McKinley	Shiras	T. Johnson	Van Devanter
Story	Curtis	J. Rutledge	Daniel	Peckham	Moore	McReynolds
Taney	Miller	Cushing	Nelson	McKenna	Trimble	Butler
Harlan I	Field	Wilson	Woodbury	Day	Barbour	Byrnes
Holmes	Bradley	Blair	Grier	Moody	Woods	Burton
Hughes	Waite	Iredell	Campbell	Lurton	H. E. Jackson	Vinson
Brandeis	E. D. White	Paterson	Clifford	J. R. Lamar		Minton
Stone	Taft	S. Chase	Swayne	Pitney		Whittaker
Cardozo	Sutherland	Ellsworth	Davis	J. H. Clarke		
Black	Douglas	Washington	S. P. Chase	Sanford		
Frankfurter	R. H. Jackson	Livingston	Strong	Roberts		
Warren	W. B. Rutledge	Todd	Hunt	Reed		
		Harlan II	Duvall	Matthews		
		Brennan	Thompson	Gray		
		Fortas	McLean	Blatchford		
		Murphy	Brewer	Baldwin		
		T. C. Clark	B. R. White	Wayne		
		Stewart	Goldberg	Catron		
		L. Q. C. Lamar	T. Marshall	Brown		
		Fuller				

Note: Ratings reflect evaluations made in June 1970 by sixty-five law school deans and professors of law, history, and political science with expertise in the judicial process.

Source: Albert P. Blaustein and Roy M. Mersky, *The First One Hundred Justices: Statistical Studies on the Supreme Court of the United States* (Hamden, Conn.: Shoe String Press, Archon Books, 1978), 37–40.

Table 9-7 Caseload of the U.S. Supreme Court, 1970-1993

Action	1970	1975	1980	1983	1984	1985	1986	1987	1988	1989	1990	1991	1992	1993
Appellate cases on docket	1,903	2,352	2,749	2,688	2,575	2,571	2,547	2,577	2,587	2,416	2,351	2,451	2,441	2,442
From prior term	325	431	527	520	539	400	476	440	466	384	365	365	379	342
Docketed during present term	1,578	1,921	2,222	2,168	2,036	2,171	2,071	2,137	2,141	2,032	1,986	2,086	2,062	2,100
Cases acted upon[a]	1,613	1,900	2,324	2,220	2,253	2,185	2,189	2,224	2,271	2,096	2,042	2,125	2,140	2,099
Granted review	214	244	167	140	167	166	152	157	130	103	114	103	83	78
Denied, dismissed, or withdrawn	1,285	1,538	1,999	1,902	1,953	1,863	1,876	1,919	1,973	1,881	1,802	1,914	1,920	1,947
Summarily decided	114	118	90	71	59	78	71	66	75	44	81	52	84	34
Cases not acted upon	290	452	425	468	322	386	358	353	316	320	309	326	301	343
Pauper cases on docket	2,289	2,395	2,371	2,394	2,416	2,577	2,564	2,675	3,056	3,316	3,951	4,307	4,792	5,332
Cases acted upon[a]	1,802	1,997	2,027	1,992	2,067	2,189	2,250	2,263	2,638	2,891	3,436	3,768	4,261	4,621
Granted review	41	28	17	9	18	20	15	23	17	19	27	17	14	21
Denied, dismissed, or withdrawn	1,683	1,903	1,968	1,968	2,050	2,136	2,186	2,210	2,577	2,824	3,369	3,716	4,209	4,566
Summarily decided	78	66	32	10	14	24	38	21	32	35	28	22	25	30
Cases not acted upon	487	398	344	402	329	388	314	412	418	425	515	539	531	711
Original cases on docket	20	14	24	18	15	10	12	16	14	14	14	12	12	12
Cases disposed of during term	7	7	7	7	8	2	1	5	2	2	3	1	1	1
Total cases available for argument	267	280	264	269	271	276	270	280	254	204	201	196	166	145
Cases disposed of	160	181	162	189	184	175	179	175	173	147	131	130	120	105
Cases argued	151	179	154	184	175	171	175	167	170	146	125	127	116	99
Cases dismissed or remanded without argument	9	2	8	5	9	4	4	8	3	1	6	3	4	6
Cases remaining	107	99	102	80	87	101	91	105	81	57	70	66	46	40
Cases decided by signed opinion	126	160	144	174	159	161	164	151	156	143	121	120	111	93

(Table continues)

Table 9-7 *(Continued)*

Action	1970	1975	1980	1983	1984	1985	1986	1987	1988	1989	1990	1991	1992	1993
Cases decided per curiam opinion	22	16	8	6	11	10	10	9	12	3	4	3	4	6
Number of signed opinions	109	138	123	151	139	146	145	139	133	129	112	107	107	84
Total cases on docket	4,212	4,761	5,144	5,100	5,006	5,158	5,123	5,268	5,657	5,746	6,316	6,770	7,245	7,786

Note: The Supreme Court begins its regular annual session on the first Monday in October. This session, known as the October term, lasts about nine months. The year shown indicates when the term began.

[a] For 1980-1993, includes cases granted review and carried over to next term, not shown separately.

Sources: 1970-1983: U.S. Bureau of the Census, *Statistical Abstract of the United States, 1977* (Washington, D.C.: U.S. Government Printing Office, 1976), 184; 1987, 168; 1984-1991: reprinted with permission from *The United States Law Week* (Washington, D.C.: The Bureau of National Affairs), vol. 56, 3102; vol. 59, 3064; vol. 61, 3098; vol. 63, 3134 (copyright © by The Bureau of National Affairs, Inc.).

Figure 9-3   Cases Filed in the U.S. Supreme Court, 1938-1993

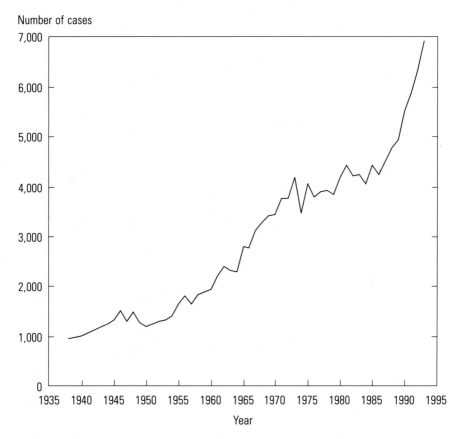

Number of cases

Sources: 1938-1969: successive volumes of *Statistical Abstract of the United States;* 1970-1983: Office of the Clerk of the Supreme Court; 1984-1993; reprinted with permission from *The United States Law Week,* vol. 56, 3102, vol. 59, 3064, vol. 61, 3098, vol. 63, 3134 (copyright © by the Bureau of National Affairs).

Table 9-8 Caseloads of U.S. Courts of Appeals, 1980-1993[a]

	1980	1985	1988	1989	1990	1991	1992	1993
Number of judgeships	132	156	156	156	156	167	167	167
Number of sitting senior judges	42	45	50	54	60	60	66	70
Number of vacant judgeship months	217.1	275.0	122.9	92.7	153.3	191.8	237.8	213.4
Appeals filed								
Prisoner	3,704	6,532	9,256	9,559	9,941	10,578	11,847	12,795
All other civil	12,141	18,660	19,213	19,190	18,886	18,742	20,716	21,639
Criminal	4,405	4,989	6,012	8,020	9,493	9,949	11,215	11,862
Administrative	2,950	3,179	3,043	2,965	2,578	2,764	3,235	3,928
Total	23,200	33,360	37,524	39,734	40,898	42,033	47,013	47,790
Appeals terminated								
Consolidations and cross appeals	2,704	2,669	2,698	2,931	3,314	4,106	4,007	3,607
Procedural	6,170	12,349	14,012	15,119	14,045	14,601	16,769	18,422
On the merits								
Prisoner	2,267	2,835	4,455	4,194	5,106	5,608	5,509	6,157
Other civil	5,861	9,208	9,989	9,839	9,867	9,665	9,942	10,087
Criminal	2,718	3,070	3,493	3,986	4,978	6,193	6,777	7,791
Administrative	1,167	1,256	1,241	1,303	1,210	1,241	1,369	1,726
Total on the merits	12,013	16,369	19,178	19,322	21,161	22,707	23,597	25,761
Total	20,887	31,387	35,888	37,372	38,520	41,414	44,373	47,790
Pending appeals	20,252	24,758	27,644	30,006	32,008	32,627	36,068	38,233
Per active judge[b]								
Termination on the merits	227	308	335	339	376	389	399	428
Procedural terminations	—	103	93	112	99	94	103	109

Note: "—" indicates not available.

[a] Data for other years can be found in previous editions of *Vital Statistics on American Politics*.
[b] Includes only judges active during the entire twelve-month period.

Sources: Director of the Administrative Office of the United States Courts, *Federal Court Management Statistics 1985* (Washington, D.C.: U.S. Government Printing Office, 1985), 29-30; *1991*, 27-31; *1992*, 29-30; and unpublished data.

Table 9-9 Caseloads of U.S. District Courts, 1980-1993[a]

	1980	1985	1988	1989	1990	1991	1992	1993
Overall								
Filings	188,487	299,164	269,174	263,896	251,113	241,420	265,612	264,038
Terminations	180,245	293,545	265,916	262,806	243,512	240,952	263,034	259,238
Pending	199,019	272,636	268,070	265,035	273,542	274,010	262,805	252,697
Number (and percentage) of civil cases over three years old	20,592 (11.7)	16,726 (6.6)	21,487 (8.8)	22,391 (9.2)	25,207 (10.4)	28,421 (11.8)	17,249 (7.7)	18,451 (8.3)
Number of judgeships	516	575	575	575	575	649	649	649
Vacant judgeship months	956.2	895.8	485.2	374.1	540.1	988.7	1,313.4	1,199.6
Per judgeship								
Civil filings	327	476	417	406	379	320	355	354
Criminal felony filings	38	44	51	53	58	52	54	53
Total filings	365	520	467	459	437	372	409	407
Pending cases	386	474	466	461	476	422	405	389
Terminations	349	511	462	457	423	371	405	399
Trials completed	38	36	35	35	36	31	32	30
Median time from filing to disposition (months)								
Criminal felony	3.7	3.7	4.3	5.0	5.3	5.7	5.9	63
Civil	8	7	9	9	9	9	9	8
Median time from issue to trial (months)								
Civil only[b]	15	14	14	14	14	15	15	16

[a] Data for other years can be found in previous editions of *Vital Statistics on American Politics*.
[b] Time is computed from the date that the answer or response is filed to the date the trial begins.

Sources: Director of the Administrative Office of the United States Courts, *Federal Court Management Statistics 1985* (Washington, D.C.: U.S. Government Printing Office, 1985), 167; 1991, 167; 1992, 167; and unpublished data.

Table 9-10 Number of Civil and Criminal Cases Filed in U.S. District Courts, 1950-1994

	Civil cases		Criminal cases	
Year	Commenced	Terminated	Commenced	Terminated
1950	44,454	42,482	36,383	37,675
1955	48,308	47,959	35,310	38,990
1960	49,852	48,847	28,137	30,512
1965	67,678	63,137	31,569	33,718
1970	87,321	79,466	38,102	36,356
1975	117,320	103,787	41,108	49,212
1980	168,789	160,481	28,932	29,297
1981	180,576	177,975	31,328	30,221
1982	206,193	189,473	32,682	31,889
1983	241,842	215,356	35,913	33,985
1984	261,485	243,113	36,845	35,494
1985	273,670	269,848	39,500	37,139
1986	254,828	266,765	41,490	39,328
1987	239,185	238,001	43,292	42,287
1988	239,634	238,753	44,585	42,115
1989	233,529	235,219	45,995	42,810
1990	217,879	213,922	48,904	44,295
1991	207,742	211,713	47,035	41,569
1992	230,509	231,304	48,356	44,147
1993	230,597	227,316	46,098	45,280
1994	238,590	227,015	45,269	44,924

Note: Data are for the twelve-month period ending on June 30 of the year shown.

Sources: 1950-1975: *Statistical Abstract of the United* States, *1971* (Washington, D.C.: U.S. Government Printing Office, 1971), 152, *1976*, 168; 1980-1992: Director of the Administrative Office of the United States Courts, *Annual Report of the Director of the Administrative Office of the United States Courts* (Washington, D.C.: U.S. Government Printing Office, 1987), 7, 13; (1989), 7, 12; (1991), 7, 10; (1992) 4,6, (1994).

Table 9-11   Types of Civil and Criminal Cases in the Federal District
Courts, 1994

Civil cases	Percentage	Criminal cases	Percentage
Contract actions	13.1	Embezzlement	3.2
Recovery of overpayments		Fraud	16.1
and enforcement of		Drunk driving and traffic	15.6
judgments	(1.9)	Narcotics	11.4
Other contract actions	(11.2)	Marijuana	7.7
Tort actions	19.5	Controlled substances	6.1
Product liability		Larceny and theft	7.4
personal injury	(8.5)	Homicide, robbery, assault,	
Other personal injury	9.7)	and burglary	5.3
Personal property damage	(1.4)	Forgery and counterfeiting	2.3
Statutory actions	64.2	Weapons and firearms	7.3
Prisoner petitions	(25.2)	Immigration	6.2
Civil rights	(17.0)	Escape	1.7
Social security	(4.6)	Auto theft	0.7
Labor laws	(6.5)	All other	9.0
Tax suits	(0.9)		
Bankruptcy	(2.2)	Total number of	
Other statutory	(8.8)	criminal cases	44,481
Real property actions	3.2		
Total number of			
civil cases	238,590		

Note: Data are for the twelve-month period ending on September 30, 1994. Data for earlier years can be found in previous editions of *Vital Statistics on American Politics*.

Source: Director of the Administrative Office of the United States Courts, *Annual Report of the Director of the Administrative Office of the United States Courts* (Washington, D.C.: Government Printing Office, 1994).

Table 9-12 Federal, State, and Local Laws Declared Unconstitutional by the Supreme Court, by Decade, 1789-1994

Years	Federal	State and local
1789-1799	0	0
1800-1809	1	1
1810-1819	0	7
1820-1829	0	8
1830-1839	0	3
1840-1849	0	9
1850-1859	1	7
1860-1869	4	23
1870-1879	7	36
1880-1889	4	46
1890-1899	5	36
1900-1909	9	40
1910-1919	6	118
1920-1929	15	139
1930-1939	13	93
1940-1949	2	58
1950-1959	5	60
1960-1969	16	149
1970-1979	20	193
1980-1989	16	162
1990-1994	3	31
Total	127	1,219

Sources: Lawrence Baum, *The Supreme Court*, 4th ed. (Washington, D.C.: CQ Press, 1992), 188, 190; Lawrence Baum, personal communication.

Figure 9-4   Economic and Civil Liberties Laws Overturned by the Supreme Court in the Twentieth Century

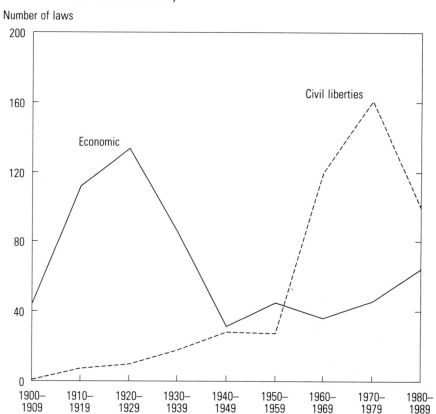

Number of laws

Note: Civil liberties category does not include laws supportive of civil liberties. Laws include federal, state, and local. From 1990-1994, thirteen economic and nineteen civil liberties laws were overturned.

Sources: Lawrence Baum, *The Supreme Court,* 4th ed. (Washington, D.C.: CQ Press, 1992), 197; Lawrence Baum, personal communication.

10

Federalism

From a statistical point of view, a major problem in studying American government below the federal level is that there are fifty state governments and thousands of local governmental units (Table 10-1). Among other things, this often makes it difficult to get accurate, up-to-date information about all relevant jurisdictions. Even for state-level data, a researcher often must turn to each of the fifty state capitals, or to fifty-one units if data about the District of Columbia are needed, or even more if Puerto Rico and areas such as the Northern Marianas Islands are included, as might be necessary for studying delegates to the national party conventions. If the researcher's interest is in counties, cities, school districts, and the like, the data collection task can be enormous—well beyond the capacity of one person.

Fortunately, organizations and publications devoted to data collection have stepped to the fore. Some, such as the Council of State Governments and the International City Management Association, are well established. The former has published the *Book of the States* since 1935, and the latter the *Municipal Year Book* since 1934. Other sources are newer, such as Congressional Quarterly's magazine *Governing*, which began publication in 1987. The U.S. Census Bureau also offers systematic collections of data covering increasingly longer spans. Two examples are the *State and Metropolitan Area Data Book* (published biennially since 1980) and the *County and City Data Book* (published with varying frequency since 1952). Such groups and publications make data collection far easier, and more systematic, and ensure higher quality than in the past.

Even when data are available, a researcher still can be frustrated by the inevitable variety that occurs across units. Simple tables or one-sentence summaries are often inadequate. Tables 6-9 and 6-10, which concern financing state election campaigns, for example, show enormous variation among states. Similarly, the listing of state fiscal discipline measures (Table 10-9) notes that provisions for passing tax bills and borrowing vary, without giving the exact requirement in each state. So much variation exists on this single point—a two-thirds majority of the legislators present and voting, two-thirds of the total number of legislators, 60 percent of the legislators present, and so on—that this book leaves it to the original sources to present the particulars.

Therefore, in studying state and local governments, their interrelationships, and their relations with the federal government, a researcher must pay attention to details. Even more than usual it is essential to read footnotes and check several sources. Differences in data collection procedures, the timing of data collection, and variations in detail of reports all become important. The user must also keep in mind the purpose for examining the data. It takes a careful researcher to know when variations can be ignored and when they become so frequent or so large that they must be an explicit part of the analysis.

Despite improvements in data collection, it is still necessary to go directly to states and localities for some information. Fortunately, this too has become easier. Publications such as the *National Directory of State Agencies* and the *State Information Book* give names and titles of specific individuals and offices, typically with addresses and phone numbers. While this will still not make a project involving twenty-five or fifty states easy, at least one can gather missing information or exact details about specific states and localities.

The recent surge in availability of information has now made possible a serious look at cities, counties, states, regions, and the relationships among all these governments. The tables in this book emphasize three topics. First, data are provided about states and localities as a whole and how they differ from the federal government and from each other (Tables 10-1 and 10-3, Figure 10-1). Second, information is given about specific states, often with an eye toward how states rank relative to one another (Tables 10-2 and 10-12). Third, considerable emphasis is given to intergovernmental relationships because of the growing fiscal interdependence between federal and state governments, state and local units, and even directly between federal and local governments (Tables 10-4 through 10-8).

As these tables amply demonstrate, students as well as professionals now have access to systematic information about all fifty states and increasingly about localities. Although users may have to make extra effort to absorb all the details provided by these tables, they are rewarded by the new possibilities for research and understanding.

Table 10-1 Composition of Federal, State, and Local Governments: Number of Units and Employees, 1942-1992

Year	Federal	State	Local government						Total
			County	Municipal	School district	Township and town	Special district[a]	Total	
1942									
Number	1	48	3,050	16,220	108,579	18,919	8,299	155,067	155,116
Employees (thousands)[b]	2,664	503[c]	333[c]	872[c]	—	223[c,d]	d	1,428[c]	5,915
1952[d]									
Number	1	50	3,052	16,807	67,355	17,202	12,340	116,756	116,807
Employees (thousands)	2,583	1,060	573	1,341	1,234	312[c]	c	3,461	7,105
1957[d]									
Number	1	50	3,050	17,215	50,454	17,198	14,424	102,341	102,392
Employees (thousands)[e]	2,439	1,300	726	1,539	1,651	394[c]	c	4,307	8,047
1962									
Number	1	50	3,043	18,000	34,678	17,142	18,323	91,186	91,237
Employees (thousands)	2,539	1,680	862	1,696	2,161	449[c]	c	5,169	9,388
1967									
Number	1	50	3,049	18,048	21,782	17,105	21,264	81,248	81,299
Employees (thousands)	2,993	2,335	1,077	1,993	2,919	549[c]	c	6,539	11,867
1972									
Number	1	50	3,044	18,517	15,781	16,991	23,885	78,218	78,269
Employees (thousands)	2,832	2,957	1,369	2,376	3,587	348	327	8,007	13,759
1977									
Number	1	50	3,042	18,862	15,174	16,822	25,962	79,862	79,913
Employees (thousands)	2,839	3,491	1,761	2,469	4,127	361	402	9,120	15,459

(Table continues)

Table 10-1 (Continued)

Year	Federal	State	County	Municipal	School district	Township and town	Special district[a]	Total	Total
					Local government				
1982									
Number	1	50	3,041	19,076	14,851	16,734	28,078	81,780	81,831
Employees (thousands)	2,862	3,744	1,824	2,397	4,194	356	478	9,249	15,841
1987									
Number	1	50	3,042	19,200	14,721	16,691	29,532	83,166	83,217
Employees (thousands)	3,121	4,115	1,963	2,541	4,620	414	537	10,076	17,311
1992									
Number	1	50	3,043	19,279	14,422	16,656	31,555	84,955	85,006
Employees (thousands)	3,047	4,595	2,253	2,665	5,134	424	627	11,103	18,745

Note: " — " indicates not available. A census of governmental units is conducted every five years.

[a] Special districts include independent public housing authorities, local irrigation units, power authorities, and other such bodies.

[b] Month for employee counts varies across years. For details, see sources. Numbers include full- and part-time employees.

[c] Employees in other than education.

[d] Townships and special districts are combined.

[e] Adjusted to include units in Alaska and Hawaii.

Sources: 1942–1967: U.S. Bureau of the Census, *Historical Statistics of the United States* (Washington, D.C.: United States Government Printing Office, 1975), 1086, 1100; 1972–1989 governmental units: U.S. Bureau of the Census, *Census of Governments, 1987* (Washington, D.C.: U.S. Government Printing Office, 1988), vi; (1993), 3; 1972–1992 employees: U.S. Office of Personnel Management, *Federal Manpower Statistics, Federal Civilian Workforce Statistics* (Washington, D.C.: U.S. Government Printing Office), various years; U.S. Bureau of the Census, *Public Employment in 1985* (Washington, D.C.: U.S. Government Printing Office, 1986), 2; 1987, vi; 1989, vi; 1992, vi, ix.

Figure 10-1   Number of Federal, State, and Local Government Employees, 1929-1992

Number of employees (millions)

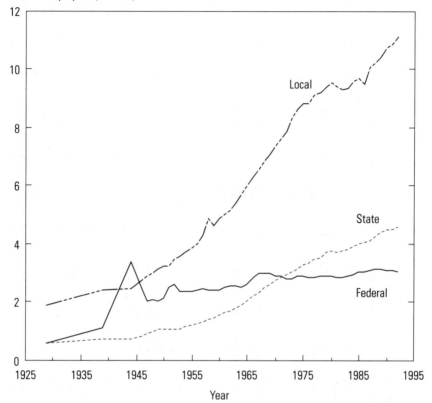

Sources: 1929-1944, 1949, 1952, 1954, 1959, 1964, 1969-1988: U.S. Advisory Commission on Intergovernmental Relations, *Significant Features of Fiscal Federalism, 1990,* vol. 2 (Washington, D.C.: U.S. Advisory Commission on Intergovernmental Relations, 1990), 177; 1989-1992: *1994,* 151; other years: U.S. Bureau of the Census, *Historical Statistics of the United States,* Series Y189-198 (Washington, D.C.: U.S. Government Printing Office, 1975), 1100.

Table 10-2 Tax Capacity and Tax Efforts of the States, 1967-1991[a]

State	1967 TC	1967 TE	1975 TC	1975 TE	1980 TC	1980 TE	1982 TC	1982 TE	1984 TC	1984 TE	1986 TC	1986 TE	1988 TC	1988 TE	1991 TC	1991 TE
Alabama	70	89	77	79	76	85	74	87	73	90	74	86	76	84	81	81
Alaska	99	104	155	76	260	166	313	180	250	141	177	168	159	127	178	119
Arizona	95	109	92	108	89	117	96	92	99	95	99	99	99	96	99	103
Arkansas	77	83	78	78	79	86	79	81	75	87	78	91	74	84	78	82
California	124	108	110	119	117	102	116	99	119	93	118	95	116	94	115	95
Colorado	104	106	106	90	113	90	121	81	121	82	117	83	107	89	109	86
Connecticut	117	93	110	99	112	100	117	99	124	99	135	94	143	90	130	99
Delaware	123	90	124	84	111	89	115	84	123	77	121	81	124	84	125	80
District of Columbia	121	90	118	94	111	131	115	145	120	138	122	143	123	154	123	157
Florida	104	84	102	74	100	74	104	72	105	74	105	77	104	82	103	86
Georgia	80	92	86	89	82	96	84	96	89	89	94	89	94	89	91	95
Hawaii	99	135	107	124	117	105	114	108	118	99	113	105	114	112	146	95
Idaho	91	105	89	90	87	88	86	85	78	91	77	90	76	93	82	94
Illinois	114	84	112	99	108	102	99	107	97	110	96	106	99	102	102	100
Indiana	99	95	98	92	92	84	89	88	87	95	87	94	87	93	90	93
Iowa	104	104	106	93	105	96	96	105	87	112	84	113	83	113	93	100
Kansas	105	96	109	85	109	88	106	88	100	95	96	96	91	104	93	100
Kentucky	80	85	85	84	83	89	82	88	77	89	76	89	81	88	83	100
Louisiana	94	90	97	87	109	78	113	82	102	81	90	91	83	90	89	89
Maine	81	105	84	104	80	111	84	107	88	105	95	99	98	105	95	102
Maryland	101	103	101	106	99	109	100	106	105	100	108	99	109	108	106	103
Massachusetts	98	121	98	129	96	135	101	119	111	105	124	103	129	94	117	101
Michigan	104	100	101	106	97	116	93	120	93	129	96	118	95	112	94	107
Minnesota	95	119	97	117	102	111	99	111	101	124	102	108	104	112	101	112
Mississippi	64	98	70	96	69	96	71	92	70	95	65	97	65	94	68	92
Missouri	97	86	96	84	94	84	91	82	89	85	93	82	90	86	91	85
Montana	105	93	103	92	112	92	110	97	95	101	88	103	85	102	91	78

State																
Nebraska	110	78	106	85	97	102	97	93	93	99	91	96	90	98	95	99
Nevada	171	71	145	70	154	60	151	63	146	65	147	65	135	69	128	73
New Hampshire	110	81	102	75	97	75	100	75	110	69	119	62	126	66	110	84
New Jersey	107	97	109	103	105	112	106	113	114	109	121	103	124	101	119	112
New Mexico	94	92	97	85	107	83	115	82	103	85	91	88	83	99	87	96
New York	108	138	98	160	90	167	92	170	98	158	107	152	109	152	103	156
North Carolina	78	94	85	86	80	97	82	94	87	89	88	92	91	93	93	87
North Dakota	92	97	101	92	108	79	115	83	106	93	94	89	86	91	91	92
Ohio	100	82	104	80	97	87	92	94	90	105	91	103	91	97	93	96
Oklahoma	102	80	98	73	117	72	126	78	113	76	98	85	89	89	87	93
Oregon	106	101	100	96	103	93	99	95	94	103	93	98	91	99	100	97
Pennsylvania	91	99	98	93	93	104	89	106	88	105	90	101	94	97	96	95
Rhode Island	91	105	88	112	84	123	81	133	86	123	92	111	99	104	89	115
South Carolina	64	97	77	85	75	95	74	96	77	95	79	94	79	96	83	90
South Dakota	91	107	94	87	90	88	87	91	83	87	78	95	78	95	86	83
Tennessee	78	87	84	79	79	84	77	86	81	81	84	84	84	83	82	82
Texas	98	75	111	68	124	65	130	66	117	69	104	79	96	88	97	87
Utah	87	111	86	89	86	101	86	97	81	106	80	107	78	106	82	94
Vermont	88	119	94	108	84	104	89	102	95	94	99	91	105	100	105	97
Virginia	86	90	93	87	95	88	94	90	96	88	101	85	104	91	103	91
Washington	112	106	98	101	103	94	102	93	99	103	98	103	98	102	108	99
West Virginia	75	96	89	85	94	82	92	86	79	100	76	98	78	88	77	102
Wisconsin	94	124	98	115	95	116	87	128	89	133	86	134	90	119	90	118
Wyoming	141	79	154	70	196	74	201	105	181	105	151	117	123	94	134	81

Note: Tax capacity (TC) measures a state's underlying economic resources and speaks to the ability to raise revenue. The tax capacity is the amount of revenue each state would raise if it applied a national average set of tax rates for twenty-six commonly used tax bases. The index above is the per capita tax capacity divided by the per capita average for all states, with the index for the average set at 100. Tax effort (TE) is the ratio of a state's actual tax collections to its tax capacity. The relative index of tax effort is created by dividing each state's tax effort by the average for all states. One hundred is the index for the U.S. average. For a more complete explanation, see the source.

[a] Data for additional years can be found in *Vital Statistics on American Politics.*

Source: U.S. Advisory Commission on Intergovernmental Relations, *Significant Features of Fiscal Federalism, 1992,* vol. 2 (Washington, D.C.: U.S. Advisory Commission on Intergovernmental Relations, 1992), 268-269; 1994, 182-183.

Table 10-3 Federal, State, and Local Taxes, by Source, 1957-1992 (percent)

Jurisdiction/ year	Property taxes	Sales, gross receipts, and customs	Individual and corporate income taxes	All other taxes
Federal				
1957		15.9	81.3	2.7
1967		13.7	83.0	3.3
1977		9.5	86.8	3.7
1982		11.3	85.7	3.0
1983		11.7	85.5	2.8
1984		11.9	85.1	3.0
1985		10.8	86.4	2.8
1986		10.0	87.3	2.7
1987		9.0	88.3	2.7
1988		9.4	88.1	2.6
1989		8.5	89.1	2.3
1990		8.5	88.6	2.8
1991		9.1	88.2	2.7
1992		9.8	87.5	2.7
State				
1957	3.3	58.1	17.5	21.1
1967	2.7	58.2	22.4	16.8
1977	2.2	51.8	34.3	11.7
1982	1.9	48.4	36.7	12.9
1983	1.9	48.9	36.7	12.4
1984	2.0	48.7	37.8	11.5
1985	1.9	48.9	37.7	11.5
1986	1.9	49.3	37.6	11.2
1987	1.9	48.5	39.2	10.4
1988	1.9	49.3	38.6	10.3
1989	1.9	48.7	39.7	9.8
1990	1.9	48.9	39.2	9.9
1991	2.0	49.4	38.5	10.0
1992	2.0	49.6	38.5	10.0
Local				
1957	86.7	7.2	1.3	4.8
1967	86.6	6.7	3.2	3.5
1977	80.5	11.1	5.0	3.4
1982	76.0	14.3	5.9	3.9
1983	76.0	14.5	5.7	3.9
1984	75.0	14.8	5.8	4.3
1985	74.2	15.6	5.9	4.3
1986	74.0	15.6	5.9	4.5
1987	73.7	15.5	6.1	4.7
1988	74.1	15.2	6.0	4.7
1989	74.3	15.1	6.0	4.6
1990	74.5	15.3	5.7	4.6
1991	75.3	14.9	5.6	4.2
1992	75.6	14.7	5.5	4.1

Source: U.S. Advisory Commission on Intergovernmental Relations, *Significant Features of Fiscal Federalism, 1992*, vol. 2 (Washington, D.C.: U.S. Advisory Commission on Intergovernmental Relations, 1992), 126-127, *1994*, 70-71.

Table 10-4   Flow of Federal Funds to and from the States, 1965-1993

State	1965-1967	1969-1971	1974-1976	1982-1984	1986-1988	1989-1991	1992-1993
Alabama	1.52	1.49	1.31	1.29	1.37	1.41	1.37
Alaska	1.01	2.76	1.82	1.01	1.16	1.19	1.21
Arizona	1.33	1.19	1.18	1.14	1.20	1.21	1.18
Arkansas	1.29	1.20	1.19	1.27	1.33	1.27	1.24
California	1.32	1.24	1.15	1.09	0.98	0.89	0.92
Colorado	1.33	1.24	1.05	0.91	1.10	1.18	1.06
Connecticut	0.92	0.88	0.92	1.02	0.84	0.77	0.69
Delaware	0.54	0.60	0.71	0.83	0.76	0.68	0.68
District of Columbia	2.16	2.99	3.23	—	5.07	5.38	5.43
Florida	1.15	1.09	0.96	1.09	1.02	1.00	1.05
Georgia	1.52	1.29	1.08	1.09	1.02	0.96	1.03
Hawaii	1.38	1.53	1.56	1.38	1.40	1.24	1.13
Idaho	1.15	0.96	1.03	1.13	1.31	1.36	1.23
Illinois	0.59	0.63	0.70	0.70	0.72	0.72	0.73
Indiana	0.75	0.81	0.74	0.83	0.89	0.89	0.88
Iowa	1.00	0.83	0.81	0.80	1.09	1.05	1.01
Kansas	1.44	1.14	0.96	1.02	1.10	1.03	1.01
Kentucky	1.32	1.14	1.17	1.10	1.23	1.27	1.19
Louisiana	1.33	1.19	1.07	0.90	1.08	1.26	1.26
Maine	1.14	1.04	1.19	1.30	1.21	1.22	1.38
Maryland	1.34	1.39	1.31	1.27	1.25	1.19	1.21
Massachusetts	0.90	0.95	1.04	1.10	1.02	0.99	0.98
Michigan	0.58	0.61	0.76	0.78	0.74	0.77	0.81
Minnesota	0.93	0.89	0.87	0.85	0.92	0.87	0.80
Mississippi	1.68	1.73	1.65	1.61	1.72	1.70	1.71
Missouri	1.09	1.10	1.12	1.43	1.31	1.32	1.24
Montana	1.53	1.18	1.17	1.07	1.37	1.43	1.38
Nebraska	1.26	0.91	0.91	0.95	1.16	1.10	1.05
Nevada	0.86	0.75	0.85	0.92	0.99	0.86	0.82
New Hampshire	0.83	0.97	0.90	0.98	0.76	0.70	0.72
New Jersey	0.71	0.75	0.79	0.70	0.64	0.63	0.67
New Mexico	1.68	1.67	1.47	1.80	2.07	2.02	1.96
New York	0.62	0.78	0.93	0.92	0.84	0.80	0.83
North Carolina	1.21	0.99	1.00	0.95	0.94	0.94	0.97
North Dakota	2.04	1.51	1.32	1.06	1.56	1.55	1.45
Ohio	0.70	0.75	0.76	0.85	0.93	0.94	0.91
Oklahoma	1.36	1.35	1.23	0.88	1.10	1.21	1.22
Oregon	0.80	0.84	0.91	0.89	0.97	0.95	0.93
Pennsylvania	0.71	0.85	0.95	0.96	0.97	0.95	0.98
Rhode Island	1.17	1.14	1.07	1.05	0.99	1.00	1.07
South Carolina	1.58	1.25	1.22	1.25	1.25	1.31	1.25
South Dakota	1.67	1.26	1.33	1.24	1.51	1.42	1.29
Tennessee	1.12	1.01	0.98	1.20	1.18	1.15	1.15
Texas	1.35	1.31	0.96	0.78	0.89	0.98	0.95
Utah	1.32	1.53	1.28	1.27	1.45	1.40	1.18

(Table continues)

Table 10-4   (*Continued*)

State	1965-1967	1969-1971	1974-1976	1982-1984	1986-1988	1989-1991	1992-1993
Vermont	1.11	1.02	1.16	1.10	0.94	0.88	0.93
Virginia	1.73	1.68	1.46	1.52	1.56	1.40	1.37
Washington	1.24	1.10	1.20	1.09	1.16	1.03	0.92
West Virginia	1.02	1.09	1.21	1.07	1.27	1.40	1.43
Wisconsin	0.67	0.71	0.76	0.82	0.84	0.85	0.82
Wyoming	1.50	1.10	1.00	0.75	1.04	1.13	1.02

Note: Numbers are the estimated amount of federal expenditures in each state for each $100 of federal taxes paid by residents of each state. Includes all federal expenditures that can be allocated by state. All figures adjusted proportionally so that overall there is $1.00 of revenue for each $1.00 of expenditure. Three-year averages (two-year for 1992-1993) for expenditures and revenue were used to ensure that unusually high or low figures in a particular state in any single year would not unduly influence the flow-of-fund ratios. The 1965-1976 figures are based on detailed analyses that take into account the precise location of taxes and expenditures (e.g., where procurement spending actually occurred as indicated by subcontracts, not just the major contract). Calculations for the 1982-1993 figures do not incorporate such adjustments (personal communication from Michael Lawson).

Sources: 1965-1984: U.S. Advisory Commission on Intergovernmental Relations, *Significant Features of Fiscal Federalism, 1985-86* (Washington, D.C.: U.S. Advisory Commission on Intergovernmental Relations, 1986), 178; 1986-1993: calculated by the editors from Bureau of the Census, Department of Commerce, *Federal Expenditures by State for Fiscal Year 1987* (Washington, D.C.: U.S. Government Printing Office, 1988), 1; *1988*, 1; *1989*, 1; *1990*, 1; *1991*, 1; *1992*, 1; *1993*, 1; and Paul G. Merski, "The 1992 Federal Tax Burden by State," *Tax Foundation Special Report*, May 1992, 6; and *Facts and Figures on Government Finance* (Washington, D.C.: Tax Foundation, 1994), 83-84.

Table 10-5 Federal Grants-in-Aid Outlays, 1950-2000

| Year | Total grants-in-aid (billions) | Federal grants as a percentage of | | State and local expenditures[c] | Gross domestic product |
| | | Federal outlays[a] | | | |
		Total	Domestic programs[b]		
1950	$2.3	5.3	—	—	0.8
1955	3.2	4.7	—	—	0.8
1960	7.0	7.6	18.0	15.0	1.4
1965	10.9	9.2	18.0	16.0	1.6
1970	24.1	12.3	23.0	20.0	2.4
1975	49.8	15.0	22.0	24.0	3.3
1980	91.5	15.5	22.0	28.0	3.5
1981	94.8	14.0	—	—	3.2
1982	88.2	11.8	—	—	2.8
1983	92.5	11.4	—	—	2.8
1984	97.6	11.5	—	—	2.6
1985	105.9	11.2	18.0	23.0	2.7
1986	112.4	11.3	—	—	2.7
1987	108.4	10.8	—	—	2.4
1988	115.4	10.8	—	—	2.4
1989	122.0	10.7	—	—	2.4
1990	135.4	10.8	17.0	20.0	2.5
1991	154.6	11.7	—	—	2.7
1992	178.1	12.9	—	—	3.0
1993	193.7	13.7	—	—	3.1
1994	210.6	14.4	21.0	24.0	3.2
1995 est.	228.0	14.8	22.0	—	3.2
1996 est.	238.5	14.8	21.0	—	3.2
1997 est.	253.2	15.0	21.0	—	3.2
1998 est.	264.4	15.2	21.0	—	3.2
1999 est.	278.9	15.3	22.0	—	3.2
2000 est.	292.9	15.4	22.0	—	3.2

Note: "—" indicates not available. Amounts in current dollars. Fiscal years.

[a] Includes off-budget outlays; all grants are on-budget.
[b] Excludes outlays for national defense, international affairs, and net interest.
[c] As defined in the national income and product accounts.

Sources: Total grants, total federal outlays, and GDP: Office of Management and Budget, *Budget of the United States Government, Fiscal Year 1996, Historical Tables* (Washington, D.C.: U.S. Government Printing Office, 1995), 175-176; domestic programs and state and local expenditures: Office of Management and Budget, *Budget of the United States Government, Fiscal Year 1996, Analytical Perspectives* (Washington, D.C.: U.S. Government Printing Office, 1995), 169.

Table 10-6   Fiscal Dependency of Lower Levels on Higher Levels of Government, 1927-1992

	Intergovernmental revenue as a percentage of total revenue		
Year	State from federal	Local from federal	Local from state[a]
1927	5.0	[b]	9.4
1934	27.3	1.3	20.7
1940	11.6	3.6	21.4
1946	9.4	0.1	21.9
1952	13.9	1.2	26.0
1957	14.2	1.2	25.2
1962	18.9	1.8	25.2
1965	20.2	2.2	32.5
1967	22.3	2.7	28.5
1970	21.6	2.9	30.2
1972	23.8	4.0	30.6
1973	24.2	6.1	31.0
1974	22.5	7.1	31.1
1975	23.0	6.8	32.0
1976	22.9	7.6	31.5
1977	22.4	8.4	30.7
1978	22.3	9.0	30.1
1979	22.1	8.8	31.6
1980	22.3	8.2	31.5
1981	21.8	7.8	30.9
1982	20.0	6.7	30.2
1983	19.3	6.2	29.1
1984	19.2	5.7	28.9
1985	19.2	5.4	28.9
1986	19.3	4.7	29.2
1987	18.5	4.2	29.1
1988	18.5	3.5	29.4
1989	18.4	3.3	29.6
1990	18.7	3.2	29.7
1991	20.4	3.1	29.8
1992	21.4	3.1	30.3

[a] Includes indirect federal aid passed through the states.
[b] Less than 0.1 percent.

Source: Calculated by the editors from U.S. Advisory Commission on Intergovernmental Relations, *Significant Features of Fiscal Federalism, 1994*, vol. 2 (Washington, D.C.: U.S. Advisory Commission on Intergovernmental Relations, 1994), 44.

Table 10-7   Variations in Local Dependency on State Aid, 1991-1992
(percent)

Rank	State	Percentage	Rank	State	Percentage
1.	New Mexico	53.4	27.	Iowa	34.4
2.	West Virginia	46.3	28.	Ohio	33.7
3.	Delaware	46.1	29.	Pennsylvania	33.4
4.	California	45.2	30.	Maine	32.7
5.	Arkansas	44.3	31.	Louisiana	32.3
6.	Wisconsin	43.1	32.	Michigan	31.9
7.	Kentucky	42.7	33.	Missouri	31.3
8.	North Carolina	42.2	34.	Virginia	30.4
9.	Idaho	42.1	35.	Vermont	30.0
10.	Wyoming	40.3	36.	Connecticut	29.2
11.	Mississippi	40.3	37.	Florida	28.5
12.	Washington	40.2	38.	Illinois	28.0
13.	Minnesota	39.8	39.	Tennessee	27.9
14.	Nevada	38.3	40.	Colorado	27.9
15.	Arizona	38.1	41.	Texas	27.5
16.	North Dakota	38.0	42.	Georgia	27.4
17.	Oklahoma	37.8	43.	Kansas	27.3
18.	Indiana	37.5	44.	Nebraska	26.9
19.	Utah	36.8	45.	Rhode Island	26.6
20.	Alaska	36.5	46.	Oregon	26.6
21.	New Jersey	36.2	47.	Maryland	26.3
22.	New York	35.3	48.	South Dakota	23.3
23.	Alabama	35.1	49.	New Hampshire	12.9
24.	South Carolina	35.0	50.	Hawaii	11.1
25.	Massachusetts	34.6			
26.	Montana	34.5		Total	34.9

Note: Percentages reflect state transfers (including "pull-through" monies from the federal government) as a percentage of total local revenues. Where ties occur, the rank order was determined by the second decimal.

Source: U.S. Bureau of the Census, *Governmental Finances in 1991-1992* (Washington, D.C.: U.S. Government Printing Office, 1994), 23.

Table 10-8 Federal Grants-in-Aid to State and Local Governments, by Function, 1940-1996 (percent)

Function	1940	1945	1950	1955	1960	1965	1970	1975	1980	1985	1990	1994	1996 est.
Health	3	11	5	4	3	6	16	18	17	23	32	41	42
Income security	39	52	59	54	38	32	24	19	20	26	27	24	23
Education, training, employment, and social services	3	14	7	10	8	10	27	24	24	17	17	16	16
Transportation	19	4	21	19	43	38	19	12	14	16	14	11	10
Natural resources and environment	-	1	1	1	2	2	2	5	6	4	3	2	2
Community and regional development	32	14	-	2	2	6	7	6	7	5	4	4	4
General purpose fiscal assistance	1	1	2	3	2	2	2	14	9	7	2	1	1
Agriculture	3	3	5	7	4	5	3	1	1	2	1	-	-
Other	-	-	-	-	-	-	-	1	2	1	1	1	1
Total	100	100	100	100	102	101	100	100	100	101	100	100	99

Note: "-" indicates 0.5 percent or less.

Sources: 1940-1990: Office of Management and Budget, *Budget Baselines, Historical Data, and Alternatives for the Future* (Washington, D.C.: U.S. Government Printing Office, 1993), 429-432; 1992-1996: Office of Management and Budget, *Budget of the U.S. Government, Fiscal Year 1996* (Washington, D.C.: U.S. Government Printing Office, 1995), 171-177.

Table 10-9 State Fiscal Discipline Measures

State	Legislature must pass or governor must sign a balanced budget	Legislative votes required to pass budget	Extraordinary vote required to pass . . .	Governor may item-veto appropriations bills	Governor may reduce budget without legislative approval	Taxes automatically adjusted for inflation[a]	May carry over a deficit	Scope of sunset legislation
Alabama	x	Majority		x	x			C
Alaska	x	Maj. elected		x				C
Arizona	x	Majority		x	x		x	S
Arkansas	x	3/4 elected	T,B	x				
California		2/3 elected	T,B	x		x	x	R
Colorado	x	Maj. present		x	x		x	
Connecticut		Maj. present		x	x		x	
Delaware	x	Maj. elected	T	x	x			C
Florida	x	Majority		x	x			R
Georgia	x	Majority		x	x			R
Hawaii	x	Maj. elected		x	x			R
Idaho	x	Majority		x	x			
Illinois	x	3/5 elected	B	x			x	R
Indiana	x	Majority			x			C
Iowa		Majority		x	x	x		
Kansas	x	Majority		x	x			
Kentucky	x	Maj. present	T	x	x			
Louisiana	x	Majority	T	x	x			C
Maine	x	Majority				x		C
Maryland	x	Majority		x	x		x	R
Massachusetts	x	Majority		x	x		x	
Michigan	x	Maj. elected		x			x	S

(Table continues)

Table 10-9 (Continued)

State	Legislature must pass or governor must sign a balanced budget	Legislative votes required to pass budget	Extraordinary vote required to pass . . .	Governor may item-veto appropriations bills	Governor may reduce budget without legislative approval	Taxes automatically adjusted for inflation[a]	May carry over a deficit	Scope of sunset legislation
Minnesota	X	Maj. elected		X	X	X		
Mississippi	X	Majority	T	X	X			
Missouri	X	Maj. elected		X	X			
Montana	X	Majority		X	X	X		
Nebraska	X	3/5 elected	B	X		X		
Nevada	X	Majority			X			
New Hampshire		Maj. present						
New Jersey	X	Majority		X	X		X	
New Mexico	X	Majority		X	X			R
New York		Majority		X	X		X	
North Carolina	X	Majority		X	X			
North Dakota	X	Majority		X	X			
Ohio	X	2/3 both houses	T,B	X	X			R,C
Oklahoma	X	Majority	T	X	X			
Oregon	X	Majority		X	X	X		S
Pennsylvania	X	Maj. elected		X	X		X	
Rhode Island	X	2/3 both houses	B		X			R
South Carolina	X	Majority		X	X	X		
South Dakota	X	Maj. elected	T	X	X			C
Tennessee	X	Maj. elected		X	X			S
Texas	X	Maj. elected		X	X		X	R
Utah	X	Majority		X	X			S
Vermont	X	Majority			X		X	
Virginia	X	Maj. elected		X	X			

Washington		Maj. present	x	x			C
West Virginia	x	Majority	x	x		x	S
Wisconsin	x	Maj. present	x				
Wyoming		Majority	x	x			
Total	40	12	43	39	8	14	24

Note: "T" indicates tax bills, "B" indicates state borrowing. "C" indicates comprehensive, "R" indicates regulatory, "S" indicates selective. There is considerable variation with respect to each type of measure. For example, an extraordinary vote may or may not be generally required but may be necessary for emergency budget requests; some states may carry over a deficit but for only a year; some states include sunset clauses in specific legislation, and so on. Considerable detail about each mechanism can be found in the source.

[a] Automatic adjustment of tax brackets, personal exemption, or standard deductions.

Source: Council of State Governments, *Book of the States, 1994-1995* (Lexington, Ky.: Council of State Governments, 1994), 141-143, 164-166, 320-321, 367.

Table 10-10 State Lottery Revenues

State/year[a]	Date established	Gross revenue (millions)	Net proceeds (millions)	Net proceeds as a percentage of state's own source revenue	Where the revenues go
Arizona					
1982	July 1981	$114.1	$45.9	1.9	
1992		234.2	91.1	1.6	Transportation
California	October 1985				
1986		1,675.7	685.6	1.8	
1992		1,278.1	469.2	0.8	Education
Colorado	January 1983				
1983		128.7	47.0	1.9	
1992		224.9	76.2	1.5	Parks and recreation, capital construction
Connecticut	February 1972				
1982		159.7	62.5	2.1	
1992		515.8	204.4	2.6	General fund
Delaware	October 1975				
1982		23.5	8.5	1.0	
1992		74.5	27.7	1.4	General fund
District of Columbia	August 1982				
1984		50.7	12.6	1.6	
1992		139.2	47.3	0.2	General fund
Florida	January 1988				
1988		621.3	200.7	1.5	Education
1992		2,071.9	865.2	4.8	Education
Georgia	—				
		—	—	—	
Idaho	July 1989				
1990		66.3	24.2	1.6	
1992		52.0	13.9	0.8	Permanent building fund

State / Year					
Illinois					
1982	July 1974	310.1	141.5	1.0	
1992		1,475.8	609.2	3.5	Education
Indiana					
1990	October 1989	378.6	132.4	1.6	
1992		359.5	116.2	1.3	"Build Indiana" fund
Iowa					
1986	August 1985	77.2	26.3	0.8	
1992		151.0	39.7	0.8	Economic development
Kansas					
1988	November 1987	62.2	19.6	0.6	
1992		73.1	19.7	0.5	Economic development
Kentucky					
1989	April 1989	118.2	45.7	0.9	
1990		401.9	104.2	1.6	Education
Louisiana					
1992	—	356.0	139.7	2.1	General fund
Maine					
1982	June 1974	9.7	2.4	0.3	
1992		114.1	41.3	1.7	General fund
Maryland					
1982	May 1973	434.1	208.3	4.9	
1992		770.8	347.5	4.0	General fund
Massachusetts					
1982	March 1972	210.0	69.4	1.2	
1992		1,610.9	482.7	3.5	Local government
Michigan					
1982	November 1972	483.1	198.3	2.4	
1992		1,120.9	473.3	3.0	Education

(Table continues)

Table 10-10 (*Continued*)

State/year[a]	Date established	Gross revenue (millions)	Net proceeds (millions)	Net proceeds as a percentage of state's own source revenue	Where the revenues go
Minnesota					
1990	April 1990	64.0	8.0	0.1	Environmental trust fund
1992		279.9	54.8	0.6	
Missouri					
1986	January 1986	196.5	80.0	1.7	General fund
1992		207.5	67.0	1.0	
Montana					
1988	June 1987	20.6	7.6	0.7	Local schools
1992		26.3	5.7	0.4	Education, environment
Nebraska	—	—	—	—	
New Hampshire					
1982	March 1964	13.3	5.3	1.0	Education
1992		99.4	36.3	2.4	
New Jersey					
1982	January 1970	$480.8	$214.9	3.0	Education
1992		1,287.0	573.8	3.2	
New York					
1982	June 1967	386.9	179.0	1.0	Education
1992		1,881.0	858.0	2.2	
Ohio					
1982	August 1974	345.3	149.6	2.0	Education
1992		1,700.6	729.6	4.4	
Oregon					
1986	April 1985	83.1	21.3	0.7	Economic development
1992		244.4	49.4	0.9	

State / Year	First year[a]				Purpose
Pennsylvania					Senior citizens
1982	March 1972	523.8	226.7	2.4	programs
1992		1,315.1	650.0	3.0	
Rhode Island					
1982	May 1974	33.8	16.6	1.2	General fund
1992		57.5	22.6	1.2	
South Dakota					
1988	September 1987	24.8	12.8	1.1	General fund
1992		60.5	43.5	4.5	General fund
Texas	—				
Vermont	February 1978		—	—	
1982		3.5	8.7	0.2	General fund
1992		48.6	16.7	1.4	
Virginia					
1989	June 1988	388.5	141.0	1.6	General fund,
1992		826.0	289.6	2.8	capital improvements
Washington					
1983	November 1982	166.8	69.7	1.4	General fund
1992		302.2	109.2	1.0	
West Virginia					
1986	January 1986	53.0	22.1	1.0	General fund
1992		85.9	28.6	0.9	
Wisconsin					
1989	June 1988	230.4	97.5	1.2	Property tax relief
1992		425.9	140.8	1.5	

Note: "—" indicates not available.

[a] First year listed is either 1982 or first year of operation.

Source: Significant Features of Fiscal Federalism, 1992, vol. 2 (Washington, D.C.: U.S. Advisory Commission on Intergovernmental Relations, 1992), 170, 172–173, 1994, 106–09.

Figure 10-2   Government Spending as a Percentage of GDP, 1934-1994

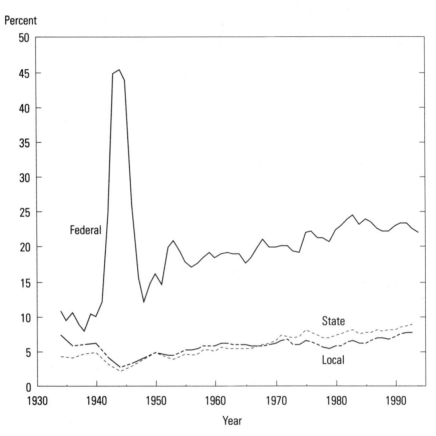

Sources: State and local expenditures: *Facts and Figures on Government Finance* (Washington, D.C.: Tax Foundation, 1994), 6; federal outlays and gross domestic product: Office of Management and Budget, *Budget of the United Sates Government, Fiscal Year 1996, Historical Tables* (Washington, D.C.: U.S. Government Printing Office, 1995), 15-16.

Table 10-11 State and Local Government Expenditures, by Function, 1902–1992 (percent)

Function	1902	1940	1952	1962	1972	1977	1982	1987	1990	1991	1992
Education	23.3	23.5	27.0	31.5	34.6	31.7	29.4	29.3	29.6	29.2	28.5
Highways	16.0	14.0	15.1	14.7	10.0	7.1	6.6	6.8	6.3	6.1	5.8
Public welfare	3.4	10.3	9.0	7.2	11.1	11.1	11.1	10.5	11.0	12.0	13.5
Health	1.6	1.4	1.4	0.9	1.4	1.7	2.0	2.2	2.5	2.5	2.6
Hospitals	3.9	4.0	5.7	5.2	5.5	5.4	5.8	5.2	5.2	5.1	5.1
Police protection	4.6	3.2	3.0	3.0	3.2	3.2	3.2	3.2	3.1	3.1	3.0
Fire protection	3.7	2.1	1.9	1.6	1.4	1.4	1.3	1.4	1.4	1.3	1.3
Natural resources	0.8	1.9	2.5	1.9	1.6	1.3	1.3	1.3	1.3	1.2	1.1
Corrections	—	—	1.1	1.1	1.1	1.3	1.6	2.2	2.5	2.6	2.5
Sanitation and sewerage	4.7	1.8	3.2	2.8	2.5	2.9	2.9	2.8	2.9	2.9	2.8
Housing and community development	—	—	2.0	1.6	1.4	1.0	1.6	1.5	1.6	1.6	1.5
Parks and recreation	2.6	1.4	1.0	1.3	1.2	1.5	1.4	1.4	1.5	1.5	1.4
Financial administration	12.9	5.0	3.9	1.5	1.3	1.4	1.5	1.7	1.7	1.6	1.6
Other government administration	—	—	—	1.8	1.8	1.9	2.7	2.9	2.9	3.0	2.8
Social insurance administration	—	0.6	0.6	0.6	0.6	0.5	0.4	0.4	0.3	0.3	0.3
Interest on general debt	6.2	5.8	1.8	2.9	3.2	3.5	3.8	5.4	5.1	4.9	4.8
Utilities	7.5	11.8	9.9	7.7	6.0	7.5	9.2	8.5	7.7	7.4	7.1
Liquor store expenditure	—	—	—	—	—	—	—	0.4	0.3	0.3	0.3
Insurance trust expenditure	—	6.1	5.5	6.9	5.5	8.1	7.5	6.6	6.5	7.0	7.9
Other	8.9	5.0	4.2	4.8	6.7	7.7	6.7	6.8	6.6	6.4	6.1
Total direct expenditure (millions)	$1,095	$11,240	$30,863	$70,547	$190,496	$324,554	$524,817	$772,864	$972,662	$1,060,167	$1,147,075

Note: "—" indicates not available. For 1902–1952, financial administration includes other government administration. For 1902–1982, utilities includes liquor store expenditures.

Sources: 1902–1982: U.S. Bureau of the Census, *Census of Governments, 1982* (Washington, D.C.: U.S. Government Printing Office, 1985), 32–33; 1987–1989: U.S. Bureau of the Census, *Governmental Finances in 1986-87* (Washington, D.C.: U.S. Government Printing Office, 1988), 13; *1989-90*, 45; *1990-91*, 45, *1991-92*, 45.

Figure 10-3   Surpluses and Deficits in Government Finances, 1947-1994

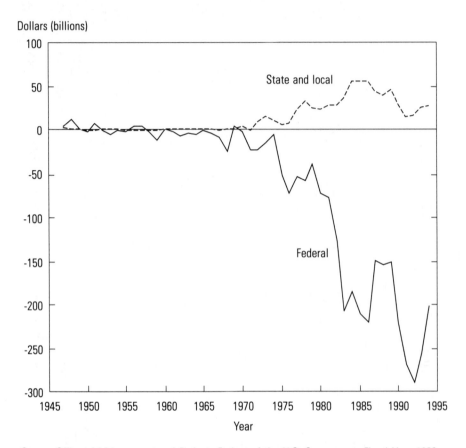

Source: Office of Management and Budget, *Budget of the U.S. Government, Fiscal Year 1996, Historical Tables* (Washington, D.C.: U.S. Government Printing Office, 1995), 241.

Figure 10-4   State and Local Government Surpluses Compared to Federal
Grants-in-Aid, 1947-1994

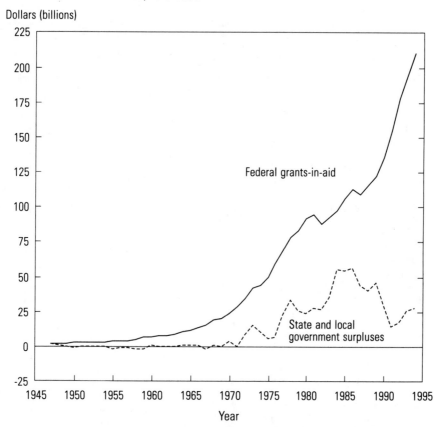

Dollars (billions)

Source: Office of Management and Budget, *Budget of the United States Government, Fiscal Year
1996, Historical Tables* (Washington, D.C.: U.S. Government Printing Office, 1995), 175, 241.

Table 10-12 Benefits and Recipients of Public Aid and Food Stamps, by State, 1994

State	Maximum AFDC grant (per month)[a]	Food stamp benefit (per month)[b]	Combined benefits as a percentage of 1993 poverty threshold[c]	Public aid recipients (percentage of population)[d]	Food stamp recipients (percentage of population)
Alabama	$164	$295	48	7.1	13.3
Alaska	923	285	101	7.0	7.1
Arizona	347	292	67	6.5	12.0
Arkansas	204	295	52	6.8	11.6
California	607	214	86	11.0	9.1
Colorado	356	289	67	4.8	7.5
Connecticut	680	192	91	6.2	6.6
Delaware	338	295	66	5.4	8.2
District of Columbia	420	270	72	15.2	15.2
Florida	303	295	62	7.2	10.7
Georgia	280	295	60	8.4	11.4
Hawaii	712	422	103	6.2	8.7
Idaho	317	295	64	3.2	7.0
Illinois	367[e]	291	69	8.0	10.0
Indiana	288	295	61	5.2	8.6
Iowa	426	268	72	5.0	6.9
Kansas	429[e]	284	74	4.8	7.4
Kentucky	228	295	55	9.8	13.9
Louisiana	190	295	51	10.2	18.0
Maine	418	271	72	7.7	11.2
Maryland	366[e]	295	69	5.9	7.5
Massachusetts	579	222	83	7.9	7.3
Michigan[f]	459[e]	258	75	9.4	10.8
Minnesota	532	236	80	5.5	6.9
Mississippi	120	295	43	11.6	20.1
Missouri	292	295	61	7.0	11.2
Montana	401	276	71	5.6	8.2
Nebraska	364	287	68	4.2	7.0
Nevada	348	292	67	3.6	6.4
New Hampshire	550	231	81	3.5	5.3
New Jersey	424[e]	276	73	6.2	6.7
New Mexico	357	289	67	8.3	14.7
New York[g]	577[e]	239	85	9.6	11.3
North Carolina	272	295	59	7.3	8.9
North Dakota	409	273	71	4.4	7.6
Ohio	341[e]	295	66	8.5	11.4
Oklahoma	324	295	65	6.4	11.4
Oregon	460[e]	293	78	5.3	9.2
Pennsylvania	421	270	72	7.1	9.8
Rhode Island	554[e]	268	86	8.4	9.3
South Carolina	200	295	52	6.9	10.8
South Dakota	417	271	72	4.6	7.8
Tennessee	185	295	50	9.3	15.0
Texas	184	295	50	6.3	14.5

Table 10-12 (*Continued*)

State	Maximum AFDC grant (per month)[a]	Food stamp benefit (per month)[b]	Combined benefits as a percentage of 1993 poverty threshold[c]	Public aid recipients (percentage of population)[d]	Food stamp recipients (percentage of population)
Utah	$414	$272	72	3.8	6.9
Vermont	638	205	88	7.2	10.0
Virginia	354	290	67	4.8	8.2
Washington	546[e]	258	84	7.0	8.7
West Virginia	249	295	57	10.0	17.7
Wisconsin	517	241	79	6.8	6.6
Wyoming	360	288	68	7.7	10.4

Note: The first two columns are maximum potential AFDC and food stamp benefits for a one-parent family of three persons. In most states the AFDC and food stamps amounts apply also to two-parent families of three (where the second parent is incapacitated or, as permitted in almost half the states, unemployed). Some, however, increase benefits for such families.

[a] In states with area differentials, figure shown is for areas with highest benefit.
[b] Food stamp benefits are based on maximum AFDC benefits shown. For assumptions about deductions, see the source.
[c] Based on the Census Bureau's 1993 poverty threshold for a family of three persons, $11,521, converted to a monthly rate of $960. For Alaska, this threshold was increased by 25 percent; for Hawaii, by 15 percent.
[d] Persons receiving AFDC (average monthly number, 1993) or Supplemental Security Income (SSI) (June, 1994).
[e] Part of the AFDC cash benefit has been designated as energy aid and is disregarded by the state in calculating food stamp benefits. The amounts disregarded vary by state. See the source for further details.
[f] Wayne County only, columns 1-3.
[g] New York City only, columns 1-3.

Sources: Benefits, AFDC recipients: U.S. Congress, House, Background Material and Data on Programs Within the Jurisdiction of the Committee on Ways and Means, 1994 Edition, 103d Cong., 2d sess., July 15, 1994 (Washington, D.C.: U.S. Government Printing Office, 1994), 366-367, 391-392, SSI; recipients: U.S. Department of Health and Human Services, Social Security Administration, Social Security Bulletin, Fall 1994 (Washington, D.C.: U.S. Government Printing Office, 1994), 129, food stamp recipients: U.S. Department of Agriculture, Food and Nutrition Service, Food Stamp Program State Activity Report Fiscal Year 1993 (Alexandria, Va.: Food and Nutrition Service, 1994), 2; state populations: U.S. Bureau of the Census, Population Distribution Branch, estimates of resident population, July 1, 1994.

11

Foreign and Military Policy

Even if one sought to understand only U.S. domestic politics, data on international relations would be essential. In the 1960 presidential campaign, for example, John Kennedy made the "missile gap" a major issue: the United States was falling behind the Soviet Union in its missile arsenal, and this imperiled the defense of the free world. The actual existence of that missile gap has been disputed, but the charge fit in with Kennedy's pledge to get the country moving again and played well to the public in the aftermath of Sputnik and the U-2 incident. Similarly, Ronald Reagan made increased military spending a cornerstone of his campaign platform in 1980.

One might think that statistics relating to foreign policy, especially the military aspects, are difficult or impossible to find, that secrecy prevents publication of important information about our defense capabilities. There are instances in which this is the case. Performance capabilities of spy satellites and the "stealth" bomber are understandably kept secret. There are also secret diplomatic and military initiatives undertaken by the Central Intelligence Agency and other organizations that the public learns about later, if at all. The sale of weapons to Iran while the United States was publicly declaring that it would have nothing to do with that country, and the use of profits from these sales to support the Nicaraguan contras, is a case in point.

Despite these examples and the obvious need for secrecy in defense-related areas, a surprisingly wide array of data is available, in part because details about military hardware are not the only kinds of relevant information. In fact, the first table in this chapter deals with public opinion data. As was evident during the 1960s, public opinion about foreign policy is extraordinarily relevant and powerful information. Public opinion on U.S. involvement in Vietnam reveals a great deal about why President Lyndon

Johnson declined to seek reelection in 1968 and why U.S. forces began to withdraw from Vietnam soon thereafter (Figure 11-1). In opposite fashion, opinions about our involvement in the 1991 Gulf War (Figure 11-1) indicate why President Bush's presidential approval ratings were, temporarily as it turned out, extraordinarily high (Figure 8-2). Public opinion on defense spending has been politically relevant, although the pattern of changes in the late 1970s and 1980s suggests that Ronald Reagan was leading as well as responding to changes in public sentiments (Table 11-12).

A great deal of other information closely relates to both defense and domestic policy, and this kind of data is emphasized here. Defense spending, for example, involves more than whether the United States has spent enough to defend itself. Elementary economics courses use the phrase "guns or butter" to express the tradeoff between defense and nondefense spending. Every dollar spent for weaponry means a dollar less that can be spent for social programs, tax reductions, and other politically worthy causes. Therefore, information on defense spending (Table 11-11) is doubly relevant.

In presenting information about defense spending, two elements arise. The first is the concept of "constant" versus "current" dollars. Current dollars are what people deal with every day. The price asked for goods is the price paid; whether the price has gone up more or less than other prices is not especially relevant. People may be aware that prices of some goods have gone up (for example, oil and gasoline in the 1970s) or down (for example, many electronic products) more than others, but the price quoted is what is most significant. Constant dollars, in contrast, take into account what has happened to prices more generally (see Table 13-2 for the Consumer Price Index). Thus, for example, most food clearly costs more in current dollars than it did years ago; in the 1960s one never heard of a loaf of bread that cost $1.00. Yet relative to other prices, the cost of bread has been reduced. Its price may have only doubled in a given period of time while other prices have tripled. In a very meaningful sense, therefore, bread and other foods are cheaper than they used to be; the "real" cost of bread has been reduced.

Another, perhaps simpler, way to express this is to say that constant dollar calculations take inflation into account. For defense spending, therefore, the question is: after taking inflation into account, has spending increased? If spending has risen only as fast as inflation, the new budget will buy only as much as the previous budget, even though nominally, that is, in current dollars, it is larger. Because this issue of real versus current dollars is so significant, Table 11-11 and many of the tables in Chapter 13 express expenditures both ways.

The second new element in presenting information about defense spending is that it is especially relevant to see what other countries are doing as well. Whether the United States is spending a lot or a little is a relative question. If foreign adversaries raise their spending, then perhaps the United States must do the same. As a consequence, information is presented on worldwide military expenditures (Table 11-13) even though the focus in this volume is on the United States.

Economic and social dimensions are also relevant to U.S. foreign and military policy, and data about these are widely available. The slippage of the U.S. trade balance (Table 11-17) and the increasing foreign investment in the United States and U.S. investment abroad (Table 11-16) are two aspects of the economic context of recent foreign policy discussions. Foreign aid, whether in the form of military (Table 11-14) or nonmilitary (Table 11-15) assistance, is another part of economic foreign policy. Immigration policy has social and economic implications, and changes in the flow of immigrants, along with future prospects, make it a most significant aspect of U.S. foreign relations (Table 11-18).

The statistical picture would be incomplete without information about military weapons and forces. Here, too, information is needed about more than just the United States. Therefore, one of many possible comparisons of superpower military strength is presented (Table 11-5), as well as existing bilateral and multilateral arms control agreements (Table 11-4). In both a contemporary and historical vein, information is given about military conflicts and personnel. Even here, however, it is impossible to avoid domestic aspects of these data. One of the tables on military personnel reports information by sex, race, and Hispanic origin (Table 11-10). This classification of personnel is obviously more relevant to U.S. domestic policy than to the question of whether the country is sufficiently prepared to meet a challenge from abroad.

Now that the Cold War is over, one might anticipate major changes in data relating to foreign and military policy. For example, information about military hardware will have to change—e.g., from how many warheads the "Soviet Union" has to how many of the old Soviet warheads are in Russia, how many are in Ukraine, and so on. And new statistics may become relevant, such as the number of U.S. military assigned to United Nations forces. It will take some time, however, for statistics of this sort to be published—both because it takes awhile to produce such numbers and because it is not immediately clear which statistics are most relevant for a "New World Order." In the meantime, the topics of these tables and figures—public opinion about wars, levels of defense spending, foreign aid, the balance of trade, and so on—and the data about them, remain as relevant as ever.

The emergence of the United States as a world power in the twentieth century has elevated the political significance of international relations so that no overview of American politics would be complete without a look at foreign and military policy. Foreign policy has often proved critical in domestic politics, and that accounts for the numbers presented here.

Table 11-1 Public Opinion on U.S. Involvement in World Affairs, 1945-1994 (percent)

Date	Active part	Stay out	No opinion
October 1945	70	19	11
September 1947	65	26	9
September 1949	67	25	8
November 1950	64	25	11
December 1950	66	25	9
October 1952	68	23	9
February 1953	73	22	5
September 1953	71	21	8
April 1954	69	25	6
March 1955	72	21	7
November 1956	71	25	4
June 1965	79	16	5
March 1973	66	31	3
March 1975	61	36	4
March 1976	63	32	5
March 1978	64	32	4
December 1978	59	29	12
March 1982	61	34	5
November 1982	53	35	12
March 1983	65	31	4
March 1984	65	29	6
March 1985	70	27	2
March 1986	65	32	4
March 1988	65	32	4
March 1989	68	28	4
March 1990	69	27	4
March 1991	73	24	2
March 1993	67	28	5
March 1994	65	32	4

Note: Question: "Do you think it would be best for the future of this country if we take an active part in world affairs, or if we stay out of world affairs?"

Sources: 1945, 1947, November 1950, December 1978, November 1982: Gallup surveys; 1949, December 1950, 1952-1965: National Opinion Research Center; all others: General Social Survey, National Opinion Research Center, University of Chicago.

Table 11-2   U.S. Diplomatic and Consular Posts, 1781-1994

Year	Diplomatic	Consular
1781	4	3
1790	2	10
1800	6	52
1810	4	60
1820	7	83
1830	15	141
1840	20	152
1850	27	197
1860	33	282
1870	36	318
1880	35	303
1890	41	323
1900	41	318
1910	48	324
1920	45	368
1930	57	299
1940	58	264
1950	74	179
1960	99	166
1970	117	122
1980	133	100
1990	170	97
1992	185	99
1994	191	90

Note: 1990 and 1992 figures are as of May, April, and August, respectively. For those years, diplomatic posts include embassies, countries with ambassadors without physical missions, branch offices, missions, and interest sections. Consular posts include consulates general and consulates.

Sources: U.S. Department of State, Office of Public Communication, *A Short History of the U.S. Department of State 1781-1981* (Washington, D.C.: U.S. Government Printing Office, 1981), 35. Updated from U.S. Department of State, *Key Officers of Foreign Service Posts* (Washington, D.C.: U.S. Government Printing Office, May 1990), vi; (1992), xi; (1994), xv.

Table 11-3 U.S.-Soviet Summit Meetings, 1945-1991

Date	Location	Leaders	Topic
July-August 1945	Potsdam	President Harry S. Truman, Soviet leader Josef Stalin, British prime ministers Winston Churchill and Clement R. Attlee	Partition and control of Germany
July 1955	Geneva	President Dwight D. Eisenhower, Soviet leader Nikolai A. Bulganin, British prime minister Anthony Eden, French premier Edgar Faure	Reunification of Germany, disarmament, European security
September 1959	Camp David, Md.	President Dwight D. Eisenhower, Soviet leader Nikita S. Khrushchev	Berlin problem
May 1960	Paris	President Dwight D. Eisenhower, Soviet leader Nikita S. Khrushchev, French president Charles de Gaulle, British prime minister Harold Macmillan	U-2 incident
June 1961	Vienna	President John F. Kennedy, Soviet leader Nikita S. Khrushchev	Berlin problem
June 1967	Glassboro, N.J.	President Lyndon B. Johnson, Soviet leader Aleksei N. Kosygin	Middle East
May 1972	Moscow	President Richard M. Nixon, Soviet leader Leonid I. Brezhnev	SALT I, antiballistic missile limitations
June 1973	Washington, D.C.	President Richard M. Nixon, Soviet leader Leonid I. Brezhnev	Détente
June-July 1974	Moscow and Yalta	President Richard M. Nixon, Soviet leader Leonid I. Brezhnev	Arms control
November 1974	Vladivostok	President Gerald R. Ford, Soviet leader Leonid I. Brezhnev	Arms control
June 1979	Vienna	President Jimmy Carter, Soviet leader Leonid I. Brezhnev	SALT II
November 1985	Geneva	President Ronald Reagan, Soviet leader Mikhail Gorbachev	Arms control, U.S.-Soviet relations
October 1986	Reykjavik	President Ronald Reagan, Soviet leader Mikhail Gorbachev	Arms control

Table 11-3 (*Continued*)

Date	Location	Leaders	Topic
December 1987	Washington, D.C.	President Ronald Reagan, Soviet leader Mikhail Gorbachev	Intermediate Nuclear Force (INF) Treaty, Afghanistan
May 1988	Moscow	President Ronald Reagan, Soviet leader Mikhail Gorbachev	Arms control, human rights
December 1988	New York	President Ronald Reagan, Soviet leader Mikhail Gorbachev	U.S.-Soviet relations
December 1989	Malta	President George Bush, Soviet leader Mikhail Gorbachev	Arms control, Eastern Europe
May-June 1990	Washington, D.C.	President George Bush, Soviet leader Mikhail Gorbachev	Arms control
September 1990	Helsinki	President George Bush, Soviet leader Mikhail Gorbachev	Middle East crisis
July 1991	Moscow	President George Bush, Soviet leader Mikhail Gorbachev	Arms control and Soviet economic and political future

Note: Prior to the dissolution of the Soviet Union, President George Bush and Soviet leader Mikhail Gorbachev met in Madrid at the opening of the Mideast Peace talks in October 1991. There was no specific agenda.

Source: Congressional Quarterly's Guide to the U.S. Presidency (Washington, D.C.: Congressional Quarterly, 1989), 520-521; updated by the editors.

Table 11-4 Arms Control and Disarmament Agreements

Issue	Participants
Nuclear weapons	
To prevent the spread of nuclear weapons	
Antarctic Treaty, 1959	37 states[a]
Outer Space Treaty, 1967	126 states[a]
Latin American Nuclear-Free Zone Treaty, 1967	31 states[a]
Nonproliferation Treaty, 1968	142 states[a]
Seabed Treaty, 1971	109 states[a]
To reduce the risk of nuclear war	
Hot Line and Modernization Agreements, 1963	United States and Soviet Union
Accidents Measures Agreement, 1971	United States and Soviet Union
Prevention of Nuclear War Agreement, 1973	United States and Soviet Union
To limit nuclear testing	
Limited Test Ban Treaty, 1963	128 states[a]
Threshold Test Ban Treaty, 1974	United States and Soviet Union
Peaceful Nuclear Explosions Treaty, 1976[b]	United States and Soviet Union
To limit nuclear weapons	
ABM Treaty (SALT I) and Protocol, 1972	United States and Soviet Union
SALT I Interim Agreement, 1972[c]	United States and Soviet Union
SALT II, 1979[d]	United States and Soviet Union
Intermediate Range Nuclear Force (INF) Missiles Treaty, 1988	United States and Soviet Union
Strategic Arms Reduction Treaty (START), 1991	United States and Soviet Union[e]
Strategic Arms Reduction Treaty, II (START II), 1993	United States and Russia[f]
Other weapons	
To prohibit use of gas	
Geneva Protocol, 1925	130 states
To prohibit biological weapons	
Biological Weapons Convention, 1972	135 states
To prohibit techniques changing the environment	
Environmental Modification Convention, 1977	77 states
To control use of inhumane weapons	
Inhumane Weapons Convention, 1981	27 states[g]

Table 11-4   *(Continued)*

Issue	*Participants*
To reduce risk of war	
Notification of Military Activities, 1986	35 states
To limit conventional weapons	
Conventional Forces in Europe Treaty, 1990	22 states[h]
To ban use, development, production, stockpiling of chemical weapons	
Chemical Weapons Convention, 1993	130 states[f]

[a] Number of parties and signatories as of December 1986.
[b] Ratified by the United States and entered into force in December 1990.
[c] Expired by its terms on October 3, 1977.
[d] Never ratified. If the treaty had entered into force, it would have expired by its terms on December 31, 1985.
[e] Ratified by the United States in October 1992; entered into force December 1994.
[f] Not ratified by the United States as of May 1995.
[g] Convention entered into force December 1983. The United States is not a signatory.
[h] Ratified by the United States in December 1991; entered into force November 1992.

Sources: U.S. Arms Control and Disarmament Agency, *Arms Control and Disarmament Agreements*, 1990 ed. (Washington: U.S. Arms Control and Disarmament Agency, 1990), and unpublished data from Office of Treaty Affairs, U.S. State Department.

Table 11-5   Strategic Offensive Forces of the Super Powers, 1992

Delivery vehicle type	United States				Commonwealth of Independent States			
	Weapon	Launchers deployed	Warheads/launcher	Total warheads	Weapon	Launchers deployed	Warheads/launcher	Total warheads
Ballistic missiles								
Intercontinental ballistic missiles (ICBM)	Minuteman II	450	1	450	SS-18	308	10	3,080
	Minuteman III	500	3	1,500	SS-24[a]	36	10	360
	MX	50	10	500	SS-25	340	1	340
					SS-11	280	1	280
					SS-13	40	1	40
					SS-17	40	4	160
					SS-19	300	6	1,800
					SS-24[b]	56	10	560
Submarine-launched ballistic missiles (SLBM)	Poseidon C-3	192	10	1,920	SS-N-6	96	1	96
	Trident C-4	384	8	3,072	SS-N-8	280	1	280
	Trident D-5	120	8	960	SS-N-18	224	3	672
					SS-N-20	120	10	1,200
					SS-N-23	112	4	448
Total ballistic missiles		1,696	-	8,402		2,232	-	9,316
START I limit				(4,900)				(4,900)

Bombers							
With air-launch cruise missiles	B-52	150	10	1,500	Tu-95H-6/H-16	61	8	488
	B-52[c]	28	20	560	Tu-160	20	8	160
Without air-launched cruise missiles	B-1B	95	1	95	Tu-95B/G	89	1	89
	B-52	278	1	278				
Total bombers		551	-	2,433		170	-	737
Grand total		2,247	-	10,835		2,402	-	10,053
START I limit		(1,600)	-	(6,000)		(1,600)	-	(6,000)

Note: "-" indicates not applicable. Data as of June 1, 1992. "START I" refers to the Strategic Arms Reduction Talks between the United States and the Soviet Union. Shown are strategic forces under START I counting rules. For additional details on warhead/launcher calculations and on START I limits, see source. The START II agreement, signed by Presidents George Bush of the United States and Boris Yeltsin of Russia in January, 1993, will yield further reductions in offensive forces if it is ratified. These reductions will not take place until later in the decade.

[a] Mobile ICBMs.
[b] Nonmobile ICBMs.
[c] START counting rules allow first 150 ACLM-capable bomber to count 10 warheads; bombers in excess of 150 count as 20.

Sources: International Institute for Strategic Studies, *The Military Balance 1991-1992* (London: Brasseys, 1992), 227-228; START I limits: *1990-1991* (1990), 212-213.

Table 11-6 Use of United States Armed Forces Abroad, 1798-1994

Decade	Number of instances	Example of use of armed forces
1798-1800	1	Undeclared naval war with France
1801-1810	4	Tripoli—First Barbary War
1811-1820	13	Caribbean—engagements with pirates, onshore and offshore
1821-1830	8	Cuba—fight, capture pirates
1831-1840	7	Fiji Islands—punish natives who attacked American explorers
1841-1850	8	China—after a clash at a trading post in Canton
1851-1860	22	Nicaragua—oppose William Walker's attempt to control country
1861-1870	13	Japan—several times, to protect American interests
1871-1880	5	Colombia—protect American interests in fighting over Panama
1881-1890	7	Hawaii—protect American interests
1891-1900	18	Philippine Islands—protect American interests; conquer islands
1901-1910	16	Colombia, Panama, Dominican Republic, Honduras, Nicaragua—protect American interests during civil turmoil
1911-1920	29	Honduras, China, Turkey, Mexico—protect American interests
1921-1930	15	Panama, Costa Rica—to prevent war over boundary dispute
1931-1940	7	Haiti—part of long-term stay to prevent chronic insurrection
1941-1950	13	Trieste—reinforce air forces after Yugoslav downing of plane
1951-1960	6	Korean War; Lebanon—protect against threatened insurrection
1961-1970	8	Vietnam War; Congo—airlift Congolese troops during rebellion
1971-1980	11	Lebanon—evacuate citizens fighting; Iran—rescue attempt
1981-1990	23	Libya—shoot down jets; Granada—restore law and order
1991-1994	23	Persian Gulf War; Somalia—food aid; Haiti—oust military

Note: The count of instances is necessarily approximate; for example, numerous engagements with pirates in the Caribbean between 1814 and 1825 are counted as only one instance. Five of the instances were declared wars: the War of 1812 (1812-1815), the Mexican War (1846-1848), the Spanish-American War (1898), World War I (1917-1918), and World War II (1941-1945). Others might be considered undeclared wars: Undeclared Naval War with France (1798-1800); First Barbary War (1801-5); Second Barbary War (1915); Korean War (1950-53); Vietnam War (1964-73); Persian Gulf War (1991). (Actions that covered more than one decade are counted as occurring in each decade.)

Source: Ellen C. Collier, "Instances of Use of United States Armed Forces Abroad, 1798-1993" (Washington, D.C.: Congressional Research Service, 1993); updated by the editors based on reports in the *New York Times*.

Table 11-7 U.S. Personnel in Major Military Conflicts

Item	Civil War[a]	Spanish-American War	World War I	World War II	Korean conflict	Vietnam conflict	Gulf War
Personnel serving (thousands)	2,213	307[b]	4,735	16,113[c]	5,720[d]	8,744[e]	541[f]
Average duration of service (months)	20	8	12	33	19	23	7
Casualties (thousands)							
Battle deaths	140	[g]	53	292	34	47[h]	[g]
Wounds not mortal	282	2	204	671	103	153[h]	[g]
Draftees: classified (thousands)	777	0	24,234	36,677	9,123	75,717[e]	0
Examined	522	0	3,764	17,955	3,685	8,611	0
Rejected	160	0	803	6,420	1,189	3,880	0
Inducted	46	0	2,820	10,022	1,560	1,759	0
Cost (millions)[i]							
Current	$2,300	$270	$32,700	$360,000	$50,000	$140,600	$7,300[j]
Constant (1967)	8,500	1,100	100,000	816,300	69,300	148,800	1,790

Note: For Revolutionary War, the number of personnel serving is not known, but estimates range from 184,000 to 250,000; for War of 1812, 286,730 served; for Mexican War, 78,718 served.

[a] Union forces only. Estimates of the number serving in Confederate forces range from 600,000 to 1.5 million; cost for the Confederacy estimated at $1 million (current dollars) and $3.7 million (constant dollars).
[b] Covers April 21, 1898 to August 13, 1898.
[c] Covers December 1, 1941 to December 31, 1946.
[d] Covers June 25, 1950 to July 27, 1953.
[e] Covers August 4, 1964 to January 27, 1973.
[f] Covers August 1, 1990 to April 30, 1992.
[g] Fewer than 500.
[h] Covers January 1, 1961 to January 27, 1973.
[i] Original direct costs only. Excludes service-connected veterans' benefits and interest payments on war loans.
[j] Total costs estimated at $61.6 billion (in current dollars). Shown is the portion of that amount estimated to have been paid by the U.S.

Sources: U.S. Bureau of the Census, *Statistical Abstract of the United States, 1991* (Washington, D.C.: U.S. Government Printing Office, 1991), 341, 346; U.S. Department of Defense, unpublished data.

Table 11-8 U.S. Military Forces and Casualties in Vietnam, 1957-1993

| Year | Military forces (thousands) | Battle deaths | | | | Wounded, nonfatal[a] | |
		Total[a]	Killed	Died of wounds	Died while missing[b]	Hospital care (thousands)	No hospital care (thousands)
1957–1964	23.3[c]	279	197	10	72	0.8	0.8
1965	184.3	1,432	1,124	111	197	3.3	2.8
1966	385.3	5,047	4,142	579	326	16.5	13.6
1967	485.6	9,463	7,525	1,598	401	32.4	29.7
1968	536.1	14,623	12,624	979	959	46.8	46.0
1969	475.2	9,426	8,117	1,168	141	32.9	37.3
1970	234.6	4,230	3,486	555	189	15.2	15.4
1971	156.8	1,376	1,082	160	134	4.8	4.2
1972	24.2	361	205	28	128	0.6[d]	0.6[d]
1973–1993	0.0	1,118	0	22	1,068	[d]	[d]
Total	[e]	47,367	38,506	5,225	3,636	153.3	150.3

Note: Military forces as of December 31. All U.S. forces withdrawn by January 27, 1973.

[a] Casualties from enemy action. Deaths exclude 10,803 servicemen who died in accidents or from disease.
[b] Includes 114 servicemen who died while captured.
[c] For 1964 only.
[d] Fewer than fifty.
[e] Not applicable.

Sources: Military forces, battle deaths: U.S. Bureau of the Census, *Statistical Abstract of the United States, 1993* (Washington, D.C.: U.S. Government Printing Office, 1993), 358; battle deaths, total: National Archives and Records Administration, unpublished data from Combat Area Casualties database, as of November 1993; wounded, nonfatal: *Statistical Abstract of the United States, 1993,* 328.

Figure 11-1 Public Opinion on U.S. Military Involvement: Vietnam, Persian Gulf, and Haiti

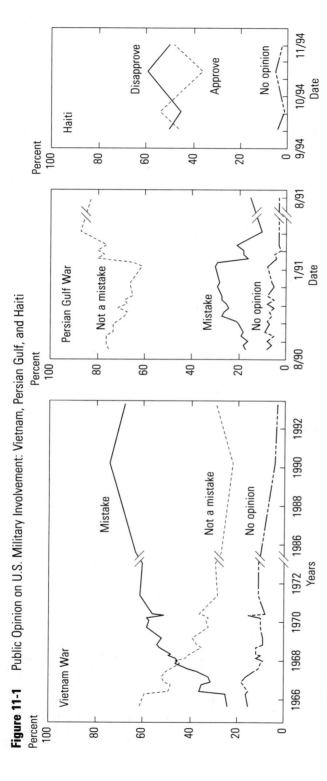

Note: Question for Vietnam War: "In view of the developments since we entered the fighting in Vietnam, do you think the United States made a mistake sending troops to fight in Vietnam?" In 1985, 1990, and 1993, the question was, "Looking back, do you think. . .?" The question was not asked between 1974 and 1984. Question for Persian Gulf War: "In view of the developments since we first sent our troops to the Persian Gulf region, do you think the United States made a mistake in sending troops to the Persian Gulf region, or not?" Prior to January 17-20, 1991, "Saudi Arabia" was used instead of the "Persian Gulf region." Results are plotted using the midpoint of the survey dates. The last two surveys were early March and mid-July 1991. The Gulf War began on January 15, 1991; a cease-fire was declared on February 28, 1991, with the surrender of all Iraqi troops occurring over the next several days. Question for Haiti: "Concerning Haiti. . . Do you approve or disapprove of the presence of U.S. troops in Haiti?"

Sources: Vietnam War: Gallup polls cited in John Mueller, *War, Presidents and Public Opinion* (New York: Wiley, 1973), 54-55 (reprinted in 1985 by University Press of America, Lanham, Md.); *The Gallup Poll, 1972-1975*, vol. I (Wilmington, Del.: Scholarly Resources, 1977), 87; *Gallup Poll Monthly*, January 1993, 37. Persian Gulf War: *Gallup Poll Monthly*, July 1991, 36. Haiti: *Gallup Poll Monthly*, October 1994, 31.

Table 11-9 U.S. Military Personnel Abroad or Afloat, by Country, 1972-1993[a] (thousands)

Country	1972	1975	1980	1983	1984	1985	1986	1987	1988	1989	1990	1991	1992	1993
Outside United States[b]	628	517	502	520	511	515	525	524	541	510	609	448	344	308
Europe[b,c]	298	314	332	342	352	358	358	354	356	341	310	285	205	166
Germany	210	220	244	254	254	247	250	251	249	249	228	203	134	105
Greece	3	4	4	4	4	4	4	3	3	3	2	1	1	1
Iceland	3	3	3	3	3	4	3	3	3	3	3	3	3	3
Italy	10	12	12	14	15	15	16	14	15	16	14	13	13	10
Spain	9	9	9	9	9	9	9	9	9	9	7	6	4	4
Turkey	7	7	5	5	5	5	5	5	5	5	4	6	5	4
United Kingdom	22	21	24	28	29	30	30	28	28	28	25	23	20	16
Afloat	28	30	22	18	25	36	33	31	33	21	18	20	17	17
East Asia and Pacific[b]	275	156	115	137	121	125	129	129	141	135	119	105	98	99
Japan[d]	65	48	46	49	46	47	48	50	50	50	47	45	46	46[d]
Philippines	17	15	13	15	15	15	16	16	17	15	14	8	2	[e]
South Korea	41	42	39	39	41	42	43	45	46	44	41	40	36	35
Thailand	47	20	[e]	[e]	[e]	[e]	[e]	[e]	[e]	[e]	[e]	[e]	[e]	[e]
Vietnam	47	0	0	0	0	0	0	0	0	0	0	0	[e]	[e]
Afloat	51	28	16	34	18	20	20	17	28	25	16	11	13	17
U.S. outlying areas[f]	29	25	2	13	13	14	13	12	12	12	11	11	12	12
Troop dependents	342	365	369	386	399	385	401	386	373	389	400	365	303	273

[a] Data for additional years can be found in previous editions of *Vital Statistics on American Politics*.
[b] Includes troops in countries not shown.
[c] Western Europe and related areas.
[d] Includes Okinawa.
[e] Fewer than 500.
[f] Primarily Guam, Panama Canal Zone, Puerto Rico, and Midway Islands.

Sources: 1972-1985: *Statistical Abstract of the United States, 1977* (Washington, D.C.: U.S. Government Printing Office, 1977), 370; *1981*, 364; *1982-1983*, 361; *1986*, 343; *1987*, 328; 1986-1990: U.S. Department of Defense, *Selected Manpower Statistics, Fiscal Year 1986* (Washington, D.C.: U.S. Government Printing Office, 1987), 44-46, 51, 163; *1987*, *1988*, 44-46, 51, 178; *1989*, 44-46, 51, 179; *1990*, *1991*, *1992*, *1993*, 44-47, 51, 176.

Table 11-10 U.S. Active Duty Forces, by Sex, Race, and Hispanic Origin, 1965-1994

Year	Female			Black			Hispanic[a]			Total[b]	
	Officers	Enlisted	Total	Officers	Enlisted	Total	Officers	Enlisted	Total	Officers (thousands)	Enlisted (thousands)
1965	3.1%	0.9%	1.2%	1.9%	10.5%	9.5%	—	—	—	339	2,317
1966	3.2	0.8	1.1	—	—	—	—	—	—	349	2,745
1967	3.3	0.8	1.0	2.1	9.9	8.9	—	—	—	385	2,992
1968	3.2	0.8	1.1	2.1	10.2	9.2	—	—	—	416	2,132
1969	3.1	0.9	1.1	2.1	9.6	8.7	—	—	—	419	3,041
1970	3.3	1.1	1.4	2.2	11.0	9.8	—	—	—	402	2,664
1971	3.5	1.3	1.6	2.3	12.1	10.7	1.3%	3.4%	3.1%	371	2,329
1972	3.8	1.6	1.9	2.4	13.5	11.9	1.2	4.0	3.6	336	1,987
1973	4.0	2.2	2.5	2.7	14.9	13.2	1.2	4.5	4.0	321	1,932
1974	4.3	3.3	3.5	3.0	16.2	14.4	1.3	4.5	3.9	303	1,860
1975	4.6	4.5	4.6	3.2	16.2	14.4	1.4	4.6	4.2	292	1,836
1976	5.0	5.3	5.2	3.6	17.1	15.2	1.3	4.6	4.2	281	1,801
1977	5.4	5.8	5.7	3.9	17.4	15.6	1.5	4.5	4.1	276	1,798
1978	6.2	6.5	6.5	4.3	19.3	17.3	1.6	4.5	4.1	274	1,788
1979	6.9	7.5	7.4	4.7	21.2	19.0	1.6	4.4	3.8	274	1,753
1980	7.7	8.5	8.4	5.0	21.9	19.6	1.2	4.0	3.6	278	1,759
1981	8.1	9.0	8.9	5.3	22.1	19.8	1.2	4.1	3.7	285	1,783
1982	8.6	9.0	9.0	5.3	22.0	19.7	1.2	4.1	3.7	292	1,804
1983	9.0	9.3	9.3	5.8	21.6	19.4	1.4	4.1	3.7	301	1,811
1984	9.4	9.5	9.5	6.2	21.1	19.0	1.4	3.9	3.6	304	1,820
1985	9.8	9.8	9.8	6.4	21.1	18.9	1.5	3.9	3.6	309	1,828
1986	10.1	10.0	10.1	6.5	21.2	19.1	1.7	4.1	3.7	311	1,845
1987	10.4	10.2	10.2	6.5	21.5	19.4	1.7	4.3	3.9	308	1,856

(Table continues)

Table 11-10 (*Continued*)

Year	Female			Black			Hispanic[a]			Total[b]	
	Officers	Enlisted	Total	Officers	Enlisted	Total	Officers	Enlisted	Total	Officers (thousands)	Enlisted (thousands)
1988	10.7	10.4	10.4	6.7	22.0	19.8	1.8	4.5	4.1	305	1,819
1989	11.1	11.0	11.0	6.9	22.8	20.3	2.0	4.8	4.4	303	1,814
1990	11.4	10.9	10.9	6.9	22.9	20.5	2.1	5.0	4.6	304	1,762
1991	11.7	10.8	10.9	7.1	22.6	20.3	2.2	5.2	4.8	298	1,711
1992	12.0	11.3	11.4	7.2	22.0	19.8	2.3	5.5	5.0	281	1,551
1993	12.4	11.5	11.7	7.1	21.6	19.4	2.4	5.8	5.3	264	1,466
1994	12.8	12.0	12.1	7.3	21.4	19.2	2.6	6.0	5.4	253	1,380

Note: "—" indicates not available.

[a] Hispanics may be of any race. Data on percent Hispanic origin from 1971 to 1979 is based on male armed forces members only.
[b] Includes other races not shown separately.

Sources: 1965-1985: *Statistical Abstract of the United States, 1976* (Washington, D.C.: U.S. Government Printing Office, 1976), 336; 1980, 375-376; 1984, 353; 1986, 341; 1987, 327; 1986-1988: Department of Defense, unpublished data; 1989 (female, total officers, total enlisted): U.S. Department of Defense, *Selected Manpower Statistics, 1989* (Washington, D.C.: U.S. Government Printing Office, 1989), 78, 87, 101; 1989 (other): U.S. Department of Defense, *Defense 90 Almanac* (Washington, D.C.: U.S. Government Printing Office, 1990), 30; 1990-1992: Defense Equal Opportunity Management Institute, *Semi-Annual Race/Ethnic/Gender Profile of the Department of Defense Active Forces, Reserve Forces, and the United States Coast Guard* (Patrick Air Force Base, Fla.: Defense Equal Opportunity Management Institute, 1990), 24; 1991, 9; 1992, 12; 1993, 12; 1994, 12.

Table 11-11 U.S. Defense Spending, 1940-2000

Year	Annual percentage change[a]		Defense outlays as a percentage of	
	Current dollars	Constant dollars	Federal outlays	Gross domestic product
1940	—	—	17.5	1.7
1941	276.5	239.1	47.1	5.7
1942	301.6	241.2	73.0	18.1
1943	159.5	137.4	84.9	38.0
1944	18.6	25.9	86.7	39.2
1945	4.9	13.3	89.5	39.1
1946	−48.6	−42.5	77.3	20.1
1947	−70.0	−73.5	37.1	5.7
1948	−28.9	−37.9	30.6	3.7
1949	45.1	38.7	33.9	5.0
1950	3.8	8.4	32.2	5.2
1951	72.3	79.1	51.8	7.5
1952	95.3	72.3	68.1	13.5
1953	14.5	4.9	69.4	14.5
1954	−6.6	−7.9	69.5	13.4
1955	−13.4	−15.6	62.4	11.1
1956	−0.5	−5.9	60.2	10.2
1957	6.8	2.5	59.3	10.4
1958	3.1	−2.6	56.8	10.4
1959	4.7	−1.2	53.2	10.2
1960	−1.8	−2.0	52.2	9.5
1961	3.1	1.6	50.8	9.6
1962	5.4	3.6	49.0	9.4
1963	2.1	−2.5	48.0	9.1
1964	2.6	0.9	46.2	8.8
1965	−7.7	−8.8	42.8	7.5
1966	14.8	9.1	43.2	7.9
1967	22.9	18.8	45.4	9.0
1968	14.7	8.4	46.0	9.7
1969	0.7	−4.5	44.9	8.9
1970	−1.0	−7.3	41.8	8.3
1971	−3.4	−10.2	37.5	7.5
1972	0.4	−5.8	34.3	6.9
1973	−3.2	−8.3	31.2	6.0
1974	3.4	−6.7	29.5	5.7
1975	9.1	−2.1	26.0	5.7
1976	3.6	−3.9	24.1	5.3
TQ[b]	c	c	23.2	5.0
1977	8.5	0.5	23.8	5.1
1978	7.5	0.5	22.8	4.8
1979	11.3	2.6	23.1	4.8
1980	15.2	3.1	22.7	5.1
1981	17.5	4.5	23.2	5.3
1982	17.7	8.1	24.8	5.9
1983	13.3	8.6	26.0	6.3

(Table continues)

Table 11-11 (*Continued*)

Year	Annual percentage change[a]		Defense outlays as a percentage of	
	Current dollars	Constant dollars	Federal outlays	Gross domestic product
1984	8.3	5.0	26.7	6.2
1985	11.1	8.8	26.7	6.4
1986	8.2	6.1	27.6	6.5
1987	3.1	2.9	28.1	6.3
1988	3.0	0.7	27.3	6.0
1989	4.5	1.5	26.6	5.9
1990	−1.4	−4.7	23.9	5.5
1991	−8.7	−11.8	20.7	4.8
1992	9.2	3.8	21.6	5.0
1993	−2.4	−5.0	20.7	4.7
1994	−3.3	−7.0	19.3	4.2
1995 est.	−3.6	−6.3	17.6	3.9
1996 est.	−3.8	−6.8	16.2	3.5
1997 est.	−1.7	−4.7	15.3	3.3
1998 est.	1.0	−3.8	14.6	3.1
1999 est.	2.0	−0.8	14.3	3.0
2000 est.	3.1	0.2	14.1	2.9

Note: "—" indicates data not available.

[a] Change from prior year.
[b] Transition quarter, July-September.
[c] Not applicable.

Sources: Annual percentage change calculated from actual dollar amounts of defense spending in Table 13-3, this volume; percent of federal outlays and GDP; Office of Management and Budget, *Budget of the U.S. Government, Fiscal Year 1996 Historical Tables* (Washington, D.C.: U.S. Government Printing Office, 1995), 82-88.

Table 11-12 Public Opinion on U.S. Defense Spending, 1960-1993
(percent)

Year	Too much	About right	Too little	No opinion
1960	18	45	21	16
1969	52	31	8	9
1971	50	31	11	8
1973	46	30	13	11
1974	44	32	12	12
1976	36	32	22	10
1977	23	40	27	10
1979	21	33	34	12
1980	14	24	49	13
1981	15	22	51	12
1982	41	31	16	12
1983	37	36	21	6
1985	46	36	11	7
1986	47	36	13	4
1987	44	36	14	6
1990 Jan.	50	35	10	5
1990 Aug.	41	40	15	4
1991 Mar.	26	60	10	4
1991 Aug.	47	38	10	5
1991 Oct.	50	36	10	4
1993 Mar.	42	38	17	3

Note: Question: "There is much discussion as to the amount of money the government in Washington should spend for national defense and military purposes. How do you feel about this? Do you think we are spending too little, too much, or about the right amount?"

Sources: *Gallup Opinion Index*, February 1980, 10; *The Gallup Report*, March 1985, 4; *The Gallup Poll* (Wilmington, Del.: Scholarly Resources, Inc., 1992), 202; *The Gallup Poll Monthly*, April 1993, 45.

Table 11-13 Worldwide Military Expenditures, 1981-1991

Country group	1981	1982	1983	1984	1985	1986	1987	1988	1989	1990	1991	Per capita 1981	Per capita 1991
Current dollars (billions)													
Worldwide, total[a]	$705.6	$791.7	$851.5	$902.6	$958.8	$995.7	$1,031.5	$1,058.4	$1,069.6	$1,086.1	$1,038.1	—	—
NATO[b]	292.3	330.4	361.2	388.3	424.7	444.3	461.1	469.0	489.4	501.3	479.9	—	—
United States	169.9	196.4	218.0	237.1	265.8	280.9	288.2	293.1	304.1	306.2	280.3	—	—
Warsaw Pact[c]	256.3	280.5	295.6	310.9	327.1	339.9	357.4	373.5	357.7	324.2	276.6	—	—
Soviet Union[d]	219.6	237.9	250.7	263.7	277.2	287.6	303.0	319.0	303.0	292.0	260.0	—	—
Constant (1991) dollars (billions)													
Worldwide, total	1,053.4	1,112.9	1,150.2	1,167.2	1,196.2	1,209.7	1,214.6	1,200.1	1,160.5	1,129.6	1,038.1	232	192
NATO[b]	436.4	464.4	487.9	502.1	529.9	539.7	542.9	531.8	531.0	521.4	479.9	703	701
United States	253.6	276.1	294.4	306.5	331.6	341.3	339.3	332.3	329.9	318.4	280.3	1,102	1,110
Warsaw Pact[c]	382.7	394.4	399.2	402.0	408.1	412.9	420.8	423.5	388.1	337.2	276.6	1,011	710
Soviet Union[d]	327.8	334.4	338.6	341.0	345.8	349.4	356.8	361.7	328.7	303.7	260.0	1,220	887

Percentage GNP[e]

Worldwide, total[a]	5.4	5.7	5.7	5.6	5.5	5.4	5.3	5.0	4.7	4.5	4.2	—	—	—
NATO[b]	4.3	4.7	4.8	4.7	4.8	4.8	4.7	4.4	4.3	4.1	3.8	—	—	—
United States	5.5	6.2	6.3	6.2	6.6	6.6	6.3	6.0	5.8	5.5	4.9	—	—	—
Warsaw Pact[c]	12.2	12.3	12.1	12.1	12.2	12.0	12.1	11.8	10.7	9.8	9.3	—	—	—
Soviet Union[d]	13.3	13.2	13.0	13.0	13.1	12.8	12.9	12.7	11.5	11.0	10.3	—	—	—

Note: "—" indicates not available.

[a] Includes countries not in NATO (North Atlantic Treaty Organization) or the Warsaw Pact.

[b] NATO includes Belgium, Canada, Denmark, France, Iceland, Great Britain, Greece, Italy, Luxembourg, the Netherlands, Norway, Portugal, Spain, Turkey, the United States, and West Germany.

[c] The Warsaw Pact countries include Bulgaria, Czechoslovakia, East Germany, Hungary, Poland, Romania, and the Soviet Union. The Warsaw Pact was formally dissolved on July 1, 1991.

[d] Estimate based on partial or uncertain data.

[e] The meaning of military expenditures as a percentage of GNP differs between most Eastern and Western bloc countries because of differing estimating procedures.

Source: U.S. Arms Control and Disarmament Agency, *World Military Expenditures and Arms Transfers 1991-1992* (Washington, D.C.: U.S. Government Printing Office, 1994), 47, 51, 81, 85.

Table 11-14 U.S. Military Sales and Military Assistance to Foreign Governments, Principal Recipients, 1950-1993 (millions)

Country	Military sales								Military assistance[a]
	1950-1986	1987	1988	1989	1990	1991	1992	1993	1950-1993
Australia	$3,718.3	$592.7	$850.1	$383.6	$266.9	$205.9	$161.8	$245.3	$0.0
Belgium	1,804.3	27.0	222.5	153.1	177.6	184.3	39.6	51.1	1,203.8
Canada	2,023.1	126.8	211.5	143.6	102.8	163.9	108.8	130.2	0.0
China (Taiwan)	3,238.7	368.4	484.3	352.7	460.1	556.1	828.3	730.3	2,554.6
France	650.8	99.4	36.8	38.2	108.5	31.8	35.0	40.7	4,045.1
Germany	8,219.6	315.4	382.3	632.6	358.7	479.5	502.1	346.6	884.8
Greece	2,010.8	78.7	129.0	137.7	113.5	123.9	171.5	206.4	1,673.2
Indochina	8.5	0.0	0.0	0.0	0.0	0.0	0.0	0.0	709.0
Iran	10,728.0	0.0	0.0	0.0	0.0	0.0	0.0	0.0	766.7
Israel	9,136.4	1,293.5	751.0	230.3	151.2	239.2	685.7	780.4	160.0
Italy	1,002.5	71.4	61.6	63.6	61.3	69.1	54.4	54.5	2,243.7
Korea	3,169.7	344.1	327.2	314.5	293.5	217.1	295.2	315.2	5,471.7
Netherlands	2,972.9	417.2	327.2	391.4	381.5	370.9	306.1	123.0	1,178.1
Saudi Arabia	18,169.7	3,139.6	970.5	629.2	890.4	2,773.5	2,464.7	3,580.3	23.9
Thailand	1,413.6	95.4	291.1	211.5	176.0	180.0	103.6	108.0	1,169.0
Turkey	2,108.7	277.1	699.9	618.7	720.1	600.6	703.4	751.3	3,170.2
United Kingdom	4,776.2	204.7	179.8	130.5	205.3	244.2	154.3	186.2	1,012.9
Vietnam	1.2	0.0	0.0	0.0	0.0	0.0	0.0	1.2	14,773.9
Total[b]	99,608.2	10,848.9	8,784.2	6,993.1	7,453.4	8,626.7	10,238.6	11,230.5	55,181.9

Note: Figures exclude training. Amounts in current dollars.

[a] Military assistance, especially to Europe, has been very low in recent years.

[b] Includes countries not shown.

Source: U.S. Defense Security Assistance Agency, *Foreign Military Sales, Foreign Military Construction Sales, and Military Assistance Facts, September 30, 1993,* (Washington, D.C.: U.S. Government Printing Office, 1993), 16-19, 78-81.

Table 11-15 U.S. Foreign Aid, Principal Recipients, 1962-1993 (millions)

Region/country	1962-1989	1990	1991	1992	1993
Asia[a]	$22,242	$873	$749	$511	$375
India	3,941	23	30	48	25
Indonesia	1,650	48	60	42	48
Korea	1,080	0	0	0	0
Pakistan	4,005	276	96	b	6
Philippines	2,075	314	328	201	83
Vietnam	4,490	0	1	1	b
Europe[a]	4,566	160	606	514	469
Turkey	2,772	14	250	1	200
Latin America[a]	16,114	1,486	1,075	855	780
Brazil	1,480	0	0	0	4
Costa Rica	1,234	78	42	24	9
Dominican Republic	879	18	14	16	19
El Salvador	2,336	200	180	234	172
Honduras	1,159	167	99	65	33
Jamaica	787	28	27	38	43
ROCAP[c]	675	30	21	12	17
Near East[a]	30,912	2,199	2,754	2,205	2,124
Egypt	11,996	900	783	893	748
Israel	15,219	1,195	1,850	1,200	1,200
Jordan	1,396	4	31	0	65
Morocco	429	31	50	41	33
Sub-Saharan Africa[a]	9,532	621	865	890	783
Cameroon	250	22	20	22	10
Chad	124	11	16	13	12
Kenya	583	36	25	20	16
Niger	268	20	28	29	17
Senegal	347	37	24	34	22
Somalia	388	1	1	11	27
Sudan	880	8	2	3	b
Zaire	548	31	22	0	0
Zambia	282	17	35	40	26
Zimbabwe	327	28	43	40	49
Oceania and other	72	18	20	20	23
Total[d]	103,341	6,964	7,668	6,819	7,059

Note: Amounts in current dollars. Shown are loans and grants made by the U.S. Agency for International Development and its predecessor agencies. Excluded are Food for Peace and "other" economic assistance. Data for individual years before 1990 can be found in earlier editions of *Vital Statistics on American Politics.*

[a] Includes countries not shown separately.
[b] Less than one million.
[c] Programs covering Costa Rica, El Salvador, Guatemala, Honduras, Nicaragua, and Panama.
[d] Includes interregional aid.

Source: U.S. Agency for International Development, *U.S. Overseas Loans and Grants and Assistance from International Organizations, Obligations and Loan Authorizations,* July 1, 1945-September 30, 1993 (Washington, D.C.: U.S. Government Printing Office, 1993), 4-203.

Table 11-16 Foreign Investment in the United States and U.S. Investment Abroad, 1950-1993 (millions)

Year	All areas	Canada	Europe	Japan
Foreign direct investment in the United States				
1950	$3,391	$1,029	$2,228	—
1960	6,910	1,934	4,707	$88
1970	13,270	3,117	9,554	229
1980	83,046	12,162	54,688	4,723
1985	184,615	17,131	121,413	19,313
1986	220,414	20,318	144,181	26,824
1987	271,788	24,013	186,076	35,151
1988	314,754	26,566	208,942	51,126
1989	368,924	30,370	239,190	67,268
1990	396,702	30,037	250,973	81,775
1991	418,780	36,341	252,692	93,787
1992	425,636	37,845	251,206	97,537
1993	445,268	39,408	270,767	96,213
U.S. investment abroad				
1950	11,788	3,579	1,733	19
1960	32,778	11,198	6,681	254
1970	78,178	22,790	24,516	1,483
1980	215,578	44,978	96,539	6,243
1985	230,250	46,909	105,171	9,235
1986	259,562	49,994	122,165	11,332
1987	314,307	57,783	150,439	15,684
1988	333,501	62,610	156,932	17,927
1989	370,091	65,548	175,213	18,488
1990	430,521	69,508	214,739	22,599
1991	467,844	70,711	235,163	25,403
1992	498,991	68,832	246,228	26,590
1993	548,644	70,395	269,158	31,393

Note: "—" indicates not available. Amounts in current dollars.

[a] Data for additional years can be found in previous editions of *Vital Statistics on American Politics*.

Sources: 1950-1960: U.S. Department of Commerce, *Foreign Business Investments in the United States: A Supplement to Survey of Current Business* (Washington, D.C.: U.S. Government Printing Office, 1962), 34; *Survey of Current Business*, August 1962, 22; others from *Survey of Current Business*: August 1973, 50; September 1973, 24; August 1982, 21-22; August 1983, 24; August 1985, 63; August 1988, 65, 80; August 1990, 41, 62-64; August 1991, 47, 87; August 1992, 89, 123-125, August 1994, 99, 134-137.

Table 11-17 U.S. Balance of Trade, 1946-1994 (millions)

Year	Merchandise trade balance[a]	Balance on current account[b]	Year	Merchandise trade balance[a]	Balance on current account[b]
1946	$6,697	$4,885	1971	−$2,260	−$1,433
1947	10,124	8,992	1972	−6,416	−5,795
1948	5,708	2,417	1973	911	7,140
1949	5,339	873	1974	−5,505	1,962
1950	1,122	−1,840	1975	8,903	18,116
1951	3,067	884	1976	−9,483	4,295
1952	2,611	614	1977	−31,091	−14,335
1953	1,437	−1,286	1978	−33,927	−15,143
1954	2,576	219	1979	−27,568	−285
1955	2,897	430	1980	−25,500	2,317
1956	4,753	2,730	1981	−28,023	5,030
1957	6,271	4,762	1982	−36,485	−11,443
1958	3,462	784	1983	−67,102	−44,460
1959	1,148	−1,282	1984	−112,492	−99,733
1960	4,892	2,824	1985	−122,173	−125,372
1961	5,571	3,822	1986	−145,081	−151,201
1962	4,521	3,387	1987	−159,557	−167,097
1963	5,224	4,414	1988	−126,959	−128,194
1964	6,801	6,823	1989	−115,249	−102,820
1965	4,951	5,431	1990	−109,033	−91,748
1966	3,817	3,031	1991	−74,068	−6,952
1967	3,800	2,583	1992	−96,097	−67,886
1968	635	611	1993	−132,575	−103,896
1969	607	399	1994	-166,364	-155,673
1970	2,603	2,331			

Note: Amounts in current dollars.

[a] "Merchandise trade balance" measures the difference between the value of goods the United States imports and the goods the United States exports.

[b] "Balance on current account" is the broadest trade gauge, measuring the difference in imports and exports of merchandise trade and trade in services; also includes certain one-way flows of money into the United States, such as pension payments.

Sources: U.S. President, *The Economic Report of the* President (Washington, D.C.: U.S. Government Printing Office, 1995, Table B-105; 1994: U.S. Department of Commerce, *News*, press release, "U.S. International Transactions: Fourth Quarter and Year 1994," March 14, 1995, 10.

Table 11-18 Immigrants, by Country, 1820-1993

| Year | Europe | | | | Asia[e] | Canada | Other western hemisphere[f] | All other[g] | Total number (thousands) |
	Northwestern[a]	Central[b]	Southern[c]	Eastern[d]					
1820-1830	62.8%	5.1%	2.1%	0.1%	—	1.6%	6.2%	22.0%	151.8
1831-1840	56.3	25.5	1.0	—	—	2.3	3.3	11.7	599.1
1841-1850	67.6	25.4	0.3	—	—	2.4	1.2	3.1	1,713.3
1851-1860	56.9	36.7	0.8	—	1.6%	2.3	0.6	1.1	2,598.2
1861-1870	53.7	34.4	0.9	0.1	2.8	6.6	0.5	0.8	2,314.8
1871-1880	48.1	28.6	2.7	1.4	4.4	13.6	0.7	0.4	2,812.2
1881-1890	44.3	35.4	6.3	4.2	1.3	7.5	0.6	0.3	5,246.6
1891-1900	30.9	32.4	19.1	14.2	1.9	0.1	1.0	0.5	3,687.6
1901-1910	17.8	28.2	26.4	20.1	2.8	2.0	2.1	0.2	8,795.4
1911-1920	14.9	18.3	25.5	17.7	3.4	12.9	7.0	0.4	5,735.8
1921-1930	21.2	20.8	14.0	4.3	2.4	22.5	14.4	0.4	4,107.2
1931-1940	15.9	30.8	15.9	3.3	3.0	20.5	9.8	0.9	528.4
1941-1950	25.4	26.3	7.7	0.6	3.5	16.6	17.7	2.1	1,035.0
1951-1960	17.7	26.0	10.6	2.9	6.1	10.9	22.5	3.1	2,515.5
1961-1970	12.2	11.2	12.2	1.3	13.2	8.6	38.9	2.3	3,321.7
1971-1980	4.3	4.0	8.0	1.8	35.9	2.6	40.4	3.1	4,493.3
1981-1990	3.9	3.1	2.3	1.6	37.0	2.1	47.1	3.0	7,338.1
1991-1993	3.3	3.4	1.9	4.3	27.6	1.8	55.0	2.8	3,705.4

Note: "—" indicates less than 0.1 percent. Data for most years are for country of last permanent residence. See source for details.

[a] United Kingdom, Ireland, Norway, Sweden, Denmark, the Netherlands, Belgium, Switzerland, and France.
[b] Germany, Poland, Czechoslovakia, Yugoslavia, Hungary, and Austria.
[c] Italy, Spain, Portugal, and Greece.
[d] USSR, Romania, Turkey, and "other Europe."
[e] Cambodia, China, Taiwan, Hong Kong, India, Iran, Israel, Japan, Korea, Philippines, Thailand, Vietnam, and "other Asia."
[f] Mexico, Caribbean, and Central and South America.
[g] Africa, Australia, and New Zealand.

Source: U.S. Department of Justice, Immigration and Naturalization Service, *Statistical Yearbook of the Immigration and Naturalization Service, 1993* (Washington, D.C.: U.S. Government Printing Office, 1994), 26-29.

12

Social Policy

The study of social policies might fairly be described as controversies informed by, but not settled by, statistics. No matter what the area, those on all sides of an issue try to support their arguments with relevant data.

The data are of many kinds and can be characterized in a variety of ways. First, there is factual information showing, for example, how many whites, blacks, and Hispanics are below the poverty line (Table 12-3), how much money is spent on social welfare (Tables 12-5 and 12-6), and how many crimes were committed in a given year (Table 12-21). Second, there are data about public opinion and social policy. Social policy concerns not only the actual crime rate but what people think about crime—for example, whether the courts are too easy on criminals (Table 12-23) and whether the death penalty is acceptable and desirable (Table 1-11). It matters not only what abortion rates are (Table 1-12) but also what people think and say about abortion (Table 1-13). One might also distinguish between data about the past or present and projections about the future. Much of the concern about Social Security payments and about health care costs is not about present payments but about what to expect in the future (Tables 12-8 and 12-9, Figure 12-2).

Social policies are inherently controversial, and so too are data relevant to such policies. Often, for example, analysts agree on a set of facts but disagree on the relevance of the material and on its interpretation. Information about numbers of people on welfare (Table 12-10), about the proportion of women and minorities elected to political office (Table 12-18), about the extent of crime and the cost of prisons (Tables 12-21 and 12-22), and so on, does not automatically answer causal questions (why the situation is as it is) any more than it answers normative questions (whether the existing situation is good and what should be done). Moreover, the importance of future projections often leads to special problems of inference. Any projection must be based on assumptions about what the future will be like. A footnote in Table 12-9, for example, should underscore the fact that no one can be certain in 1993 what health or Social Security costs will be in 2070.

In the face of enormous problems of inference, of controversy about almost every fact, and of the need to deal with future unknowns, one might well ask whether all these numbers are useful or necessary when discussing social policies. There are at least two answers to this question. The first is highly pragmatic. Some analysts will surely have factual information at their disposal; those who do not or cannot understand data and are unable or unwilling to provide any of their own will be hostage to others' information and interpretations.

From a more theoretical perspective, one can note that although data are always subject to some error and interpretation, people often do agree on the facts and on roughly how they should be interpreted. There is no disagreement, for example, that—barring major unforeseen catastrophes or extremely large and unlikely changes in immigration—there will be a considerably smaller ratio of young people to old people in the first half of the next century. Knowing this does not solve the problems implicit in this fact, but it tells analysts that there will be problems and that the country needs to be thinking of solutions. It also suggests possible solutions—raising the retirement age, lowering Social Security payments or raising Social Security taxes, encouraging private pension plans so that the elderly need less government support, and so on.

In the area of social policy, as in other areas, data do not speak for themselves. They must be analyzed and interpreted. The facts alone will settle few arguments about causality or about normative questions. Still, data and an ability to interpret them are essential ingredients in the arsenal of any well-educated social analyst, commentator, or student.

Figure 12-1   U.S. Population: Total, Urban, and Rural, 1790-2050

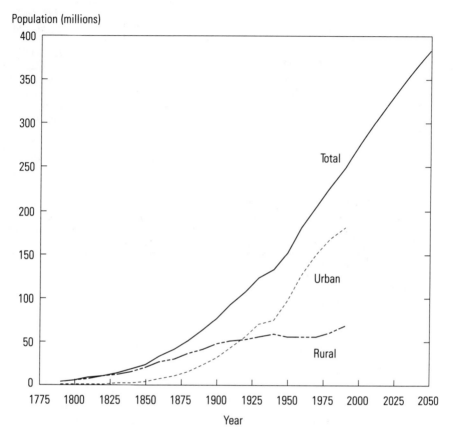

Note: Urban places, in general, are those with a population of 2,500 or more. A change in definition in 1950 resulted in about 5 percent more individuals being classified as urban than under the old definition. For details on definitions and projections, see sources.

Sources: Urban, rural, and total resident population, 1790-1970: U.S. Bureau of the Census, *Historical Statistics of the United States* (Washington, D.C.: U.S. Government Printing Office, 1975), 8, 11; total resident population, 1980 and 1990: see source in this volume, Table 12-1; urban and rural population, 1980-1990: U.S. Bureau of the Census, *Current Population Reports* (Washington, D.C.: U.S. Government Printing Office, 1992), Series P-20, no. 457, 13; population projections: U.S. Bureau of the Census, *Current Population Reports* (Washington, D.C.: U.S. Government Printing Office, 1992), P25-1104, 1.

Table 12-1   U.S. Population, 1790-1990

Year	Resident population	Year	Resident population
1790	3,929,214	1900	75,994,575
1800	5,308,483	1910	91,972,266
1810	7,239,881	1920	105,710,620
1820	9,638,453	1930	122,775,046
1830	12,866,020	1940	131,669,275
1840	17,069,453	1950	150,697,361
1850	23,191,876	1960	179,323,175
1860	31,443,321	1970	203,235,298
1870	39,818,449	1980	226,545,805
1880	50,155,783	1990	248,709,873
1890	62,947,714		

Sources: 1790-1970: U.S. Bureau of the Census, *Historical Statistics of the United States* (Washington, D.C.: U.S. Government Printing Office, 1975), 11; 1980: U.S. Bureau of the Census, *1980 Census of Population: General Population Characteristics* (Washington, D.C.: U.S. Government Printing Office, 1980), Series PC80-1-B1, 1-19; 1990: U.S. Bureau of the Census, *1990 Census of Population and Housing: Summary Population and Housing Characteristics* (Washington, D.C.: U.S. Government Printing Office, 1990), Series 1990 CPH-1-1, 360.

Table 12-2 Median Family Income, by Race and Hispanic Origin, 1950-1993

Year	Median income in current dollars				Median income in constant (1993) dollars				Annual percentage change in median income of all families	
	All families[a]	White	Black	Hispanic origin[b]	All families[a]	White	Black	Hispanic origin[b]	Current dollars	Constant dollars
1950	$3,319	$3,445	$1,869[c]	—	$18,305	$19,000	$10,308	—	—	—
1955	4,418	4,613	2,544[c]	—	21,938	22,906	12,633	—	6.6[d]	3.9[d]
1960	5,620	5,835	3,230[c]	—	25,220	26,185	14,495	—	5.4[d]	3.0[d]
1965	6,957	7,251	3,993[c]	—	29,394	30,637	16,871	—	4.8[d]	3.2[d]
1970	9,867	10,236	6,279	—	34,523	35,814	21,969	—	8.4[d]	3.1[d]
1971	10,285	10,672	6,440	—	34,482	35,780	21,591	—	4.2	−0.2
1972	11,116	11,549	6,864	$8,183	36,177	37,586	22,339	$26,632	8.1	4.8
1973	12,051	12,595	7,269	8,715	36,893	38,559	22,254	26,680	8.4	2.0
1974	12,902	13,408	8,006	9,540	35,922	37,331	22,290	26,561	7.1	−3.5
1975	13,719	14,268	8,779	9,551	35,274	36,686	22,572	24,557	6.3	−2.6
1976	14,958	15,537	9,242	10,259	36,388	37,796	22,483	24,957	9.0	3.1
1977	16,009	16,740	9,563	11,421	36,603	38,274	21,865	26,113	7.0	0.5
1978	17,640	18,368	10,879	12,566	37,763	39,321	23,289	26,901	10.2	2.3
1979	19,587	20,439	11,574	14,169	38,248	39,991	22,601	27,668	11.0	−0.2
1980	21,023	21,904	12,674	14,716	36,912	38,458	22,253	25,838	7.3	−5.5
1981	22,388	23,517	13,266	16,401	35,905	37,716	21,276	26,303	6.5	−3.5
1982	23,433	24,603	13,598	16,227	35,419	37,188	20,553	24,527	4.7	−1.4
1983	24,674	25,837	14,561	16,930	35,797	37,484	21,125	24,562	5.3	2.0
1984	26,433	27,686	15,431	18,832	36,762	38,505	21,461	26,191	7.1	2.7
1985	27,735	29,152	16,786	19,027	37,246	39,149	22,543	25,552	4.9	1.3
1986	29,458	30,809	17,604	19,995	38,838	40,620	23,210	26,362	6.2	4.3

(Table continues)

Table 12-2 (Continued)

Year	Median income in current dollars				Median income in constant (1993) dollars				Annual percentage change in median income of all families	
	All families[a]	White	Black	Hispanic origin[b]	All families[a]	White	Black	Hispanic origin[b]	Current dollars	Constant dollars
1987	$30,970	$32,385	$18,406	$20,300	$39,394	$41,194	$23,413	$25,822	5.1	1.4
1988	32,191	33,915	19,329	21,769	39,320	41,426	23,610	26,590	3.9	-0.2
1989	34,213	35,975	20,209	23,446	39,869	41,922	23,550	27,322	6.3	1.4
1990	35,353	36,915	21,423	23,431	39,086	40,813	23,685	25,905	3.3	-2.0
1991	35,939	37,783	21,548	23,895	38,129	40,085	22,861	25,351	1.7	-2.4
1992	36,812	38,909	21,161	23,901	37,688	39,828	21,735	24,260	2.4	-1.9
1993	36,959	39,300	21,542	23,654	36,959	39,300	21,542	23,654	0.4	-1.9

Note: "—" indicates not available.

[a] Includes other races not shown separately.
[b] Persons of Hispanic origin may be of any race.
[c] For 1950-1965, black and other races.
[d] Calculated by annualizing the five-year change.

Sources: 1950-1965: *Statistical Abstract of the United States, 1987* (Washington, D.C.: U.S. Government Printing Office), 436; 1970-1991: U.S. Bureau of the Census, Current Population Reports, "Money Income of Households, Families and Persons in the United States: 1991" (Washington, D.C.: U.S. Government Printing Office, 1992), Series P-60, no. 180, 40-43, B9-B10; 1992-1993: U.S. Bureau of the Census, Current Population Reports, "Income, Poverty, and Valuation of Noncash Benefits: 1993" (Washington, D.C.: U.S. Government Printing Office, 1995), 7-10, A3, D5-D7.

Table 12-3 Persons Below the Poverty Level, by Race and Hispanic Origin, 1959-1993 (percent)

Year	White	Black	Hispanic origin[a]	Total[b]
1959	18.1	55.1	—	22.4
1960	17.8	—	—	22.2
1961	17.4	—	—	21.9
1962	16.4	—	—	21.0
1963	15.3	—	—	19.5
1964	14.9	—	—	19.0
1965	13.3	—	—	17.3
1966	11.3	41.8	—	14.7
1967	11.0	39.3	—	14.2
1968	10.0	34.7	—	12.8
1969	9.5	32.2	—	12.1
1970	9.9	33.5	—	12.6
1971	9.9	32.5	—	12.5
1972	9.0	33.3	—	11.9
1973	8.4	31.4	21.9	11.1
1974	8.6	30.3	23.0	11.2
1975	9.7	31.3	26.9	12.3
1976	9.1	31.1	24.7	11.8
1977	8.9	31.3	22.4	11.6
1978	8.7	30.6	21.6	11.4
1979	9.0	31.0	21.8	11.7
1980	10.2	32.5	25.7	13.0
1981	11.1	34.2	26.5	14.0
1982	12.0	35.6	29.9	15.0
1983	12.1	35.7	28.0	15.2
1984	11.5	33.8	28.4	14.4
1985	11.4	31.3	29.0	14.0
1986	11.0	31.1	27.3	13.6
1987	10.4	32.4	28.0	13.4
1988	10.1	31.3	26.7	13.0
1989	10.0	30.7	26.2	12.8
1990	10.7	31.9	28.1	13.5
1991	11.3	32.7	28.7	14.2
1992	11.9	33.4	29.6	14.8
1993	12.2	33.1	30.6	15.1

Note: "—" indicates not available.

[a] Persons of Hispanic origin may be of any race.
[b] Includes other races not shown separately.

Source: U.S. Bureau of the Census, Current Population Reports, "Income, Poverty, and Valuation of Noncash Benefits: 1993" (Washington, D.C.: U.S. Government Printing Office, 1995), Series P-60, no. 188, D13-D16.

Table 12-4   Persons Below the Poverty Line, 1992

Group	Percentage of group that is poor	Group as a percentage of all poor people
Race/ethnicity		
White	11.9	66.4
Black	33.4	28.5
Hispanic origin[a]	29.6	20.0
Family status		
Female householder, no husband present		
White	31.0	18.9
Black	53.0	18.3
Hispanic[a]	53.2	7.5
All other families		
White	7.2	31.0
Black	15.4	6.0
Hispanic[a]	22.3	10.6
Age		
Under 15	23.2	35.3
65 or over	12.9	10.3
Dwelling		
Metropolitan residents	14.2	74.7
Nonmetropolitan residents	16.9	25.3
Region		
Northeast	12.6	16.9
Midwest	13.3	21.2
South	17.1	40.0
West	14.8	21.9
All persons	14.8	100.0

[a] Persons of Hispanic origin may be of any race.

Source: U.S. Bureau of the Census, Current Population Reports, "Income, Poverty, and Valuation of Noncash Benefits: 1993" (Washington, D.C.: U.S. Government Printing Office, 1995), Series P-60, no. 188, B-4, D13-D16.

Table 12-5   Social Welfare Expenditures, 1950-1991

	Federal		State and local		Total expenditures	
Year	Total (billions)	Percentage of total federal outlays	Total (billions)	Percentage of total state and local outlays	Total (billions)	Percentage of total GDP[a]
1950	$10.5	26.2	$13.0	59.2	$23.5	8.2
1955	14.6	22.3	18.0	55.3	32.6	8.2
1960	25.0	28.1	27.3	60.1	52.3	10.3
1965	37.6	32.6	39.5	61.7	77.1	11.5
1966	45.2	34.9	42.6	60.0	87.8	11.9
1967	53.2	35.0	46.3	57.8	99.5	12.6
1968	60.2	35.1	53.4	60.0	113.6	13.4
1969	68.1	37.5	58.8	58.8	127.0	13.7
1970	77.1	40.0	68.4	57.9	145.6	14.8
1971	92.3	44.8	78.9	59.3	171.3	16.3
1972	105.9	47.2	84.4	60.4	190.3	16.6
1973	122.2	50.3	91.1	59.3	213.3	16.7
1974	136.7	52.1	101.9	58.1	238.7	17.0
1975	166.9	53.7	122.3	61.6	289.2	19.1
1976	196.7	56.8	134.8	63.2	331.5	19.7
1977	217.9	56.1	142.4	63.2	360.3	19.3
1978	239.4	55.2	154.4	63.2	393.8	18.2
1979	263.2	54.8	166.6	62.1	429.9	17.7
1980	303.2	54.4	189.5	62.9	492.7	18.6
1981	346.5	54.3	207.4	62.3	553.8	18.7
1982	370.2	52.9	230.9	61.1	601.1	19.2
1983	402.3	53.1	247.1	61.0	649.4	19.5
1984	421.2	50.8	256.9	59.9	678.1	18.3
1985	450.8	48.7	281.5	59.9	732.2	18.4
1986	472.8	48.6	309.0	64.2	781.8	18.5
1987	497.9	50.2	336.2	66.6	834.1	18.7
1988	527.0	49.5	360.5	67.0	887.5	18.4
1989	565.1	49.5	392.3	68.0	957.4	18.5
1990	616.5	49.2	433.6	—	1,050.2	19.2
1991	676.4	51.1	485.8	—	1,162.2	20.5

Note: Amounts in current dollars.

[a] GNP for 1950-1960.

Sources: 1950-1960: U.S. Department of Health and Human Services, Social Security Administration, *Social Security Bulletin*, November 1988 (Washington, D.C.: U.S. Government Printing Office, 1988), 27-28; 1965-1991: *Social Security Bulletin*, Winter 1992, 55-56; Spring 1994, 98-99, 101.

Table 12-6 Social Welfare Expenditures, by Category, 1950-1991[a]

Year	Social insurance	Public aid	Health and medical programs[b]	Veterans programs	Education	Housing	Other social welfare[c]	All health and medical care[d]	Total social welfare outlays
Federal (millions)									
1950	$2,103	$1,103	$604	$6,386	$157	$15	$174	$1,362	$10,541
1955	6,385	1,504	1,150	4,772	485	75	252	1,948	14,623
1960	14,307	2,117	1,737	5,367	868	144	417	2,918	24,957
1965	21,807	3,594	2,660	6,011	2,470	238	812	4,482	37,592
1970	45,246	9,649	4,568	8,952	5,876	582	2,259	16,363	77,132
1975	99,715	27,276	7,890	16,570	8,629	2,541	4,264	33,469	166,885
1980	191,162	49,394	12,840	21,254	13,452	6,278	8,786	68,939	303,166
1985	310,175	63,474	18,029	26,704	13,796	11,059	7,548	122,139	450,785
1990	422,236	92,858	27,121	30,428	18,374	16,612	8,905	187,864	616,535
1991	453,538	113,235	29,713	32,331	19,062	18,696	9,831	—	676,406
State and local (millions)									
1950	2,844	1,393	1,460	480	6,517	—	274	1,704	12,967
1955	3,450	1,499	1,953	62	10,672	15	367	2,473	18,017
1960	4,999	1,984	2,727	112	16,758	33	723	3,478	27,337
1965	6,316	2,670	3,495	20	25,638	80	1,254	4,942	39,473
1970	9,446	6,839	5,038	126	44,970	120	1,886	8,698	68,425
1975	23,298	14,171	8,852	449	72,205	631	2,683	17,932	122,289
1980	38,592	23,309	14,423	212	107,597	601	4,813	31,320	189,547
1985	59,420	34,882	21,024	338	158,253	1,540	6,004	49,146	281,461
1990	91,565	53,019	36,669	488	240,011	2,856	9,012	83,666	433,621
1991	107,641	67,176	39,652	526	258,063	2,826	9,949	—	485,833

Total (millions)

Year									
1950	4,947	2,496	2,064	6,866	6,674	15	448	3,065	23,508
1955	9,835	3,003	3,103	4,834	11,157	89	619	4,421	32,640
1960	19,307	4,101	4,464	5,479	17,626	177	1,139	6,395	52,293
1965	28,123	6,264	6,155	6,031	28,108	318	2,066	9,424	77,065
1970	54,692	16,488	9,606	9,078	50,846	702	4,145	25,061	145,557
1975	123,013	41,447	16,742	17,019	80,834	3,172	6,947	51,401	289,174
1980	229,754	72,703	27,263	21,466	121,049	6,879	13,599	100,259	492,713
1985	369,595	98,356	39,053	27,042	172,049	12,599	13,522	171,285	732,246
1990	513,801	145,877	63,790	30,916	258,385	19,468	17,917	—	1,050,156
1991	561,179	180,411	69,365	32,857	277,125	21,522	19,780	—	1,162,239

Percentage of total expenditures

Year									
1950	21.0	10.6	8.8	29.2	28.4	0.1	1.9	13.0	100.0
1955	30.1	9.2	9.5	14.8	34.2	0.3	1.9	13.5	100.0
1960	36.9	7.8	8.5	10.5	33.7	0.3	2.2	12.2	100.0
1965	36.5	8.1	8.0	7.8	36.5	0.4	2.7	12.2	100.0
1970	37.6	11.3	6.6	6.2	34.9	0.5	2.8	17.2	100.0
1975	42.5	14.3	5.8	5.9	28.0	1.1	2.4	17.8	100.0
1980	46.6	14.8	5.5	4.4	24.6	1.4	2.8	20.3	100.0
1985	50.5	13.4	5.3	3.9	23.5	1.7	1.9	23.4	100.0
1990	48.9	13.9	6.1	2.9	24.6	1.9	1.7	—	100.0
1991	48.3	15.5	6.0	2.8	23.8	1.9	1.7	—	100.0

Percentage federal of total

Year									
1950	42.5	44.2	29.2	93.0	2.3	100.0	38.9	44.4	44.8
1955	64.9	50.1	37.1	98.7	4.3	84.3	40.7	44.1	44.8
1960	74.1	51.6	38.9	98.0	4.9	81.4	36.6	45.6	47.7
1965	77.5	57.4	43.2	99.7	8.8	74.8	39.3	47.6	48.8
1970	82.7	58.5	47.6	98.6	11.6	82.9	54.4	65.3	53.0

(Table continues)

Table 12-6 (*Continued*)

Year	Social insurance	Public aid	Health and medical programs[b]	Veterans programs	Education	Housing	Other social welfare[c]	All health and medical care[d]	Total social welfare outlays
1975	81.1	65.8	47.1	97.4	10.7	80.1	61.4	65.1	57.7
1980	83.2	67.9	47.1	99.0	11.1	91.2	64.6	68.7	61.5
1985	83.9	64.5	46.2	98.8	8.0	87.8	55.7	71.3	61.6
1990	82.2	63.7	42.5	98.4	7.1	85.3	49.7	—	58.7
1991	80.8	62.8	42.8	98.4	6.9	86.9	49.7	—	58.2

Note: "—" indicates not available. Amounts in current dollars. Figures for fiscal years ending in year shown.

[a] Data for additional years can be found in earlier editions of *Vital Statistics on American Politics*.

[b] Excludes medical services parts of social insurance, public aid, veterans, and other social welfare.

[c] Includes outlays for vocational rehabilitation, institutional care, child nutrition and welfare, and social welfare expenditures not elsewhere classified.

[d] Combines health and medical programs with medical services included in social insurance, public aid, veterans, vocational rehabilitation, and antipoverty programs.

Sources: 1950-1960: U.S. Department of Health and Human Services, Social Security Administration, *Social Security Bulletin*, November 1988 (Washington, D.C.: U.S. Government Printing Office, 1988), 27-28; 1965-1988: *Social Security Bulletin*, Winter 1992, 55-57, Spring 1994, 99-100.

Table 12-7 Private Social Welfare Expenditures, by Category and as a Percentage of GDP, 1972-1991 (millions)

	Private[a]					Public total[d]	Percentage of gross domestic product		
Year	Health	Income maintenance[b]	Education	Welfare services[c]	Total		Private[e]	Public[f]	Total[g]
1972	$57,200	$15,955	$14,935	$7,545	$95,635	$190,315	7.9	16.6	23.7
1973	63,200	18,063	16,146	8,297	105,706	212,314	7.8	16.7	23.7
1974	69,400	19,660	17,718	8,970	115,748	237,132	7.9	17.0	24.1
1975	102,000	21,910	19,993	10,067	153,970	289,173	9.7	19.1	27.7
1976	113,900	25,004	22,095	11,748	172,747	331,425	9.8	19.7	28.4
1977	113,900	30,662	23,581	13,535	181,678	360,314	9.2	19.3	27.5
1978	113,900	36,743	26,361	16,590	193,594	393,830	8.7	18.2	25.9
1979	126,900	42,628	28,774	19,540	217,842	431,007	8.8	17.7	25.5
1980	145,000	51,169	32,667	22,776	251,612	492,714	9.3	18.6	26.9
1981	168,500	58,741	36,521	25,728	289,490	554,189	9.6	18.7	27.2
1982	191,300	70,096	40,570	28,067	330,033	601,345	10.5	19.2	28.5
1983	210,900	82,414	44,639	31,369	369,322	649,229	10.8	19.6	29.3
1984	230,000	93,235	48,435	34,699	406,369	678,112	10.8	18.3	27.9
1985	248,000	116,207	53,167	38,914	456,288	732,250	11.3	18.4	28.5
1986	265,200	140,793	57,574	43,086	506,653	781,725	11.9	18.5	29.1
1987	286,100	140,433	64,423	47,429	538,385	834,142	11.9	18.7	29.3
1988	318,900	145,380	71,003	53,218	588,501	887,542	12.0	18.5	29.2
1989	351,000	163,138	79,245	59,466	652,849	957,394	12.4	18.5	29.6
1990	390,000	160,876	85,974	65,329	702,129	1,050,155	12.7	19.2	30.5
1991	421,800	171,016	92,095	71,454	756,365	1,165,136	13.3	20.5	32.4

Note: Amounts in current dollars.

[a] Calendar year basis.

(Notes continue)

Table 12-7 (*Continued*)

b These expenditures represent outlays for private employee benefit plans including private pension plans, group life insurance, sickness and disability insurance, paid sick leave, and supplemental unemployment benefits.

c Expenditures include individual and family social services, adoption services, emergency and disaster services, child day care centers, senior citizen centers, residential care, recreation and group work, civic, social, and fraternal organizations, job training, and vocational rehabilitation.

d Fiscal year basis.

e Calendar year expenditures as a percentage of calendar year gross domestic product.

f Fiscal year expenditures as a percentage of federal fiscal year gross domestic product.

g The sum of public and private expenditures as a percentage of gross domestic product, after adjustment to eliminate overlap that occurs when public or private income maintenance payments are used to purchase medical care, educational services, or residential care.

Source: U.S. Department of Health and Human Services, Social Security Administration, *Social Security Bulletin*, Spring 1994 (Washington, D.C.: U.S. Government Printing Office, 1994), 88.

Table 12-8   Health Insurance Trust Fund: Income, Expenditures, and
Balance, 1993-2001 (billions)

Year	Income	Disbursements	Net increase in fund	Fund at end of year
1993	$98.2	$94.4	$3.8	$127.8
1994	107.5	107.2	0.3	128.1
1995	119.0	116.6	2.4	130.5
1996	124.1	127.7	−3.6	126.9
1997	129.4	138.8	−9.4	117.5
1998	134.7	151.3	−16.6	100.9
1999	139.9	165.2	−25.3	75.6
2000	145.3	180.5	−35.2	40.4
2001	150.7	197.2	−46.4	Depleted

Note: The Hospital Insurance Program (Medicare Part A) pays for inpatient hospital care and other related care for those aged sixty-five or older and for the long-term disabled. It represents more than half of all Medicare expenses. Income for the fund is derived from a 1.45 percent payroll tax on employees and employers. Figures for 1993 represent actual experience. Figures for 1994 and beyond are "intermediate" projections; see source for details. Amounts in current dollars.

Source: U.S. Congress, House, "1994 Annual Report of the Board of Trustees of the Federal Hospital Insurance Trust Fund," 103d Cong., 2d sess., House Document 103-230, April 12, 1994, 14.

Table 12-9   Social Security (OASDI) Covered Workers and
Beneficiaries, 1945-2070

Year	Covered workers[a] (thousands)	Beneficiaries[b]			Covered workers per OASDI beneficiary	Beneficiaries per 100 covered workers
		OASI	DI	Total		
1945	46,390	1,106	—	1,106	41.9	2
1950	48,280	2,930	—	2,930	16.5	6
1955	65,200	7,563	—	7,563	8.6	12
1960	72,530	13,740	522	14,262	5.1	20
1965	80,680	18,509	1,648	20,158	4.0	25
1970	93,090	22,618	2,568	25,186	3.7	27
1975	100,200	26,998	4,125	31,123	3.2	31
1980	112,212	30,385	4,734	35,119	3.2	31
1985	119,481	32,776	3,874	36,650	3.3	31
1986	121,962	33,349	3,972	37,321	3.3	31
1987	125,028	33,918	4,035	37,953	3.3	30
1988	129,121	34,343	4,077	38,420	3.4	30
1989	131,687	34,754	4,105	38,859	3.4	29
1990	132,548	35,266	4,204	39,470	3.4	30
1991	131,774	35,785	4,388	40,173	3.3	30
1992	132,467	36,314	4,716	41,030	3.2	31
1993	135,209	36,758	5,083	41,841	3.2	31
1994	137,178	37,213	5,456	42,669	3.2	31
1995	139,068	37,654	5,830	43,484	3.2	31
2000	146,543	39,418	7,471	46,889	3.1	32
2005	152,642	41,379	8,884	50,223	3.0	33
2010	157,424	44,689	9,812	54,502	2.9	35
2015	159,944	50,489	10,214	60,703	2.6	38
2020	160,999	57,728	10,321	68,049	2.4	42
2025	161,726	64,574	10,570	75,144	2.2	46
2030	162,821	69,822	10,520	80,342	2.0	49
2035	164,443	72,991	10,398	83,389	2.0	51
2040	166,017	73,949	10,473	84,421	2.0	51
2045	167,063	74,595	10,885	85,480	2.0	51
2050	167,661	75,840	11,120	86,961	1.9	52
2055	168,087	77,956	11,274	89,230	1.9	53
2060	168,576	80,188	11,198	91,386	1.8	54
2065	169,091	81,917	11,187	93,104	1.8	55
2070	169,607	83,314	11,279	94,593	1.8	56

Note: "—" indicates not available; "OASI" indicates Old-Age and Survivors' Insurance; "DI" indicates Disability Insurance. Projections (1994-2070) are the so-called Intermediate projections. See source for further details.

[a] Workers who pay OASDI taxes at some time during the year.
[b] Beneficiaries with monthly benefits in current-payment status as of June 30.

Source: U.S. Congress, House, House Committee on Ways and Means, "1994 Annual Report of the Board of Trustees of the Federal Old-Age and Survivors Insurance and Disability Insurance Trust Funds," 103d Cong., 2d sess., April 12, 1994, 119.

Figure 12-2   Social Security Receipts, Spending, and Reserve Estimates, 1992-2025

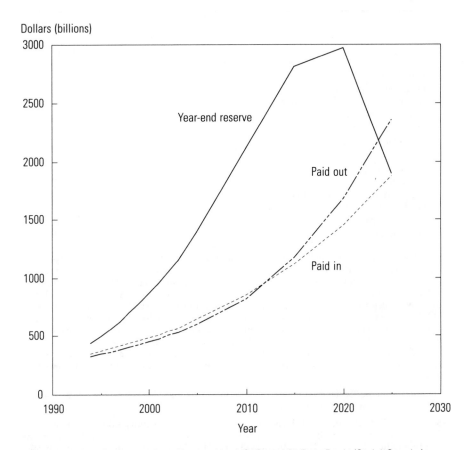

Note: In billions of current dollars. The combined OASI and DI Trust Funds (Social Security) are estimated to become exhausted during 2029 under intermediate cost projections. For details see source.

Source: U.S. Congress, House, House Committee on Ways and Means, "1994 Annual Report of The Board of Trustees of the Federal Old-Age and Survivors Insurance and Disability Insurance Trust Funds," 103d Cong., 2d sess., April 12, 1994, 178.

Table 12-10 Recipients of Social Insurance Programs, 1992

Program	Number of recipients (thousands)	Percentage of population[a]
Nonmeans-tested		
Social Security (OASDI)	41,507	16.0
Medicare (hospital insurance)	35,154	13.4
Veterans programs	3,448	1.4
Railroad programs	873	0.4
State unemployment insurance	2,620	1.0
Means-tested		
Medicaid	30,926	10.2
Supplemental Security Income	5,647	2.0
Aid to Families with Dependent Children	13,773	4.7
Food stamps	25,403	8.1
General assistance	1,184	0.5

Note: "Means-tested" refers to the requirement of demonstration of financial need based on income and assets. People may receive benefits from more than one program. For example, in 1985, 16 percent of U.S. households received one or more means-tested benefits; in addition to the programs listed above, these include free or reduced-price school lunches and publicly owned or subsidized housing. OASDI beneficiaries as of December 31. Medicare enrollees as of July 1. Veterans program beneficiaries as of December 31. Railroad programs beneficiaries as of December 31 (except for unemployment). State unemployment insurance is the average weekly number in December. Medicaid is the number of recipients during the year. SSI is the number of recipients in December. AFDC is the average number of monthly recipients. Food stamp number is the average during the year. General assistance is the average monthly number.

[a] Population in the "Social Security area," which includes Puerto Rico and other outlying areas, adjusted for Census undercount; for details, see source.

Sources: U.S. Department of Health and Human Services, Social Security Administration, *Social Security Bulletin, Annual Statistical Supplement, 1994* (Washington, D.C.: U.S. Government Printing Office, 1994), 181, 285, 309-310, 325, 343, 346, 355; note: U.S. Bureau of the Census, *Current Population Reports*, "Receipt of Selected Noncash Benefits: 1985" (Washington, D.C.: U.S. Government Printing Office, 1987), Series P-60, no. 155, 2.

Table 12-11 Aid to Families with Dependent Children Versus the
Poverty Line, 1936-1993

Year	Average monthly benefit per family	Yearly benefit	Average poverty threshold
1936	$28.15	$337.80	—
1940	31.98	383.76	—
1945	48.18	578.16	—
1950	71.33	855.96	—
1955	84.17	1,010.04	—
1960	105.75	1,269.00	$3,022
1961	110.97	1,331.64	3,054
1962	116.30	1,395.60	3,089
1963	120.19	1,442.28	3,128
1964	126.88	1,522.56	3,169
1965	133.20	1,598.40	3,223
1966	142.83	1,713.96	3,335
1967	155.19	1,862.28	3,410
1968	168.41	2,020.92	3,553
1969	174.89	2,098.68	3,743
1970	183.13	2,197.56	3,968
1971	187.16	2,245.92	4,137
1972	188.87	2,266.44	4,275
1973	190.91	2,290.92	4,540
1974	204.27	2,451.24	5,038
1975	219.44	2,633.28	5,500
1976	236.10	2,833.20	5,815
1977	246.27	2,955.24	6,191
1978	253.89	3,046.68	6,662
1979	262.86	3,154.32	7,412
1980	280.03	3,360.36	8,414
1981	282.04	3,384.48	9,287
1982	303.02	3,636.24	9,862
1983	312.82	3,753.84	10,178
1984	325.44	3,905.28	10,609
1985	342.15	4,105.80	10,989
1986	355.04	4,260.48	11,203
1987	361.37	4,336.44	11,611
1988	374.07	4,488.84	12,092
1989	383.14	4,597.68	12,674
1990	391.67	4,700.04	13,359
1991	390.44	4,685.28	13,924
1992	373.71	4,484.52	14,335
1993 (prelim.)	—	—	14,764

Note: "—" indicates not available. Poverty threshold is the annual income for a family of four. Amounts in current dollars.

Source: U.S. Department of Health and Human Services, Social Security Administration, *Social Security Bulletin, Annual Statistical Supplement, 1994* (Washington, D.C.: U.S. Government Printing Office, 1994), 151, 343.

Table 12-12 Persons Who Have Completed High School or College, by Race, Hispanic Origin, and Sex, 1940-1993 (percent)

| | 25 years and over | | | | | | 25-29 years | | | | | |
| | White | | Black[a] | | Hispanic[b] | | White | | Black[a] | | Hispanic[b] | |
Level/Year	Male	Female	Male	Female	Male	Female	Male	Female	Male	Female	Male	Female
Completed four years of high school or more												
1940	24.2	28.1	6.9	8.4	—	—	38.9	43.4	10.6	13.6	—	—
1947	33.2	36.7	12.7	14.5	—	—	52.9	56.8	19.6	24.7	—	—
1959	44.5	47.7	19.6	21.6	—	—	66.9	67.4	40.6	38.6	—	—
1970	57.2	57.6	32.4	34.8	—	—	79.2	76.4	54.5	57.9	—	—
1980	71.0	70.1	51.1	51.3	46.4	44.1	86.8	87.0	74.8	78.1	58.3	58.8
1990	79.1	79.0	65.8	66.5	50.3	51.3	84.6	88.1	81.5	81.8	56.6	59.9
1993	81.8	81.3	69.6	71.1	52.9	53.2	86.1	88.5	85.0	80.9	58.3	64.0
Completed four years of college or more[d]												
1940	5.9	4.0	1.4	1.2	—	—	7.5	5.3	1.5	1.7	—	—
1947	6.6	4.9	2.4	2.6	—	—	6.2	5.7	2.6	2.9	—	—
1959	11.0	6.2	3.8	2.9	—	—	15.9	8.1	5.6	3.7	—	—
1970	15.0	8.6	4.6	4.4	—	—	21.3	13.3	6.7	8.0	—	—
1980	22.1	14.0	7.7	8.1	9.7	6.2	25.5	22.0	10.5	12.5	8.4	6.9
1990	25.3	19.0	11.9	10.8	9.8	8.7	24.2	24.3	15.1	11.9	7.3	9.1
1993	25.7	19.7	11.9	12.4	9.5	8.5	24.4	25.1	12.6	13.8	7.1	9.8

Note: "—" indicates data not available.

a Data are for black and other races for 1940 to 1960; for 1970-1993, data are for black persons only.

b Persons of Hispanic origin may be of any race.

c Beginning 1992, high school graduate or more.

d Beginning 1992, bachelor's degree or more.

Source: U.S. Bureau of the Census, Current Population Reports, "Educational Attainment in the United States: March 1993 and 1992" (Washington, D.C.: U.S. Government Printing Office, 1994), Series P20, no. 476, 96-98.

Table 12-13 School Desegregation, by Region, 1968-1991[a]

Region/year	Percentage of black students in schools with more than half minority students	Percentage of Hispanic students in schools with more than half minority students	Percentage of black students in schools 90-100 percent minority	Percentage of Hispanic students in schools 90-100 percent minority
South 1968	80.9	69.6	77.8	33.7
1972	55.3	69.9	24.7	31.4
1976	54.9	70.9	22.4	32.2
1980	57.1	76.0	23.0	37.3
1984	56.9	75.4	24.2	37.3
1986	58.0	75.2	25.1	38.6
1988	56.5	80.2	24.0	37.9
1991	60.8	76.8	26.6	38.6
Change 1968 to 1991	−20.1	+7.2	−51.2	+4.9
Border 1968	71.6	—	60.2	—
1972	67.2	—	54.7	—
1976	60.1	—	42.5	—
1980	59.2	—	37.0	—
1984	62.5	—	37.4	—
1986	59.3	29.9	35.6	—
1988	59.6	—	34.5	—
1991	59.3	37.4	33.2	10.8
Change 1968 to 1991	−12.3	—	−27.0	—
Northeast 1968	66.8	74.8	42.7	44.0
1972	69.9	74.4	46.9	44.1
1976	72.5	74.9	51.4	45.8
1980	79.9	76.3	48.7	45.8
1984	73.1	77.5	47.4	47.1
1986	72.8	78.2	49.8	46.4
1988	77.3	79.7	48.0	44.2
1991	76.2	78.1	50.1	46.2
Change 1968 to 1991	+9.4	+3.3	+7.4	+2.2
Midwest 1968	77.3	31.8	58.0	**6.8**
1972	75.3	34.4	57.4	**9.5**
1976	70.3	39.3	51.1	**14.1**
1980	69.5	46.6	43.6	19.6
1984	70.7	53.9	43.6	24.2
1986	69.8	54.3	38.5	23.5
1988	70.1	52.3	41.8	24.9
1991	69.9	53.5	39.4	21.1
Change 1968 to 1991	−7.4	+21.7	−18.6	+14.3

(Table continues)

Table 12-13 (*Continued*)

Region/year	Percentage of black students in schools with more than half minority students	Percentage of Hispanic students in schools with more than half minority students	Percentage of black students in schools 90-100 percent minority	Percentage of Hispanic students in schools 90-100 percent minority
West 1968	72.2	42.4	50.8	11.7
1972	68.1	44.7	42.7	11.5
1976	67.4	52.7	36.3	13.3
1980	66.8	63.5	33.7	18.5
1984	66.9	68.4	29.4	22.9
1986	68.2	69.9	28.3	24.7
1988	67.1	71.3	28.6	27.5
1991	69.7	73.5	26.4	29.7
Change 1968 to 1991	−2.5	+31.1	−24.4	+18.0
Total 1968	76.6	54.8	64.3	23.1
1972	63.6	56.6	38.7	23.3
1976	62.4	60.8	35.9	24.8
1980	62.9	68.1	33.2	28.8
1984	63.5	70.6	33.2	31.0
1986	63.3	71.5	32.5	32.2
1988	63.2	—	32.1	—
1991	66.0	73.4	33.9	34.0
Change 1968 to 1991	−10.6	+18.6	−30.4	+10.9

Note: "—" indicates not available. For composition of regions, see Appendix Table A-4.

[a] 1968-1969 to 1991-1992 school years.

Sources: 1968-1980: Gary Orfield, testimony before the House Subcommittee on Civil and Constitutional Rights, *Civil Rights Implications of the Education Block Grant Program*, September 9, 1982, 67-72; 1984-1986: Reprinted with permission from Gary Orfield, Franklin Monfort, Melissa Aaron, "Status of School Desegregation 1968-1986" (Alexandria, Va.: National School Boards Association, 1989), 5,7; 1988: Reprinted with permission from Gary Orfield and Franklin Monfort, "Status of School Desegregation: The Next Generation" (Alexandria, Va.: National School Boards Association, 1992), 3, 7-8. 1991: Gary Orfield, "The Growth of Segregation in American Schools: Changing Patterns of Separation and Poverty Since 1968" (Alexandria, Va: National School Boards Association, 1993), 9. Copyright 1989, 1992, and 1993 National School Boards Association. All rights reserved.

Table 12-14 Public Opinion of Whites on School and Neighborhood
Integration, 1942-1990 (percent)

Date	Blacks and whites should attend		
	Same schools	Separate schools	Don't know
June 1942	30	66	4
September 1956	48	49	3
December 1963	65	29	6
June 1964	62	32	5
October 1965	68	28	4
April 1970	74	24	3
March 1972	85	14	2
November 1972	80	15	5
March 1976	83	15	3
March 1977	85	14	2
March 1980	86	12	2
March 1982	88	9	2
March 1984	90	8	2
March 1985	92	7	1

Date	If blacks lived next door			
	Would definitely move	Might move	Would not move	Don't know
1958	21	23	56	—
1963	20	25	55	—
1965	13	22	65	—
1966	13	21	66	—
1967	12	23	65	—
1978	4	9	84	3
1990	1	4	93	2

Date	If many blacks lived in neighborhood			
	Would definitely move	Might move	Would not move	Don't know
1958	50	30	21	—
1963	49	29	22	—
1965	40	29	31	—
1966	39	31	30	—
1967	40	31	29	—
1978	20	31	45	4
1990	8	18	68	6

Note: "—" indicates not available. School questions: "Do you think white students and
(Negro/black) students should go to the same schools or to separate schools?" Asked of whites
only. Neighborhood questions: "If (colored/black) people came to live next door, would you
move?" "Would you move if (colored/black) people came to live in great numbers in your
neighborhood?" Asked of nonblacks only.

Sources: Schools (1942-1970): November 1972, National Opinion Research Center; (March 1972,
1976-1985): General Social Survey, National Opinion Research Center, University of Chicago;
neighborhood integration: *Gallup Poll Monthly*, June 1990, 27; and unpublished data from the
Gallup Poll.

Table 12-15 Public Opinion of Whites on School Integration, by Racial Composition of School, 1958-1994 (percent)

| Date | Object to own children attending school with | | |
	A few blacks	Half blacks	More than half blacks
September 1958	25	53	70
February 1959	20	47	71
May 1963	25	52	75
April 1965	16	42	67
June 1965	20	44	68
May 1966	11	41	67
July 1969	11	38	66
March 1970	8	32	66
April 1970	10	34	63
March 1972	6	25	55
August 1973	9	36	67
March 1974	4	33	67
March 1975	6	38	66
September 1975	7	35	62
March 1977	7	26	64
March 1978	4	24	61
July 1978	7	36	67
December 1980	6	28	62
March 1982	4	21	54
March 1983	3	25	65
March 1985	4	22	60
March 1986	4	24	64
March 1988	3	21	62
March 1989	4	23	58
March 1990	2	20	59
March 1991	4	26	62
March 1993	2	19	54
March 1994	4	21	54

Note: Question: "Would you, yourself, have any objection to sending your children to a school where a few of the children are (Negroes/blacks)?" If no: "Where half of the children are (Negroes/blacks)?" If no: "Where more than half of the children are (Negroes/blacks)?" Those saying "don't know" were assumed to have expressed some objection. Question asked of non-blacks with school-age children only.

Sources: 1958-1970, 1973, September 1975, July 1978, 1980: Gallup surveys; other years: General Social Survey.

Table 12-16 Black Elected Officials, by Category of Office, 1970-1993

Year	Federal	State	Substate regional	County	Muni-cipal	Judicial, law en-forcement	Educa-tion	Total
1970	10	169	—	92	623	213	362	1,469
1971	14	202	—	120	785	274	465	1,860
1972	14	210	—	176	932	263	669	2,264
1973	16	240	—	211	1,053	334	767	2,621
1974	17	239	—	242	1,360	340	793	2,991
1975	18	281	—	305	1,573	387	939	3,503
1976	18	281	30	355	1,889	412	994	3,979
1977	17	299	33	381	2,083	447	1,051	4,311
1978	17	299	26	410	2,159	454	1,138	4,503
1979	17	313	25	398	2,224	486	1,144	4,607
1980	17	323	25	451	2,356	526	1,214	4,912
1981	18	341	30	449	2,384	549	1,267	5,038
1982	18	336	35	465	2,477	563	1,266	5,160
1983	21	379	29	496	2,697	607	1,377	5,606
1984[a]	21	389	30	518	2,735	636	1,371	5,700
1985	20	396	32	611	2,898	661	1,438	6,056
1986	20	400	31	681	3,112	676	1,504	6,424
1987	23	417	23	724	3,219	728	1,547	6,681
1988	23	413	22	742	3,341	738	1,550	6,829
1989	24	424	18	793	3,595	760	1,612	7,226
1990	24	423	18	810	3,671	769	1,655	7,370
1991	26	458	15	810	3,683	847	1,638	7,480
1992	26	484	15	857	3,697	847	1,623	7,552
1993	39	533	13	913	3,903	922	1,689	8,015

Note: "—" indicates not available. Figures are for January of the year indicated. In 1992 and 1993 the total includes two shadow senators and one shadow representative from the District of Columbia.

[a] The 1984 figures reflect blacks who took office during the seven-month period between July 1, 1983, and January 30, 1984.

Source: Black Elected Officials: A National Roster. (Washington, D.C.: Joint Center for Political and Economic Studies Press, 1994), xxii.

Table 12-17 Black Elected Officials and Black Voting-Age Population (VAP), by State, 1993

State	Number of black elected officials	Total number of elected officials	Percentage of blacks among elected officials	Percentage black VAP	Ratio of percent black elected officials to percent black VAP[a]
Alabama	699	4,315	16.2	22.9	.707
Alaska	3	1,757	.2	3.8	.053
Arizona	15	3,183	.5	2.8	.179
Arkansas	380	8,331	4.6	13.7	.336
California	273	19,236	1.4	7.4	.189
Colorado	20	8,035	.2	3.9	.051
Connecticut	62	8,489	.7	7.8	.090
Delaware	23	1,227	1.9	16.4	.116
District of Columbia	198	325	60.9	64.3	.947
Florida	200	5,256	3.8	11.8	.322
Georgia	545	6,556	8.3	24.6	.338
Hawaii	0	160	.0	2.1	.000
Idaho	0	4,678	.0	.4	.000
Illinois	465	38,936	1.2	13.9	.086
Indiana	72	11,355	.6	7.3	.082
Iowa	11	17,044	.1	1.5	.067
Kansas	21	16,410	.1	5.4	.019
Kentucky	63	7,388	.9	6.7	.134
Louisiana	636	4,966	12.8	28.5	.449
Maine	1	6,978	.0	.3	.000
Maryland	140	1,943	7.2	24.4	.295
Massachusetts	30	13,631	.2	4.9	.041
Michigan	333	19,923	1.7	13.2	.129
Minnesota	16	18,887	.1	1.9	.053
Mississippi	751	4,944	15.2	32.0	.475
Missouri	185	17,115	1.1	9.8	.112
Montana	0	5,646	.0	.2	.000
Nebraska	6	15,064	.0	3.3	.000
Nevada	10	1,174	.9	5.9	.153
New Hampshire	2	6,721	.0	.6	.000
New Jersey	211	9,345	2.3	13.1	.176
New Mexico	3	2,096	.1	1.8	.056
New York	299	25,999	1.2	16.1	.075
North Carolina	468	5,531	8.5	20.2	.421
North Dakota	0	15,141	.0	.4	.000
Ohio	219	19,750	1.1	10.0	.110
Oklahoma	123	9,290	1.3	6.7	.194
Oregon	10	8,367	.1	1.5	.067
Pennsylvania	158	29,586	.5	8.7	.057
Rhode Island	12	1,120	1.1	3.7	.297
South Carolina	450	3,692	12.2	27.1	.450
South Dakota	3	9,249	.0	.2	.000
Tennessee	168	6,841	2.5	14.6	.171

Table 12-17 (*Continued*)

State	Number of black elected officials	Total number of elected officials	Percentage of blacks among elected officials	Percentage black VAP	Ratio of percent black elected officials to percent black VAP[a]
Texas	472	26,932	1.8	11.5	.157
Utah	0	2,588	.0	.7	.000
Vermont	2	8,021	.0	.2	.000
Virginia	155	3,112	5.0	17.8	.281
Washington	19	8,032	.2	2.8	.071
West Virginia	21	2,838	.7	2.9	.241
Wisconsin	30	18,242	.2	4.3	.047
Wyoming	1	2,340	.0	.6	.000
Total	7,984	497,785	1.6	11.0	.146

Note: Numbers of black elected officials are as of January 1993.

[a] Ratios calculated before rounding.

Sources: number of black elected officials and total number of elected officials: Joint Center for Political and Economic Studies, *Black Elected Officials: A National Roster* (Washington, D.C.: Joint Center for Political and Economic Studies, 1993), xxiii; voting-age population: U.S. Bureau of the Census, Current Population Reports, "Projections of the Population of Voting Age for States: November 1992" (Washington, D.C.: U.S. Government Printing Office, 1992), Series P-25, no. 1085, 5-10.

Table 12-18 Blacks, Hispanics, and Women as a Percentage of State Legislators and State Voting-Age Population, 1995

State	Total number of legislators	Blacks				Hispanics				Women			
		Legislators	Percentage	Percentage VAP	Ratio[a]	Legislators	Percentage	Percentage VAP	Ratio[a]	Legislators	Percentage	Percentage VAP	Ratio[a]
Alabama	140	35	25.0	23.0	1.087	0	.0	.6	.000	5	3.6	53.1	.067
Alaska	60	1	1.7	3.7	.450	1	1.6	3.0	.556	14	23.3	47.3	.456
Arizona	90	4	4.4	2.7	1.646	10	11.1	17.6	.631	27	30.0	51.4	.697
Arkansas	135	13	9.6	13.6	.708	1	.7	1.0	.741	17	12.6	52.8	.182
California	120	9	7.5	7.3	1.027	12	10.0	24.7	.405	25	20.8	50.4	.463
Colorado	100	3	3.0	3.9	.769	9	9.0	11.8	.763	31	31.0	51.0	.668
Connecticut	187	13	7.0	7.9	.880	12	6.4	6.4	1.003	50	26.7	52.4	.480
Delaware	62	3	4.8	16.5	.293	0	.0	2.1	.000	13	21.0	52.2	.277
Florida	160	20	12.5	12.1	1.033	14	8.8	13.1	.668	31	19.4	52.5	.334
Georgia	236	42	17.8	25.0	.712	0	.0	1.8	.000	43	18.2	52.4	.332
Hawaii	76	0	.0	2.4	.000	2	2.6	7.1	.371	16	21.1	49.6	.475
Idaho	105	0	.0	.2	.000	1	1.0	5.1	.187	30	28.6	50.8	.600
Illinois	177	22	12.4	14.0	.888	6	3.4	7.7	.440	42	23.7	52.2	.444
Indiana	150	12	8.0	7.4	1.081	2	1.3	1.8	.741	33	22.0	52.3	.368
Iowa	150	1	.7	1.8	.370	0	.0	1.2	.000	27	18.0	52.3	.280
Kansas	165	7	4.2	5.6	.758	4	2.4	3.7	.655	46	27.9	51.6	.551
Kentucky	138	5	3.6	6.8	.533	0	.0	.6	.000	11	8.0	52.4	.080
Louisiana	144	30	20.8	28.5	.731	3	2.1	2.5	.833	14	9.7	52.9	.131
Maine	186	0	.0	.2	.000	0	.0	.5	.000	50	26.9	52.1	.598
Maryland	188	36	19.1	25.1	.763	0	.0	2.8	.000	54	28.7	52.4	.447
Massachusetts	200	8	4.0	5.0	.800	0	.0	4.6	.000	48	24.0	52.8	.434
Michigan	148	16	10.8	13.5	.801	0	.0	2.1	.000	33	22.3	52.3	.375
Minnesota	201	1	.5	1.9	.262	2	1.0	1.2	.829	50	24.9	51.6	.530
Mississippi	174	47	27.0	32.0	.844	0	.0	.7	.000	20	11.5	53.4	.205
Missouri	197	16	8.1	9.9	.820	0	.0	1.2	.000	39	19.8	52.7	.366

State	Total legislators	Black: Number	Black: % of legislators	Black: % of voting-age pop	Black: Ratio[a]	Hispanic: Number	Hispanic: % of legislators	Hispanic: % of voting-age pop	Hispanic: Ratio[a]	Women: Number	Women: % of legislators	Women: % of voting-age pop	Women: Ratio[a]
Montana	150	0	.0	.2	.000	0	.0	1.3	.000	36	24.0	51.0	.377
Nebraska	49	1	2.0	3.4	.600	0	.0	2.4	.000	12	24.5	52.0	.391
Nevada	63	6	9.5	6.1	1.561	1	1.6	11.2	.142	22	34.9	49.5	.550
New Hampshire	424	1	.2	.4	.590	0	.0	.9	.000	128	30.2	51.7	.653
New Jersey	120	11	9.2	13.3	.689	1	.8	10.2	.080	16	13.3	52.5	.238
New Mexico	112	2	1.8	1.8	.992	43	38.4	37.2	1.032	23	20.5	51.4	.380
New York	211	26	12.3	16.5	.747	10	4.7	11.9	.398	38	18.0	53.0	.304
North Carolina	170	24	14.1	20.3	.695	0	.0	1.2	.000	27	15.9	52.3	.347
North Dakota	147	0	.0	.4	.000	0	.0	.7	.000	22	15.0	50.7	.321
Ohio	132	16	12.1	10.2	1.188	0	.0	1.3	.000	32	24.2	52.7	.402
Oklahoma	149	5	3.4	6.7	.501	0	.0	2.6	.000	16	10.7	52.1	.180
Oregon	90	3	3.3	1.5	2.222	0	.0	3.8	.000	24	26.7	51.4	.518
Pennsylvania	253	18	7.1	8.7	.818	1	.4	2.0	.198	30	11.9	53.0	.186
Rhode Island	150	8	5.3	3.8	1.404	1	.7	4.8	.139	36	24.0	52.7	.465
South Carolina	170	31	18.2	27.5	.663	0	.0	.9	.000	21	12.4	52.4	.246
South Dakota	105	1	1.0	.4	2.381	0	.0	.8	.000	19	18.1	51.3	.388
Tennessee	132	16	12.1	14.5	.836	0	.0	.4	.000	18	13.6	52.8	.229
Texas	181	15	8.3	11.4	.727	35	19.3	24.9	.777	33	18.2	51.5	.312
Utah	104	0	.0	.7	.000	1	1.0	4.8	.200	15	14.4	51.0	.263
Vermont	180	1	.6	.2	2.778	0	.0	.5	.000	53	29.4	51.7	.652
Virginia	140	13	9.3	17.9	.519	0	.0	2.7	.000	16	11.4	51.6	.221
Washington	147	2	1.4	2.7	.504	3	2.0	4.3	.475	58	39.5	50.9	.776
West Virginia	134	3	2.2	2.7	.829	0	.0	.6	.000	20	14.9	52.9	.309
Wisconsin	132	8	6.1	4.6	1.318	0	.0	1.7	.000	32	24.2	51.8	.527
Wyoming	90	0	.0	.6	.000	1	1.1	5.8	.192	18	21.1	50.1	.488
United States	7,424	555	7.5	11.4	.656	176	2.4	7.8	.304	1,535	20.7	52.0	.392

Note: Hispanics may be of any race. The counts of legislators are as of January 1995.

a The ratio between the group's indicated percentage of state legislators and the group's percentage of the state voting-age population. Calculated before rounding.

Sources: Total number of legislators and women legislators: Center for the American Woman and Politics, Eagleton Institute of Politics, Rutgers University, "Women in State Legislatures 1995," March 1995; black legislators: Joint Center for Political and Economic Studies; Hispanic legislators: National Association of Latino Elected and Appointed Officials Educational Fund, 1994 National Roster of Hispanic Elected Officials (Washington, D.C.: NALEO Educational Fund), and unpublished data; voting-age population, U.S. Bureau of the Census, Current Population Reports, "Projections of the Voting Age Population for States: November 1994" (Washington, D.C.: U.S. Government Printing Office, 1994), Series P-25, no. 1117, 8-16.

Table 12-19 State and Local Government Employment and Salary, by Sex, Race, and Hispanic Origin, 1973-1993 (thousands)

| | Employment | | | | | | | Median annual salary | | | | | | |
| | | | | | Minority | | | | | | | Minority | | |
Year	Male	Female	White[a]	Total	Black[a]	Hispanic	Total[b]	Male	Female	White[a]	Total	Black[a]	Hispanic	Total[b]
1973	2,486	1,322	3,115	3,809	523	125	693	$9.6	$7.0	$8.8	$8.6	$7.4	$7.4	$7.5
1975	2,436	1,464	3,102	3,899	602	147	797	11.3	8.2	10.2	9.8	8.6	8.9	8.8
1977	2,737	1,678	3,480	4,415	705	175	935	12.4	9.1	11.3	10.9	9.5	9.9	9.7
1978	2,711	1,736	3,481	4,447	723	181	966	13.3	9.7	12.0	11.7	10.1	10.7	10.4
1979	2,761	1,816	3,568	4,576	751	192	1,008	14.1	10.4	12.8	12.3	10.6	11.4	10.9
1980	2,350	1,637	3,146	3,987	619	163	842	15.2	11.4	13.8	13.3	11.5	12.3	11.8
1981	2,740	1,925	3,591	4,665	780	205	1,074	17.7	13.1	16.1	15.6	13.3	14.7	13.5
1983	2,674	1,818	3,423	4,492	768	219	1,069	20.1	15.3	18.5	18.0	15.6	17.3	15.9
1984	2,700	1,880	3,458	4,580	799	233	1,121	21.4	16.2	19.6	19.1	16.5	18.4	17.4
1985	2,789	1,952	3,563	4,742	835	248	1,179	22.3	17.3	20.6	19.9	17.5	19.2	18.4
1986	2,797	1,982	3,549	4,779	865	259	1,230	23.4	18.1	21.5	—	18.7	20.2	19.6
1987	2,818	2,031	3,600	4,849	872	268	1,249	24.1	18.9	22.4	—	19.3	21.1	20.9
1989	3,030	2,227	3,863	5,257	961	308	1,394	26.1	20.6	24.1	—	20.7	22.7	22.1
1990	3,071	2,302	3,918	5,374	994	327	1,456	27.3	21.8	25.2	—	22.0	23.8	23.3
1991[c]	3,110	2,349	3,965	5,459	1,011	340	1,494	28.4	22.7	26.4	25.5	22.7	24.5	—
1993	2,820	2,204	3,588	5,024	948	341	1,436	30.6	24.3	28.5	27.7	24.2	26.8	—

Note: "—" indicates not available. Full-time employment as of June 30, excludes school systems and educational institutions. Amounts in current dollars.

[a] Non-Hispanic.

[b] Includes other minority groups, not shown separately.

[c] Due to reporting changes, data from 1993 are not comparable to previous years.

Sources: 1975-1991: U.S. Equal Employment Opportunity Commission, *State and Local Government Information Report* (Washington, D.C.: U.S. Government Printing Office), annual volumes; 1993: U.S. Equal Employment Opportunity Commission, *Job Patterns for Minorities and Women in State and Local Government,* 1993.

Table 12-20 Federal Employment, by Government Service (GS) Salary
Level, Race/Ethnic Group, and Sex, 1993

Government service (GS) salary level	Total number	Percentage black	Percentage Hispanic	Percentage female
GS-01 $12,141-15,183	3,891	40.0	12.6	72.5
GS-02 $13,650-17,174	7,888	34.2	9.8	67.3
GS-03 $14,895-19,368	42,562	27.9	8.8	67.0
GS-04 $16,721-21,734	123,304	28.4	6.7	73.1
GS-05 $18,707-24,323	186,177	24.6	6.5	74.2
GS-06 $20,852-27,107	114,413	25.2	5.7	75.9
GS-07 $23,171-30,119	153,113	21.9	6.3	65.5
GS-08 $25,662-33,357	42,956	24.1	6.1	64.2
GS-09 $28,345-36,850	156,301	15.3	6.2	49.9
GS-10 $31,215-40,584	33,452	14.4	6.2	56.9
GS-11 $34,295-44,582	210,488	12.2	5.5	40.5
GS-12 $41,104-54,434	247,951	10.4	4.2	31.6
GS-13 $48,878-63,539	167,645	8.5	3.3	25.2
GS-14 $57,760-75,085	95,079	6.3	2.6	20.3
GS-15 $67,941-88,326	53,041	4.6	2.5	16.4
Total, all pay plans	2,110,510	16.7	5.6	43.7
Total, GS and related	1,638,241	16.6	5.3	49.5

Note: Amounts in current dollars. Pay schedules effective January 1995.

Source: Office of Personnel Management, unpublished data.

Table 12-21 Crime Rates, 1960-1993

	Violent crime					Property crime				Total
Year	Murder	Rape	Robbery	Aggravated assault	Total	Burglary	Larceny theft	Vehicle theft	Total	
1960	5.1	9.6	60	86	161	509	1,035	183	1,729	1,887
1965	5.1	12.1	72	111	200	663	1,329	257	2,249	2,249
1970	7.9	18.7	172	165	364	1,085	2,079	457	3,621	3,985
1975	9.6	26.3	218	227	482	1,526	2,805	469	4,800	5,282
1980	10.2	36.8	251	299	597	1,684	3,167	502	5,353	5,950
1981	9.8	36.0	259	290	594	1,650	3,140	475	5,264	5,858
1982	9.1	34.0	239	289	571	1,489	3,085	459	5,033	5,604
1983	8.3	33.7	217	279	538	1,338	2,869	431	4,637	5,175
1984	7.9	35.7	205	290	539	1,264	2,791	437	4,492	5,031
1985	7.9	36.7	209	303	556	1,287	2,901	462	4,651	5,207
1986	8.6	37.9	225	346	618	1,345	3,010	508	4,863	5,480
1987	8.3	37.4	213	351	610	1,330	3,081	529	4,940	5,550
1988	8.4	37.6	221	370	637	1,309	3,135	583	5,027	5,664
1989	8.7	38.1	233	383	663	1,276	3,171	630	5,077	5,740
1990	9.4	41.2	257	424	732	1,236	3,195	658	5,089	5,820
1991	9.8	42.3	273	433	758	1,252	3,229	659	5,140	5,898
1992	9.3	42.8	264	442	758	1,168	3,103	632	4,903	5,660
1993	9.5	40.6	256	440	746	1,099	3,032	605	4,737	5,483

Note: Figures are rates per 100,000 inhabitants. For definitions of crimes, see the sources. Data for additional years can be found in previous editions of *Vital Statistics on American Politics.*

Sources: 1960-1987: *Statistical Abstract of the United States, 1976* (Washington, D.C.: U.S. Government Printing Office, 1976), 153, *1987,* 155, *1989,* 166; 1988-1989: U.S. Department of Justice, Federal Bureau of Investigation, *Crime in the United States: Uniform Crime Reports 1989* (Washington, D.C.: U.S. Government Printing Office, 1990), 7, 14, 17, 22, 26, 31, 37; 1990-1991: *1991,* 5, 10, 13, 23, 26, 31, 35, 38, 43, 49; 1992-1993: 5, 10, 13, 23, 26, 31, 35, 38, 43, 49.

Table 12-22 Number of Federal and State Prisoners, 1925-1993, and Cost per Prisoner per Year, 1980-1993

Year	Number of prisoners	Rate (per 100,000 population)	Cost per prisoner per year
1925	91,669	79	—
1930	129,453	104	—
1935	144,180	113	—
1940	173,706	131	—
1945	133,649	98	—
1950	166,123	109	—
1955	185,780	112	—
1960	212,953	117	—
1965	210,895	108	—
1970	196,429	96	—
1973	204,211	96	—
1974	218,466	102	—
1975	240,593	111	—
1976	262,833	120	—
1977	285,456	129	—
1978	294,396	132	—
1979	301,470	133	—
1980	315,974	138	$10,350
1981	353,167	153	13,570
1982	394,374	170	15,830
1983	419,820	179	16,250
1984	443,398	188	17,320
1985	480,568	200	14,590
1986	522,084	216	15,220
1987	560,812	228	15,890
1988	603,732	244	16,320
1989	680,907	271	16,950
1990	739,980	292	17,550
1991	789,610	310	17,706
1992	847,271	330	18,330
1993	910,462	351	19,119

Note: "—" indicates not available. Definition of prisoners has varied somewhat over the years. See sources for details. Costs are in current dollars and are the averages for federal and state agencies. Costs are approximate due to variations in reporting practices. Data for additional years can be found in earlier editions of *Vital Statistics on American Politics.*

Sources: Number of prisoners and rate, 1925-1992: U.S. Department of Justice, Bureau of Justice Statistics, *Sourcebook of Criminal Justice Statistics, 1993* (Washington, D.C.: U.S. Government Printing Office, 1994), 600; 1993: U.S. Department of Justice, Bureau of Justice Statistics Bulletin, *Prisoners in 1993* (Washington, D.C.: U.S. Government Printing Office, 1994), 2; cost per prisoner: Criminal Justice Institute, *The Corrections Yearbook* (South Salem, N.Y.: Criminal Justice Institute), annual volumes, 1981-1993.

Table 12-23 Public Opinion on the Courts, 1965-1994

Date	Too harsh	About right	Not harsh enough	Don't know
April 1965	2	34	48	16
August 1965	2	27	60	12
February 1968	2	19	63	16
January 1969	2	13	74	10
March 1972	7	16	66	11
December 1972	4	13	74	8
March 1973	5	13	73	9
March 1974[a]	5	6	60	29
March 1974	6	10	78	7
March 1975	4	10	79	7
March 1976	3	10	81	6
March 1977	3	8	83	6
March 1978	3	7	85	5
March 1980	3	8	83	6
January 1981	3	13	77	7
March 1982[a]	4	5	76	14
March 1982	3	8	86	4
March 1983	4	6	85	4
March 1984	3	11	82	4
March 1985	3	9	84	3
March 1986	3	8	85	4
March 1987	3	12	79	6
March 1988	4	10	82	5
March 1989	3	9	84	4
March 1990	3	9	83	5
March 1991	4	11	80	5
March 1993	3	10	81	6
March 1994	3	8	85	5

Note: Question: "In general, do you think the courts in this area deal too harshly or not harshly enough with criminals?"

[a] In 1974 and 1982 half of the General Social Survey sample was asked the question as noted above and half the sample was asked the same question but with the phrase "or don't you have enough information about the courts to say" added at the end. The "don't know" column for these rows includes those saying "not enough information."

Sources: 1965-1969, December 1972: Gallup survey; 1981: *Los Angeles Times* survey; others: General Social Survey.

13

Economic Policy

Economic policy makers labor under the burden of an overabundance of numbers. Statistics recording various aspects of the economy's performance appear regularly—often monthly. These statistics are important, not simply because of the conditions they report, but for the way they filter into economic calculations: expectations and reactions to indicators of past performance are critical determinants of how the economy performs in the future. Moreover, there is a direct link to politics because the public's perceptions of economic performance help shape choices in the voting booth: properly or not, presidents often get blamed when the economy turns down and (less often) praised when it recovers. President Ronald Reagan's public approval ratings plummeted as an economic downturn continued through 1982 (Figure 8-2). The subsequent economic recovery played a substantial role in shaping the mood of the voters to secure Reagan's 1984 reelection in a landslide.

When one turns to even simple economic matters, fundamental issues and terms arise that distinguish the discourse from that in other areas of politics. One is the overall size of the economy, usually measured by the gross domestic product, or GDP (Table 13-1).[1] Knowing what the GDP is and what it means is important to even a minimal understanding of economic statistics and policy. Without some sense of the size of the economy, it is impossible to make informed judgments about economic matters. For example, a trillion-dollar national debt is unquestionably large, but many argue that it is not overburdening because it in fact represents the same proportion of the total economy as numerically smaller deficits did in earlier years (Figure 13-2).

A second key concept is that of constant dollars, which is explained in the introduction to Chapter 11 in connection with defense spending. A few additional points are appropriate here. Note that the basis for many constant dollar calculations is the Consumer Price Index, or CPI (Table 13-2). One can see from this index that a market basket of goods that cost $100 in 1982-1984 would have cost $29.60 in 1960. Unfortunately, while 1982-1984 is the base period in Table 13-2, other tabulations, such as those in Table 13-1, use a different base. This makes it more difficult to compare the data. However, the concept of a constant dollar is unchanged by which year is used as the base. (However, the CPI is not always used as the basis for such adjustments, and here it is not possible to move precisely from the figures in Table 13-2 to those in 13-1.)

During Ronald Reagan's and George Bush's presidencies, economic news was dominated by the deficit. The growth in the federal deficit (Table 13-6) helped focus public attention on government spending and taxing, as politicians and economists alike tried to assess ways of reducing the gap between income and expenditures. Economic growth could provide the basis for greater tax revenues to balance the budget and reduce the deficit ("Grow our way out," as Reagan insisted). But as the national debt has continued to mount in relation to GDP (Figure 13-2), the political and economic demands for reduction of the debt have constrained government spending and compelled consideration of additional revenue sources. Tax increases are one means of reducing the federal deficit: Table 13-7 displays the revenue loss to the federal government from selected tax breaks, some of which have already been curtailed to raise revenue.

Cutting spending is another means of deficit reduction. Although federal budget outlays by function (Table 13-4) may give the impression of vast sums and a variety of programs suitable for cuts, the data in Table 13-5 show that mandatory programs account for half of federal budget outlays. An increasing proportion of the federal budget has become relatively uncontrollable from the president's standpoint. Reducing spending in the mandatory category would require that Congress rewrite laws affecting payments to which beneficiaries are entitled on the basis of past commitments. Programs that fall under this heading, such as Social Security, are referred to as entitlement programs.

Unemployment and inflation are two other noteworthy features of the economic landscape that merit inclusion when considering politics. The large-scale entry of women into the labor force since World War II (Table 13-8), the fluctuations in the annual unemployment rate since 1929 (Table 13-9), and the relatively high unemployment rates among black teenagers (Table 13-10) document critical economic trends with political ramifications.

Because economic issues are an important aspect of political policy making and because economic conditions affect voter choices, economic data rank among the most vital of vital statistics on American politics.

Notes

1. Beginning in 1991, the Bureau of Economic Analysis began using gross domestic product (GDP), rather than gross national product (GNP), as the primary measure of U.S. production. Other government agencies have also switched to GDP. Consequently, many of the tables in this volume use the GDP base. In some instances, however, the reporting agency has not yet made the shift, and of necessity we rely on the values as reported. So that readers can have some sense of the magnitude of this change, which is generally very small, we present both GDP and GNP in Table 13-1. A detailed accounting of the meaning of, and difference between, the two measures is U.S. Department of Commerce, *National Income and Product Accounts of the United States*, (Washington, D.C.: U.S. Government Printing Office, 1993), volume 1, M-5.

Table 13-1 Gross National and Gross Domestic Products, 1929-1994 (billions)

Year	Current dollars		Annual percentage change		Constant (1987) dollars		Annual percentage change	
	GNP	GDP	GNP	GDP	GNP	GDP	GNP	GDP
1929	$103.9	$103.1	—	—	$827.4	$821.8	—	—
1930	91.1	90.4	-12.3	-12.4	754.2	748.9	-8.8	-8.9
1931	76.3	75.8	-16.2	-16.2	695.5	691.3	-7.8	-7.7
1932	58.3	58.0	-23.6	-23.5	603.0	599.7	-13.3	-13.3
1933	55.9	55.6	-4.1	-4.1	589.9	587.1	-2.2	-2.1
1934	65.4	65.1	17.0	17.1	634.8	632.6	7.6	7.7
1935	72.7	72.3	11.2	11.1	684.1	681.3	7.8	7.7
1936	83.0	82.7	14.2	14.4	780.0	777.9	14.0	14.2
1937	91.2	90.8	9.9	9.8	814.5	811.4	4.4	4.3
1938	85.3	84.9	-6.5	-6.5	782.2	778.9	-4.0	-4.0
1939	91.3	90.8	7.0	7.0	844.2	840.7	7.9	7.9
1940	100.4	100.0	10.0	10.2	908.8	906.0	7.7	7.8
1941	125.5	125.0	25.0	25.0	1,074.4	1,070.6	18.2	18.2
1942	159.0	158.5	26.7	26.8	1,288.4	1,284.9	19.9	20.0
1943	192.8	192.4	21.3	21.3	1,543.6	1,540.5	19.8	19.9
1944	211.5	211.0	9.7	9.7	1,673.3	1,670.0	8.4	8.4
1945	213.5	213.1	1.0	1.0	1,605.0	1,602.6	-4.1	-4.0
1946	212.6	211.9	-0.4	-0.6	1,276.0	1,272.1	-20.5	-20.6
1947	235.5	234.3	10.8	10.6	1,258.5	1,252.8	-1.4	-1.5
1948	261.8	260.3	11.2	11.1	1,307.0	1,300.0	3.9	3.8
1949	260.7	259.3	-0.4	-0.4	1,311.8	1,305.5	0.4	0.4
1950	288.5	287.0	10.7	10.7	1,425.6	1,418.5	8.7	8.7
1951	333.6	331.6	15.6	15.5	1,567.4	1,558.4	9.9	9.9
1952	351.8	349.7	5.5	5.4	1,634.3	1,624.9	4.3	4.3
1953	372.0	370.0	5.7	5.8	1,694.2	1,685.5	3.7	3.7
1954	373.1	370.9	0.3	0.2	1,683.3	1,673.8	-0.6	-0.7

Year								
1955	406.8	404.3	9.0	9.0	1,779.0	1,768.3	5.7	5.6
1956	429.1	426.2	5.5	5.4	1,815.5	1,803.6	2.1	2.0
1957	451.8	448.6	5.3	5.2	1,850.9	1,838.2	1.9	1.9
1958	457.5	454.7	1.3	1.4	1,839.7	1,829.1	-0.6	-0.5
1959	497.0	494.2	8.6	8.7	1,939.6	1,928.8	5.4	5.5
1960	516.6	513.4	3.9	3.9	1,982.8	1,970.8	2.2	2.2
1961	535.4	531.8	3.6	3.6	2,037.1	2,023.8	2.7	2.7
1962	575.8	571.6	7.5	7.5	2,143.3	2,128.1	5.2	5.2
1963	607.7	603.1	5.5	5.5	2,231.9	2,215.6	4.1	4.1
1964	653.0	648.0	7.5	7.4	2,358.2	2,340.6	5.7	5.6
1965	708.1	702.7	8.4	8.4	2,489.0	2,470.5	5.5	5.5
1966	774.9	769.8	9.4	9.5	2,633.2	2,616.2	5.8	5.9
1967	819.8	814.3	5.8	5.8	2,702.6	2,685.2	2.6	2.6
1968	895.5	889.3	9.2	9.2	2,815.7	2,796.9	4.2	4.2
1969	965.6	959.5	7.8	7.9	2,890.9	2,873.0	2.7	2.7
1970	1,017.1	1,017.7	5.3	5.3	2,891.6	2,873.9	0.0	0.0
1971	1,104.9	1,097.2	8.6	8.6	2,976.0	2,955.9	2.9	2.9
1972	1,215.7	1,207.0	10.0	10.0	3,128.8	3,107.1	5.1	5.1
1973	1,362.3	1,349.6	12.1	11.8	3,298.6	3,268.6	5.4	5.2
1974	1,474.3	1,458.6	8.2	8.1	3,282.4	3,248.1	-0.5	-0.6
1975	1,599.1	1,585.9	8.5	8.7	3,247.6	3,221.7	-1.1	-0.8
1976	1,785.5	1,768.4	11.7	11.5	3,412.2	3,380.8	5.1	4.9
1977	1,994.6	1,974.1	11.7	11.6	3,569.0	3,533.3	4.6	4.5
1978	2,254.5	2,232.7	13.0	13.1	3,739.0	3,703.5	4.8	4.8
1979	2,520.8	2,488.6	11.8	11.5	3,845.3	3,796.8	2.8	2.5
1980	2,742.1	2,708.0	8.8	8.8	3,823.4	3,776.3	-0.6	-0.5
1981	3,063.8	3,030.6	11.7	11.9	3,884.4	3,843.1	1.6	1.8
1982	3,179.8	3,149.6	3.8	3.9	3,796.1	3,760.3	-2.3	-2.2
1983	3,434.4	3,405.0	8.0	8.1	3,939.6	3,906.6	3.8	3.9
1984	3,801.5	3,777.2	10.7	10.9	4,174.5	4,148.5	6.0	6.2
1985	4,053.6	4,038.7	6.6	6.9	4,295.0	4,279.8	2.9	3.2

(Table continues)

Table 13-1 *(Continued)*

Year	Current dollars		Annual percentage change		Constant (1987) dollars		Annual percentage change	
	GNP	GDP	GNP	GDP	GNP	GDP	GNP	GDP
1986	$4,277.7	$4,268.6	5.5	5.7	$4,413.5	$4,404.5	2.8	2.9
1987	4,544.5	4,539.9	6.2	6.4	4,544.5	4,539.9	3.0	3.1
1988	4,908.2	4,900.4	8.0	7.9	4,726.3	4,718.6	4.0	3.9
1989	5,266.8	5,250.8	7.3	7.2	4,852.7	4,838.0	2.7	2.5
1990	5,567.8	5,546.1	5.7	5.6	4,916.5	4,897.3	1.3	1.2
1991	5,740.8	5,724.8	3.1	3.2	4,882.3	4,867.6	-0.7	-0.6
1992	6,025.8	6,020.2	5.0	5.2	4,985.7	4,979.3	2.1	2.3
1993	6,347.8	6,343.3	5.3	5.4	5,140.3	5,134.5	3.1	3.1
1994	6,738.4	6,726.9	6.2	6.0	5,337.3	5,344.0	3.8	4.1

Note: "—" indicates data not available.

Sources: U.S. Department of Commerce, *Survey of Current Business* (Washington, D.C.: U.S. Government Printing Office, September 1994), 38, 41; 1994: (March 1995), 9.

Table 13-2 Consumer Price Index, 1950-1994

Year	All items	Food	Shelter	Fuel, oil, and other household fuel commodities	Gas and electricity	Apparel and upkeep	Transportation Private[a]	Transportation Public	Medical care	All commodities	All services
1950	24.1	25.4	—	11.3	19.2	40.3	24.5	13.4	15.1	29.0	16.9
1955	26.8	27.8	22.7	12.7	20.7	42.9	26.7	18.5	18.2	31.3	20.4
1960	29.6	30.0	25.2	13.8	23.3	45.7	30.6	22.2	22.3	33.6	24.1
1961	29.9	30.4	25.4	14.1	23.5	46.1	30.8	23.2	22.9	33.8	24.5
1962	30.2	30.6	25.8	14.2	23.5	46.3	31.4	24.0	23.5	34.1	25.0
1963	30.6	31.1	26.1	14.4	23.5	46.9	31.6	24.3	24.1	34.4	25.5
1964	31.0	31.5	26.5	14.4	23.5	47.3	32.0	24.7	24.6	34.8	26.0
1965	31.5	32.2	27.0	14.6	23.5	47.8	32.5	25.2	25.2	35.2	26.6
1966	32.4	33.8	27.8	15.0	23.6	49.0	32.9	26.1	26.3	36.1	27.6
1967	33.4	34.1	28.8	15.5	23.7	51.0	33.8	27.4	28.2	36.8	28.8
1968	34.8	35.3	30.1	16.0	23.9	53.7	34.8	28.7	29.9	38.1	30.3
1969	36.7	37.1	32.6	16.3	24.3	56.8	36.0	30.9	31.9	39.9	32.4
1970	38.8	39.2	35.5	17.0	25.4	59.2	37.5	35.2	34.0	41.7	35.0
1971	40.5	40.4	37.0	18.2	27.1	61.1	39.4	37.8	36.1	43.2	37.0
1972	41.8	42.1	38.7	18.3	28.5	62.3	39.7	39.3	37.3	44.5	38.4
1973	44.4	48.2	40.5	21.1	29.9	64.6	41.0	39.7	38.8	47.8	40.1
1974	49.3	55.1	44.4	33.2	34.5	69.4	46.2	40.6	42.4	53.5	43.8
1975	53.8	59.8	48.8	36.4	40.1	72.5	50.6	43.5	47.5	58.2	48.0
1976	56.9	61.6	51.5	38.8	44.7	75.2	55.6	47.8	52.0	60.7	52.0
1977	60.6	65.6	54.9	43.9	50.5	78.6	59.7	50.0	57.0	64.2	56.0
1978	65.2	72.0	60.5	46.2	55.0	81.4	62.5	51.5	61.8	68.8	60.8
1979	72.6	79.9	68.9	62.4	61.0	84.9	71.7	54.9	67.5	76.6	67.5

(Table continues)

Table 13-2 (Continued)

Year	All items	Food	Shelter	Fuel, oil, and other household fuel commodities	Gas and electricity	Apparel and upkeep	Transportation[b] Private[b]	Public	Medical care	All commodities	All services
1980	82.4	86.8	81.0	86.1	71.4	90.9	84.2	69.0	74.9	86.0	77.9
1981	90.9	93.6	90.5	104.6	81.9	95.3	93.8	85.6	82.9	93.2	88.1
1982	96.5	97.4	96.9	103.4	93.2	97.8	97.1	94.9	92.5	97.0	96.0
1983	99.6	99.4	99.1	97.2	101.5	100.2	99.3	99.5	100.6	99.8	99.4
1984	103.9	103.2	104.0	99.4	105.4	102.1	103.6	105.7	106.8	103.2	104.6
1985	107.6	105.6	109.8	95.9	107.1	105.0	106.2	110.5	113.5	105.4	109.9
1986	109.6	109.0	115.8	77.6	105.7	105.9	101.2	117.0	122.0	104.4	115.4
1987	113.6	113.5	121.3	77.9	103.8	110.6	104.2	121.1	130.1	107.7	120.2
1988	118.3	118.2	127.1	78.1	104.6	115.4	107.6	123.3	138.6	111.5	125.7
1989	124.0	125.1	132.8	81.7	107.5	118.6	112.9	129.5	149.3	116.7	131.9
1990	130.7	132.4	140.0	99.3	109.3	124.1	118.8	142.6	162.8	122.8	139.2
1991	136.2	136.3	146.3	94.6	112.6	128.7	121.9	148.9	177.0	126.6	146.3
1992	140.3	137.9	151.2	90.7	114.8	131.9	124.6	151.4	190.1	129.1	152.0
1993	144.5	140.9	155.7	90.3	118.5	133.7	127.5	167.0	201.4	131.5	157.9
1994	148.2	144.3	160.5	88.8	119.2	133.4	131.4	172.0	211.0	133.8	163.1

Note: "—" indicates not available. 1982–1984 equals 100. Data beginning in 1978 are for all urban consumers; earlier data are for urban wage earners and clerical workers. Data beginning 1983 incorporate a rental equivalence measure for homeowners' costs and therefore are not strictly comparable with earlier figures. Data for additional years can be found in earlier editions of *Vital Statistics on American Politics.*

[a] Includes direct pricing of new trucks and motorcycles beginning September 1982.

Sources: U.S. President, *Economic Report of the President* (Washington, D.C.: U.S. Government Printing Office, 1995), Table B-59.

Table 13-3 Federal Budget: Total, Defense, and Nondefense
Expenditures, 1940-2000 (billions)

	Current dollars			Constant (1987) dollars		
Year	National defense	Non-defense	Total	National defense	Non-defense	Total
1940	$1.7	$7.8	$9.5	$18.6	$78.2	$96.8
1941	6.4	7.2	13.7	64.9	70.4	135.3
1942	25.7	9.5	35.1	222.7	92.3	315.1
1943	66.7	11.9	78.6	537.9	116.9	655.2
1944	79.1	12.2	91.3	670.1	117.3	787.1
1945	83.0	9.7	92.7	731.6	81.2	812.6
1946	42.7	12.6	55.2	380.4	82.2	463.0
1947	12.8	21.7	34.5	101.6	129.0	230.6
1948	9.1	20.7	29.8	72.0	120.8	192.9
1949	13.2	25.7	38.8	97.1	148.3	245.5
1950	13.7	28.8	42.6	101.1	159.4	260.5
1951	23.6	21.9	45.5	171.5	114.4	285.9
1952	46.1	21.6	67.9	310.4	105.6	416.0
1953	52.8	23.3	76.1	332.1	112.5	444.5
1954	49.3	21.6	70.9	305.6	96.0	401.4
1955	42.7	25.7	68.4	261.8	118.2	380.0
1956	42.5	28.1	70.6	243.7	126.7	370.4
1957	45.4	31.1	76.6	245.0	134.6	379.7
1958	46.8	35.6	82.4	241.6	146.4	388.0
1959	49.0	43.1	92.1	233.2	176.2	409.5
1960	48.1	44.1	92.2	220.1	172.1	392.1
1961	49.6	48.1	97.7	221.2	184.7	406.0
1962	52.3	54.5	106.8	228.0	208.1	436.0
1963	53.4	57.9	111.3	222.9	214.7	437.6
1964	54.8	63.8	118.5	224.0	232.7	456.6
1965	50.6	67.6	118.2	203.9	242.1	446.1
1966	58.1	76.4	134.5	225.9	266.6	492.4
1967	71.4	86.0	157.5	269.1	290.8	560.0
1968	81.9	96.2	178.1	295.5	313.0	608.6
1969	82.5	101.1	183.6	282.5	311.4	593.9
1970	81.7	114.0	195.6	262.9	333.1	596.1
1971	78.9	131.3	210.2	236.9	362.3	599.1
1972	79.2	151.5	230.7	219.7	397.8	617.5
1973	76.7	169.0	245.7	197.2	423.1	620.3
1974	79.3	190.0	269.4	185.3	440.0	625.4
1975	86.5	245.8	332.3	183.9	514.6	698.5
1976	89.6	282.2	371.8	177.8	551.6	729.3
TQ[a]	22.3	73.7	96.0	42.4	139.2	181.5
1977	97.2	312.0	409.2	176.8	564.2	740.9
1978	104.5	354.3	458.7	177.2	596.7	773.9
1979	116.3	387.1	503.5	180.4	601.2	781.7
1980	134.0	457.0	590.9	187.1	645.0	832.1
1981	157.5	520.7	678.2	198.2	669.5	867.7

(Table continues)

Table 13-3 *(Continued)*

Year	Current dollars			Constant (1987) dollars		
	National defense	Non-defense	Total	National defense	Non-defense	Total
1982	$185.3	$560.4	$745.7	$214.3	$676.8	$891.1
1983	209.9	598.5	808.4	230.4	690.8	921.1
1984	227.4	624.4	851.8	241.7	691.7	933.5
1985	252.7	693.6	946.3	261.2	740.1	1,001.3
1986	273.4	717.0	990.3	276.4	740.8	1,017.3
1987	282.0	721.9	1,003.9	282.0	721.9	1,003.9
1988	290.4	773.8	1,064.1	283.3	743.8	1,027.1
1989	303.6	839.6	1,143.2	285.9	771.3	1,057.2
1990	299.3	953.4	1,252.7	272.6	837.7	1,110.4
1991	273.3	1,050.1	1,323.4	240.5	882.7	1,123.2
1992	298.4	1,082.5	1,380.9	249.7	883.7	1,133.4
1993	291.1	1,117.6	1,408.7	237.2	888.6	1,125.8
1994	281.6	1,179.4	1,460.9	220.6	919.7	1,140.3
1995 est.	271.6	1,267.3	1,538.9	206.7	961.5	1,168.1
1996 est.	261.4	1,350.7	1,612.1	192.6	993.4	1,186.0
1997 est.	257.0	1,427.7	1,684.7	183.6	1,017.0	1,200.6
1998 est.	254.5	1,490.7	1,745.2	176.7	1,029.5	1,206.2
1999 est.	259.7	1,562.5	1,822.2	175.2	1,046.6	1,221.8
2000 est.	267.8	1,637.5	1,905.3	175.5	1,063.7	1,239.2

[a] Transitional quarter when fiscal year start was shifted from July 1 to October 1.

Source: Office of Management and Budget, *Budget of the United States Government, Fiscal Year 1996, Historical Tables* (Washington, D.C.: U.S. Government Printing Office, 1995), 82-88.

Table 13-4 Federal Budget Outlays, by Function, 1970-1995 (billions)

Function	1970	1975	1980	1985	1990	1991	1992	1993	1994	1995 (est.)
National defense	$81.7	$86.5	$134.0	$252.7	$299.3	$273.3	$298.4	$291.1	$281.6	$271.6
Human resources	75.3	173.2	313.4	471.8	619.3	689.7	772.4	827.5	869.4	926.0
Education, training, employment, and social services	8.6	16.0	31.8	29.3	38.8	43.4	45.2	50.0	46.3	56.1
Health	5.9	12.9	23.2	33.5	57.7	71.2	89.5	99.4	107.1	115.1
Income security	15.6	50.2	86.5	128.2	147.0	170.3	196.9	207.2	214.0	223.0
Social Security and Medicare[a]	36.5	77.5	150.6	254.4	346.7	373.5	406.6	435.1	464.3	493.4
Veterans' benefits and services	8.7	16.6	21.2	26.3	29.1	31.3	34.1	35.7	37.6	38.4
Physical resources	15.6	35.4	66.0	56.8	125.5	134.2	74.8	45.9	69.7	66.3
Commerce and housing credit[a]	2.1	9.9	9.4	4.2	67.1	75.3	10.1	-22.7	-5.1	-12.0
Community, regional development	2.4	4.3	11.3	7.7	8.5	6.8	6.8	9.1	10.5	12.6
Energy	1.0	2.9	10.2	5.7	3.3	2.4	4.5	4.3	5.2	4.6
Natural resources and environment	3.1	7.3	13.9	13.4	17.1	18.6	20.0	20.2	21.1	21.9
Transportation	7.0	10.9	21.3	25.8	29.5	31.1	33.3	35.0	38.1	39.2
Net interest[a]	14.4	23.2	52.5	129.5	184.2	194.5	199.4	198.8	203.0	234.2
Other functions[b]	17.3	27.5	45.0	68.2	60.9	71.1	75.1	82.7	75.0	82.2
Administration of justice	1.0	3.0	4.6	6.3	10.0	12.3	14.4	15.0	15.3	17.6
Agriculture	5.2	3.0	8.8	25.6	12.0	15.2	15.2	20.5	15.1	14.4
General government	2.3	10.4	13.0	11.6	10.7	11.7	13.0	13.0	11.3	14.5
General science, space, technology	4.5	4.0	5.8	8.6	14.4	16.1	16.4	17.0	16.2	17.0
International affairs	4.3	7.1	12.7	16.2	13.8	15.9	16.1	17.2	17.1	18.7
Undistributed offsetting receipts[a]	-8.6	-13.6	-19.9	-32.7	-36.6	-39.4	-39.3	-37.4	-37.8	-41.4
Total outlays[a]	195.6	332.3	590.9	946.4	1,252.7	1,323.4	1,380.9	1,408.7	1,460.9	1,538.9

Note: Amounts in current dollars. For 1940-1975, ending June 30. Beginning 1980, ending September 30. Data for earlier years can be found in previous editions of *Vital Statistics on American Politics.*

[a] Includes both on- and off-budget amounts.

[b] Includes other outlays not shown separately.

Sources: Office of Management and Budget, *Budget of the U.S. Government, Fiscal Year 1996, Historical Tables* (Washington, D.C.: U.S. Government Printing Office, 1995), 36-42.

Figure 13-1   Federal Outlays as a Percentage of GNP/GDP, 1869-2000

Percent of GNP/GDP

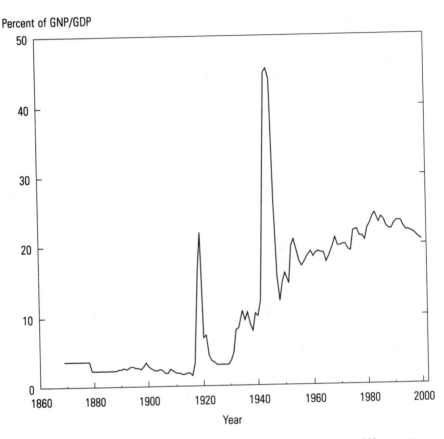

Year

Note: Averaged by decade for 1869-1888. Percentage of GNP is shown through 1933, percentage of GDP thereafter.

Sources: 1869-1933: U.S. Bureau of the Census, *Historical Statistics of the United States* (Washington, D.C.: U.S. Government Printing Office, 1975), 224, 1114; 1934-2000: Office of Management and Budget, *Budget of the United States Government, Fiscal Year 1996, Historical Tables* (Washington, D.C.: U.S. Government Printing Office, 1995), 15-16.

Table 13-5 Mandatory and Discretionary Federal Budget Outlays, 1962-1995

Outlays	1962	1965	1970	1975	1980	1985	1990	1994	1995 (est.)
Mandatory and related programs outlays, total[a]	$32.0	$36.4	$71.2	$170.1	$315.0	$531.0	$751.0	$915.3	$985.1
Health	0.1	0.2	2.8	7.1	14.7	23.9	42.9	86.6	92.5
Income security	8.7	8.9	14.7	46.7	75.7	109.1	123.6	178.4	183.9
Medicare	[b]	[b]	5.8	12.2	31.0	64.1	95.8	141.8	154.4
Social Security	14.0	15.5	29.6	63.6	117.1	186.4	246.5	316.9	333.7
Veterans' benefits and services	4.4	4.3	6.6	12.5	14.0	15.9	15.9	20.3	20.2
Net interest[c]	6.9	8.6	14.4	23.2	52.5	129.4	184.2	203.0	234.2
Undistributed offsetting receipt[c]	-5.3	-5.9	-8.6	-13.6	-19.9	-32.7	-36.6	-37.8	-41.4
Discretionary programs outlays, total[a]	74.9	81.8	124.5	162.2	275.9	415.3	501.7	545.6	553.8
Domestic, total[a]	16.8	26.1	38.6	66.4	128.5	145.4	182.5	242.6	259.6
Education, training, employment, and social services	0.9	1.8	7.3	12.9	25.6	21.7	27.6	37.3	40.2
General science, space, and technology	1.7	5.8	4.5	4.0	5.8	8.6	14.4	16.2	16.9
Health	1.1	1.5	3.1	5.8	8.5	9.6	14.9	20.5	22.6
Income security	0.5	0.5	0.9	3.5	10.8	19.1	23.5	35.6	39.1
Natural resources and environment	2.3	2.8	3.4	7.8	14.9	14.8	17.8	20.8	21.6
Transportation	4.2	5.7	6.9	10.6	21.1	25.3	29.1	37.8	38.7
International affairs	5.5	4.7	4.0	8.2	12.8	16.8	19.1	20.8	22.1
National defense	52.6	51.0	81.9	87.6	134.6	253.1	300.1	282.2	272.1
Total outlays	106.8	118.2	195.6	332.3	590.9	946.3	1,252.7	1,460.9	1,538.9
Mandatory program outlays as a percentage of total outlays	30.0	30.8	36.4	51.2	53.3	56.1	60.0	62.7	64.0

Note: Amounts in billions of current dollars.

[a] Includes other outlays not shown separately.
[b] Medicare outlays began in fiscal year 1967.
[c] Includes both on- and off-budget amounts.

Source: Office of Management and Budget, Budget of the U.S. Government, Fiscal Year 1996, Historical Tables (Washington, D.C.: U.S. Government Printing Office, 1995), 99-113.

Table 13-6 The National Debt, 1940-2000

Year	Debt held by the public (millions)	As a percentage of GDP	Year	Debt held by the public (millions)	As a percentage of GDP
1940	$42,772	44.8	1971	$303,037	28.8
1941	48,223	42.9	1972	322,377	28.1
1942	67,753	47.8	1973	340,910	26.8
1943	127,766	72.8	1974	343,699	24.5
1944	184,796	91.6	1975	394,700	26.1
1945	235,182	110.9	1976	477,404	28.3
1946	241,861	113.8	TQ[a]	495,509	27.8
1947	224,339	100.6	1977	549,103	28.6
1948	216,270	87.7	1978	607,125	28.2
1949	214,322	81.6	1979	640,308	26.4
1950	219,023	82.4	1980	709,838	26.8
1951	214,326	68.4	1981	785,338	26.5
1952	214,758	63.1	1982	919,785	29.5
1953	218,383	60.0	1983	1,131,596	34.1
1954	224,499	61.0	1984	1,300,498	35.2
1955	226,616	58.9	1985	1,499,908	37.8
1956	222,156	53.4	1986	1,736,709	41.2
1957	219,320	50.0	1987	1,888,680	42.4
1958	226,336	50.5	1988	2,050,799	42.7
1959	234,701	48.9	1989	2,189,882	42.3
1960	236,840	46.9	1990	2,410,722	44.0
1961	238,357	46.1	1991	2,688,137	47.4
1962	248,010	44.7	1992	2,998,834	50.6
1963	253,978	43.5	1993	3,247,471	51.9
1964	256,849	41.1	1994	3,432,213	51.7
1965	260,778	38.9	1995 est.	3,640,149	51.8
1966	263,714	35.9	1996 est.	3,857,300	52.1
1967	266,626	33.6	1997 est.	4,101,157	52.5
1968	289,545	34.2	1998 est.	4,334,920	52.6
1969	278,108	30.0	1999 est.	4,571,167	52.5
1970	283,198	28.7	2000 est.	4,805,437	52.3

Note: Amounts in current dollars.

[a] Transitional quarter when fiscal year start was shifted from July 1 to October 1.

Source: Office of Management and Budget, *Budget of the U.S. Government, Fiscal Year 1996, Historical Tables* (Washington, D.C.: U.S. Government Printing Office, 1995), 89.

Figure 13-2   The National Debt as a Percentage of GDP, 1940-2000

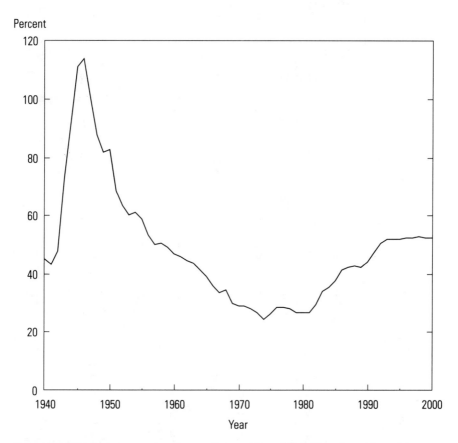

Note: 1995-2000 percentages are estimates. Figures reflect debt held by the public and do not include debt held by federal government accounts.

Source: Office of Management and Budget, *Budget of the U.S. Government, Fiscal Year 1996, Historical Tables* (Washington, D.C.: U.S. Government Printing Office, 1995), 89.

Table 13-7 Revenue Loss Estimates for Selected Tax Expenditures, 1980–1999 (millions)

Type of tax expenditure	1980	1985	1990	1993	1994	1995	1996	1999
Commerce and housing credit								
Exclusion of interest on life insurance savings	$3,490	$2,175	$7,265	$7,565	$9,145	$10,075	$10,085	$13,480
Deductibility of interest on consumer credit	4,745	15,530	1,525	0	0	0	0	0
Deductibility of mortgage interest on owner-occupied homes	15,615	24,785	37,580	45,145	48,430	51,270	54,165	63,960
Deductibility of property tax on owner-occupied homes	7,310	9,315	9,520	13,100	14,020	14,845	15,680	18,520
Deferral of capital gains on home sales	1,010	1,775	12,635	13,925	16,640	17,140	$17,850	19,290
Exclusion of capital gains on home sales for persons age 55 and over	535	830	3,230	4,265	4,690	4,820	4,920	5,125
Investment credit, other than ESOP's, rehabilitation of structures, energy property, and reforestation expenditures	18,250	24,445	0	0	0	0	0	0
Accelerated depreciation of machinery and equipment	—	20,145	18,655	15,750	14,765	16,120	17,105	20,805
Education, training, employment, and social services								
Deductibility of charitable contributions (education)	1,090	1,345	1,195	1,290	1,450	1,535	1,630	1,930
Credit for child and dependent care expenses	885	2,700	3,895	2,685	2,820	2,900	2,995	3,195
Deductibility of charitable contributions, other than education and health	6,270	10,175	10,870	11,745	13,235	14,015	14,835	17,605
Health								
Exclusion of employer contributions for medical insurance premiums and medical care	12,075	21,095	26,360	46,055	56,000	60,670	66,620	86,245
Deductibility of medical expenses	3,150	3,620	2,860	2,840	3,380	3,660	3,965	5,035
Exclusion of interest on state and local debt for private nonprofit health facilities	425	1,405	2,765	865	870	895	920	1,015
Deductibility of charitable contributions (health)	1,370	1,615	1,225	1,320	1,480	1,570	1,660	1,970

Social Security and Medicare								
Exclusion of Social Security benefits								
Disability insurance benefits	690	1,170	1,210	1,655	1,815	1,895	2,100	2,750
OASI benefits for retired workers	6,890	12,955	16,040	18,190	18,295	16,875	17,395	19,840
Benefits for dependents and survivors	1,015	3,755	2,995	3,545	3,620	3,610	3,730	4,365
Income security								
Exclusion of workmen's compensation benefits	2,200	2,225	2,735	3,750	4,240	4,475	4,860	5,645
Net exclusion of pension contributions and earnings								
Employer plans	19,785	48,525	45,385	53,840	48,750	55,540	59,010	60,400
Individual Retirement Accounts	—	12,695	6,620	5,210	5,185	6,245	6,375	4,970
Keoghs	1,925	1,960	1,460	2,835	3,915	4,435	4,825	6,025
Veterans benefits and services								
Exclusion of veterans disability compensation	1,065	1,695	1,580	1,760	1,910	1,985	1,930	2,180
General purpose fiscal assistance								
Deductibility of nonbusiness state and local taxes other than on owner-occupied homes	14,690	21,455	18,875	25,300	25,745	27,250	28,795	34,000

Note: "—" indicates not available. Amounts in current dollars. Fiscal year basis. Tax expenditures are defined as revenue losses attributable to provisions of the federal tax laws which allow a special exclusion, exemption, or deduction from gross income or which provide a special credit, a preferential rate of tax, or a deferral of liability. The Internal Revenue Service collected slightly under $500 billion in 1987 through individual and corporate income taxes.

Sources: 1980-1991: Office of Management and Budget, *Budget of the U.S. Government* (Washington, D.C.: U.S. Government Printing Office), annual; 1992: Office of Management and Budget, *Budget Baselines, Historical Data, and Alternatives for the Future* (Washington, D.C.: U.S. Government Printing Office, 1993), 546-549; 1994-2000: Office of Management and Budget, *Budget of the U.S. Government, Analytical Perspectives* (Washington, D.C.: U.S. Government Printing Office, 1995), 43-46.

Table 13-8   Civilian Labor Force Participation Rate, Overall and by Sex and Race, 1948-1994 (percent)

Year	Total	Male	Female	White	Black and other nonwhite
1948	58.8	86.6	32.7	—	—
1950	59.2	86.4	33.9	—	—
1955	59.3	85.4	35.7	58.7	64.2
1956	60.0	85.5	36.9	59.4	64.9
1957	59.6	84.8	36.9	59.1	64.4
1958	59.5	84.2	37.1	58.9	64.8
1959	59.3	83.7	37.1	58.7	64.3
1960	59.4	83.3	37.7	58.8	64.5
1961	59.3	82.9	38.1	58.8	64.1
1962	58.8	82.0	37.9	58.3	63.2
1963	58.7	81.4	38.3	58.2	63.0
1964	58.7	81.0	38.7	58.2	63.1
1965	58.9	80.7	39.3	58.4	62.9
1966	59.2	80.4	40.3	58.7	63.0
1967	59.6	80.4	41.1	59.2	62.8
1968	59.6	80.1	41.6	59.3	62.2
1969	60.1	79.8	42.7	59.9	62.1
1970	60.4	79.7	43.3	60.2	61.8
1971	60.2	79.1	43.4	60.1	60.9
1972	60.4	78.9	43.9	60.4	60.2
1973	60.8	78.8	44.7	60.8	60.5
1974	61.3	78.7	45.7	61.4	60.3
1975	61.2	77.9	46.3	61.5	59.6
1976	61.6	77.5	47.3	61.8	59.8
1977	62.3	77.7	48.4	62.5	60.4
1978	63.2	77.9	50.0	63.3	62.2
1979	63.7	77.8	50.9	63.9	62.2
1980	63.8	77.4	51.5	64.1	61.7
1981	63.9	77.0	52.1	64.3	61.3
1982	64.0	76.6	52.6	64.3	61.6
1983	64.0	76.4	52.9	64.3	62.1
1984	64.4	76.4	53.6	64.6	62.6
1985	64.8	76.3	54.5	65.0	63.3
1986	65.3	76.3	55.3	65.5	63.7
1987	65.6	76.2	56.0	65.8	64.3
1988	65.9	76.2	56.6	66.2	64.0
1989	66.5	76.4	57.4	66.7	64.7
1990	66.4	76.1	57.5	66.8	63.7
1991	66.0	75.5	57.3	66.6	63.1
1992	66.3	75.6	57.8	66.7	63.8
1993	66.2	75.2	57.9	66.7	63.1
1994	66.6	75.1	58.8	67.1	63.9

Note: "—" indicates not available. Figures are for persons sixteen years of age and over. The participation rate is the percentage of adults considered to be in the labor force. It is roughly those persons who are working, temporarily laid off, or looking for work. For details, see U.S. Bureau of the Census, *Statistical Abstract of the United States, 1992* (Washington, D.C.: Government Printing Office, 1992), 378.

Source: U.S. President, *Economic Report of the President* (Washington, D.C.: U.S. Government Printing Office, 1995), Table B-37.

Table 13-9   Unemployment Rate Overall, 1929-1994, and by Sex and Race, 1948-1994 (percent)

Year	Civilian workers	Male	Female	White	Nonwhite
1929	3.2	—	—	—	—
1933	24.9	—	—	—	—
1939	17.2	—	—	—	—
1940	14.6	—	—	—	—
1941	9.9	—	—	—	—
1942	4.7	—	—	—	—
1943	1.9	—	—	—	—
1944	1.2	—	—	—	—
1945	1.9	—	—	—	—
1946	3.9	—	—	—	—
1947	3.9	—	—	—	—
1948	3.8	3.6	4.1	3.5	5.9
1949	5.9	5.9	6.0	5.6	8.9
1950	5.3	5.1	5.7	4.9	9.0
1951	3.3	2.8	4.4	3.1	5.3
1952	3.0	2.8	3.6	2.8	5.4
1953	2.9	2.8	3.3	2.7	4.5
1954	5.5	5.3	6.0	5.0	9.9
1955	4.4	4.2	4.9	3.9	8.7
1956	4.1	3.8	4.8	3.6	8.3
1957	4.3	4.1	4.7	3.8	7.9
1958	6.8	6.8	6.8	6.1	12.6
1959	5.5	5.2	5.9	4.8	10.7
1960	5.5	5.4	5.9	5.0	10.2
1961	6.7	6.4	7.2	6.0	12.4
1962	5.5	5.2	6.2	4.9	10.9
1963	5.7	5.2	6.5	5.0	10.8
1964	5.2	4.6	6.2	4.6	9.6
1965	4.5	4.0	5.5	4.1	8.1
1966	3.8	3.2	4.8	3.4	7.3
1967	3.8	3.1	5.2	3.4	7.4
1968	3.6	2.9	4.8	3.2	6.7
1969	3.5	2.8	4.7	3.1	6.4
1970	4.9	4.4	5.9	4.5	8.2
1971	5.9	5.3	6.9	5.4	9.9
1972	5.6	5.0	6.6	5.1	10.0
1973	4.9	4.2	6.0	4.3	9.0
1974	5.6	4.9	6.7	5.0	9.9
1975	8.5	7.9	9.3	7.8	13.8
1976	7.7	7.1	8.6	7.0	13.1
1977	7.1	6.3	8.2	6.2	13.1
1978	6.1	5.3	7.2	5.2	11.9
1979	5.8	5.1	6.8	5.1	11.3
1980	7.1	6.9	7.4	6.3	13.1
1981	7.6	7.4	7.9	6.7	14.2
1982	9.7	9.9	9.4	8.6	17.3
1983	9.6	9.9	9.2	8.4	17.8
1984	7.5	7.4	7.6	6.5	14.4

(Table continues)

Table 13-9   (*Continued*)

Year	Civilian workers	Male	Female	White	Nonwhite
1985	7.2	7.0	7.4	6.2	13.7
1986	7.0	6.9	7.1	6.0	13.1
1987	6.2	6.2	6.2	5.3	11.6
1988	5.5	5.5	5.6	4.7	10.4
1989	5.3	5.2	5.4	4.5	10.0
1990	5.5	5.6	5.4	4.7	10.1
1991	6.7	7.0	6.3	6.0	11.1
1992	7.4	7.8	6.9	6.5	12.7
1993	6.8	7.1	6.5	6.0	11.7
1994	6.1	6.2	6.0	5.3	10.5

Note: "—" indicates not available. 1929-1947 figures are for persons fourteen years of age and over. 1948-1992 figures are for persons sixteen years of age and over.

Source: U.S. President, *Economic Report of the President* (Washington, D.C.: U.S. Government Printing Office, 1993), 382, 390, (1993), Table B-40.

Table 13-10 Unemployment, by Race, Sex, and Age, 1955-1994 (percent)

	White				Black[a]			
	Male		Female		Male		Female	
Year	16-19	20 and over	16-19	20 and over	16-19	20 and over	16-19	20 and over
1955	11.3	3.3	9.1	3.9	13.4	8.4	19.2	7.7
1960	14.0	4.2	12.7	4.6	24.0	9.6	24.8	8.3
1965	12.9	2.9	14.0	4.0	23.3	6.0	31.7	7.5
1970	13.7	3.2	13.4	4.4	25.0	5.6	34.5	6.9
1972	14.2	3.6	14.2	4.9	31.7	7.0	40.5	9.0
1973	12.3	3.0	13.0	4.3	27.8	6.0	36.1	8.6
1974	13.5	3.5	14.5	5.1	33.1	7.4	37.4	8.8
1975	18.3	6.2	17.4	7.5	38.1	12.5	41.0	12.2
1976	17.3	5.4	16.4	6.8	37.5	11.4	41.6	11.7
1977	15.0	4.7	15.9	6.2	39.2	10.7	43.4	12.3
1978	13.5	3.7	14.4	5.2	36.7	9.3	40.8	11.2
1979	13.9	3.6	14.0	5.0	34.2	9.3	39.1	10.9
1980	16.2	5.3	14.8	5.6	37.5	12.4	39.8	11.9
1981	17.9	5.6	16.6	5.9	40.7	13.5	42.2	13.4
1982	21.7	7.8	19.0	7.3	48.9	17.8	47.1	15.4
1983	20.2	7.9	18.3	6.9	48.8	18.1	48.2	16.5
1984	16.8	5.7	15.2	5.8	42.7	14.3	42.6	13.5
1985	16.5	5.4	14.8	5.7	41.0	13.2	39.2	13.1
1986	16.3	5.3	14.9	5.4	39.3	12.9	39.2	12.4
1987	15.5	4.8	13.4	4.6	34.4	11.1	34.9	11.6
1988	13.9	4.1	12.3	4.1	32.7	10.1	32.0	10.4
1989	13.7	3.9	11.5	4.0	31.9	10.0	33.0	9.8
1990	14.2	4.3	12.6	4.1	32.1	10.4	30.0	9.6
1991	17.5	5.7	15.2	4.9	36.5	11.5	36.1	10.5
1992	18.4	6.3	15.7	5.4	42.0	13.4	37.2	11.7
1993	17.6	5.6	14.6	5.1	40.1	12.1	37.5	10.6
1994	16.3	4.8	13.8	4.6	37.6	10.3	32.6	9.8

[a] Black and other prior to 1972.

Source: U.S. President, *Economic Report of the President* (Washington, D.C.: U.S. Government Printing Office, 1995), Table B-41.

Figure 13-3 Consumer Confidence, 1952–1995

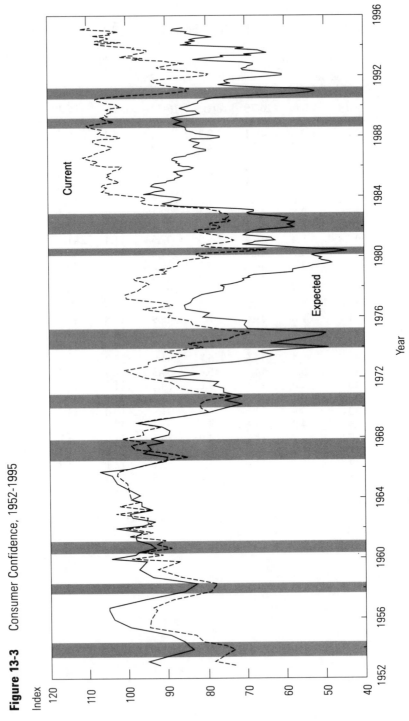

Note: Shaded areas indicate periods of economic recession, as determined by the National Bureau of Economic Research. Figures above reflect data from surveys conducted two or three times a year before 1960, quarterly from 1960 through 1977, and as a three-month moving average since 1978 based on monthly survey data. "Current" indicates the Index of Current Economic Conditions (ICC) and "Expected" the Index of Consumer Expectations (ICE).

The current index includes the following survey questions: (X1) "We are interested in how people are getting along financially these days. Would you say that you (and your family living there) are better off or worse off financially than you were a year ago?" (X5) "About the big things people buy for their homes—such as furniture, a refrigerator, stove, television, and things like that. Generally speaking, do you think now is a good or a bad time for people to buy major household items?"

The expected index includes the following survey questions: (X2) "Now looking ahead—do you think that a year from now you (and your family living there) will be better off financially, or worse off, or just about the same as now?" (X3) "Now turning to business conditions in the country as a whole—do you think that during the next twelve months we'll have good times financially, or bad times, or what?" (X4) "Looking ahead, which would you say is more likely—that in the country as a whole we'll have continuous good times during the next five years or so, or that we will have periods of widespread unemployment or depression?"

As a first step in calculating each index, a relative score is calculated from the percent giving favorable replies minus the percent giving unfavorable replies, plus 100 percent, for each question used. Each relative score is rounded to the nearest whole number. Using the following equation for each index, the relative scores of the appropriate survey questions are summed, divided by the 1966 base period constant for the index, and 2 is added (a constant to correct for sample design changes from the 1950s).

$$ICC = ((X1 + X5)/2.6424) + 2.0$$
$$ICE = ((X2 + X3 + X4)/4.1134) + 2.0$$

The Index of Consumer Sentiment is a weighted average of the current and expected indexes.

Sources: 1952-1990: Surveys of Consumers, *Historical Data* (Ann Arbor: Institute for Social Research, University of Michigan, 1991), 10-14; 1991-1995: Survey of Consumers, unpublished data; questions and equations from Surveys of Consumers, "Index Calculations" (Ann Arbor: Institute for Social Research, University of Michigan, n.d.); recession periods determined by the National Bureau of Economic Research and listed (through 1990) in Surveys of Consumers, *December 1990* (Ann Arbor: Institute for Social Research, University of Michigan, 1991).

Appendix

Table A-1   Regions as Defined by the U.S. Census Bureau

Northeast	Midwest	South	West
New England	East north central	South Atlantic	Mountain
Connecticut	Illinois	Delaware	Arizona
New Hampshire	Indiana	District of	Colorado
Maine	Michigan	Columbia	Idaho
Massachusetts	Ohio	Florida	Montana
Rhode Island	Wisconsin	Georgia	Nevada
Vermont	West north central	Maryland	New Mexico
Middle Atlantic	Iowa	North Carolina	Utah
New Jersey	Kansas	South Carolina	Wyoming
New York	Minnesota	Virginia	Pacific
Pennsylvania	Missouri	West Virginia	Alaska
	Nebraska	East south central	California
	North Dakota	Alabama	Hawaii
	South Dakota	Kentucky	Oregon
		Mississippi	Washington
		Tennessee	
		West south central	
		Arkansas	
		Louisiana	
		Oklahoma	
		Texas	

Source: U.S. Bureau of the Census, *Statistical Abstract of the United States, 1992* (Washington D.C.: U.S. Government Printing Office, 1992), Figure 1.

Table A-2 Regions as Defined by Congressional Quarterly, Gallup Poll, *New York Times*/CBS News Poll, and Voter Research & Surveys

East	Midwest	South	West
Connecticut	Illinois	Alabama	Alaska
Delaware	Indiana	Arkansas	Arizona
District of Columbia	Iowa	Florida	California
Maine	Kansas	Georgia	Colorado
Maryland	Michigan	Kentucky	Hawaii
Massachusetts	Minnesota	Louisiana	Idaho
New Hampshire	Missouri	Mississippi	Montana
New Jersey	Nebraska	North Carolina	Nevada
New York	North Dakota	Oklahoma	New Mexico
Pennsylvania	Ohio	South Carolina	Oregon
Rhode Island	South Dakota	Tennessee	Utah
Vermont	Wisconsin	Texas	Washington
West Virginia		Virginia	Wyoming

Sources: The Gallup Organization; Congressional Quarterly.

Table A-3 Regions for Partisan Competition Table (Table 4-3)

New England	Middle Atlantic	Midwest	Plains
Connecticut	Delaware	Illinois	Iowa
Maine	New Jersey	Indiana	Kansas
Massachusetts	New York	Michigan	Minnesota
New Hampshire	Pennsylvania	Ohio	Nebraska
Rhode Island		Wisconsin	North Dakota
Vermont			South Dakota

South	Border	Rocky Mountain	Pacfic Coast
Alabama	District of	Arizona	Alaska
Arkansas	Columbia	Colorado	California
Georgia	Maryland	Montana	Oregon
Louisiana	Missouri	Nevada	Washington
Mississippi	Oklahoma	New Mexico	
North Carolina	West Virginia	Utah	
South Carolina		Wyoming	
Tennesse			
Texas			
Virginia			

Table A-4   Regions for School Desegregation Table (Table 12-13)

South	Border	Northeast	Midwest	West	Excluded
Alabama	Delaware	Connecticut	Illinois	Arizona	Alaska
Arkansas	District of	Maine	Indiana	California	Hawaii
Florida	Columbia	Massachusetts	Iowa	Colorado	
Georgia	Kentucky	New	Kansas	Idaho	
Louisiana	Maryland	Hampshire	Michigan	Montana	
Mississippi	Missouri	New Jersey	Minnesota	Nevada	
North	Oklahoma	New York	Nebraska	New Mexico	
Carolina	West Virginia	Pennsylvania	North	Oregon	
South		Rhode Island	Dakota	Utah	
Carolina		Vermont	Ohio	Washington	
Tennessee			South	Wyoming	
Texas			Dakota		
Virginia			Wisconsin		

Source: Gary Orfield, and Franklin Monfort, "Status of School Desegregation: The Next Generation" (Alexandria, Va.: National School Boards Association, 1992), 2.

Guide to References
for Political Statistics

General

Alonso, William, and Paul Starr, eds. *The Politics of Numbers.* New York: Russell Sage, 1987.
> Excellent analysis of issues relating to the collection and publication of statistics, especially the U.S. census.

Austin, Erik W., and Jerome M. Clubb. *Political Facts of the United States Since 1789.* New York: Columbia University Press, 1986.
> Convenient one-volume compilation of otherwise all-too-often elusive data on politics in the nation; one strength is the long time series.

Congressional Information Service. *American Statistics Index: A Comprehensive Guide and Index to the Statistical Publications of the U.S. Government.* Washington, D.C.: Congressional Information Service, 1973-. Annual, with monthly supplements.
> Definitive guide, multiply indexed, to statistics "of probable research significance" in government publications; 1974 "Annual and Retrospective Edition" includes not only items in print but also significant items published over the preceding decade.

Congressional Information Service. *Statistical Reference Index: A Selective Guide to American Statistical Publications from Sources Other than the U.S. Government.* Washington, D.C.: Congressional Information Service, 1980-. Annual, with bimonthly supplements.
> A complement to *American Statistics Index*, indexes statistics from private and public sources other than the U.S. federal government.

Congressional Quarterly Weekly Report. Washington, D.C.: Congressional Quarterly, 1945-. Weekly.
> Newsweekly covering political developments in Congress, the presidency, the Supreme Court, and national politics; individual voting records on all roll-call votes in the House and Senate; texts of presidential press conferences and major statements.

407

Maier, Mark H. *The Data Game: Controversies in Social Science Statistics.* Armonk, N.Y.: Sharpe, 1991.
  Discussion of statistical source material, with an emphasis on inaccuracies, ambiguities, misinterpretations, and unavailability as well as on the relationship between statistics and important social questions.

National Journal. Washington, D.C.: National Journal, Inc., 1969-. Weekly.
  Newsweekly about government; reviews recent actions and features analyses of policy and political issues.

U.S. Bureau of the Census. *Historical Statistics of the United States, Colonial Times to 1970.* Bicentennial edition. Washington, D.C.: U.S. Government Printing Office, 1975.
  Invaluable, broad-ranging collection of more than 12,000 time series covering the nation's history; often the series can be updated by the annual *Statistical Abstract of the United States* (see below).

U.S. Bureau of the Census. *Statistical Abstract of the United States.* Washington, D.C.: U.S. Government Printing Office, 1879-. Annual.
  Strong, indispensable collection of nationally significant statistics from public and private sources on economics, politics, and society; generally worth checking first; also a useful guide to sources for additional statistics; indicates which time series update those in *Historical Statistics of the United States* (see above).

The Constitution

Balinski, Michel, and H. P. Young. *Fair Representation.* New Haven, Conn.: Yale University Press, 1982.
  Analysis of methods of apportionment of representatives among the states.

Congressional Research Service. *The Constitution of the United States: Analysis and Interpretation.* Washington, D.C.: U.S. Government Printing Office, 1987. 99th Cong., 1st sess., S.Doc. 99-16. Supplement issued 100th Cong., 1st sess., S.Doc. 100-9.
  Not statistics laden, but an essential document with commentary and annotations of Supreme Court decisions; tables on proposed constitutional amendments pending and unratified, laws (congressional, state, or local) held unconstitutional by the Supreme Court, and Supreme Court decisions overruled by subsequent decisions; U.S. law requires a new edition every ten years with biennial supplements between editions to keep this work current.

Reapportionment Law: The 1990s. Denver: National Conference of State Legislatures, 1989.
  Detailed discussion of law relating to redistricting.

Redistricting Provisions: 50 State Profiles. Denver: National Conference of State Legislatures, 1989.
  Compilation of state constitutional and statutory requirements regarding congressional and state legislative districting.

U.S. Congress. House. *Constitution, Jefferson's Manual, and Rules of the House of Representatives of the United States.* Washington, D.C.: U.S. Government Printing Office. Biennial.
Solid reference on the Constitution with full notes on all ratifications; indexed.

The Mass Media

ADI Book. Beltsville, Md.: Arbitron Television. Annual.
Reports of television usage, including demographic and market analyses.

Broadcasting Publications. *Broadcasting Cablecasting Yearbook.* Washington, D.C.: Broadcasting Publications, 1982-. Annual. Continues *Broadcasting Cable Yearbook,* which combined *Broadcasting Yearbook* (1968-1979) and *Broadcasting Cable Sourcebook* (1973-1979).
International directory of radio, television, and cable industries as well as related fields; presents some statistical overviews.

Editor & Publisher—The Fourth Estate. New York: Editor & Publisher Co., 1884-. Weekly.
Weekly periodical covering the media.

Magazine Index. Belmont, Calif.: Information Access Co., 1977-.
Indexes a long list of magazines, including a number of political news magazines.

Multimedia Audiences: Television Audiences. New York: Mediamark Research, Inc., 1979-. Semiannual.
Detailed reports of demographic and marketing segments of media audiences.

National Newspaper Index. Belmont, Calif.: Information Access Co., 1977-.
Indexes major national newspapers. The current list includes the *New York Times, Wall Street Journal, Christian Science Monitor, Los Angeles Times,* and the *Washington Post.* The *New York Times* has its own longstanding index.

Newsbank. New Canaan, Conn.: NewsBank, 1971-.
Microfiche collection of indexed articles from hundreds of American newspapers, from 1970 to the present, with newspapers from every state.

Nexus. Dayton, Ohio: Meade Data Central, Inc. On-line.
Full text of a number of newspapers and news, business, and medical magazines. Coverage varies, but is often since about 1980.

Nielsen Television Index. Northbrook, Ill.: A. C. Nielsen, 1955. Annual.
Overall and market section reports on television viewing and network program audiences.

Public Affairs Video Archives Catalogue. West Lafayette, Ind.: Public Affairs Video Archives, Purdue University, 1988-.

Archives of C-SPAN programming. Partial coverage 1987-September 1988, complete coverage since October 1988. Some other items, such as campaign commercials.

Sterling, Christopher H. *Electronic Media: A Guide to Trends in Broadcasting and Newer Technologies: 1920-1983*. New York: Praeger, 1984.
Data on growth, ownership, economics, employment and training, contents, audience and regulation of radio, television, and cable; strong on trends and time series.

Cable and Station Coverage Atlas, 1986. Indianapolis, Ind.: Warren Publishing, 1986-. Annual.
Data on television stations and the growing reach of cable systems.

Television Digest. *Television and Cable Factbook*. Washington, D.C.: Television Digest, 1946-. Annual.
Data on cable, television, and related industries; published in two volumes: "Stations" and "Cable and Services."

Television News Index and Abstracts. Nashville, Tenn.: Vanderbilt Television News Archives, Vanderbilt University, 1972-. Monthly.
Archives of nightly network news.

Elections and Campaigns

Alexander, Herbert E., and Monica Bauer. *Financing the 1988 Election*. Boulder, Colo.: Westview, 1991.
Detailed statistical coverage of fund-raising and spending in all phases of the presidential campaign; continues a series of books by Alexander on financing presidential campaigns since 1960.

Bartley, Numan V., and Hugh D. Graham. *Southern Elections: County and Precinct Data, 1950-1972*. Baton Rouge, La.: Louisiana State University Press, 1978.
Gubernatorial and senatorial contests, primaries, and referenda in southern states; some socioeconomic and geographic analysis of the elections.

Brace, Kim, et al. *The Election Data Book*. Lanham, Md.: Bernan Press, 1993-. Biennial.
Extensive compilation of general election and primary vote totals, by state and county, for president, governor, and U.S. senator and representative. Voter registration and turnout figures by state since 1948; by country for most recent election. Information on voting precincts, registration methods, and voting equipment. State maps with county and congressional districts boundaries.

Congressional Quarterly. *Congressional Quarterly's Guide to U.S. Elections*. 3d ed. Washington, D.C.: Congressional Quarterly, 1994.

Superb collection of vote returns for presidential, gubernatorial, and House elections since 1824, electoral college votes since 1789, senatorial elections since 1913, presidential primaries since 1912, and primaries for governor and senator since 1956 (in southern states since 1919); general and candidate indexes; biographies of presidential and vice-presidential candidates; lists of governors and senators since 1789; discussions of and data on political parties and presidential nominating conventions throughout the nation's history.

Federal Election Commission. *Annual Report.* Washington, D.C.: U.S. Government Printing Office, 1976-.
Cumulative figures since the mid-1970s on contributions and spending in federal election campaigns; also information on political action committee (PAC) growth and activities.

Federal Election Commission. *Reports on Financial Activity.* Washington, D.C.: U.S. Government Printing Office, 1980-.
Multi-volume work reporting revenues and spending in congressional and presidential campaigns by candidates, party, and nonparty political committees (PACs); reports typically cover a two-year campaign cycle (for example, 1987-1988).

Glashan, Roy R. *American Governors and Gubernatorial Elections, 1775-1978.* Westport, Conn.: Meckler, 1979.
Details about state governors (such as birthdates, party affiliations, principal occupations, terms of office) and election data.

Heard, Alexander E. *The Costs of Democracy.* Chapel Hill, N.C.: University of North Carolina Press, 1960.
A classic work, published in 1960 when hard data on campaign contributions and spending were hard to secure.

Kallenbach, Joseph E., and Jessamine S. Kallenbach. *American State Governors, 1776-1976.* Dobbs Ferry, N.Y.: Oceana Publications, 1977-1982.
Election results and biographical data on governors.

Makinson, Larry. *The Price of Admission: An Illustrated Atlas of Campaign Spending in the 1988 Congressional Elections.* Washington, D.C.: Center for Responsive Politics, 1989.
Convenient compilation of total and PAC receipts for winners, total spending for winners and losers.

McGillivray, Alice V. *Congressional and Gubernatorial Primaries: 1991-1992.* Washington, D.C.: Congressional Quarterly, 1993.
County-by-county primary results for governors and for U.S. senators and representatives.

McGillivray, Alice V. *Presidential Primaries and Caucuses: 1992.* Washington, D.C.: Congressional Quarterly, 1992.
County-by-county results for presidential primaries in 1992. Voter registration figures by county.

McGillivray, Alice V., and Richard M. Scammon, eds., *America at the Polls: A Handbook of Presidential Election Statistics.* Washington, D.C.: Congressional Quarterly, 1994.
Two volumes span 1920-1992, providing popular votes (state and county) for president as well as state presidential primary results. Available on disk.

Mullaney, Marie. *American Governors and Gubernatorial Elections, 1979-1987.* Westport, Conn.: Meckler, 1988.
Details about state governors (such as birthdates, party affiliations, principal occupations, terms of office) and election data.

Nomination and Election of the President and Vice President of the United States. Washington, D.C.: U.S. Government Printing Office, 1960-. Quadrennial.
Compilation of federal and state laws and party rules governing nomination and election of the President.

Republican National Committee. *The (Year) Republican Almanac: State Political Profiles.* Washington, D.C.: Republican National Committee, 1973-. Biennial.
In its most recent edition, a voluminous statistical report of political, especially election, data about each state of the nation.

Runyon, John H., Jennefer Verdini, and Sally S. Runyan, eds. *Source Book of American Presidential Campaign and Election Statistics, 1948-1968.* New York: Frederick Ungar, 1971.
Information on presidential campaign staffs, candidate itineraries, media exposure, campaign costs, and public opinion polls.

Scammon, Richard M., and Alice V. McGillivray, eds. *America Votes: A Handbook of Contemporary American Election Statistics.* Washington, D.C.: Congressional Quarterly, Elections Research Center, 1956-. Biennial.
Convenient compilation of vote totals and statistics by state for general elections and primaries for president, governor, senator, principally since 1945 (comparable district-level data for members of Congress); county-level totals and statistics for most recent general election for president, governor, and senator; state maps with county and congressional districts boundaries.

U.S. Bureau of the Census. Current Population Reports. Population Characteristics, Series P-20. *Voting and Registration in the Election of November (Year).* Washington, D.C.: U.S. Government Printing Office, 1964-. Biennial.
Survey results on voter registration and turnout in presidential and midterm general elections for the nation and regions (and sometimes states and metropolitan areas) for various groups.

Political Parties

Bain, Richard C., and Judith H. Parris. *Convention Decisions and Voting Records.* 2d ed. Washington, D.C.: Brookings, 1973.
    Data on convention actions through 1972.

Congressional Quarterly. *National Party Conventions, 1831-1992.* 6th ed. Washington, D.C.: Congressional Quarterly, 1995.
    Summarizes conventions, with results of ballots, nominees, and party profiles.

Cotter, Cornelius P., James L. Gibson, John F. Bibby, and Robert J. Huckshorn. *Party Organizations in American Politics.* New York: Praeger, 1984.
    Contains information on the characteristics of state parties and assessments of their organizational strength as of the late 1970s. Also rates states on support for and regulation of political parties.

David, Paul T. *Party Strength in the United States, 1872-1970.* Charlottesville, Va.: University Press of America, 1972. Updated for 1972 in *Journal of Politics* 36 (1972): 785-796; for 1974 in *Journal of Politics* 38 (1974): 416-425; for 1976 in *Journal of Politics* 40 (1976): 770-780.
    Measures of party competition in the states covering several offices and an admirably lengthy historical span.

Miller, Warren E., and M. Kent Jennings. *Parties in Transition.* New York: Russell Sage, 1986.
    Descriptions and analyses of delegates to the 1972-1980 Republican and Democratic national conventions.

Schapsmeier, Edward L., and Frederick H. Schapsmeier. *Political Parties and Civic Action Groups.* Westport, Conn.: Greenwood Press, 1981.
    Brief descriptions of political organizations, current and past. Includes political parties, civic organizations, and all types of special interest groups.

Public Opinion

The American Enterprise. Washington, D.C.: American Enterprise Institute for Public Policy Research, 1990-. Bimonthly.
    Regular "Public Opinion and Demographic Report" section presents poll data from several sources on selected topics; a more limited continuation of *Public Opinion*, previously published (1978-1989) by the same organization.

Converse, Philip E., Jean D. Dotson, Wendy J. Hoag, and William H. McGee III. *American Social Attitudes Data Sourcebook, 1947-1978.* Cambridge, Mass.: Harvard University Press, 1980.
    Compendium of national polling data from the Survey Research Center at the University of Michigan, ranging across major social issues.

Dey, E. L., A. W. Astin, and W. F. Korn. *The American Freshman: Twenty-five Year Trends.* Los Angeles: Higher Education Research Institute, University of California, Los Angeles, 1991. *National Norms for Fall,* 1991-. Annual.
Reports of national surveys of college freshmen, including attitudes toward jobs, subject interests, liberalism/conservatism.

The Gallup Poll: Public Opinion 1935-71. 3 vols. New York: Random House, 1972. Wilmington, Del.: Scholarly Resources, Inc., 1972-. Annual. Years 1972-1977 contained in 2 vols.
Poll data from thousands of Gallup surveys since 1935 on then-current topics, presented chronologically.

The Gallup Report: Political, Social and Economic Trends. Princeton, N.J.: American Institute of Public Opinion, 1965-. Monthly. Previously titled *Gallup Opinion Index* and *The Gallup Political Report.*
Compilation of recent Gallup public opinion data on political and social issues, often presented with historical trends.

Miller, Warren E., and Santa Traugott. *American National Election Studies Data Sourcebook, 1952-1986.* Cambridge, Mass.: Harvard University Press, 1989.
Compendium of polling data from the National Election Studies covering presidential and congressional election years.

Niemi, Richard G., John E. Mueller, and Tom W. Smith. *Trends in Public Opinion.* Westport, Conn.: Greenwood Press, 1989.
Public opinion polls on numerous political and other topics; based primarily on the General Social Survey. Provides time series, often quite long, of identically worded questions.

Opinion Research Service. *American Public Opinion Index.* Louisville, Ky.: Opinion Research Service, 1981-. Annual.
Indexes scientifically drawn samples of national, state, and local universes.

POLL (The Public Opinion Location Library). Storrs, Ct.: Roper Center for Public Opinion Research.
A computer-based information retrieval system for public opinion survey data. Extensive coverage for 1955 to the present; some coverage of earlier years.

Public Opinion Quarterly. Chicago: University of Chicago Press, 1937-. Quarterly.
Analysis of the mechanics and findings of survey research; regular thematic presentation of poll results.

The Public Perspective: A Roper Center Review of Public Opinion and Polling. Storrs, Ct.: The Roper Center for Public Opinion Research, 1989-. Bimonthly.
Poll results and articles on public opinion and polling.

Wood, Floris W., ed. *An American Profile—Opinions and Behavior, 1972-1989.* Detroit: Gale, 1990.
> Poll results of the General Social Survey plus a chronology of world events.

Interest Groups

Cigler, Allan J., and Burdett A. Loomis. *Interest Group Politics.* 3d ed. Washington, D.C.: CQ Press, 1991.
> Examines interest groups in the policy-making process—a rapidly changing field.

Close, Arthur C., and John P. Gregg. *Washington Representatives.* Washington, D.C.: Columbia Books, 1977-. Annual.
> Lists Washington representatives of major corporations, unions, and national associations as well as registered foreign agents and the organizations represented by an individual or an office in Washington.

Congressional Quarterly. *The Washington Lobby.* 5th ed. Washington, D.C.: Congressional Quarterly, 1987.
> Lobbying developments in strategies and techniques, highlighting political action committees (PACs); explores federal laws, regulations, and court cases that govern lobbyists as well as interest group ratings of members of Congress.

Foundation for Public Affairs. *Public Interest Profiles.* Washington, D.C.: Congressional Quarterly, 1977-. Biennial.
> Profiles of 250 "public interest" groups, including single-cause organizations (e.g., Greenpeace), board coalitions (e.g., Common Cause), and think tanks (e.g., Brookings). Includes evaluation of the effectiveness of each group.

Greevy, David U., Chadwick R. Gore, and Marvin I. Weinberger. *The PAC Directory.* Cambridge, Mass.: Ballinger, 1984.
> Useful, though now dated, assemblage of information on political action committees in the political process.

Interstate Bureau of Regulations. *State Political Action Legislation and Regulations: Index and Directory of Organizations.* Westport, Conn.: Quorum Books, 1984.
> Information on regulation of political action committees in the states.

Koek, Karin E., Susan B. Martin, and Annette Novallo, eds. *Encyclopedia of Associations.* Detroit, Mich.: Gale Research, Inc., 1960-. Annual.
> Guide to over 23,000 organizations, both national and international, spanning various sectors of society.

Makinson, Larry. *Open Secrets: The Encyclopedia of Congressional Money and Politics.* 3d ed. Washington, D.C.: Congressional Quarterly, 1994.

Summary information about individual and PAC contributions, plus a listing of members of Congress and their sources of PAC money.

Malbin, Michael J. *Parties, Interest Groups, and Campaign Finance Laws.* Washington, D.C.: American Enterprise Institute for Public Policy Research, 1980.
Early (1980) collection pulling together analyses in an increasingly investigated area.

Troy, Leo, and Neil Sheflin. *U.S. Union Sourcebook.* West Orange, N.J.: Industrial Relations Data and Information Services, 1985.
Excellent source of statistical information on membership in American and Canadian unions; long historical coverage.

Congress

Barone, Michael, and Grant Ujifusa. *The Almanac of American Politics.* Washington, D.C.: National Journal, 1972-. Biennial.
Data-rich political analyses of each state, congressional district, representative, senator, and governor; current composition of committees; state maps with congressional district and county boundaries.

Congressional Quarterly. *American Leaders 1789-1994.* 3d ed. Washington, D.C.: Congressional Quarterly, 1994.
Material on more than 11,000 members of Congress: age, religion, occupations, women, blacks, turnover, and shifts between chambers; data on congressional sessions, party composition, and leadership. Also includes biographical summaries of presidents, vice presidents, Supreme Court justices, and governors.

Congressional Quarterly. *Congress A to Z.* 2d ed. Washington, D.C.: Congressional Quarterly, 1993.
Mostly essays but contains a number of useful listings of hard-to-find material such as treaties killed by the Senate, impeachment trials, women members of Congress, etc.

Congressional Quarterly. *Congress and the Nation.* Washington, D.C.: Congressional Quarterly, 1965-. Quadrennial. Years 1945-1964 contained in 1 vol.
Akin to *Congressional Quarterly Almanac* (see below), but each volume now covers a presidential term.

Congressional Quarterly. *Congressional Districts in the 1990s.* Washington, D.C.: Congressional Quarterly, 1993.
Profiles of each congressional district containing statistics on election returns, economic makeup, and demographics.

Congressional Quarterly. *Congressional Quarterly Almanac.* Washington, D.C.: Congressional Quarterly, 1945-. Annual.

Each volume now covers legislation for a single session of Congress, appendices contain particularly useful data on Congress and politics.

Congressional Quarterly. *Congressional Roll Call.* Washington, D.C.: Congressional Quarterly, 1974-. Annual.

Annual compilation of every roll-call vote by every member of Congress and summary voting measures (ideology, party unity, presidential support, and voting participation).

Congressional Quarterly. *Guide to Congress.* 4th ed. Washington, D.C.: Congressional Quarterly, 1991.

Massive, rich accounting of how Congress works and how it developed. Check here first for data covering all but the most recent years.

Congressional Quarterly. *Guide to 1990 Congressional Redistricting,* Parts I and II. Washington, D.C.: Congressional Quarterly, 1993.

Descriptions and maps of 1990s districts. Contains a summary of the process by which districting plans were adopted.

Congressional Quarterly. *Landmark Legislation 1789-1994.* Washington, D.C., Congressional Quarterly, 1995.

Summary and historical and political background of major legislation and treaties.

Congressional Quarterly. *Politics in America.* Washington, D.C.: Congressional Quarterly, 1981-. Biennial.

Data-rich political analyses of each state, congressional district, representative, and senator; current composition of committees; state maps with congressional district and county boundaries.

(Year) Congressional Staff Directory. Mt. Vernon, Va.: Congressional Staff Directory, Ltd., 1959-. Biannual.

Names, addresses, phone numbers, and numerous biographies of senators' and representatives' personal staffs and the staffs of congressional committees and subcommittees.

Martis, Kenneth C., and Gregory A. Elmes. *The Historical Atlas of State Power in Congress, 1790-1990.* Washington, D.C.: Congressional Quarterly, 1993.

Maps, tables, and text describing changes in apportionment among the states.

Ornstein, Norman J., Thomas E. Mann, and Michael J. Malbin, eds. *Vital Statistics on Congress.* Washington, D.C.: Congressional Quarterly, 1980-. Biennial.

Data on characteristics of members, elections, campaign finance, committees, staff, expenses, workload, budgeting, and voting alignments; most data series stretch back to World War II, some longer.

Parsons, Stanley B., William W. Beach, Dan Hermann, and Michael J. Dubin. *United States Congressional Districts and Data.* 2 vols. Westport, Conn.: Greenwood Press, 1978, 1986.

Demographic and geographic data about American congressional districts. Currently two volumes available, covering 1789-1883.

Sharp, J. Michael. *The Directory of Congressional Voting Scores and Interest Group Ratings.* 2 vols. New York: Facts on File, 1988.
Contains voting scores (e.g., presidential support) and interest group ratings (eleven groups, as available) for all members of Congress from 1947 to 1985.

U.S. Bureau of the Census. *Congressional District Atlas.* Washington, D.C.: U.S. Government Printing Office, 1960-. Frequency varies.
Detailed maps of congressional districts.

U.S. Bureau of the Census. *Congressional District Data Book.* Washington, D.C.: U.S. Government Printing Office, 1961-. Frequency varies.
Census data by congressional district with maps.

U.S. Congress. Joint Committee on Printing. *Official Congressional Directory.* Washington, D.C.: U.S. Government Printing Office, 1865-. Biennial (in recent years).
Biographical data on current members, statistics on the sessions of Congress, useful reference source on committees and subcommittees, foreign representatives and consular offices in the United States, press representatives, and state delegations.

U.S. Congress. Senate. *Biographical Directory of the American Congress, 1774-1989.* Washington, D.C.: U.S. Government Printing Office, 1989. 100th Cong., 2d sess., S.Doc. 100-34.
Biographies of U.S. senators and representatives to January 3, 1989.

The Presidency and the Executive Branch

Congressional Quarterly. *Congressional Quarterly's Guide to the Presidency,* Michael Nelson, ed. Washington, D.C.: Congressional Quarterly, 1989.
Detailed coverage of numerous aspects of presidents and administrations. Focus on the institution complements CQ's volumes on elections.

Congressional Quarterly. *Federal Regulatory Directory.* Washington, D.C.: Congressional Quarterly, 1979-. Frequency varies.
Descriptions and data provide extensive profiles of the major and minor regulatory agencies—more than 100 in all.

Congressional Quarterly. *Presidential Elections Since 1789.* 6th ed. Washington, D.C.: Congressional Quarterly, 1995.
Facts and figures on presidential elections; electoral college vote since 1789; primary returns since 1912; major-party candidate vote shares state-by-state; minor candidate vote totals; recent turnout and party support trends.

Congressional Quarterly. *Washington Information Directory.* Washington, D.C.: Congressional Quarterly, 1975-. Annual.

Names, addresses, phone numbers, and heads of thousands of federal government and private, nonprofit agencies in and about Washington, D.C.

DeGregorio, William A. *The Complete Book of U.S. Presidents*. New York: Dembner, 1984.

Biographies of presidents and cabinet members.

(Year) Federal Staff Directory. Mt. Vernon, Va.: Congressional Staff Directory, Ltd., 1982-. Biannual.

Names, addresses, phone numbers, and numerous biographies of key executives and assistants in the executive branch of the federal government.

Kane, Joseph Nathan. *Facts About the Presidents: A Compilation of Biographical and Historical Information*. 6th ed. New York: H. H. Wilson, 1993.

Chapter on each president and comparative statistics on all presidents.

Ragsdale, Lyn. *Vital Statistics on the Presidency*. Washington, D.C.: CQ Press, 1996.

Data on presidents, their careers, elections, speeches and appearances, approval ratings, congressional relationships; focus is on postwar presidencies, with some longer time series.

U.S. Government Organization Manual. Washington, D.C.: U.S. Government Printing Office, 1935-. Annual.

Official federal government handbook detailing the organization, activities, and current officials in legislative, judicial, and executive governmental units. Weekly Compilation of Presidential Documents. Washington, D.C.: U.S. Government Printing Office.

Weekly Compilation of Presidential Documents. Washington, D.C.: U.S. Government Printing Office.

Highly useful collection of presidential activities; includes texts of proclamations, executive orders, speeches, and other presidential communications; supplements include acts gaining presidential approval, nominations submitted for Senate confirmation, and a list of White House press releases; indexed.

The Judiciary

The American Bench. Sacramento, Calif.: Reginald Bishop Forster & Associates, 1977-. Biennial.

Comprehensive listing of all judges in the United States, along with brief biographies of approximately 18,000 judges.

Congressional Quarterly. *Guide to the U.S. Supreme Court*. 2d ed. Washington, D.C.: Congressional Quarterly, 1990.

Solid, broad coverage of the Supreme Court and the development of the law; an excellent source that also refers readers to additional references.

The Corrections Yearbook. South Salem, N.Y.: Criminal Justice Institute, 1980-. Annual.
> Inmate populations, budgets, facilities, staff, and other data for jails with average daily populations of 200 or more.

Curran, Barbara A., et al. *The Lawyer Statistical Report: A Statistical Profile of the U.S. Legal Profession in the 1980s.* Chicago: American Bar Foundation, 1985. *U.S. Legal Profession in 1985 (Supplement to Statistical Report),* 1987.
> A statistical profile of a changing profession, by age, gender, and place of employment; also profiles 1980 lawyer populations within states, metropolitan, and nonmetropolitan areas.

Director of the Administrative Office of the United States Courts. *Annual Report.* Washington, D.C.: U.S. Government Printing Office, 1940-. Annual.
> Numerous statistics about the kind, timing, and disposition of cases in the federal courts and about numbers and workloads of federal judges.

Dornette, W. Stuart, and Robert R. Cross. *Federal Judiciary Almanac.* New York: Wiley, 1987.
> Data on various aspects of the federal judiciary.

Epstein, Lee, Jeffrey Segal, Harold J. Spaeth, and Thomas A. Walker. *Supreme Court Compendium.* Washington, D.C.: CQ Press, 1994.
> Data on characteristics of justices, caseload, voting alignments, public opinion, and legal developments.

Friedman, Leon, and Fred L. Israel, eds. *The Justices of the United States Supreme Court.* 5 vols. New York: Chelsea House, 1978.
> Biography on each justice including several typical opinions; tables showing acts of Congress held unconstitutional, decisions overruled by subsequent decisions, and summary biographical data.

Judges of the United States. 2d ed. Washington, D.C.: U.S. Government Printing Office, 1983.
> Biographies of all federal judges through 1983.

(Year) Judicial Staff Directory. Mt. Vernon, Va.: Congressional Staff Directory, Ltd., 1986-. Annual.
> Personnel listings for federal courts, maps of court jurisdictions, biographies of judges and staffs.

State Court Caseload Statistics: Annual Report. Williamsburg, Va.: Conference of State Court Administrators and the National Center for State Courts, 1976-. Annual.
> Data on judicial workload in the state courts.

Widman, Iris J., and Mark J. Handler, comps. *Federal Judges and Justices: A Current Listing of Nominations, Confirmations, Elevations, Resignations, Retirements.* Littleton, Colo.: Rothman, 1987.
> Useful compendium with revealing subtitle.

Federalism

Alexander, Herbert E., and Mike Eberts. *Public Financing of State Elections: A Data Book and Election Guide to Public Funding of Political Parties and Candidates in Twenty States.* Los Angeles: Citizens' Research Foundation, 1986.
> Important compendium for understanding and comparing state regulation of campaign finances.

Beyle, Thad, ed. *State Government.* Washington, D.C.: Congressional Quarterly, 1985-. Annual.
> Analysis of recent developments in state governments; reprints articles from a diverse set of state publications.

The Book of the States. Lexington, Ky.: Council of State Governments, 1935-. Biennial.
> Definitive reference to the current data on state government activities across the board.

Campaign Finance: Ethics and Lobby Law Blue Book. Lexington, Ky.: Council on Governmental Ethics Laws, Council of State Governments, 1990.
> Information about ethics laws, campaign finance reports and limits, personal disclosure requirements, and lobby laws in the states and in the Canadian provinces.

Campaign Finance Law. Washington, D.C.: D. T. Skelton Service Associates, Inc., Federal Election Commission's National Clearinghouse of Election Administration, 1981-. Annual.
> Rules and regulations for campaign financing in the states and nation.

Carpenter, Allan. *Facts About the Cities.* New York: H.W. Wilson, 1992.
> Data on 300 cities, culled from federal sources. Includes limited political information (e.g., number of women in governing body).

The County Year Book. Washington, D.C.: National Association of Counties and International City Management Association, 1975-. Annual.
> Surveys issues and trends in county government and administration; a reliable source of data on county government.

Holli, Melvin G., and Peter Jones, eds. *Biographical Dictionary of American Mayors, 1820-1980.* Westport, Conn.: Greenwood Press, 1981.
> Covers 679 mayors in over a dozen cities; contains lists categorizing mayors by characteristics such as party, religion, and ethnicity.

Hornor, Edith R., ed. *Almanac of the 50 States: Basic Data Profiles with Comparative Tables.* Palo Alto, Calif.: Information Publications, 1985-. Annual.
> State-level summaries of data on government and elections, state expenditures, federal aid, population characteristics, crime, etc.

International City Management Association. *The Municipal Year Book.* New York: International City Management Association, 1934-. Annual.
Reliable source for urban data and developments.

Lilley III, William, Laurence J. DeFranco, and William M. Diefenderfer III. The Almanac of State Legislatures. Washington, D.C., Congressional Quarterly, 1995.
Maps and statistical profiles of the geographic, economic, and political composition of state legislative districts.

Marlin, John Tepper, and James S. Avery. *The Book of American City Rankings.* New York: Facts on File, 1983.
Nearly 300 thematic tables with data on the 100 largest U.S. cities.

National Directory of State Agencies. Bethesda, Md.: National Standards Association, 1976-. Annual since 1986.
Names of agency heads, addresses, and phone numbers of state agencies.

The New Book of American Rankings. New York: Facts on File, 1984.
State rankings and statistics on over 300 items. Some of the material is now dated.

Significant Features of Fiscal Federalism. Washington, D.C.: U.S. Advisory Commission on Intergovernmental Relations, 1976-. Annual.
Convenient compilation of comparative state data on revenues, expenditures, and related matters; tables and figures present comparisons across states as well as state-by-state in-depth treatment.

State Administrative Officials Classified by Functions. Lexington, Ky.: Council of State Governments, 1977-. Biennial.
Lists state administrative officials by function; before 1977 issued as a supplement to *The Book of the States.*

State Elective Officials and the Legislatures. Lexington, KY.: Council of State Governments, 1977-. Biennial.
Lists state elected officials and legislators; before 1977 issued as a supplement to *The Book of the States.*

State Information Book. Rockville, Md.: Infax, 1973-. Biennial.
Some statistics, but emphasizes names, addresses, phone numbers, and heads of departments and agencies, plus county seats and phone numbers.

State Legislative Sourcebook. Topeka, Kan.: Government Research Service, 1986-. Annual.
Tells how to find detailed information about state legislative activity, including offices, addresses, phone numbers, and price lists.

State Policy Data Book. McConnellsburg, Pa.: Brizius & Foster, 1984-. Annual.
State-by-state rankings, with percentages, averages, or other entries, on numerous items, including demographics, economics, health, and education.

State statistical abstracts.
> A list of state statistical abstracts (or near equivalents) can be found in recent editions of the *Statistical Abstract of the United States*. They are of widely varying quality.

Tax Foundation. *Facts and Figures on Government Finance*. Englewood Cliffs, N.J.: Prentice Hall, 1941-. Annual.
> Data on government revenues, spending, and debt at the federal, state, and local levels.

The Transformation in American Politics: Implications for Federalism. Washington, D.C.: U.S. Advisory Commission on Intergovernmental Relations, 1986.
> Wide-ranging treatment (much broader than the subtitle implies) of major recent trends in American politics with emphasis on relevant data.

U.S. Bureau of the Census. *Census of Governments*. Washington, D.C.: U.S. Government Printing Office, 1972-. Frequency varies.
> Numbers and characteristics of governments, including special district governments dealing with subjects such as schools, parks and recreation, and sewage.

U.S. Bureau of the Census. *City Government Finances; Government Finances; State Government Finances*. Washington, D.C.: U.S. Government Printing Office, 1909-; 1965-; 1916-. Annual.
> These three series summarize government finances at city and state levels; great detail for states and the larger cities.

U.S. Bureau of the Census. *County and City Data Book*. Washington, D.C.: U.S. Government Printing Office, 1952-. Frequency varies.
> Demographic, economic, health, agricultural, and other information about counties, cities, and towns. Presidential voting by county.

U.S. Bureau of the Census. *State and Metropolitan Area Data Book*. Washington, D.C.: U.S. Government Printing Office, 1979-. Frequency varies.
> Demographic, economic, health, education, and other data about states and metropolitan statistical areas.

Foreign and Military Policy

Cochran, Thomas B., William A. Arkin, and Milton M. Hoenig. *Nuclear Weapons Databook*. Cambridge, Mass.: Ballinger, 1987.
> Descriptions, specifications, and deployments of American and Soviet nuclear weapons systems.

Joint Chiefs of Staff. *Military Posture for Fiscal Year (Year)*. Washington, D.C.: U.S. Government Printing Office. Annual.

Brief review of all aspects of military preparedness of the U.S. and of the world military environment.

The Military Balance. London: International Institute of Strategic Studies, 1959-. Annual.
Statistical analysis of military forces and defense spending; figures given for countries and regional organizations such as NATO (North Atlantic Treaty Organization).

U.S. Arms Control and Disarmament Agency. *World Military Expenditures and Arms Transfers.* Washington, D.C.: U.S. Government Printing Office, 1965-. Annual (title varies).
Annual statistical accounts of military spending and the arms race.

U.S. Department of State. *Patterns of Global Terrorism.* Washington, D.C.: U.S. Department of State, 1983-. Annual.
Details on terrorist incidents around the world.

World Armaments and Disarmament: SIPRI Yearbook. Stockholm: Almqvist & Wiksell, New York: Oxford University Press, 1970-. Annual.
Overview of the arms race and efforts to promote disarmament; detailed data on world military spending.

Social Policy

Black Elected Officials: A National Roster. Washington, D.C.: Joint Center for Political and Economic Studies, 1971-. Annual.
Lists black elected officials by office and address with summary tabulations on the historical trends and comparative state figures.

Bogue, Donald J. *The Population of the United States: Historical Trends and Future Projections.* New York: Free Press, 1985.
Extensive description of nation's population characteristics, focusing on the years since 1960; topics include poverty, income, housing, educational attainment, ethnicity, migration, and so forth.

Center for the American Woman and Politics, National Information Bank on Women in Public Office, Eagleton Institute of Politics, Rutgers University.
Various reports provide data on women in public office, electoral turnout of women, and so forth. Both historical and contemporary information.

National Center for Health Statistics. *Monthly Vital Statistics Report.* Hyattsville, Md.: U.S. Department of Health and Human Services. 1952-.
Statistical reports and analyses of various aspects of health.

National Roster of Hispanic Elected Officials, (Year). Washington, D.C.: National Association of Latino Elected and Appointed Officials Education Fund, no date. Annual.

> Lists Hispanic elected officials by office and state.

Schick, Frank L., and Renee Schick. *Statistical Handbook on U.S. Hispanics.* Phoenix: Oryx, 1991.

> Numerous tables about social and political characteristics of U.S. Hispanics.

The State of Black America. New York: National Urban League, 1976-. Annual.

> Yearly review assessing the conditions of blacks in the nation.

U.S. Department of Education. Center for Statistics. *Digest of Education Statistics.* Washington, D.C.: U.S. Government Printing Office, 1962-. Annual.

> Current data on school enrollments, teachers, retention rates, educational attainment, finances, achievement, schools and school districts, federal education programs, and so forth.

U.S. Department of Education. Office of Educational Research and Improvement. *The Condition of Education: A Statistical Report.* Washington, D.C.: U.S. Government Printing Office, 1975-.

> Data survey reviewing trends in elementary, secondary, and higher education; data portray student characteristics and performance as well as fiscal, material, and human resources deployed in education.

U.S. Department of Energy. Energy Information Administration. *Annual Energy Review.* Washington, D.C.: U.S. Government Printing Office, 1977-.

> Data on energy supply and disposition, exploration, and reserves.

U.S. Department of Justice. Bureau of Criminal Justice Statistics. *Sourcebook of Criminal Justice Statistics.* Washington, D.C.: U.S. Government Printing Office, 1974-. Annual.

> Brings together nationwide statistical data on the criminal justice system, public opinion, illegal activities, persons arrested, judicial proceedings, and persons under correctional supervision.

U.S. Department of Justice. Federal Bureau of Investigation. *Uniform Crime Reports for the United States.* Washington, D.C.: U.S. Government Printing Office, 1930-. Annual.

> Variety of charts and tables on types and frequencies of crimes, persons arrested, and law enforcement personnel; several forty-year trends.

Economic Policy

(Year) Historical Chart Book. Washington, D.C.: Board of Governors of the Federal Reserve System, 1965-. Annual.

Long-range financial and business data, mostly from series maintained by the Federal Reserve Board.

Frumkin, Norman. *Guide to Economic Indicators*. Armonk, N.Y.: M.E. Sharpe, 1990.
Content, accuracy, relevance, and sources for fifty economic indicators.

Hoel, Arline Alchian, Kenneth W. Clarkson, and Roger LeRoy Miller. *Economics Sourcebook of Government Statistics*. Lexington, Mass.: Lexington Books, 1983.
Ranges across inflation, general business conditions, interest rates, employment and earnings, international finance and trade, and the budget; critical discussions of over fifty major statistical series produced by the federal government in these areas; also refers to primary and secondary sources containing the series.

Office of Management and Budget. *Budget of the United States Government*. Washington, D.C.: U.S. Government Printing Office. Annual.
Multi-volume annual presentation of data on federal revenues and expenditures; while the details of the federal budget documents may be numbing to the uninitiated, even the novice can find two volumes particularly useful: *Historical Tables* and *The Budget in Brief,* both of which are designed for the general public.

O'Hara, Frederick M., and Robert Sicignano. *Handbook of United States Economic and Financial Indicators*. Westport, Conn.: Greenwood Press, 1985.
Defines several hundred economic indicators culled from over fifty sources; provides information on publication schedules and historical trends.

U.S. Bureau of Labor Statistics. *Employment and Earnings*. Washington, D.C.: U.S. Government Printing Office, 1961-. Annual.
Various statistics on the nation's nonfarm workforce, including lengthy time series with data beginning in 1909.

U.S. Bureau of Labor Statistics. *Handbook of Labor Statistics*. Washington, D.C.: U.S. Government Printing Office, 1927-. Frequency varies.
Collection of data concerning employment, unemployment, earnings, school enrollment and educational attainment, productivity, prices, strikes, and so forth.

U.S. Bureau of Labor Statistics. *Monthly Labor Review*. Washington, D.C.: U.S. Government Printing Office, 1915-.
Covers most Bureau of Labor Statistics series, giving data concerning employment, hours, pay, strikes, prices and inflation, and so forth.

U.S. Council of Economic Advisers. *Economic Indicators*. Washington, D.C.: U.S. Government Printing Office, 1948-. Monthly.
Data on total output, income, and spending; employment, unemployment, and wages; production and business activity; prices, currency, credit, and security markets; and federal finance.

U.S. Department of Agriculture. *Agricultural Statistics.* Washington, D.C.: U.S. Government Printing Office, 1937-. Annual.
> Vast array of agricultural data, including politically relevant displays, such as farm economic trends, price-support programs, and agricultural imports and exports.

U.S. Department of Commerce. *Survey of Current Business.* Washington, D.C.: U.S. Government Printing Office, 1921-. Monthly.
> Monthly publication with data on U.S. income and trade developments.

U.S. President. *The Economic Report of the President.* Washington, D.C.: U.S. Government Printing Office, 1947-. Annual.
> Reviews the national economic situation; presents a substantial appendix with long time series of critical economic data.

World Bank. *World Development Report.* New York: Oxford University Press, 1978-. Annual.
> Analysis of and data on worldwide capital and economic indicators, with an emphasis on development.

Miscellaneous

Some politically relevant information is found in general purpose almanacs. Such information is usually very limited, but these sources have the advantage of being very readily available.

Information Please Almanac: Atlas and Yearbook. Boston: Houghton Mifflin, 1947-. Annual.

Reader's Digest Almanac. Pleasantville, N.Y.: Reader's Digest, 1966-. Annual.

The World Almanac and Book of Facts. New York: Pharos Books, 1868-. Annual since 1886.

Index

Abortion
  amendment, public opinion on, 20-22
  amendment, state action on, 18-19
  frequency, by race, 34-35
  public opinion on, 36
ACU (American Conservative Union), ratings of congressional voting, 207-232
ADA (Americans for Democratic Action), ratings of congressional voting, 207-232
AFDC (Aid to Families with Dependent Children)
  benefit compared to poverty line, 363
  benefit per family, 363
  recipients, 362
AFL-CIO, ratings of congressional voting, 207-232
African-Americans. See Race/ethnicity
Age
  and congressional composition, 187
  and congressional vote, 101
  and Democratic presidential primary voting, 92
  and educational attainment, 364
  and media usage, 48
  and national convention delegate participation, 139
  and partisan identification, 149
  and persons below poverty line, 352

and presidential vote, 97, 99
and voter registration, turnout, 79
Amendments. See Constitutions
Arms control and disarmament agreements, 324-325

Balance of trade, 343
Balance on current trade account, 343
Balanced budget
  amendment, public opinion on, 20
  amendment, state action on, 18-19
  requirement, states, 303-305
Bill of Rights, applied to states, 17
Black elected officials
  and black voting-age population, 370-371
  legislators, federal, 40-41, 187
  legislators, state, 372-373
  by office, 369
Blacks. See Race/ethnicity
Budget, U.S. See also Military spending; Social welfare spending
  controllability, 391
  defense and nondefense, 387-388
  federal outlays, 390
  outlays by function, 389
Budget deficit, 312. See also Debt, U.S.

C-SPAN viewing, 48
Cabinet
  current officials, 245-246
  nominations rejected by Senate, 260
Cable television, viewing, 48
Campaign finance. See also PACs